EXTREME TOURISM: LESSONS FROM THE WORLD'S COLD WATER ISLANDS

ADVANCES IN TOURISM RESEARCH

Series Editor: Professor Stephen J. Page
University of Stirling, UK
s.j.page@stir.ac.uk

Advances in Tourism Research series publishes monographs and edited volumes that comprise state-of-the-art research findings, written and edited by leading researchers working in the wider field of tourism studies. The series has been designed to provide a cutting edge focus for researchers interested in tourism, particularly the management issues now facing decision-makers, policy analysts and the public sector. The audience is much wider than just academics and each book seeks to make a significant contribution to the literature in the field of study by not only reviewing the state of knowledge relating to each topic but also questioning some of the prevailing assumptions and research paradigms which currently exist in tourism research. The series also aims to provide a platform for further studies in each area by highlighting key research agendas, which will stimulate further debate and interest in the expanding area of tourism research. The series is always willing to consider new ideas for innovative and scholarly books. Inquiries should be made directly to the series editor.

Published:
Destination Marketing Organisations
PIKE

Small Firms in Tourism: International Perspectives
THOMAS

Tourism and Transport
LUMSDON & PAGE

Tourism Public Policy and the Strategic Management of Failure
KERR

Managing Tourist Health and Safety in the New Millennium
WILKS & PAGE

Indigenous Tourism
RYAN AND AICKEN

Taking Tourism to the Limits
RYAN, PAGE & AICKEN

An International. Handbook on Tourism Education
AIREY & TRIBE

Tourism in Turbulent Times
WILKS, PENDERGAST & LEGGAT

Benchmarking National Tourism Organisations and Agencies
LENNON, SMITH, COCKEREL & TREW

Forthcoming titles include:

Tourism and Small Businesses in the New Europe
THOMAS & AUGUSTYN

Tourism Micro-clusters & Networks: The Growth of Tourism
MICHAEL

Related Elsevier Journals — sample copies available on request
Annals of Tourism Research
International Journal of Hospitality Management
Tourism Management
World Development

EXTREME TOURISM: LESSONS FROM THE WORLD'S COLD WATER ISLANDS

GODFREY BALDACCHINO

Island Studies Programme
University of Prince Edward Island, Canada

ELSEVIER

Amsterdam • Boston • Heidelberg • London • New York • Oxford
Paris • San Diego • San Francisco • Singapore • Sydney • Tokyo

Elsevier
The Boulevard, Langford Lane, Kidlington, Oxford OX5 1GB, UK
Radarweg 29, PO Box 211, 1000 AE Amsterdam, The Netherlands

First edition 2006

British Library Cataloguing in Publication Data
A catalogue record for this book is available from the British Library

Library of Congress Cataloging-in-Publication Data
A catalog record for this book is available from the Library of Congress

ISBN-13: 978-0-08-044656-1
ISBN-10: 0-08-044656-6

For information on all Elsevier publications
visit our website at books.elsevier.com

Printed and bound in The Netherlands

06 07 08 09 10 10 9 8 7 6 5 4 3 2 1

Working together to grow
libraries in developing countries
www.elsevier.com | www.bookaid.org | www.sabre.org
ELSEVIER   BOOK AID
International   Sabre Foundation

Contents

List of Maps

List of Figures

List of Tables

Contributors

Rosemarie Ankre is a Ph.D. student in Spatial Planning at the Blekinge Technology Institute and the European Tourism Research Institute, Mid-Sweden University in Östersund, Sweden. E-mail: rosemarie.ankre@etour.se.

Godfrey Baldacchino is the Canada Research Chair in Island Studies at the University of Prince Edward Island, Canada, and a visiting professor of Sociology at the University of Malta, Malta. E-mail: gbaldacchino@upei.ca.

Suzanne de la Barre is a Ph.D. candidate in the Faculty of Physical Education and Recreation at the University of Alberta, Canada. E-mail: sd@ualberta.ca.

Thomas G. Bauer is an assistant professor of Tourism at the School of Hotel and Tourism Management, The Hong Kong Polytechnic University, Hong Kong SAR, China. E-mail: hmthomas@polyu.edu.hk.

Tom Baum is a professor of International Tourism and Hospitality Management at the Scottish Hotel School, University of Strathclyde, Scotland, UK. E-mail: t.g.baum@strath. ac.uk.

Ted Berry is the technology coordinator for Alaska's Lower Kuskokwim School District, including the Island of Nunivak, the largest island in the Bering Strait. E-mail: tedberry_aus@yahoo.com.

Richard W. Butler, formerly professor of Tourism at the University of Surrey, UK, is now professor of International Tourism at the Scottish Hotel School, University of Strathclyde, Scotland, UK. E-mail: r.butler2@btinternet.com.

Andrew Cardow lectures in the Department of Management and International Business at Massey University, New Zealand. E-mail: A.cardow@massey.ac.nz.

Graham M. S. Dann is a professor in the Department of Tourism and Leisure, Luton Business School, UK. E-mail: graham.dann@luton.ac.uk.

Claire F. Ellis is the director of Destination Development at Tourism Tasmania, Hobart, Australia. E-mail: Claire.Ellis@tourism.tas.gov.au.

Regena Farnsworth is a professor of Organizational Behaviour and Human Resource Management at the University of New Brunswick, Saint John NB, Canada. E-mail: rfarnswo@unbsj.ca.

Stefan Gössling is an associate professor of Cultural Geography and Human Ecology in the Department of Service Management at Lund University, Helsingborg Campus, Sweden, and a former tour guide to Iceland in his spare time.
E-mail: stefan.gossling@ msm.lu.se.

C. Michael Hall is a professor and head in the Department of Tourism at the School of Business, University of Otago, New Zealand, and a docent in the Department of Geography at the University of Oulu, Finland. E-mail: CMHall@business.otago.ac.nz.

Nick Holmes is an honorary research associate at the Centre for Environmental Studies, University of Tasmania, Australia. E-mail: ndholmes@utas.edu.au.

Lee Jolliffe is the director of International Office and associate professor in the Faculty of Business at the University of New Brunswick, Saint John NB, Canada.
E-mail: ljolliff@unbsj.ca.

Berit C. Kaae is a senior researcher at the Danish Centre for Forest, Landscape and Planning, KVL, and has undertaken an extensive study of tourism research and documents in Greenland. E-mail: bck@kvl.dk.

Lorne K. Kriwoken is a senior lecturer at the School of Geography and Environmental Studies, and a research associate at Antarctic Climate and Ecosystems Cooperative Research Centre, University of Tasmania, Australia. E-mail: L.K.Kriwoken@utas.edu.au.

Sarah Marsh is a research & planning coordinator for Tourism and Parks in the Department of Industry, Tourism and Investment, Government of the Northwest Territories, Canada. E-mail: Sarah_Marsh@gov.nt.ca.

Jerome L. McElroy is a professor of Economics at Saint Mary's College, Notre Dame, IN, USA. E-mail: jmcelroy@saintmarys.edu.

Simon Milne is a professor of Tourism & director of the New Zealand Tourism Research Institute, Auckland University of Technology, New Zealand and is a visiting professor at the Graduate School of Management, La Trobe University, Australia.
E-mail: simon.milne@ aut.ac.nz.

Julia Nevmerzhitskaya, from Archangelsk, Russia, is a Ph.D. candidate at Vaasa University and a senior lecturer in Marketing at Laurea Polytechnic, both in Finland.
E-mail: Julia.Nevmerzhitskaya@laurea.fi.

Per-Åke Nilsson is a tourism researcher affiliated to the Centre for Tourism and Regional Research, Bornholm, Denmark. E-mail: per-ake.nilsson@miun.se.

Bruce Potter is the president and CEO of Island Resources Foundation and a founding director of the Global Islands Network. E-mail: bpotter@irf.org.

Stephen A. Royle is a reader in Geography at the School of Geography, Archaeology and Palaeoecology, Queen's University Belfast, Northern Ireland. E-mail: s.royle@qub.ac.uk

Callum Thomson is a consulting archaeologist specializing in circumpolar and North Atlantic cultures, a former government archaeologist and museum curator and a guide on many small expedition cruises in the North Atlantic, Arctic and Antarctic.
E-mail: thomsonheritage@canada.com.

Jane Sproull Thomson is a lecturer in Native Art History at the University of Calgary, and a research associate with the Arctic Institute of North America, a past curator of Ethnology with the Newfoundland Museum and the Glenbow Museum, Calgary and a cruise ship guide to the far North. E-mail: jsthomso@ucalgary.ca.

Arvid Viken is associate professor at Finnmark University College, Alta, Norway.
E-mail: arvid@ hifm.no.

Peter Wiltshier now lectures at the School of Tourism and Hospitality, Derby University, UK, and was formerly with the Department of Applied Management, UNITEC Institute of Technology, Auckland, New Zealand. E-mail: P.Wiltshier@derby.ac.uk.

Acknowledgements

Page 2 — Isotherm plus Islands Locator Map drawn by Maura Pringle, School of Geography, Archaeology and Palaeoecology, Queen's University Belfast, Northern Ireland, UK.

Page 62 — Map of Nunivak, Alaska, prepared by Robert Drozda for Nuniwarmiut Piciryarata Tamaryalkuti, 2004.

Page 74 — Map of the Northwest Territories and Banks Island, made available by the Department of Industry, Tourism & Investment, Government of the Northwest Territories, Canada.

Page 88 — Map of Baffin Island, Nunavut, prepared by the New Zealand Tourism Research Institute, Faculty of Business, Auckland University of Technology, New Zealand.

Page 100 — Underlay map of Greenland reproduced with permission from Greenland Tourism.

Page 114 — Map of Iceland prepared for Stefan Gössling by the staff at the Department of Geography, University of Freiburg, Germany.

Page 128 — Map of Svalbard reproduced with permission from the Norsk Polarinstitutt — www.npolar.no.

Page 140 — Visual publicity material by Svalbard Tourism reproduced with permission from the Svalbard Tourist Bureau.

Page 144 — Map of Luleå Archipelago reproduced with permission from the National Land Survey, Sweden, and modified by Egil Nilsson.

Page 158 — Solovetsky map reproduced with permission from Nordic Travel, Russia — www.nordictravel.ru.

Page 168 — Arctic cruise ship tourism map: favourite ports of call. Prepared by Callum Thomson and Jane Sproull Thomson.

Page 180 — Falkland Islands map drawn by Gill Alexander of the School of Geography, Archaeology and Palaeoecology, Queen's University Belfast, Northern Ireland, UK, from material provided by Falkland Islands Tourism.

Page 192 — Macquarie Island map drawn by June Pongratz, Senior Technical Officer, School of Earth Sciences, University of Tasmania, Hobart, Tasmania, Australia.

Page 204 — Chatham Islands map reproduced with permission from the Chatham Islands Enterprise Board — www.chathams.com.

Page 218 — Map of Stewart Island reproduced with permission from the Department of Conservation, Government of New Zealand.

Page 234 — Map of South Shetlands reproduced from www.wikipedia.org.

Page 234 — Map of the islands around the Antarctic Peninsula reproduced courtesy of the University Libraries, the University of Texas at Austin, USA.

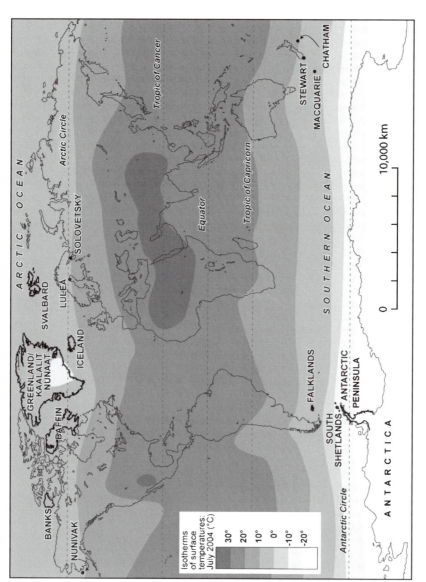

Image 1: Isotherm map.

Editorial Introduction

Godfrey Baldacchino

> I try in vain to be persuaded that the Pole is the seat of frost and desolation; it ever presents itself to my imagination as the region of beauty and delight.
>
> Mary Shelley, *Frankenstein* (1818)

Rationale

The picture gracing the cover of a typical text on island tourism is likely to include a handsome couple frolicking in knee-deep, crystal-clear water, with sun-drenched sand and a beach resort under cloudless blue skies. Conlin and Baum (1995) is one of many such texts. Only one out of the nine chapters dedicated to "management practice" deals with a "cold water" location (Corner Brook, in Newfoundland); out of 93 different islands or island regions listed in its index, only five at most could be considered as "cold water" ones (Antarctica, Falklands, Newfoundland, New Zealand and Prince Edward Island).

Islands, it seems, could only be *warm* for tourism purposes. For example, Canada's *Globe and Mail* thought fit to feature Barbados — "one of the top gourmet destinations in the Caribbean" — in its weekly travel supplement of 16 October 2004. Yet a feature on cold and windy Devon Island, Nunavut, located in the Canadian North, carried in the same issue of the tabloid, was relegated to the "focus" section. It seems that Devon Island's "Mars on Earth" climate renders it attractive only to "scientists" and "researchers", *not* tourists (Ferguson, 2004; Stevenson, 2004).

It may prove difficult to identify the rationale behind the connection: islands are credited to offer that "something different" to tourists, as if there were "something special" about a place merely because people get to it by means of boat or plane. The island appeal has been related to feelings of separateness, of authenticity, of somehow being able to "do the place" or to "take it all in" in a short time (Baum, 2000; Butler, 1993). Whatever the link between the ultimate lure of islandness and tourism, the association between small (especially small and tropical) islands and the tourism industry has surely been one of the best branding exercises in the history of destination marketing. The island mystique forms an essential part of the millenary tradition of the West, dating back to such ancient Greek epics as the *Odyssey*, repackaged in Western Europe's voyages of discovery and perpetuated by pioneer anthropologists like Margaret Mead (Baldacchino, 1997, p. 59; 2004; Gillis, 2004; Patton, 1996,

p. 1). The image of islands as "Eden without apples" lingers on (Pitt, 1970, pp. 1–3; Conlin & Baum, 1995), and it is now exploited also by the media (in movies like *Cast Away* or in TV serial blockbusters like *Survivor*). Yet such popularity is not without its costs. Islands are amongst the world's most "penetrated" tourism locations (McElroy, 2003); large scale hospitality and infrastructure constructions have filled in salt ponds, disfigured shorelines and polluted near-shore waters with sewage (Pearce, 1987); mass tourism has swamped local culture, contributed to domestic inflation and damaged insular ecosystems (Beller, D'Ayala, & Hein, 1990; Briguglio, Archer, Jafari, & Wall, 1996a; Briguglio, Butler, Harrison, & Leal Filho, 1996b; Lanfant, Allcock, & Bruner, 1995).

The image of tourist destinations as alluring undiscovered paradises has much to do with islands. But this trope is based on one crucial premise: a warm and arguably pleasant climate. So, for example, "… the natural beauty and attractive climate of many island states have enabled them to develop a relatively large tourist industry, by exploiting the advantages bestowed upon them by nature" (Briguglio, 1996, p. xii). Nature does not always act or appear as benign: indeed, nature may present itself as the principal, insurmountable enemy to a tourism industry. The "mass market practice common in islands" (McElroy & de Albuquerque, 1992) assumes that all islands are warm water islands. But it is not so.

Tourism Heats Up

The world is full of islands. Over 10 percent of the world's population today lives on islands: tropical, temperate and polar. Yet, the notion of a "cold-water" island taunts us as if it were a myth, an impossibility, a contradiction-in-terms, an oxymoron. Have we been socialized into expecting islands (and islanders) to be only lush, malleable and exotic?: as represented, for example, in William Shakespeare's *The Tempest,* Daniel Defoe's *Robinson Crusoe,* Jonathan Swift's *Gulliver's Travels,* Johann Wyss' *Swiss Family Robinson,* Jules Verne's *Mysterious Island* (as texts) and *Blue Lagoon* and *Live and Let Die* (as films)? Moreover, most island *states* do happen to lie astride the world's temperate and tropical regions. They include both small sovereign states (the majority of which are to be found in the Caribbean Sea, South Pacific and Indian Oceans); and larger ones — like the sprawling and heavily populated archipelagos of Indonesia, Japan, the Philippines and of course, Great Britain.

If one of the star attractions of islandness is remoteness, then part of the island tourism mystique lies in the affirmation of distance (and therefore also difference) while still ensuring access. Cold water temperatures and inclement weather contribute to this sense of isolation. Remote locations, once identified and recognized as potential destinations for non-residents, generally tend to attract few visitors, each of whom however stays longer, justifying the time, effort and expense of travel. A "cold water" scenario could be expected to exacerbate this trend. But remoteness is a relative term, and easily overcome by technology. One of the most noticeable characteristics of recent tourism growth has been the "continuous thrust to the periphery" (Butler, 2002, p. 3). In this trend, space-as-marginal and low temperatures enter into an uncanny alliance since the movement from metropolitan to marginal could be easily compared to the transition from mature to frontier destinations, and from the tropical through the temperate to the frigid regions of the globe. Meanwhile, and as a sinister parallel, global warming may be steadily reducing the temperature differential, gradually rendering hitherto cold water islands more akin to their warm weather cousins. In this process, one could expect the standard island "paradise myth" of the tourist package to become extended to ever-larger stretches of island candidates in higher latitudes. Will this be a lost opportunity for cold water islands and islanders to craft a different set of self-images as tourism destinations, where the challenges of cold and harsh surroundings (obvious obstacles to tourism marketing in warmer climes) are transformed into assets? Or would islands and islanders prefer to walk the well-trodden path, and be subject to the same imagery, processes of market commoditization, but also environmental degradation, as their warmer counterparts?

This Book

Thus emerged the germ of an idea and structure for this volume. It builds on a track record of islands traditionally informing some of the best theoretically informed research in tourism due to more clearly identifiable impacts and effects, as in the case of Bryden (1973) for the Caribbean and Britton (1987) for the Pacific. The idea led to an investigation of the tourism practices in some of the world's cold water islands, located at or close to the northern and southern antipodes; followed by a conceptual analysis of what these experiences tell us with regard to key transversal themes. Moreover, touching base with the additional allure of islands as naturally framed and convenient laboratories (e.g. Evans, 1973; Patton, 1996, pp. 2–5), the contents of this book could serve as lessons for other, non-island locations.

This collection goes to print with a representative set of case study chapters from Northern latitudes: Nunivak (Alaska, USA), Banks (Northwest Territories, Canada), Baffin (Nunavut, Canada), Greenland/Kalaallit Nunaat, Iceland, Luleå (Sweden), Svalbard (Norway) Solovetsky (Russia), plus the particular vantage point of Arctic cruise ship tourism. Another, smaller, set of case study chapters hails from Southern latitudes: Falklands (UK), the Antarctic Peninsula and South Shetlands, Macquarie (Australia), Stewart and the Chathams (associated with New Zealand).

Four conceptual chapters are presented first, even though they were actually the last to be written. They have obliged their authors to examine the 14 case study chapters in so much as they provide insights into the key tourism management issues: (a) *human resources* (labour market features; sourcing; recruitment; retention; training; career progression and flexible specialization); (b) *environment* (the representation of nature in island tourism profiling; ecological issues in typically fragile habitats; waste management policies and practices and sustainability concerns); (c) *promotion* (advancing destination difference and linking it with "cold islandness"; developing tourism and linking it with "islandness", location, size and "island culture"; targeting and profiling actual and potential clients in terms of matching island attributes with the motivational needs of visitors; portraying "friendly natives" living in a hostile natural environment and presenting the appropriate discourse on "island" and "extremeness") and (d) *seasonality* (should it be embraced, tolerated or challenged? Or does being cold all year round eliminate talk of seasonality altogether?)

In the fifth and final conceptual chapter, the intention is to bring together the various themes raised in this book into a unified and cohesive format, while suggesting the future research and policy leads. This conclusion takes a sober look at the overall nature of cold-water island tourism, and its relationship to "islandness", space–time compression and globalizations.

Literature

Unlike tourism in/on warm water islands, the literature on tourism in cold-water islands, like these destinations themselves, is relatively hard to come by (Hall & Johnston (1995) is one notable exception). Part of the paucity could be explained by the absence of cold-water island *jurisdictions* (with Iceland as the single and notable exception) — after all, political autonomy improves the likelihood of a location being regarded as the focus of a specific policy. Comments have already been made on the contents of Conlin and Baum (1995). A regional focus, as with Apostolopoulos and Gayle (2002), excludes cold water considerations completely. From their titles, Briguglio et al. (1996a,b) might suggest that they cover cold-water islands too; but only 1 out of the 29 chapters does so, with a focus on the Shetland Islands (Butler, 1996). Lockhart and Drakakis-Smith (1997) do somewhat better: three (opening) chapters address themes largely relevant to islands beyond the tropical "pleasure periphery". However, once the text goes into case study mode, only 3 out of 14 chapters are not sourced from warm climes: Butler on Orkney & Shetland; Royle on the South Atlantic Islands, which includes the Falklands and Aronsson on Swedish islands. Gradus and Lithwick (1996) and Krakover and Gradus (2002), in spite of promising titles that highlight frontier regions, do not discuss islands at all. Royle (2001) is a commendable academic attempt at a multi-disciplinary review of islands on a global scale. His tourism chapter is sensitive to both non-tropical and non-sovereign locations, reviewing such islands as Heligoland (Germany) and Kulusuk (Greenland). There is a useful discussion of concepts and arguments that could be applied to cold water islands, but which are not specifically addressed in a limited and condensed, 20-page, chapter. Finally, as a singly authored text, King (1997) does tackle islands comparatively. However, the focus is (once again) restricted to Oceanic and Pacific territories. In other cases, the connection between tourism and islandness is not articulated or problematized, a common neglect among researchers who do not have an "island studies" imagination.

A systematic initiative, which has tried to redress this dearth of relevant research material has emerged from the North Atlantic Islands Programme, coordinated by the Institute of Island Studies at the University of Prince Edward Island, Canada along with NordRefo (now NordRegio), the Nordic Centre for Spatial Development, based in Stockholm, Sweden (Baldacchino & Greenwood, 1998; Baldacchino & Milne, 2000; Baum & Hagen, 1999; Hagen, 1998). Another cooperative effort between Canadian and Scandinavian researchers, coordinated by the European Tourism Research Institute (ETOUR) at the Mid-Sweden University in Östersund, has investigated *peripheral* (though not explicitly *island*) tourism in Northern Canada and Sweden (Sahlberg, 2001). The latter product is part of a growing interest in extreme and adventure tourism (e.g. Swarbrooke, Beard, Leckie, & Pomfret, 2003; Turner, 2003; Grenier, 2004), a fascination bolstered by popularized publications of tales of explorers from a bygone age (e.g. Lundgren, 2001, p. 12). Yet, none of these texts is so far known to consider islands in this context, let alone be specific to them.

Seven Research Themes

Seven distinct yet interrelated, fundamental research themes have inspired this book. They have been assembled from the sporadic literature on tourism in cold-water island destinations. These themes, and the associated questions that they raise, are the ones to which the authors of the case studies in the second section of this volume have been asked to respond, thus hopefully balancing the necessarily idiosyncratic descriptive aspects of each of their cases with themes that lend themselves to comparison and contrast *across* cases. In the process, some interesting conceptualizations about island tourism are suggested. It is the latter that have been grasped and commented upon by the more critical, analytic and comparative chapters that comprise the first section of the book.

Serving Paradise Cold

In spite of the huge amounts of text that have been devoted to the topic, understanding what is the island "lure" (Lockhart, 1997), or what it is exactly that attracts visitors to islands and "islandness" remains largely "speculative" (Baum, 2000, p. 215). The physical separation from the mainland, necessitating a conscious decision to cross the water, the opportunity to get away from it all in a slower-paced environment, and the ability to seek out and take in the totality of a destination are presented as three explanations for the inherently distinct adventurism of a trip to an island, especially a *small* island (Baum, 1997, p. 21; 2000, pp. 215–216). How do islands on the extremities of the Earth's geography and climate seek to promote themselves as tourism destinations, and develop the so-called tourism product? The myth of the island as paradise has been a powerful one (e.g. King, 1993; Harrison, 2001); so has the discourse of the frontier (Dann, 1996). But could the two metaphors happily co-exist in a cold location? What happens when these images are combined? And is the result compatible with the type of tourism that is desirable and appropriate to the locality and its people?

Remoteness: Blessing or Curse?

Given their extreme and insular location, and shorn of the "paradise" hype of sun, sand, sea (and sex?), islands at the top and bottom of the world could be seen starkly as the most remote and forbidding destinations on the planet. Their appeal appears naturally limited with respect to the conventional mass market. The islanders themselves, of course, may beg to differ. Or do they? Is this condition actually a distinct advantage in (self-) regulating tourism flows and in preventing an often-irreversible trend towards mass tourism and the serious erosion of (often fragile) island ecosystems that so many other destinations have espoused, either by design or default? (McElroy & de Albuquerque, 2002, p. 22). After all, "… while it may be desirable that access be improved for local benefit, such steps may well remove the greatest asset that an island may have in controlling the numbers, type and scale of tourism development" (Butler, 1996, pp. 16–17). Their appeal may relate to the "very real feeling of separateness and difference, caused in part to their being physically separate, and perhaps therefore different from adjoining mainlands" (Butler, 1993, p. 71). Jurisdictional specificity (such as being a sovereign state or being a province) could be expected to enhance such a condition of differentiation and, therefore, of intrinsic appeal.

Planning or Thwarting Access Improvement

The idea of "distance decay" suggests that the extent of spatial interaction is inversely related to distance (Tobler, 1970). Now, access to islands is usually "… complicated, expensive, hazardous, time-consuming, irregular and unreliable, or any combination of the above" (Butler, 1996, p. 16) — leading to expectations of low tourism interest and presence. To what extent should access to islands be remedied? (Of course, ease of access may be changing anyway, irrespective of human planning: for example, because of global warming.) What brand of economic development, inclusive of means of (air/land/sea) transportation and infrastructure (or mix thereof), lends itself to a sustainable tourism strategy? Or are such decisions taken with other concerns in mind, and tourism policy is only "muddled through"? Who actually takes these decisions, especially in the (most common) case of islands where political control is vested somewhere else?

Impact of Volatility

Small islands are characterized by "… resource and market scarcity and intense openness" (McElroy & de Albuquerque, 2002, p. 17). This statement suggests that changes brought about by an exogenous variable such as tourism will be rapid, deep and intimate. Intense openness also means that a small island economy could quickly become dependent on the tourism industry with visitors from faraway, foreign lands, with often-fickle tastes: a hazardous proposition. Moreover, the policies and practices of just one tour operator, one airline, perhaps one hotel, could make or break tourism. Service providers in the industry, as with other enterprises in cold-water locations, tend towards being oligopolies or monopolies. Is there such volatility and boom-bust orientation in the tourism industry of cold-water islands? Is there a tendency towards concentration of capital, skill or service? With what effects?

Cold Tourists?

Specific tourist types are concerned with a search for the novel and the authentic (e.g. MacCannell, 1989). Islands, like frontier regions, have a particular appeal to those tourist types keen on natural environments, traditional cultures and unorthodox scenarios. Moreover, prevailing and challenging weather conditions may be less significant features for visitors to cold water islands than to other locations, since most activities are not highly weather dependent and in some cases may actually depend on *adverse* weather conditions (Butler, 1996, pp. 23–24). To what extent do "cold water tourists" exist as a special type of tourist (*after* Cohen, 1972)? And how do they differ, if at all, from their warm water cousins? Are they, for example, more environmentally conscious?

Conflicting Models of Land Use and Development

If the tourism "area cycle" evolutionary model generally holds (*after* Butler, 1980), then the last "raw" outposts of civilization to be discovered by the tourism industry (*after* King, 1997) could be assumed to be cold water, island locations. As communities in destination regions face the downside of tourism, and as tourists become thwarted by the non-primitive and/or non-authentic character of the "natives", the urge to seek out even more remote, genuine, pristine and extreme locations remains strong (Butler, 2002, p. 5). It may be just a question of time before all corners of the world are fully integrated into a global tourism vice, as technology continues to make the planet smaller and more accessible. But, it is a big IF. What if a small, cold-water island has a totally different competitive advantage, which suggests its own evolutionary pattern? Can such a location develop its own response to the "changing spatial patterns of international tourism" (Williams, 1998)? Is the "island as a prison" its greatest, ultimate asset (Royle, 2001, p. 224)? If this is the case, then its "relative inaccessibility, the absence of much development and the presence of few other tourists" (Butler, 2002, p. 5) have been features of the competitive tourism advantage of a cold-water island. But this also means that the scale and type of tourism and its development must be closely managed. This task may be easier to carry out in frontier sites where the land area is typically large and population levels are minimal. In contrast, on small islands, land is finite and the contact between tourists and residents is impossible to avoid, and potentially tense. Locals may have needs that run counter to arguments about their own tourism industry's sustainability; land use conflicts are also more likely (e.g. Latimer, 1985).

Political Geography

Extreme island regions tend to lie on the political periphery, especially when they have small populations: un/under-represented in the corridors of power; largely forgotten by centralized policy makers suffering from "the urban bias"; dismissed as insignificant backwaters other than, perhaps, in strategic (military and resource) terms (Butler, 1993; Wilkinson, 1994). A weak local political influence may, in turn, suggest a precarious status that attracts a bold entrepreneurial tourism elite (Butler, 2002). However, such a frontier mentality may also bring about the haphazard and dependent development of a tourism industry that suffers from benign domestic neglect: with non-domestic tourist visitors being catered for by non-local businesses, resulting in massive economic leakages; and with common resources liable to over-use and erosion (Getz, 1983). The long-term consequences of such a condition may not be pleasant. In contrast, sound local management could conspire with climate and relative inaccessibility to limit tourism to small scale, low-impact, dispersed and genuinely sustainable development (e.g. Butler, 1997, p. 78).

Islands *In Extremis* are Cool

Every island is unique. Yet, a comparative "island studies" perspective alerts us to some underlying patterns lurking within the diversity of cold water islands reviewed in this text: apart from the obvious pronouncement that the water is too cold to swim in. Our profiled, cold-water island locations tend to have harsh as well as pristine and fragile natural environments, characterized by wide-open spaces; this makes them support low populations at best. They become contexts for an exceptional and expensive form of vigorous, outdoor, adventure or cultural tourism, and direct encounters with nature (observing penguins, bears or wild flowers; hunting wild game and visiting parks); history (whaling stations, abandoned mines, battle sites, research stations and explorer routes); and local culture (indigenous people, their lifestyle and artifacts): definitely not places to laze about and relax in hotel precincts. Indeed, there may not even be a hotel. The locals, where they exist, are not particularly enthusiastic about visitors; few of the locals owe their livelihoods to tourism anyway, and they are usually in agreement that visitor numbers must remain low — and especially so if the locals happen to be a bunch of scientists. Specific local interests — a company, a monastery, a corporation, apart from the scientific community — can have inordinate influences on local public policy, since there is a tighter, more compact and more identifiable resident elite. The anomaly in our set remains Iceland, since 1944 the world's coolest sovereign state: it has by far the largest population, highest tourism numbers and strongest tourism infrastructure in our set.

In Andrea Barrett's novel *The Voyage of the Narwhal*, a despondent, unmarried naturalist from the metropolitan USA sees an opportunity to both make his reputation and redeem himself by signing on for a voyage to the Arctic in 1855, in search of Sir John Franklin's lost expedition (Barrett, 1999). Personal and territorial exploration, along with their hazards and tribulations, are deftly intertwined. Similarly, the travails of visitors to the white island expanses of the north and south today could be felt to recreate the journeys of the Vikings and other intrepid explorers. The personal audacity of these pioneers, their awe and wonder at the marvels of nature they stumbled upon, and their encounters with natives, seem to capture the imagination of those contemporary tourists who wish, and could afford, to reach beyond the typical vacation and travel periphery (Lundgren, 2001, p. 12), while, thereby claiming some of the glory of "doing" these harsh yet seductive island environments for themselves. Before global warming thaws it all away. Truly chilling.

References

Apostolopoulos, Y., & Gayle, D. J. (Eds). (2002). *Island tourism and sustainable development: Caribbean, Pacific and Mediterranean experiences*. Westport, CT: Praeger.

Baldacchino, G. (1997). *Global tourism & informal labour relations: The small scale syndrome at work*. London: Mansell.

Baldacchino, G. (2004). Island studies comes of age. *Tijdschrift voor Economische en Sociale Geografie, 95*, 272–283.

Baldacchino, G., & Greenwood, R. (Eds). (1998). *Competing strategies of socio-economic development from small islands*. Charlottetown, Canada: Institute of Island Studies, University of Prince Edward Island.

Baldacchino, G., & Milne, D. (Eds). (2000). *Lessons from the political economy of small islands: The resourcefulness of jurisdiction*. Basingstoke: Macmillan, & New York: St. Martins Press (in association with Institute of Island Studies, University of Prince Edward Island, Canada).

Barrett, A. (1999). *The voyage of the Narwhal*. New York: W.W. Norton.

Baum, T. G. (1997). The fascination of islands: A tourist perspective. In: D. G. Lockhart, & D. Drakakis-Smith (Eds), *Island tourism: Trends and prospects* (pp. 21–35). London: Mansell.

Baum, T. G. (2000). Tourism and cold water islands in the North Atlantic. In: G. Baldacchino, & D. Milne (Eds), *Lessons from the political economy of small islands: The resourcefulness of jurisdiction* (pp. 214–229). Basingstoke: Macmillan.

Baum, T. G., & Hagen, L. (1999). Responses to seasonality: The experiences of peripheral destinations. *International Journal of Tourism Research*, *1*, 299–312.

Beller, W., D'Ayala, P., & Hein, P. (Eds). (1990). *Sustainable development and environmental management of small islands*. Paris: UNESCO-Parthenon.

Briguglio, L. (1996). Preface to L. Briguglio, B. Archer, J. Jafari, & G. Wall, (Eds), *Sustainable tourism in islands & small states: Issues and policies* (pp. xii–xiii.). London: Pinter.

Briguglio, L., Archer, B., Jafari, J., & Wall, G. (Eds). (1996a). *Sustainable tourism in small and island states: Issues and policies*. London: Pinter.

Briguglio, L., Butler, R., Harrison, D., & Leal Filho, W. (Eds). (1996b). *Sustainable tourism in small and island states: Case studies*. London: Pinter.

Britton, S. G. (1987). Tourism in Pacific island states: Constraints and opportunities. In: S. Britton, & W. Clarke (Eds), *Ambiguous alternatives: Tourism in small developing countries* (pp. 113–139). Suva, Fiji: Institute of Pacific Studies, University of the South Pacific.

Bryden, J. M. (1973). *Tourism and development: A case study of the commonwealth Caribbean*. London: Cambridge University Press.

Butler, R. W. (1980). The concept of a tourist area-cycle of evolution: Implications for the management of resources. *Canadian Geographic*, *14*, 5–12.

Butler, R. W. (1993). Tourism development in small islands: Past influences and future directions. In: D. G. Lockhart, D. Drakakis-Smith, & J. A. Schembri (Eds), *The development process in small island states* (pp. 71–91). London: Routledge..

Butler, R. W. (1996). Problems and possibilities of sustainable tourism: The case of the Shetland Islands. In: L. Briguglio, R. W. Butler, D. Harrison, & W. Leal Filho (Eds), *Sustainable tourism in islands & small states: Case studies* (pp. 11–31). London: Pinter.

Butler, R. W. (1997). Tourism in the Northern Isles: Orkney and Shetland. In: D. G. Lockhart, & D. Drakakais-Smith (Eds), *Island tourism: Trends and prospects* (pp. 59–80). London: Pinter.

Butler, R. W. (2002). The development of tourism in frontier regions: Issues and approaches. In: S. Krakover, & Y. Gradus (Eds), *Tourism in frontier areas* (pp. 3–19). Lanham, MD: Lexington Books.

Cohen, E. (1972). Towards a sociology of international tourism. *Social Research*, *39*, 164–182.

Conlin, M., & Baum, T. G. (Eds). (1995). *Island tourism: Management principles and practices*. Chichester: Wiley.

Dann, G. M. S. (1996). *The language of tourism: A socio-linguistic perspective*. Wallingford: CAB International.

Evans, J. D. (1973). Islands as laboratories for the study of cultural processes. In: A. C. Renfrew (Ed.), *The explanation of cultural change: Models in prehistory* (pp. 517–520). London: Duckworth.

Ferguson, J. (2004). Tasting the Bajan bounty. *The Globe and Mail*. Canada, October 16th, Travel Supplement, p. 4.

Getz, D. (1983). Capacity to absorb tourism: Concepts and implications for strategic planning. *Annals of Tourism Research*, *10*, 239–263.

Gillis, J. R. (2004). *Islands on our mind: How the human imagination created the atlantic world*. London: Palgrave Macmillan.

Gradus, Y., & Lithwick, I. (Eds). (1996). *Frontiers in regional development*. Lanham, MD: Rowman & Littlefield.

Grenier, A. A. (2004). *The nature of nature tourism*, published dissertation. Rovaniemi: University of Lapland, Faculty of Social Sciences.

Hagen, L. (1998). *Seasonality in tourism in the small islands of the North Atlantic.* Charlottetown, Canada: Institute of Island Studies, University of Prince Edward Island.

Hall, C. M., & Johnston, M. E. (Eds). (1995). *Polar tourism: Tourism in the Arctic and Antarctic regions.* Chichester: Wiley.

Harrison, D. (2001). Islands, image and tourism. *Tourism Recreation Research, 26,* 9–14.

King, E. M. (1997). *Creating island resorts.* London: Routledge.

King, R. (1993). The geographical fascination of islands. In: D. G. Lockhart, D. Drakakis-Smith, & J. Schembri (Eds), *The development process in small island states* (pp. 13–37). London: Routledge.

Krakover, S., & Gradus, Y. (Eds). (2002). *Tourism in frontier areas.* Lanham, MD: Lexington Books.

Lanfant, M. F., Allcock, J. B., & Bruner, E. M. (1995). *International tourism: Identity and change.* London: Sage.

Latimer, H. (1985). Developing island economies: Tourism versus agriculture. *Tourism Management, 6,* 32–42.

Lockhart, D. G. (1997). Tourism and islands: An overview. In: D. G. Lockhart, & D. Drakakis-Smith (Eds), *Island tourism: Trends and prospects* (pp. 3–20). London: Pinter.

Lockhart, D. G., & Drakakis-Smith, D. (Eds). (1997). *Island tourism: Trends and prospects.* London: Pinter.

Lundgren, J. O. J. (2001). Arctic tourism prologue. In: B. Sahlberg (Ed.), *Going North: peripheral tourism in Canada and Sweden* (pp. 9–12). Östersund, Sweden: Etour Publishers.

MacCannell, D. (1989). *The tourist: A new theory of the leisure class* (revised ed.). New York: Schocken Books.

McElroy, J. L. (2003). Tourism development in small islands across the world. *Geografiska Annaler B, 85,* 231–242.

McElroy, J. L., & de Albuquerque, K. (1992). Caribbean small-island tourism styles and sustainable strategies. *Environmental Management, 16,* 615–632.

McElroy, J. L., & de Albuquerque, K. (2002). Problems for managing sustainable tourism in small islands. In: Y. Apostolopoulos, & D. J. Gayle (Eds), *Island tourism & sustainable development: Caribbean, Pacific & Mediterranean experiences* (pp. 15–34). Westport, CT: Praeger.

Patton, M. (1996). *Islands in time: Island socio-geography and Mediterranean prehistory.* London: Routledge.

Pearce, D. (1987). *Tourism today: A geographical analysis.* New York: Longman.

Pitt, D. (1970). *Tradition and economic progress in Samoa.* London: Oxford University Press.

Royle, S. A. (2001). *A geography of islands: Small island insularity.* London: Routledge.

Sahlberg, B. (Ed.). (2001). *Going North: Peripheral tourism in Canada and Sweden.* Östersund, Sweden: Etour Publishers.

Stevenson, M. (2004). Mars on earth. *The Globe and Mail.* Canada, October 16th, Focus Section, p. 9.

Swarbrooke, J., Beard, C., Leckie, S., & Pomfret, G. (2003). *Adventure tourism. The new frontier.* Amsterdam: Butterworth Heinemann.

Tobler, W. (1970). A computer movie. *Economic Geography, 46,* 234–240.

Turner, C. (2003). *Adventure tour guides: Life on extreme outdoor adventures.* New York: Rosen Publishing.

Wilkinson, P. F. (1994). Tourism and small island states: Problems of resource analysis, management and development. In: A. V. Seaton (Ed.), *Tourism: The state of the art* (pp. 41–51). Chichester: Wiley.

Williams, S. (1998). *Tourism geography.* London: Routledge.

SECTION I

CONCEPTUAL THEMES

Chapter 1

Promotional Issues

Graham M.S. Dann

Introduction

How does the tourism industry promote "island-ness" when it seems to be so unilaterally associated with the paradise myth of the tropical, exotic and erotic? What are the opposing attributes of a cold-water island as a "place" that comprises a unique medley of pull factor appeals for potential visitors, and how is this verbal and pictorial amalgam formulated in "the language of tourism"? (Dann, 1996). What, in turn, are the corresponding push factor motivations and activities of the tourists who are drawn to such peripheral regions and how are their attitudes and behaviour articulated by publicity? Finally, as and where they have an actual presence, how are the inhabitants of these extreme locations described in such a way that touristic interaction with Other is viewed as an attraction in itself?

This chapter seeks to address most of these issues by adopting a triangulated approach. It does so, first, by content analysing some recent British travelogues featuring a number of cold-water islands, thereby allowing the characteristics of these isolated locales to emerge inductively from the text. Travelogues are chosen as the preferred medium of communication since, with the exception of word-of-mouth, they have the singular ability to demote as well as promote. All have been drawn from the online files of the same newspaper (Sunday Telegraph, 2005) over an eight-year period from 1997 to 2004 in order to control for cultural and national contamination had a variety of journalistic sources been alternatively selected as the research base. Second, these impressionistic accounts are supplemented by neo-classical travel writing and scholarly commentary from within and without the current volume, both of which provide a corresponding (dis)-confirmation. Through such complementary description and interpretation, several characteristics of place, hosts and their visitors are derived. They are contrasted with their induced counterparts of tropical islands in order to reinforce their distinctiveness and subsequently act as a promotional framework.

Place

Place may be considered according to its constituent elements of space and time.

Space

The myth of paradise   Tropical-island destinations typically rely on perpetuating the myth of paradise — an alluring, undiscovered, unspoiled Garden of Eden whose inhabitants are epitomised by lives of simplicity, *joie de vivre* and community spirit (Tresse, 1990). In such an idyllic setting, the ancient myths of the Fountain of Youth, Heliopolis, the Golden Age and the Horn of Plenty can flourish and be enacted (Dufour, 1978). Paradisiacal myths of this nature are pre-figured in classical and more modern literature, as places where anything wonderful can happen, and in paintings with their images of flowers, beautiful women and perpetual sunshine (Cohen, 1982, p. 13).

However, this type of paradise, argues Cohen (1982, p. 9), is largely contrived and meaningless. It has lost its original (religious) sense, and has instead become a flattened, secularised, post-Fall paradise, the supreme pseudo-event, a place of post-modern conspicuous consumption. In order to regain a traditional "paradise lost", it is necessary for seekers to engage in a quest for re-creation and self-renewal (Cohen, 1982, p. 8), possibilities which can only materialise in remote locations of prelapsarian innocence that are virtually untouched by the machinations of the tourism industry. This is the other side of paradise, an image of the frontier (Echtner, 2000), where 'as long as there is wilderness there is hope' (Theroux, 1992, p. 11).

As far as promotion is concerned, the paradise myth of sultry tropical islands will no doubt continue to be peddled via the visual and written cliché of such hackneyed icons as waving palm trees, azure skies (Krippendorf, 1987) and friendly natives welcoming the visitor with their beguiling charms (Cohen, 1982, p. 17) — key elements which are taken directly from popular literature and placed into advertising copy. However, there is a difficulty in producing a sufficient supply of promised happy and "lei-d back" indigenes, as well as the concomitant problematic realisation that such a paradise of inertia can be quite boring (Cohen, 1982, pp. 15, 19). There needs to be adventure and wilderness action, as well as motivational emphases on separation and difference — appeals that, as will be seen later, cold-water islands can arguably more readily satisfy than their warm and exotic counterparts.

The periphery   Accompanying the notion of a hot tropical paradise is its remoteness — the idea that it must be physically, and hence psychologically removed from the hurly burly of everyday life. At the same time, however, such a paradise must not be *so* distant that it is hard to reach — optimally it should be no more than a non-stop, long-haul flight and an easy connection away. Once they have arrived there, tourists can be given the illusion of isolation via a process of encapsulation (Bhattacharyya, 1997). To this end, they are typically confined and controlled in the all-inclusive equivalents of eggs, cocoons, bubbles, wombs, resorts, villages and clubs. The promotional language is one of safe insularity (Cazes, 1987, pp. 11–12) and protection from a hostile, outside world (Theroux, 1992, p. 535).

By contrast, cold-water islands are often much more difficult to reach. Transportation links are complicated, expensive, irregular, unreliable and frequently in the monopolistic hands of a lone operator. Therein lies their anti-tourist appeal — "the fact that few people go there is one of the most persuasive reasons for travelling to a place" (Theroux, 1992, p. 387). Alternatively stated, and as can be seen in the Greenland chapter, depending on one's point of view, access can be a problem or a safety barrier (against the advent of mass tourism). Many of these territories are located in the spatial periphery. The Hebrides, for example, are spoken of as "the indigo skerry at Europe's edge" (MacClean, 2004, p. 1). Such a description is parallelled in many of the current contributions. Svalbard, for example, is said to be located "on the edge of the world" and the Chatham Islands are referred to as "living on the edge" (see Newton, 2004). The Falklands are described as lying "east of the end of the world", Chatham as an "outpost of New Zealand" and Stewart Island as an "outpost of the world". The act of travel to these peripheral locations often becomes a greater challenge than the actual sojourn, and the art of narrating the danger-filled odyssey even more so.

Just as there is frequently an absence of signposts on a cold-water island, such an a-semiotic situation stands in sharp contrast to a sign-laden tropical island that depends on verbal instruction in order to control its clients (Dann, 2003), comprising notices that range in intensity from simple purveyors of information to menacing messages that threaten the confined and surveyed inmates.

In some cases, too, lack of signage on cold-water islands may also be due to their relatively minuscule size. Although a few of these islands are immense, being tiny and remote is often closest to their stereotype (Cohen, 1982, p. 18). Yet, smallness indicates as well that, for an islander, vagueness in direction has no meaning unless the island is considered as a microcosm (Theroux, 1992, p. 440) where everything can be taken in. Lowliness of stature can additionally be applied to a person as a condition of humility. As Theroux (1992, p. 21) puts it, "the smaller one feels on the earth, dwarfed by mountains and assailed by weather, the more respectful one has to be — and, unless we are very arrogant, the less likely we are to poison or destroy it" (Theroux, 1992, p. 21). Such a statement is also reflected in the case-study account of a Baffin Island resident flying into Pangnirtung:

> The plane begins its descent and I try to reassure myself that the mountains
> in front of me are scenery, not obstacles. Dwarfing both the aircraft and the
> town site below, it makes me realise how small I really am.

Finally, the periphery is not just located at the *end* of the world — it is often spoken of in terms of the *beginning* of the world, of the act of creation itself. Thus, in one of the travelogues, Iceland is said to be one of a "few places so other worldly, so elemental" (Keeble, 2004, p. 1). By way of confirmation, among the contributions to this volume, Macquarie is said to be the only island in the world to be formed from the oceanic crust, while the west coast of Greenland has been created from the oldest rocks on earth. Iceland goes one stage further in claiming to be a place where, metaphorically at least, one can witness the very "birth of the earth".

As far as publicity is concerned, a warm-water island has to strike a delicate balance between remoteness and attainability. Such a strategy is generally achieved by stressing the accessibility of the travel component and the isolation of the sojourn experience. Another way of bringing about a similar promotional effect is by showing that the destination, if not physically, is socially and culturally close to the generating point of touristic origin. In this regard, Puerto Rico, for example, was for years competitively promoted as being part of America for inhabitants from the United States mainland. It was thus said to be unnecessary, and perhaps unpatriotic, for them to travel to other (stranger) islands in the Caribbean or to rival countries like Brazil with similar scenery (Puerto Rico Tourism Company, 1992; Dann, 1996, pp. 205–206).

Cold-water islands, on the other hand, precisely because they are so remote and inaccessible, need to stress the adventure in getting there. Being located in the physical, environmental, climatic and political periphery, cold-water islands can usefully build on the idea that they constitute the last places of their kind. Thus, people need to get there before it is too late, before these fragile locations are lost to development (Ateljevic, 2000, pp. 198–200; Butler, 2002, p. 7; MacCannell, 1989, p. 88) or to global warming. This scenario implies a quest for the genuine and pre-modern before they are changed for the worse. Instead, such islands must be experienced as they are: "the good with the bad, the safe with the unsafe" (Kernan and Domzal, 2000, p. 96). Hence, the risk and challenge involved.

The pure   In tropical islands, nature must typically first be conquered in order to provide a safe and hygienic environment for paying guests. Air conditioning thus counteracts the stultifying humidity, fumigation can reduce infestation and a policy of cleanliness overcomes the risk of disease. Many warm-water islands have additionally spawned a number of health resorts where various luxury treatments are administered. One reason for their success is that the external environment is not conducive to physical well being. Hence, the accent on imported beneficial artificiality within the confines of the spa.

For their part, cold-water islands stress some of the benefits of water itself, especially that it must be clean and potable. Iceland, for instance, is said to have "exceptionally clear air [and] some of the cleanest water in the world" (Mohammadi, 2004, p. 1). Such a situation stands in sharp contrast to much of the tropical Third World where a potable water supply free from disease often cannot be guaranteed. In emphasising health, cold-water islands tend to market their outdoor activities to individuals who, though chronologically elderly, are nevertheless physically fit, whereas tropical islands may have greater appeal to those in need of rejuvenation via the use of the hotel gym.

In other travel accounts, the notion of purity is also associated with the original ("this pristine environment [of the Lofoten] is much as the ice age left it 10,000 years ago" Eames, 2004, p. 1). Such a situation is confirmed by two of the current case studies and their allusions to the pristine environment of Svalbard and the unspoilt nature of Stewart Island. More often than not, travel writers refer to a past where sensory perception is less distorted by artificiality. Thus, in Tasmania, and partly also because of its reduced scale, things are said to have a clearer definition: the oysters are more luscious, cheeses taste sharper and the air seems tangier. Even the peaks seem more gothic and the past darker (Borthwick, 2004b, p. 1).

Taking these various characteristics of purity together on cold-water islands, it is just a short step to the grander notion of "quality of life": a comprehensive state of existence that predates the undesired consequences of tourism (Butler, 2002, p. 11). Here, in travel writing, a direct comparison is often made between the destination and the contemporary touristic society of origin. Via a series of contrasts, it is then suggested that a return to another era and a different place can frequently yield a higher standard of well-being. Thus, Norfolk Island has no income tax, no McDonalds, no foreign debt, no dole, no graffiti and no major crime since 1855 (Borthwick, 2004a, p. 1). Parallels in this volume include the analogous observations that Iceland has one of the highest standards of living in Europe, a high-tech, low-pollution, hydrogen society with the luxury of under-street heating. Then there is Svalbard that not only nostalgically relies on its heritage; it is also a duty-free haven. Similarly, on the Falklands, there has never been a mugging or a pick pocketing through-out the entire course of its history. It is thus important to discover how the residents per-ceive their own quality of life (Stewart Island) and the ways in which they attempt to preserve it in the face of development (Chatham Islands).

However, in many, tropical, especially New World, islands, such dips into the past are simply not viable. More often than not, they come up against a legacy of exploitation and slavery, hardly the stuff of quality of life, and certainly not worth risking as part of any suc-cessful tourism promotion. Cold-water islands are in a more fortunate position. That is why in their publicity they not only refer to the "big outdoors" and associated well-being, but, via competitive advertising, they can suggest that the alternative tropical experience of indoor relaxation is just not cool. Hence, the latest campaign from the Scottish Tourist Board that simply says: "So if you prefer a holiday where you get out rather than chill out, there are few better places than Scotland. Live it. Visit Scotland" (Visit Scotland.com 2004, p. 1).

The sacred   From the quality of life in general, there is a smooth transition to spiritual well-being. In the case of a tropical island, this situation is constituted by a pseudo or dis-enchanted paradise (Cohen, 1982). For a cold-water island, by contrast, it comprises the sacred as a place of inner renewal (Butler, 2002, p. 10), an existential attribute that, accord-ing to travelogues, is manifested in several ways.

The first manner in which the sacred is associated with such peripheral locations is through their *hagiography* and *religious architectural heritage*. One learns, for example, that "Barra is reputedly named after St. Finbarr of Cork (AD 550–623) who converted the inhabitants to Christianity" (Robinson, 2004, p. 9). A similar connection is noted for Greenland in this volume with an allusion to its evangelisation by Lief the Happy over 1000 years ago, as also for Iceland which is said to have been discovered by Irish monks. Then there is Aran which is "littered with ancient fortresses and early chapels" (Seal, 2004, p. 1); and there are parallel references to the sacred Moriori carvings on the Chatham Islands. Of all the case studies in this collection, it is the Solovetsky archipelago that is best known for its association with the sacred. With its ancient holy labyrinths and the estab-lishment of a monastery that have become an important political and religious centre in Russia from the 16th century onwards, it comes as no surprise to learn that today the Solovetsky Islands are a UNESCO World Heritage Site and about a quarter of their visi-tors are pilgrims, many working at the monastery in exchange for food and accommoda-tion, and all seeking that peace so necessary for contemplation.

The second characteristic of the sacred is its relationship with *cemeteries*. Iona, for example, has a famous graveyard wherein are interred the bodies of many saints, prelates and up to 50 Scottish kings. After all, "for 1,000 years after St. Columba's mission, Iona was considered the most venerable ground that anyone could be buried in" (Somerville, 2004a, p. 1), a point echoed on the chapter on Arctic cruise tourism, and once more in relation to the Solovetsk archipelago with its many funerary monuments and burial cairns.

Apart from feeling obliged to sketch in these historical details for their readers, several travel writers also allude to *contemporary celebrations of life and death*. Robinson (2004, p. 9), for instance, describes a funeral on Barra. Somerville (2004b, p. 1), in turn, provides a lengthy description of a burial on Omey Island in order to make the point that it is "one of the few places in Ireland where people are brought from the mainland to be buried on an island", because it is such a sacred place with a cemetery going back "thousands of years". Here the whole community mourns with the bereaved, thereafter to "honour death and celebrate life" (Somerville, 2004b, p. 1). Tropical islands also have similar elaborate celebrations, though participation is strictly limited to local residents. For many tourists, by contrast, especially those from the West, even the word "death" is strictly taboo.

Finally, sacred connotations are established by direct or implicit reference to *the divine*. As regards the former, and according to one travel writer, in Greenland, for instance, the inhabitants are said to survive "by using all that the Lord provides" (Tisdall, 2004, p. 1). "This far north the sun never sets between mid-May and the end of July — just bows toward the horizon as if God were tweaking his heavenly dimmer switch" (Tisdall, 2004, p. 2). In relation to the latter, it is observed that on Macquarie Island, the emotive richness of a natural experience can sometimes be considered spiritual. Some clients of tropical islands, on the other hand, are rarely described as believers, either religious or secular. In this respect, they may indirectly suffer the negative consequences of desacralisation. Similarly, in the sole such adverse reference in the present volume, the 1930s' inhabitants of Nunivak experienced the direct effects of an evangelical Eskimo missionary ban on their language, artefacts and dance, whose cultural revival has taken over 70 years to recover.

Time

Since contemporary society may be unattractive for the tourist, the resulting alienation can bring about not just a *Fernweh*, or longing for distant places, but also a *Zeitweh* — a yearning for far off times. Hence, the language of tourism's stress of "trips to simple and remote people which emphasise the antiquity and changeless nature of their life-ways" (Cohen, 1986, p. 14; Dann, 1996, p. 49).

Much of tourism promotion, particularly that related to tropical islands, makes the distinction between the ordinary and quantitative time of home and the out-of-ordinary qualitative time of away, where the luxury of the latter is portrayed as sleeping all day and partying all night, free from temporal constraints. Only sightseers, it would seem, come under the regulatory ordering of the tour schedule. Cold-water *aficionados*, on the other hand, are depicted not just as free *from* the restrictions of the clock, but rather as free *to* engage in a number of worthwhile activities. For them, the time inversion passivity of tropical island enthusiasts would be a colossal waste of time. What, then, are the major temporal advantages of cold-water environments as described by travel writers? The answer appears to lie in the twin concepts of pace and memory.

Pace   Theroux (1992, p. 470) confesses that visitors to tropical islands tend to adjust their pace to the lives of the inhabitants. If the latter make plans and then subsequently procrastinate, tourists are likely to do the same. After all, he says, "paradise hasn't got a calendar or seasons" (Theroux, 1992, p. 505).

On cold-water islands, by contrast, trips often require careful organisation ("No one goes to the Arctic on impulse. It needs planning" (Davis, 1998, p. 118)). In this vein, visitors to Banks Island are said to research their trip and prepare well. There can also be disorienting experiences of time, as for instance, on Orkney with the shops opening and closing at odd hours (Chalmers, 1987, p. 143). Nevertheless, it is still possible to deny time by removing, for example, all timepieces, as travel writer Birkett does, for instance, in the Stockholm archipelago. In such a manner, one can experience freedom "from the anxieties of modern life" (Birkett, 2004, p. 2).

Memory   A link with the past, along with the realisation that it is in many ways superior to the present, constitutes the frequently encountered travel motive of "nostalgia". This two-phase phenomenon, argues Theroux (1992, p. 255), is successful to the extent that "remote places could induce in me the most intense reveries of home". An alien landscape or foreign culture is not for losing oneself in. Rather, it triggers a harking back to an earlier stage in one's life where mistakes are recognised. Yet the total experience comprises a juxtaposition of the two phases — past and present (Theroux, 1992, pp. 16–17).

Tourists

Having considered the demand side of the equation in terms of place, the supply dimension from the point of view of the tourist's motivation and activities is now examined.

Motivation

Strangerhood and familiarity   Referring to Tasmania, travel writer Borthwick speaks of a peculiar "Penny Farthing championship" (2004b, p. 1) and of "odd" place names like "Break-O' Day River" and "Break-Me-Neck Hill" (2004b, p. 2). Meanwhile, fellow author Tully (2004, p. 1) refers to such "oddities" of Stewart Island as men with "beards ranging from neatly trimmed to ZZ top, and to a juke box "creaking" under the weight of "seventies rock classics". Absence of the familiar is also remarked upon, as for instance, van Dongen's (2004, p. 1) comment on Great Barrier Island where there is "not a member of the chattering classes in sight". Both types of experience are disorienting — positive strangeness, and its negative counterpart — lack of familiarity. Together, they act as a motivational amalgam for visiting cold-water islands.

The distinction between strangeness and familiarity is not new. Indeed, it may be said to underpin some of the earliest typologies of the tourist (Cohen, 1972, 1974, 1979). In turn, this taxonomy relies on the sociological contributions of Schutz (1944) and Simmel (1950). According to Cohen, familiarity and strangeness lie on extreme ends of a motivational continuum. The former relates to the mass tourist whose alienation from the society of origin is merely of the recreational or diversionary variety. The latter is evident in the tourist types of wanderer and drifter, and in the corresponding phenomenological categories of experiential, experimental and existential who seek increasing novelty in the "Centre-out-there" — the alternative society of the Other.

It is easy to see how familiarity and strangeness are respectively associated with tropical and cold-water islands. The warm-water island, typically epitomised by the isolated resort hotel, is deliberately cut off from the surrounding (strange) native environment. It is, by contrast, a self-sufficient locale of incompatible luxury, replete with touristic reminders of home ranging from four-poster beds to bacon and egg breakfasts. The cold-water island, on the other hand, positively *embraces* strangeness in terms of the place and its people. Novelty and adventure are key ingredients to this type of break from everyday life. It is therefore not surprising to find their promotional appeal couched in a contemporary language of difference. Such a lingo of uniqueness is often replete with superlatives that are applied by advertising, brochure copy and travel writing to the natural and built environment. This dichotomy between home and away is confirmed by two offerings in the present volume. The Luleå archipelago is said to constitute a contrast between the ordinary society of the visitor and the out-of-ordinary of the visited; while in Greenland, such difference is referred to as a pull factor. The former account goes on to state that difference is accentuated by a series of multi-sensory activities that relate exclusively to ice (such as dining on ice and ice-breaker conferences). In other contributions, however, difference is spoken of in relation to superlatives. Natural phenomena and areas of outstanding natural beauty are referred to in such a manner in the case of Macquarie; while Iceland boasts of Europe's largest waterfalls, geysers and hot springs. Similarly, Banks Island possesses the northernmost navigable river in America and the highest density of musk oxen in the world; while the Chatham Islands are described in terms of their *unique* flora, fauna and culture, an epithet that is applied to Iceland's language, artistes and food, as well as to those of Nunivak.

Strangeness is also directly associated with a correspondingly frequent use of simile and metaphor (see Dann, 1992). Examples from travel articles include:

- natural environment (e.g., Barra: "cliff-edged islands are strewn like giant boulders hurled by an irate Cyclops" (Robinson, 2004, p. 9)),
- built environment (e.g., Lofoten islands: "houses built like the hotels in Monopoly, plonked unceremoniously on the sward" (Eames, 2004, p. 3)),
- tourist activities (e.g., Iceland: "volcanic hangovers" (Keeble, 2004, p. 2)),
- local people and culture (e.g., Stockholm archipelago: "The boat taxi's skipper seemed to have swaggered from the pages of a Jack London novel" (Birkett, 2004, p. 1)).

Interestingly, in the travel articles examined, as many as 142 similes/metaphors were employed, in contrast to 88 more prosaic signifiers of difference. Additionally, and particularly with respect to tropical islands, the more familiar the island to the reader, the less the perceived need for the writer to utilise simile or metaphor (Dann, 1996, p. 173). Correspondingly, differences are downplayed in favour of similarities, several examples of which are provided by the French scholar, Tresse (1990, pp. 9, 15–17), in relation to a number of Francophone territories in Africa.

Finally, some contributors to the present volume associate the cold-water *motif* of strangeness with curiosity. This is so in relation to the Chatham Islands and Falklands. In the case of the latter, however, curiosity is linked to such oddities as driving on the left, having a 21-gun salute on the Queen's birthday and the presence of a minefield that doubles as a golf course.

Safety   Safety is another consideration in the motivation of tourists and in the corresponding promotion of destinations. Tropical islands tend to deal with this feature by protecting their clients from humans and (other) animals deemed to be dangerous. Cold-water islands, on the other hand, adopt a more ambivalent stance. While a certain sense of excitement and adventure is engendered in the direct encounter with such wild fauna as polar bears, there is also an underlying nostalgic appeal to quasi-biblical times when animals and humans peacefully co-existed (see Isaiah (11: 1ss)). Thus, writing of the Falklands in a travel article, Vitaliev (2004, p. 3) notes that "most of the birds are totally unafraid of humans and are easily approachable". The concept of safety is further extended in the case study of Iceland as a feeling of security even when travelling alone. It thus ties in with the motivational appeal to self-fulfilment.

Alienation–freedom–control   It has been argued by Cohen (1979) that the quest for strangeness beyond the tourist's society of origin is directly related to the prior degree of alienation experienced in the home environment. Those in search of cold-water islands, therefore, are more prone to leave behind domesticity and all its trappings than are those who gravitate towards tropical luxury. In relation to Svalbard, Viken (2003, pp. 240–241), in an earlier paper, calls the former tendency the "de-objectification of nature" — the abandonment of the material things of life and their substitution with (the spirituality of) nature itself. This point is reflected in the current offering when it is noted that most of the inhabitants of that place do not own property. It is also echoed in an observation from the chapter on Arctic cruise tourism that the locals' "closely guarded sense of community" is predicated on the perception that real human values lie beyond the notion of purchasing power. Theroux (1992, p. 13) captures the idea in the following passage:

> Everything you need is on your back. All inessentials have been left behind
> as you enter a world of natural beauty which has not been violated, where
> money has no value, and possessions are a dead weight. The person with
> the fewest possessions is the freest.

The connection with freedom becomes all the more evident when this situation is compared with its converse. On warm-water islands, such as Hawaii, for instance, all the paraphernalia that tourists bring with them, or purchase at the destination, become status symbols, denoting who their owners are in terms of the social advantages gained through conspicuous consumption.

However, freedom is more deeply felt in cold-water environments free from material constraint. Thus, "if in the Arctic, you follow the Inuit rules of survival, you too survive". However, if instead you bring the accoutrements of home with you (such as cigars and silver dinner plates) you perish (as did the British explorers) (Davis, 1998, p. 120). Here these pseudo adventurers might as well have been on a tropical island surrounded by creature comforts, to the point where the latter controlled them.

Finally, the notion of freedom, and its correlative — possessions, is extended to the concept of (dis)-possessing islands themselves. In this scenario, and carrying the foregoing logic to its extreme, there is clearly an inverse relationship between freedom and ownership. On cold-water islands, when this topsy-turvy feeling is at its most intense, there is absolutely no wish on the part of visitors to possess these territories. According to travel writer Birkett (2004, p. 2), such islands belong to the inhabitants, or, in their absence, to scientists or nature. Visitors, if they become more than visitors (such as prospective purchasers), are decidedly unwelcome.

It is on the tropical island that the latter connection materialises in the familiar mainland fantasy of buying a piece of paradise (as indeed do some cruise companies and airlines). For the academic, however, such consumerism may involve a masculine language of appropriation which itself becomes part of the discourse of promotion. The tropical island territory is thus described in terms of virginity waiting like a maiden to be possessed, of emptiness, abundance and seizure — an Orientalist discourse (Said, 1991) of male capture. It comes as little surprise, therefore, that it is reflected in such advertising as "Greece belongs to you", "Bali offers everything" and "The Maldives are yours" (Cazes, 1987, p. 5).

Self-discovery   From the previous section it follows that the major difference between cold-water islands and their tropical counterparts is that, whereas the former are *places to see*, unhampered by material concerns, the latter are *places to be seen in* (Hack, 1997, p. 145). Indeed, on warm-water islands it is easier to amass status points on location as well as through the parallel ego-enhancing activity of "trip dropping" in front of friends, neighbours and work-mates when the tourist returns home. However, as one contributor to this volume demonstrates, these "Veblen effects" can also extend to cold-water territories such as Iceland, on account of their higher prices and the consequent exclusiveness they connote. Whatever the situation, however, this difference is based on another, more fundamental respective distinction — that between self-discovery and love of self.

Self-discovery, ("self-fulfilment" or "reaffirmation of identity" in the Iceland case study), that quality primarily associated with cold-water environments, places humankind in a direct confrontation with nature, an exposure that evokes humility in the subject and, with it, the enabling spiritual exercises of contemplation, purification and rebirth. In such a manner, individuals become lovers of nature, the condition for seeing themselves as part of nature.

On tropical islands, however, self-discovery is not usually possible, since the distinction between humanity and nature is rarely made. Indeed, because nature is constantly being conquered, and humankind is continuously being protected from hostile nature, humanity is lost in the process.

Activities

Natural   Since self-discovery is so closely associated with direct contact with nature, it follows that the behavioural counterpart to motivation — activity — must itself be natural. In a cold-water context, this means that related pursuits are often not weather dependent. Bird watching, white water rafting, and so on, can actually become more adventuresome when the weather is bad; while equivalent tropical island activities (such as paragliding and sunbathing) may have to be cancelled through fear of danger or inconvenience associated with inclement weather. The former situation is a challenge to self-development; the latter is an obstacle to the quest for hedonistic happiness.

Experiences can also be said to be natural, to the extent that they are *polysensual* (Jacobsen, 1994). Nature, especially in cold-water islands, involves far more than mere sight-seeing. (Indeed, as far as sight is concerned, there may be very little to see except for bland whiteness). The natural also includes the senses of touch, taste, sound and smell, descriptions of which travel writers are only too ready to supply. Nor are these recorded sensations always pleasant. Smell, for instance, can be described as neutral and negative, as well as positive. It can also be particularly evocative of the past (see the section on memory). Yet, as has been noted, the multi-sensorial nature of the deep-embodied experiences associated with cold-water islands, such as Iceland, are evident in feeling the heat of underground volcanoes, the omnipresent odour of sulphur, the hissing of steam and the taste of rotten shark.

Tropical islands, by contrast, are ocular-centric. With regard to their nature, where odours are banished, and touch, taste and sound are similarly excluded on the grounds of hygiene or in the name of progress, the remaining conquering gaze is the "monarch-of-all-that-is-surveyed" variety — of the possessor rather than the possessed (Theroux, 1992, p. 515).

Educational   As Morgan and Pritchard (1998, p. 172) observe: "when we visit an island paradise we cast off not only our normal form but also "normal" standards of behaviour." This island paradise, which is typically of the tropical variety, places the accent firmly on rest, relaxation, play and fantasy.

By contrast, Jacobsen notes that recuperation is of minimal significance for first-time journeys to such cold-water destinations as the Arctic region of northern Scandinavia. Here: "experiences, participation and learning appear to be more important factors of tourism … the wish to encounter something not yet seen or known … to come to terms with oneself and to discover one's own abilities" (1994, p. 82). It is in this last sentence that the educational factor is linked with the previously discussed motive of self-discovery. Another reason why cold-water islands satisfy the twin quest for knowledge and re-affirmation of identity is that they are authentic. As travel writer Borthwick (2004b, p. 2) notes in relation to Tasmania: "in an era when many destinations are presented like theme parks, Tasmania still permits its travel-lers witness to *real* history and nature" (emphasis added). It is presumably for this reason that several contributors to this volume note that cold-water islands are deliberately targeted at the well educated (e.g., Svalbard, Macquarie, Banks and Baffin). As the chapter on Arctic cruise tourism points out, learning as a related activity is here considered more important than mind-less entertainment (often associated with warm-water islands).

Interaction with Locals

Contact with the Other

From what has been stated earlier with respect to motivation, it should be clear that on cold-water islands the desire for strangeness, encounters with a culture out there and the need for self-awareness imply a contact with the "Other". Quite the opposite motivational characteristics, however, are to be found among *aficionados* of tropical islands who require large doses of familiarity with reminders of home and simultaneous protection from the hostile "Other".

As Theroux (1992, p. 431) implies, the reason why the self can progress in a cold-water environment is that "living on an island … [means] … that you [are] never alone". Where they exist, the inhabitants all know one another and are often inter-related. They thus tend to treat visitors in a similar fashion to their mutual advantage. Hence, in relation to Rathlin Island, Scott (2004, p. 2) observes, "You can easily be *alone* if you want to be. But you'll never be *lonely*. Sooner or later a McFaul or a McCurdy will be along saying Richard or Paddy are looking for you in the pub" (emphases added). Even so, it is noted in relation to the Falklands that locals, however friendly, do not have to defer to tourists simply because they are from away. Rather, hosts and guests learn from each other, often because there are no hotels (e.g., Banks Island), but instead, and as in the chapter on Arctic cruise tourism, "tiny communities with big hearts".

Such a situation stands in sharp contrast to temporary sojourn on a tropical island where visitors only have themselves for company. The latter state-of-affairs, argues Urbain (2003, p. 193) is "not a society of difference but of paraded sameness … When a seaside vacationer looks at another he [sic] is looking at himself". It is an *égotisme à deux*.

The Other as Brother, the Other as Mother

Clearly, if a cold-water island visitor is to be open to the "Other", that "Other" must be treated as equal. Treating *alter* on par with *ego* has been described in terms of "the Other as brother" (Dann, 2004). Here the "Other" is regarded in terms of work rather than leisure, as serious rather than playful, just as visitors are similarly working at their vacations. For that reason, it is not surprising to find allusions to the industrious "Other" among the travel accounts of cold-water islands. In Barra, for example, there is an old fisherman with little time for an outside world that has been "ruined by mechanisation", who admits that, "here we still work with our hands. It's hard but it's real at least" (Robinson, 2004, p. 9).

Yet, a transition occurs whenever a place, instead of simply welcoming visitors, gravitates towards tourism. Such change is epitomised on tropical islands, where an (often Third World) "Other as mother" is introduced as someone inferior and servile catering to the tourist's every whim and fancy. She is the "noble savage" of plantation tourism, the house slave of the Great House fulfilling the desires of the new "massa" from the same colonial origins as the landlord of yesteryear.

Conclusion: Cold is Cool and Hot is Not

This chapter has examined a number of travel narratives that are deeply embedded in Western culture (Rassing and Sørensen, 2001), recurring inductive themes that depict cold-water islands, in an effort to discover their elements of attractiveness from both the supply and demand sides of the tourism equation, when contrasted with their warm-water counterparts. While cold-water islands stress *locational* difference, remoteness, pre-modern authenticity, spirituality, absence of signs, slow pace and nostalgia, tropical islands respectively emphasise sameness, accessibility, abundance post-modern thematisation, hedonism, surfeit of signs, scheduling and living for the here-and-now. Whereas cold-water islands underline *touristic* novelty, lack of possessions, self-discovery through nature and learning through polysensual experiences, warm-water islands place the equivalent accent on homeliness, ego-enhancement through the display of status symbols, love of self via conquered nature and mastery through the ocular-centric. Cold-water islands view the *local inhabitants* as an opportunity for socialisation. Tropical islands regard the natives as inimical to narcissistic love and thus to be avoided via the process of touristic encapsulation.

There remain a number of problems associated with promoting tropical islands, and many have been highlighted in the literature. They range from the irresponsible use of cliché (Dann, 2001) to the sort of unsustainable tourism to which such promotion can easily lead. To these may be added the following disadvantages that have been noted directly or indirectly in the present account:

- The "enclavisation" of resorts.
- The polarisation of a destination society into "us" (the natives) and "them" (tourists and their imitators).
- The (often racist) stereotyping of locals as happy, pleasure-loving, laid-back, inferior and lazy people catering to the leisure needs of visitors.
- The local resentment accruing from the above and its heightening through the parading of foreign affluence against a backdrop of indigenous poverty.
- The re-awakening of relationships based on plantation slavery in those locations with such an historical memory.

Less glaring, though nonetheless worthy of final comment, are some persisting difficulties connected with the promotion of cold-water islands. The first is linked to the success of such publicity. If it leads to a substantial increase in visitor arrivals it could, in turn, militate against the uncrowded, anti-tourist nature of the place that attracted people initially. For that reason, carefully controlled doses of demotion — such as limiting the number of cruise ships or the number of annual visitors — should arguably accompany any promotion. Second, and by way of paradox, if, as has been shown (Rassing and Sørensen, 2001), highly satisfying visitor experiences on cold-water islands are not conducive to repeat visitation (maybe because such tourists require ever-increasing novelty), how can such locales attract the right sort of clientèle? Third, if alienation from the home society characterises the *aficionados* of cold-water islands, is there not a real danger that these visitors who are disenchanted with their society of origin may find it more difficult to adapt to local conditions elsewhere than those who simply come to have a good time (the enthusiasts of tropical climes)? Fourth, if a dearth of wealth and possessions is associated with patrons of cold-water islands, how can their chosen relative lack of affluence help the host society economically? Finally, if a desired slow pace and nostalgic evocations of yesteryear are paramount considerations for the cold-water visitor, surely such a situation is problematic for the development of a destination society, caught as it is in a resulting promotional time-warp.

The foregoing are just some of the potential and actual pitfalls associated with the successful promotion and visitation of cold-water islands. Part of their solution clearly resides in how their inhabitants wish to portray themselves and the places in which they live, and whether or not the tourism industry of the future will thus empower them to provide self-imagery in place of an imagery imposed by outsiders.

References

Ateljevic, L. (2000). Tourist motivation, values and perceptions. In: A. Woodside, G. Crouch, J. Mazanec, M. Oppermann, & M. Sakai (Eds), *Consumer psychology of tourism, hospitality and leisure* (pp. 193–209). Wallingford: CABI.

Bhattacharyya, D. (1997). An analysis of a guidebook. *Annals of Tourism Research*, *24*(2), 371–389.

Birkett, D. (2004). The Stockholm archipelago. http://www.travelintelligence.net/wsd/articles/art4print_41.html (accessed 20/10/05).

Borthwick, J. (2004a). Norfolk island. www.travelintelligence.net/wsd/articles/art4print_2147.html (accessed 20/10/05).

Borthwick, J. (2004b). Tasmania: Australia's 'Other Half'. www.travelintelligence.net/wsd/articles/art4print_2154.html, (accessed 20/10/05).

Butler, R. (2002). The development of tourism in frontier regions: Issues and approaches. In: S. Krakover, & Y. Gradus (Eds), *Tourism in frontier areas* (pp. 3–29). Lanham, MD: Lexington Books.

Cazes, G. (1987). L'Île tropicale, figure emblematique du tourisme international. *Cahiers du tourisme.* Série C, no. 112.

Chalmers, J. (1987). *Wish you were here? 50 of the best holidays*. London: Queen Anne Press.

Cohen, E. (1972). Toward a sociology of international tourism. *Social Research 39* (1), 164–182.

Cohen, E. (1974). Who is a tourist? A conceptual clarification. *Sociological Review*, *22*(4), 527–555.

Cohen, E. (1979). A phenomenology of tourist experiences. *Sociology*, *13*(2), 179–201.

Cohen, E. (1982). The Pacific Islands from utopian myth to consumer product: The disenchantment of paradise. *Cahiers du tourisme*, Série B, no. 27.

Cohen, E. (1986). Tourism and time. *World Leisure and Recreation*, *28*(3), 13–16.

Dann, G. (1992). Travelogs and the management of unfamiliarity. *Journal of Travel Research*, *30*(4), 59–63.

Dann, G. (1996). *The language of tourism. A sociolinguistic perspective*. Wallingford: CABI.

Dann, G. (2001). Self-admitted use of cliché in the language of tourism. *Tourism, Culture and Communication*, *3*(1), 1–14.

Dann, G. (2003). Noticing notices: Tourism to order. *Annals of Tourism Research*, *30*(2), 465–484.

Dann, G. (2004). (Mis)-representing the Other in the language of tourism. *Journal of Eastern Caribbean Studies*, *29*(2), 76–94.

Davis, W. (1998). Force of nature. *Condé Nast Traveler*, January, pp. 110–121, 197–200.

Dufour, R. (1978). Des mythes du Loisir/tourisme weekend. Aliénation ou libération? *Cahiers du tourisme*, Série C, no. 47.

Eames, A. (2004). Lofoten islands www.travelintelligence.net/wsd/articles/art4print_2625.html (accessed 20/10/05).

Echtner, C. (2000). *The representation of the third world in tourism marketing*. Unpublished doctoral dissertation. University of Calgary, Calgary.

Hack, S. (1997). Rock à la mode. *Condé Nast Traveler*, July, pp. 94–103, 145–149.

Jacobsen, J. (1994). *Arctic tourism and global tourism trends*. Report 37. Thunder Bay, Ontario: Lakehead University Centre for Northern Studies.

Keeble, J. (2004). A weekend to remember in Iceland. www.travelintelligence.net/wsd/articles/art4print_3062.html (accessed 20/10/05).

Kernan, J., & Domzal, T. (2000). Playing on the post-modern edge: Action, leisure and self-identity. In: A. Woodside, G. Crouch, J. Mazanec, M. Oppermann, & M. Sakai (Eds), *Consumer psychology of tourism, hospitality and leisure* (pp. 91–101). Wallingford: CABI.

Krippendorf, J. (1987). *The holidaymakers. Understanding the impact of leisure and travel*. Oxford: Heinemann.

MacCannell, D. (1989). *The tourist. A new theory of the leisure class.* (2nd ed.). New York: Schocken Books.

Maclean, R. (2004). Islands among islands. www.travelintelligence.net/wsd/articles/art4print_601.html (accessed 20/10/05).

Mohammadi, K. (2004). Over the rainbow: The best of Iceland www.travelintelligence.net/wsd/articles/art4print_1810.html (accessed 20/10/05).

Morgan, N., & Pritchard, A. (1998). *Tourism promotion and power. Creating images, creating identities.* Chichester: Wiley.

Newton, R. (2004). Chatham Islands: The end of the world. www.travelintelligence.net/wsd/articles/art4print_3303.html (accessed 20/10/05).

Puerto Rico Tourism Company. (1992). Advertisement. *Condé Nast Traveler,* October, p. 153.

Rassing, C., & Sørenson, A. (2001). Once-only visitors and the Faroe islands: Notes on the topic of non-repeat tourism. Paper presented at the 10th Nordic tourism and hospitality research symposium, Vasa, Finland, 18–20 October.

Robinson, P. (2004). Scots on the rocks. *Sunday Telegraph Travel,* 21 March, p. 9.

Said, E. (1991). *Orientalism. Western conceptions of the orient.* Harmondsworth: Penguin.

Scott, D. (2004). Rathlin island. www.travelintelligence.net/wsd/articles/art4print_3256.html (accessed 20/10/05).

Schutz, A. (1944). The stranger: An essay in social psychology. *American Journal of Sociology, 49*(6), 495–507.

Seal, J. (2004). The Aran islands www.travelintelligence.net/wsd/articles/art4print_643.html (accessed 20/10/05).

Simmel, G. (1950). The stranger. In: K. Wolff (Ed.), *The sociology of Georg Simmel.* Glencoe, IL: Free Press.

Somerville, C. (2004a). Iona. www.travelintelligence.net/wsd/articles/art4print_752.html (accessed 20/10/05).

Somerville, C. (2004b). Omey island www.travelintelligence.net/wsd/articles/art4print_910.html (20/10/05).

Sunday Telegraph. (2005). http://www.telegraph.co.uk. (accessed 20/10/05).

Theroux, P. (1992). *The happy isles of Oceania. Paddling the Pacific.* London: Hamish Hamilton.

Tisdall, N. (2004). Dog-sledding in Greenland. www.travelintelligence.net/wsd/articles/art4print_1496.html (accessed 20/10/05).

Tresse, P. (1990). L'Image des civilisations Africaines à travers les Publications des Services Officiels du Tourisme des Pays d'Afrique Francophone. *Cahiers du tourisme,* Série C (110).

Tully, C. (2004). Next stop Antarctica. www.travelintelligence.net/wsd/articles/art4print_3128.html (accessed 20/10/05).

Urbain, J.-D. (2003). In: C. Porter (Trans.). [*At the beach.*] Minneapolis MN: University of Minnesota Press.

van Dongen, Y. (2004). Ourselves, alone. www.travelintelligence.net/wsd/articles/art4print_772.html (accessed 20/10/05).

Viken, A. (2003). Tourist environmental concern: Attitudes, identity or good behaviour. In: K. Pedersen, & A. Viken (Eds). *Nature and identity: Essays on the culture of nature* (pp. 221–245). Kristiansand: Høyskoleforlaget.

Visit Scotland.com (2004). Scotland's natural heritage www.visitscotland.com. (accessed 20/10/05).

Vitaliev, V. (2004). Falkland islands www.travelintelligence.net/wsd/articles/art4print_585.html (accessed 20/10/05).

Chapter 2

Sustainability Issues

Jerome L. McElroy and Bruce Potter

Introduction

Given accelerating ecosystem damage and the decline in biodiversity on a global scale, the search for sustainability pervades contemporary development discourse and will likely dominate the economic-environmental debate across the 21st century. However broadly defined — a rising standard of living for a growing population experiencing expanding economic choice and political autonomy over generations — sustainable growth will likely be considered the holy grail of the present generation. Since tourism has become the largest industry in the world economy — accounting for roughly 10% of global GDP, employment, exports and investment (WTTC, 2005) — and since its long-standing viability depends on environmental durability, it is not surprising that sustainable tourism (ST) has become the dominant paradigm (Hunter, 1995) in both tourism theory and practice as well as an issue that continues to be hotly debated (Velikova, 2001).

This ST emphasis is particularly appropriate for many small islands engaged in postwar economic restructuring toward tourism diversification. This transformation has been driven by a confluence of push and pull factors. First, export revenues from traditional colonial staples (like sugar, bananas and copra) have declined because of loss of preferential (high-price) markets and rising transport costs (WTO, 2004). Second, domestic agriculture has been buffeted by import competition as trade barriers have fallen. Third, the demand for an island holiday has been fueled by postwar affluence in the industrial North and the availability of jet access to and transport infrastructure in the once remote island tropics. The appeal of insular separation, distinctness and boundedness (Baum, 1997) has made the paradise getaway a fixture in the middle-class imagination. Finally, the focus on ST is timely since, according to Fennell and Ebert (2004, p. 269), coming decades will witness an acceleration of long-haul tourism converging on the more remote and ecologically vulnerable ecosystems like the cold-water islands examined in this volume where tourism experience and planning are relatively limited.

Extreme Tourism: Lessons from the World's Cold Water Islands
Copyright © 2006 by Elsevier Ltd.
All rights of reproduction in any form reserved
ISBN: 0-08-044656-6

Background

The recent gestation of the ST concept is sourced in two related phenomena: (1) the rapid and damaging global spread of international tourism across the island periphery especially since 1960 and (2) the changing emphases of the tourism research chronicling these impacts. In the former case, resort construction and road networks on steep mountain slopes have caused deforestation, erosion, lagoon pollution and reef damage (McElroy & de Albuquerque, 1998). Overgrowth in the Mediterranean has spawned over-burdened sewage and solid waste systems, disfigured shorelines and created intense seasonal congestion (Bramwell, 2004). Several Greek island landscapes have been spoiled by rapid and unplanned coastal development (Andriotis, 2004). Even the less tourism penetrated Pacific — with its history of unsustainable logging, mining and fishing (Overton & Scheyvens, 1999) — has not escaped the scars of change (Apostolopoulos & Gayle, 2002). In short, Bianchi's summary (2004, p. 499) applies: a generation of palpable economic benefits have come at a high price — rising environmental damage, dependency and cultural dislocation.

   Against this backdrop of change, early researchers in the 1960s touted the economic benefits of tourism diversification to drive post-colonial insular modernization (Jafari, 2002). As the negative ecosystem spillovers associated with rapid mass tourism growth surfaced during the 1970s, this advocacy platform was followed by a critical literature emphasizing tourism's ecological and socio-cultural intrusions. Since the 1980s a new so-called 'adaptancy platform' has emerged seeking to address the concerns of the critics in two different directions. The first emphasizes small, low-impact, locally controlled alternatives to mass tourism (Weaver, 1998). It includes both the expansion of ecotourism and other special interest forms (agro, adventure, cultural, etc.) as well as the greening of conventional tourism through reduced utility consumption and waste production (Spilanis & Vayanni, 2004).

   The second strand emphasizes developing more holistic approaches to better capture tourism's complexity and volatility. Some authors stress expanding the horizon of possibilities for Butler's (1980) lifecycle model of tourism evolution (Briassoulis, 2004). For example, Papatheodorou (2004) emphasizes a systems approach with core and periphery nodes in a destination and multiple equilibrium solutions. Others press for longer-run, non-linear frameworks that borrow from science and use trans-disciplinary thinking (Farrell & Twining-Ward, 2004, 2005). For example, McKercher (1999) favors a chaos/complexity framework that treats tourism as a living ecological community with keystone (primary) attractions. In a similar vein, Russell and Faulkner (2004) use chaos theory to understand entrepreneurial vagaries and resort development. Among other things, the interplay between these two strands — both the new thinking and improved tourism styles — has produced the groundswell of interest in ST.

The Problem

Despite these advances in theory and practice, sustainability remains elusive in island tourism for at least four reasons. First, despite tourism's pervasiveness, most studies continue to be conducted within single disciplinary boundaries and generate narrow policy outcomes that fail to gauge the widespread impacts of tourism. Second, planning tourism development in small islands is particularly difficult because of their inherent fragility on two fronts: extreme interdependence on the inside; and openness to external intrusion from the outside. The former is especially problematic because of the delicate linkages between terrestrial and marine ecosystems in volcanic islands that complicate planning options. Inappropriate hillside resort construction accelerates runoff and pollutes lagoons while sand dredging destabilizes coastlines, erodes beaches and chokes coral growth. Third, island tourism is a moving target. As Butler (1980) has argued, successful destinations tend to pass through successive stages of increasing visitor density, facility size, external control and bio-cultural damage until saturation and/or their appeal wanes. This movement is principally due to the scale discontinuity between the large-scale mass market international throughput tourist economy and the small relatively closed insular ecology: a scale discrepancy that almost guarantees island natural and social carrying capacities will be threatened (McElroy, 1975). Fourth, there is no univocal definition of sustainability. Most formulations are rooted in the 1987 Brundtland Report (Brundtland, 1987): development in the present that does not compromise options for future generations; yet much debate has centered on 'hard' (constant natural assets: Collins, 1999) versus 'soft' (allowing for human-made replacements: McKercher, 1993) sustainability. One tends, however, to agree with (Clarke, 1997, p. 229) that: "... the absence of a precise good definition is less important than general movement in the correct direction."

Commonalities

Despite these differences, however, a sampling of definitions suggests ST does contain a core of common elements. This core embraces balance among economic, ecological and socio-cultural processes. Various formulations may express particular emphases. For example, at the top of the list for the World Tourism Organization (WTO, 2004, p. 62) is maintaining essential ecological stability. On the other hand, a recent textbook (Tribe, 2005, p. 380) defines sustainability "as growth which is not threatened by feedback, for example, from pollution, resource depletion or social unrest." Several authors stress the importance of ST's favorable local impacts: ecosystem conservation and improvement in host quality of life (Weaver, 1998, p. 17); developing domestic decision-making capacity or empowerment (Sofield, 2003); and contributing "beyond the confines of the resort community" to the sustainable development of the non-tourist economic sectors (Hunter, 1995, p. 160). Most definitions tend to underline two additional imperatives: proactive, comprehensive planning over long time horizons (Fennell & Ebert, 2004, p. 468; Khan, 2005), and maintaining "a high level of tourist satisfaction..." (WTO, 2004, p. 62).

One short-hand way to understand the meaning of ST is to summarize its formidable challenge, that is, to simultaneously satisfy the needs of the major stakeholders: hosts, guests, entrepreneurs and bio-cultural assets (Hunter, 1995, p. 156). As a working definition based on this challenge, we propose the so-called four-cornered "sustainability diamond" — a rough but useful reference point for briefly analyzing the cold-water cases to follow. This embraces the following (McElroy, 2002, p. 152):

1. durable natural and cultural assets;
2. improved host life quality;

3. enduring visitor enjoyment; and
4. long-term enterprise profitability.

Accordingly, a destination is said to be moving in the right direction when one or more of the following barometers of ST surfaces at least to some degree:

1. Islanders becoming major beneficiaries of tourism;
2. Visitors developing a strong return ethos;
3. Developers respecting the integrity of the native "genius of the place"; and
4. Public decision-makers committing to long-term planning, impact monitoring and controlling "visitor numbers, activities and investments, if intrusive and damaging to insular scale" (McElroy, 2002, p. 165).

Moreover, there are a number of lessons from warm-water island experience deserving mention. Royle (2001, p. 206) cautions that "Tourism everywhere is a double-edged sword..." creating both costs and benefits. The WTO (2004, p. 61) warns that any tourism activity "even at low levels of intensity" will produce environmental and socio-cultural impacts. According to Cater (1993, p. 89): "There is no example of tourist use that is completely without impact." In fact, even low-density alternatives to mass tourism like ecotourism are no panacea, especially when they access delicate amenities in poor regions lacking appropriate regulations and monitoring. In addition, they often are susceptible to rapid change and foreclose local participation to aggressive outsiders (Cater, 1993). In a similar vein, Weaver (1998, p. 25) argues that "successful" styles can infiltrate "backstage regions" in the search for authentic local interaction, disrupt the pace and pattern of community living, and "pave the way for less benign forms of tourism." Even in cases where ecotourism seems sustainable on the local level, Gössling et al. maintain "... it may not be sustainable from a global point of view" when it involves long-haul travel since 90% of the environmental impact is contributed by air transport to and from the destination.

The lifecycle literature is particularly revealing about how destinations at different stages of development face different planning challenges: establishing infrastructure and identity in emergence, controlling the pace of change during growth and managing visitor densities and vacation quality in maturity (McElroy & de Albuquerque, 1998). A number of case studies suggest also that ST may be more easily achieved in truly diversified insular economies like Bermuda, Mauritius and Seychelles where tourism is not the sole engine of growth. Viable alternative economic activities tend to blunt the pressure to promote tourism beyond insular ecological and social carrying capacities. In addition, for most warm-water destinations across all oceanic basins, usually the most determinative factor in tourism's historical gestation has been the establishment of an international airport. This underlines the overwhelming significance of access on insular amenities and populations.

Finally, given a generation of unprecedented tourism development in small islands "at the expense of the natural world and local identity and traditional cultures" (Fennel & Ebert, 2004, p. 461), and given the likelihood that future growth thrusts will envelop even more remote, unexploited ecosystems, sustainability may require occasional use of the Precautionary Principle. According to Myers (1993, p. 74), this places "a premium on a cautious and conservative approach to human interventions in environmental

sectors that are: (1) usually short on scientific understanding, and (2) usually susceptible to significant injury ...". Such an approach seems appropriate for the delicate assets
in new tourism areas of cold-water islands where carrying capacities cannot be easily
assessed, recovery to disturbance is slow, and "both the probability and value of irre-
versible damage are uncertain" (Fennell & Ebert, 2004, p. 466). As a tool in the plan-
ner's arsenal, the PP appropriately "... puts the onus on the present population to address
current actions that might lead to potential risks and negative outcomes for future generations" (*ibid.*, p. 468).

Cold Cases

The limited literature on cold water islands does identify many strategic advantages and
shortcomings that circumscribe tourism growth. In his examination of the northern islands
of Orkney and Shetland, Butler (1997) stresses rural ambience and heritage assets, wildlife
and unique scenery and the possibilities of adventure activity. In their analysis of North
Atlantic islands, Baum and others (2000) emphasize three major development limitations:
insufficient tourism recognition by policy-makers, extreme seasonality because of
inclement weather, and restricted high-cost access because of remoteness. However, they
also underscore the advantages of a small-scale visitor industry: enhanced local ownership,
reduced income leakages, and the availability of infrastructure and services "... which
island populations could not otherwise sustain" (Baum et al., 2000, p. 217).

The cases assembled in this volume differ widely in size: from Greenland, the largest
island in the world, and Iceland (population 300,000) to tiny Macquarie Island in Australia
(34 km^2), Banks Island in the Canadian Arctic (population 153), and the Luleå Archipelago
in Sweden (population 80). They also exhibit a variety of distinct traditions including,
among others, the Inuit culture in Baffin Island, Canada, Viking history across the North
Atlantic Islands, and the Maori muttonbird harvesting in Stewart Island, New Zealand.
Although most are recently emerging as international destinations, they differ somewhat
in the stages of tourism development. The major contrast is between Iceland (a mass tourist
destination with over 300,000 annual tourists, roughly 20,000 cruise visitors and over 6000
hotel rooms) and the rest of the pack: most notably less than 500 yearly tourists to
Macquarie Island, the Luleå Archipelago, and Nunivak Island, and only 50 hotel rooms
and two hotels in the Falklands and Chatham Island respectively, and no dedicated tourism
infrastructure in Antarctica. Between these extremes are half a dozen destinations with
30–60 thousand annual stay-over or cruise visitors. In comparison with other small island
tourist economies across the globe, all these are low-impact destinations, with the possible
exception of Iceland (McElroy, 2003).

Despite such differences, these cases possess a similarity in assets that define them as
cold-water destinations. These include isolation, unusual terrestrial and marine wildlife
and scenery, unique geologic and atmospheric features and ample opportunity for adventure holidays (such as hunting, fishing and sledding) and cultural experiences. By and
large, they also illustrate the constraints on tourism development imposed by climate-
induced seasonality and difficult and expensive access. Again excepting Iceland as well as

Antarctica, they also exemplify small-island economies undergoing tourism diversification in the face of declining traditional sectors (mining, fishing, agriculture). Many face the similar challenges of determining destination identity, the small-scale ecotourism attractions compatible with that native natural and cultural "genius of the place," and establishing the infrastructure/facilities to access them. Unlike Iceland (which may, in coming decades, need to begin seriously managing visitor densities), these destinations are in the initial stages of visitor marketing and promotion to establish international visibility. Fortunately, at their early position in the resort cycle, they have ample time and room to plan a sustainable industry.

Special Issues

Waste management and climate change will provide particular challenges for cold-water island planners. In the first case, since at least the 1994 Barbados Programme of Action for Small Island Developing States, waste management has been acknowledged as one of the most significant and pervasive sustainable development problems for small islands (UN CSD, 1998; UN, 2005). In cold water islands, cold temperatures slow the biochemical processes of decomposition that frequently 'de-toxify' the toxic elements of solid waste. Thus these toxic and hazardous substances persist for much longer in cold climes, and under some conditions they are concentrated or distilled over time to the point that they represent health and safety problems. Attention was drawn to this subject in the early 1980s with Arctic studies of atmospheric deposition of organo-chlorines (Davis, 1981). This interest has gradually extended to other solid waste issues (AMAP, 2002). Recent research reported in *Science* magazine indicates that birds and other species in Arctic food chains are also serving as aggregators (rather than just consumers) of toxics (Fountain, 2005).

Research also suggests concentrations of Persistent Organic Pollutants (POPs) and some heavy metals are increasing in the fatty tissues of most birds and mammals in high latitude areas including resident human (frequently Inuit) populations. Although the health impacts on employees or even tourists at cold water tourism facilities are unlikely, based on what is now known the existence of hot spots (or hot toxic species) should be examined. In addition, to avoid contributing to increasing 'toxic loads' on high latitude environments — and in light of the sometimes severe constraints on traditional solid waste burial strategies in such areas — many ST facilities in cold water islands will have to consider strategies that include exporting waste streams (perhaps after burning non-toxic elements for facility heating needs) to temperate areas where they can be treated in more traditional fashion. With respect to liquid wastes, although cold water islands are likely to have access to some form of deepwater or offshore discharge, these can be costly systems to build and maintain. Given these difficulties, the Alaska Science Forum (1992) recommends water-conserving systems for new and expanded settlement areas as well as the use of composting toilets.

Moreover, climate change scenarios for high latitude areas generally predict temperature increases over the next 50 years of 5–7°C: substantially above other areas of the globe. One effect of this change will be to reduce seasonal sea ice or permanent sea pack ice around many cold water islands, with unknown effects on both local ecosystems, the livelihoods of local residents, and on the natural amenities for which tourism plans are currently being made. Such eventualities suggest the need for a long-term planning horizon and a certain caution about mounting large-scale grandiose developments.

While Arctic warming can contribute to increases in observed levels of contaminants like POPs, heavy metals and radionuclides (AMAP, 2002), a secondary, and perhaps more dramatic impact will be to release large pulses of toxic substances as dumps and trash middens are rather suddenly thawed after being frozen for decades or generations. This is perhaps the most dramatic result of the general conditions referred to in the AMAP recommendations mentioned above. Associated with Arctic warming and melting of the ice packs will be changes in precipitation patterns that may impact snow and ice conditions that are now features of tourism, such as ski or snowshoe trekking or 'ice hotels'. If and when these climate trends become more visible to and generally understood by cold island populations, planners may have to exercise some control over tourism entrepreneurs to avoid non-sustainable and damaging growth thrusts spawned by the 'make hay while the sun shines' mentality common in some 'boom-bust' insular economies (Vernicos, 1990). In addition, in the medium term and at a minimum, for cold water islands with permafrost conditions, Arctic warming will require rehabilitation of existing construction which is built on permafrost footings, and new forms of construction based on seasonal freezing and thawing of ground conditions.

Finally, to assist in long-range planning and environmental monitoring in these fragile ecosystems, cold water islands need accurate mapping of basic geography, land cover and other natural resources. Such mapping can also provide accurate orientation tools — probably in combination with modern navigations tools such as GPS receivers — for tourists who may be trekking and camping on relatively unmarked terrain (Savitsky, Allen, & Blackman, 1999).

Conclusions

The majority of these islands at least in the near term are on the path toward sustainable ecotourism destinations. A broad-brush overview suggests that, with some exceptions, there is sufficient environmental awareness, legislation and training for protecting natural assets and, in some cases, for interpreting cultural mores. Given the relatively high level of repeat visitation in several islands, visitor satisfaction seems satisfactory and enduring. Progress is needed in target-marketing and developing new attractions (and in coordinating tourism policy in a few instances) in order to more firmly establish the industry on a strong economic footing so that a threshold of community members have a financial stake in tourism's future. The strength of the non-tourist sectors and the double limitations of difficult access and high cost provide future safeguards against the non-sustainable visitor expansion characteristic of postwar mass tourism growth in warm-water islands. To this must be added the limited appeal of what often has been described as 'the holiday adventure of a lifetime'.

On the other hand, local decision-makers must exercise a healthy dose of precaution and policy control. Tourism is extremely dynamic and "tends to take on a life of its own once development appears successful" (Butler, 2002, p. 12). To achieve sustainability, it must be carefully managed, a far-ranging task in such a pervasive and fragmented industry involving a multitude of actors and common natural and cultural resources over which "no agency has responsibility for their overall well-being and continued existence" (*ibid.,* p. 13). Whatever the outcome, these low-density cold-water destinations will provide an interesting laboratory for future scholars in their search for the holy grail. Perhaps the result will be what Butler (1997, p. 78) forecast for Orkney and Shetland: "... these islands may prove to be one of the few genuine cases of sustainable tourism development."

References

Andriotis, K. (2004). Problems of island tourism development: The Greek insular regions. In: B. Bramwell, (Ed.), *Coastal mass tourism* (pp. 114–132). Clevedon, UK: Channel View Publications.

Apostolopoulos, Y., & Gayle, D. G. (Eds). (2002). *Island tourism and sustainable development: Caribbean, Pacific & Mediterranean experiences.* Westport, CT: Praeger.

Arctic Monitoring and Assessment Programme. (2002). *2002 Assessment of Arctic pollution issues.* Oslo: AMAP.

Baum, T. G. (1997). The fascination of islands: A tourist perspective. In: D. G. Lockhart, & D. Drakakis-Smith (Eds), *Island tourism: Trends and prospects* (pp. 21–35). London: Pinter.

Baum, T. G., Hagen-Grant, L., Jolliffe, L., Lambert, S., & Sigurjonsson, B. (2000). Tourism and cold water islands in the North Atlantic. In: G. Baldacchino, & D. Milne (Eds), *Lessons from the political economy of small islands*: *The resourcefulness of jurisdiction* (pp. 214–229). New York: St. Martin's Press.

Bianchi, R.V. (2004). Tourism restructuring and the politics of sustainability: A critical view from the European periphery (The Canary Islands). *Journal of Sustainable Tourism, 12*(6), 495–529.

Bramwell, B. (Ed.). (2004). *Coastal mass tourism: Diversification and sustainable development in Southern Europe.* Clevedon, UK: Channel View Publications.

Briassoulis, H. (2004). Crete: Endowed by nature, privileged by geography, threatened by tourism? In: B. Bramwell (Ed.), *Coastal mass tourism* (pp. 48–67). Clevedon, UK: Channel View Publications.

Brundtland, H. (1987). *Our common future: The World Commission on environment and development.* Oxford: Oxford University Press.

Butler, R. W. (1997). Tourism in the Northern Isles: Orkney and Shetland. In: D. G. Lockhart, & D. Drakakis-Smith (Eds), *Island tourism*: *Trends and prospects* (pp. 59–80). London: Pinter.

Butler, R. W. (1980). The concept of a tourist area cycle of evolution: Implications for management of resources. *Canadian Geographer, 24*(1), 5–12.

Butler, R. W. (2002). The development of tourism in frontier regions. In: S. Krakover, & Y. Gradus (Eds), *Tourism in frontier areas* (pp. 4–19). Lanham, MD: Lexington Books.

Cater, E. (1993). Ecotourism in the Third World: Problems for sustainable development. *Tourism Management, 12*(1), 85–90.

Clarke, J. (1997). A framework of approaches to sustainable tourism. *Journal of Sustainable Tourism, 5*(3), 224–233.

Collins, A. (1999). Tourism development and natural capital. *Annals of Tourism Research, 26*(1), 98–109.

Davis, T. N. (1981). Arctic haze confirmed. *Alaska Science Forum*, June 15th. Available at http://www.gi.alaska.edu/ScienceForum/ASF4/490.html

Farrell, B., & Twining-Ward, L. (2004). Reconceptualizing tourism. *Annals of Tourism Research, 31*(2), 274–295.

Farrell, B., & Twining-Ward, L. (2005). Seven steps towards sustainability: Tourism in the context of new knowledge. *Journal of Sustainable Tourism, 13*(2), 109–122.

Fennell, D. A., & Ebert, K. (2004). Tourism and the precautionary principle. *Journal of Sustainable Tourism, 12*(6), 461–479.

Fountain, H. (2005). Toxic mementos left behind in Arctic. *New York Times*, July 19th.

Gössling, S., Hansson, C. B., Horstmeier, O., & Saggel, S. (2002). Ecological footprint analysis as a tool to assess tourism sustainability. *Ecological Economics, 43*(2–3), 199–211.

Hunter, C. J. (1995). On the need to re-conceptualize sustainable tourism development. *Journal of Sustainable Tourism, 3*(3), 155–165.

Jafari, J. (2002). Tourism's landscape of knowledge. *Revista: Harvard's review of Latin America*. http://drclas.fas.harvard.edu/revista/?issue_id=13&article_id=35 (accessed 25/10/2005).

Khan, C. (2005). Sustaining a viable future for South Pacific tourism. *Travel wire news online*. www.travelwirenews.com/cgi-script/csArticles/articles/000043/004371.htm (accessed 25/10/2005).

McElroy, J. L. (1975). Tourist economy and island environment: An overview of structural disequilibrium. *Caribbean Educational Bulletin, 2*(1), 40–58.

McElroy, J. L. (2002). The impact of tourism in small islands: A global comparison. In: F. Di Castri, & V. Balaji (Eds), *Tourism, biodiversity and information* (pp. 151–167). Leiden, The Netherlands: Backhuys Publishers.

McElroy, J. L. (2003). Tourism development in small islands across the World. *Geografiska Annaler, 85B*(4), 231–242.

McElroy, J. L., & de Albuquerque, K. (1998). Tourism penetration index for the small-island Caribbean. *Annals of Tourism Research, 25*(1), 145–168.

McKercher, B. (1993). The unrecognized threat to tourism: Can tourism survive sustainability? *Tourism Management, 14*(2), 131–136.

McKercher, B. (1999). A chaos approach to tourism. *Tourism Management, 20*(4), 425–434.

Myers, N. (1993). Biodiversity and the precautionary principle. *Ambio, 22*(2–3), 74–79.

Overton, J., & Scheyvens, R. (1999). *Strategies for sustainable development: Experiences from the Pacific*. Sydney: University of New South Wales Press.

Papatheodorou, A. (2004). Exploring the evolution of tourism resorts. *Annals of Tourism Research, 31*(1), 219–237.

Royle, S. A. (2001). *A geography of islands: Small island insularity*. London: Routledge.

Russell, R., & Faulkner, B. (2004). Entrepreneurship, chaos and the tourism area life cycle. *Annals of Tourism Research, 31*(3), 556–579.

Savitsky, B., Allen, J., & Blackman, K. F. (1999). The role of geographic information systems (GIS) in tourism planning and rural economic development. *Tourism Analysis, 4*(3–4), 187–199.

Sofield, T. H. B. (2003). *Empowerment for sustainable tourism development*. Oxford: Elsevier.

Spilanis, I., & Vayanni, H. (2004). Sustainable tourism: Utopia or necessity? The role of new tourism in the Aegean Islands. In: B. Bramwell (Ed.), *Coastal mass tourism* (pp. 269–291). Clevedon, UK: Channel View Publications.

Tribe, J. (2005). *The economics of recreation, leisure and tourism* (3rd ed.). Oxford: Elsevier.

United Nations (2005). *Small islands: Big stakes. Mauritius Conference — January 10–14th*. www.un.org/smallislands2005 (accessed 20/10/2005).

United Nations, Commission on Sustainable Development. (1998). *Management of wastes in small island developing states*: Progress in the implementation of the programme of action for the sustainable development of small island developing states, Report of the Secretary General — Addendum, Sixth Session, UN General Assembly (20 April–1 May), New York: UNCSD, E/CN.17/1998/7/Add.2 of 10, February.

Velikova, M. P. (2001). How sustainable is sustainable tourism? *Annals of Tourism Research*, *28*(2), 496–499.

Vernicos, N. (1990). The islands of Greece. In: W. Beller, P. d'Ayala, & P. Hein (Eds), *Sustainable development and environmental management of small islands* (pp. 141–168). Paris: UNESCO.

Weaver, D. B. (1998). *Ecotourism in the less developed world*. Wallingford, UK: CABI.

World Tourism Organisation (2004). *Making tourism work for small island developing states*. Madrid: WTO, Department of Sustainable Development of Tourism.

World Travel and Tourism Council (2005). *2005 tourism satellite accounting highlights*. Available at www.wttc.org/2005tsa/pdf/world.pdf (accessed 25/10/2005).

Chapter 3

Human Resource Issues

Tom Baum

Introduction

In an era of increasing emphasis on quality in the delivery of tourism services, service quality and human support, such service demands can be looked upon as a competitive opportunity as well as a strategic issue. Consideration of the role of human resources in creating quality and its efficient management has widely been recognised as one of the most important methods to improve quality and competitiveness. At the same time, the tourism industry, worldwide, is characterised by ambiguous attitudes to investment in human capital, inflexible employment practices and an unsustainable approach to its development (Jithendran & Baum, 2000). Often perceived purely in operational terms (Baum, 1993), the management and development of human resources in tourism is readily described as an example of *adhocism* in that formal planning of a long-term and strategic nature rarely takes place within the sector. It is also an area of activity that has repercussions far beyond the operational domain in organisations and clearly impacts on the marketing and financial effectiveness of tourism businesses.

This generic analysis with respect to the role of human resources in tourism is of direct relevance in the context of tourism services and experiences, which are located in what co-authors to this volume describe as extreme tourism destinations, whether extremity in this context relates to remote location, insularity or climate or, indeed, a combination of all the three. Indeed, this chapter will endeavour to demonstrate that the challenges faced by organisations operating within extreme tourism destinations with respect to: (1) labour market features; (2) sourcing and recruitment of staff to work in the sector; (3) employee retention; (4) training and development; and (5) career progression, are different in both kind and extent from the issues faced by destinations located in more 'normal' tourism environments.

Discussion of issues relating to human resource management and development in the extreme island tourism context in the literature is very limited. Indeed, the majority of contributions to what is a growing body of knowledge in the field of small island tourism make little more than a passing reference to the employment and skills environment within such destinations. There are some exceptions. Baum and Conlin (1994) and Conlin and Baum (2003) explore some of the practical issues faced by tourism organisations in small island locations in terms of the impact of seasonality, limited skills within the local labour market and issues of access to formal education and training for the tourism sector. These general points about human resource challenges within tourism are demonstrated specifically in the context of one small island environment, that of the Aland Islands in the Baltic, by Baum (1996). Baum and Lundtorp (2000) address the impact of seasonality on the sustainability of employment in tourism and the challenges which attendant problems present for service and product quality in more remote and highly seasonal destinations of which the islands provide some of the best examples. The impact of seasonality on employment in small islands in the North Atlantic is explored by Baum and Hagen (1999). Hall (in this volume) notes the importance of tourism employment in Stewart Island, a very significant 26% of total work offered in that location. Likewise, Thomson and Thomson (also in this volume) make a passing reference to the skills requirements of an extreme cruise tourism but focus primarily on the role of the guide and lecturer rather than the wider array of service staff employed on ships of this kind.

This chapter focuses on the management and development of people within the context of extreme small island tourism against the five key areas of human resource practice and activity identified above.

Labour Market Features of Extreme Small Island Destinations

A discussion of the human resource characteristics of extreme small island destinations must be underpinned by recognition of the typically weak labour market features that operate within tourism generally (Riley, 1996). Riley is useful in his application of the weak–strong internal labour market model to illustrate the relationship between the wider labour market and a number of key characteristics of tourism work, notably educational requirements, points of entry into the workforce, workplace pay differentials and level of trade union membership. This analysis has important ramifications for the status of tourism work and the perceived attractiveness of the sector both for employment and educational/training opportunities. Keep and Mayhew (1999, pp. 8, 9) summarise a list of the characteristics of tourism work that confirm Riley's weak internal labour market attribution:

- Tendency to low wages, except where shortage of skills act to counter this.
- Prevalence of unsocial hours and family unfriendly shift patterns.
- Rare incidence of equal opportunities policies and male domination of higher level, better-paid work.
- Poor or non-existent career structures.
- Informal recruitment practices.
- Failure to adopt formalised 'good practice' models of human resource management and development.
- Lack of any significant trade union presence.
- High levels of labour turnover.
- Difficulties in recruitment and retention.

The last two of these relate to seasonality constraints in the cold-water destinations reviewed in this book. However, in small self-contained labour markets, the turnover may typically be very low, a cause in itself, of particular challenges.

The skills profile of tourism, in turn, is influenced by the labour market that is available to it, both in direct terms and via educational and training establishments. The weak internal labour market characteristics in themselves impose downward pressures on the skills expectations that employers have of their staff and this, in turn, influences the nature and level of training which the educational system delivers. There is an evident cycle of downskilling, not so much in response to the actual demands of tourism work or of consumer expectations of what it can deliver, but as a result of the perceptions of potential employees and the expectations that employers have of them.

Small islands, generally and in extreme locations in particular, do not always conform to the wider generalisations addressed above. Nevertheless, they do exhibit labour market characteristics that create real challenges for the delivery of quality tourism products and services. Tourism in the various locations discussed in this volume and in other similar destinations, is characterised by extreme seasonality, possibly depending on operating seasons of two to three months per year. The tourism sector is also relatively immature in most extreme island destinations, responding to market demand for new forms of tourism in locations, until very recently, totally off the beaten track for all but the most intrepid travellers. In such situations, the tourism labour market cannot be seen as an embedded part of the wider employment environment for a significant number of the resident population. Rather, employment in tourism can be a transitory activity, which is taken up either:

- by local residents who work in tourism enterprises alongside other economic activity or periods of extended economic inactivity or unemployment. However, the immaturity of extreme island destinations in terms of tourism means that the resident workforce is frequently not well equipped to avail of opportunities demanding more than the most basic of skills levels; or
- by "incomers" who choose to migrate to island destinations for the short season from mainland locations or from other seasonal islands in search of work or to participate in some of the lifestyle activities which the island has to offer. Adler and Adler (2004) describe such transitory, lifestyle-seeking tourism workers in some detail in their exploration of hotel work in Hawaii (hardly an extreme island location, admittedly). They talk of a substantial number of tourism workers who spend part of their year working and playing in ski resorts in the USA and Canada and the balance of surfing and working in Hawaii. "Incomers" such as these satisfy both their personal, usually sporting ambitions and their economic needs while also providing a range of skills, which may be unavailable within the resident labour market. In extreme forms, this lifestyle form of incomer migration means that worker motivations for being in a destination can mirror those of the paying guests and the two become almost indistinguishable for much of their respective stays. Arnould and Price (1993) discuss the context of white-water rafting and reveal that experiential themes — personal growth, self-renewal, communities and harmony with nature — are significant in explaining the underlying dimensions of satisfaction for both tourists and many of those who work with them as guides and instructors. This motivational convergence between guests and employees is a theme

that is emergent within wider tourism (Baum, 1997), particularly in what might be called the aesthetics of labour, within which it becomes difficult to distinguish the two in terms of interests, behaviour and appearance (Warhurst, Nickson, Witz, & Cullen, 2000). Thomson and Thomson (in this volume) likewise describe the proximity of guests and employees in the cruise ship context and their shared experiences.

> In many extreme island destinations, the "incomer" role is played by work-
> ers from a mainland location with close cultural and political ties to the
> island. Thus Danes fulfill this role in Greenland/Kaalaalit Nunaat; British
> workers do likewise in the Falkland Islands; mainland Russians in the
> Solovetsky Islands; and continental Americans are most commonly found
> in remote Alaskan tourism destinations.

Seasonality impacts upon the extent to which the resident community is able to provide specialist skills required in extreme tourism destinations. Some of these may be closely associated with the day-to-day lifestyle of such communities — marine activities (fishing, wildlife viewing), mountain activities (abseiling, climbing, hunting) or winter sports (dog sledging) — but others have little in common with other economic and leisure activities in the destination, notably those related to the delivery of hospitality and service. Thus, the labour market in extreme tourism island destinations frequently suffers from a tourism skills deficiency and this, in turn, may have serious consequences for the ability of the destination to compete in the international tourism arena.

Tourism businesses in extreme island destinations are, characteristically, micro to small operations, employing few staff and are often family owned (e.g. Baum, 1996, writing about the Åland Islands). The impact of larger, multiple operations (hotels, local travel companies) is virtually non-existent in most extreme small island locations. Smaller tourism businesses, universally, have distinctive characteristics in their operations and organisation that have wider labour market implications in terms of the sustainability of the work that is on offer, opportunities for career progression and their investment in the skills development of those who work within the businesses (Baum, 1999). Small tourism businesses frequently operate alongside (or as part of) wider economic activities such as agriculture or fishing, in a family context. There is also a merging of personnel between the two functions, often as a result of differing seasonal demands.

The characteristics of the labour markets within which tourism businesses in extreme island destinations operate, therefore, dictate to a significant extent the manner in which more specific human resource management functions are carried out in such locations, notably the impact of seasonality, their immaturity as tourism destinations, a dependence on external labour and the size and structure of the locally based tourism businesses that are able to operate.

Sourcing and Recruitment of Staff to Work in the Sector

Extreme island locations have small and constrained labour pools upon which to draw when developing tourism as an area of economic activity. The immaturity of the sector and seasonality of its operation means that tourism may not always offer attractive opportunities to island residents. In this context, as suggested above, 'incomers' with lifestyle motivations, may be more willing and able to seize the more attractive employment opportunities offered within the tourism sector. Creating greater business and employment viability within the tourism sector is frequently a challenge addressed by public sector authorities as they seek to embed tourism within the local economy. Diversifying product as a means to extend the tourism season beyond the core summer period is a common response and is one that can be successful. Iceland, although perhaps not the most extreme of island destinations, has developed its urban tourism product in Reykjavik and, to a lesser extent, Akureyri, so that shoulder and off-season winter tourism in the form of short breaks and cultural tours are now important complements to the main season. Such measures provide opportunities for longer and more sustainable employment and, therefore, assist in enhancing the recruitment 'offer' within the resident community.

Many of the specialist and 'authentic' skills demanded by tourists visiting extreme island destinations, whether an activity based, sporting or cultural, may be uniquely located within the local resident community but need to be harnessed in a way that is complementary to the existing economic activity. Recruitment of, for example, land-based or marine guides, cultural animators, exponents of traditional crafts or extreme sports instructors, for whom such activities may be an extension of their "normal" lives, may require a 'selling' of the tourism concept to the community in a manner that goes beyond economic criteria. Persuading the community that opening its doors to tourism is in the general good must underpin and, indeed, precede more formal measures to recruit staff for specific tourism functions. The hesitation and ambivalence of island communities to such a 'buy-in' is evident in this volume (a case in point is Stewart Island).

The small business culture of tourism in extreme island destinations has its limitations but also provides an opportunity to encourage resident participation, providing core business skills are available within the community. Such participation can be fostered through targeted training in entrepreneurial skills and appropriate business development support to encourage people to use their existing skills within the context of tourism. While not recruitment in the traditional human resource management sense, such strategies increase the labour pool within the community who have an economic and skills commitment to tourism.

Notwithstanding measures to increase the tourism operating season and, with it, core employment, there are limitations to the extent to which sustained work can be offered by tourism businesses in extreme island destinations. Therefore, particular focus is required on measures to recruit seasonal staff for the key periods when tourism activity is high and to ensure that they are fully equipped in skills terms to undertake the tasks required of them. The Scottish Highlands and Islands SHEP programme is an example of how the tourism industry, the education sector and public authorities can collaborate to provide a recruitment vehicle for seasonal businesses in remoter areas. SHEP is targeted at secondary school students seeking seasonal summer work and provides them with classroom and industry skills training during school time in anticipation of employment opportunities during their main vacation. As a result of this recruitment and training initiative, school students are more likely to remain in their home locations during the tourism season and more likely to opt for tourism work in preference to other areas of employment (Baum & Farquharson, 2000).

When local recruitment measures do not meet the demand for labour within extreme island destinations, external recruitment is inevitable. The "selling" point in this context is frequently lifestyle related, seeking to attract people, generally younger workers with few family ties, to enable them to combine activity and cultural interests with what in effect becomes a working vacation. The challenge, within local labour markets, of this "incomer" model is that such employees may have skills and experience that exceed that available locally. In addition, for lifestyle reasons, they may be willing and able to work for remuneration and in conditions that are inferior to those demanded locally.

Employee Retention

Seasonality is perhaps the main barrier to long-term employee retention in the tourism sectors of extreme island destinations. The reality of tourism in extreme island destinations is that it is not an economic sector that can offer sustained employment opportunities on a year-round basis, excepting for a very small proportion of staff in management or marketing functions. Thus, retention in the normal use of the term, is not a real issue in that seasonal commitment to employment is generally good.

However, investment in training for seasonal employment can be relatively high and, therefore, there are significant costs attached to the loss of trained staff at the end of the main operating season unless measures are in place to attract them back again the following year. Therefore, in extreme island destinations, the concept of retention can take on a meaning, which relates to the ability of organisations to attract the same operational team back on an annual basis, whether they are local residents or 'incomers'. The value of this form of retention lies in savings with respect to training and the ability of such staff to 'hit the ground running' and deliver products and services to the organisational standard immediately. Where other industrial seasons complement tourism (as can be the case with forestry, the fishery or agriculture), this form of retention is a realistic proposition and island residents can operate within defined seasons and industrial sectors on a long-term basis. Conflict can emerge when tourism seeks to extend its seasonal activity outside the traditional time frame because then employees may be torn between two loyalties and opportunities. Another retention model adopted by innovative tourism employers in extreme seasonal destinations is to support employees to seek alternative tourism work during the down season so that they can return the following year with enhanced skills and experience. Hotels in the far south-west of Ireland, for example, have partnered with counterparts in ski destinations in Switzerland in trading employees during their respective off seasons to the benefit of both sets of operators.

Training and Development

Issues relating to the training and development of tourism employees in extreme island destinations are also strongly predicated upon the structure of the sector and its operating cycle. The lack of continuous employment on offer to employees, not to mention the daunting logistics and costs of getting trainers and trainees together, can make both employers and employees reluctant to invest in training and development beyond the minimal, on-the-job induction required to meet the immediate demands of the job. The dominant expectation is that most staff will learn through experience once in position. At the same time, ensuring that the staff is able to meet the service and product standards of the business is essential if tourism operators are to be competitive in the international marketplace. The notion that travellers will accept what they would see as sub-standard services because they are in remote and extreme locations is questionable, given that such locations are frequently high cost in terms of access and destination services. Chan and Baum (2005) explore traveller expectations of accommodation in remote eco-tourism sites in Sabah, Malaysia and note that, while some compromise in terms of luxury is acceptable, core service standards and comfort levels are expected by international visitors. The implications are that there are few compromises that can be made with respect to the skills sets of tourism employees in remote locations.

The small business structure of tourism businesses in extreme island locations also militates against the effective training and development of employees. This is noted as a general issue with respect to tourism training in most contexts of the sector (Baum, 2002). Tourism businesses in general, and smaller operations specifically, do not invest significantly in employee training and development unless compelled to do so by legal or market pressures.

Few of the extreme island locations cased in this volume have the critical population masses within which to provide a full range of pre-entry or in-service educational opportunities in the tourism sector. The smaller the island community, the greater is the likelihood that potential entrants to the tourism sector will be required to go "off island" in order to avail of educational and training opportunities. While this may be feasible for young school leavers with an ambition to develop a sustained livelihood in tourism, it is not always a realistic option for more mature aspirants or those seeking to enter tourism after an experience in another sector of the economy. While similar barriers are faced with respect to educational opportunity for other sectors, combining this reality with other structural barriers in tourism exacerbates this problem further. Furthermore, tourism education and training, especially in applied areas, is not wholly appropriate for delivery via remote technologies and cannot look to such substitutes for direct classroom and laboratory learning.

Career Progression

The concept of a career in tourism within extreme island destinations must, again, be tempered by the structural and demand-side reality of a highly seasonal industry, with a preponderance of small business operators. In this situation, conventional notions of progressive and developmental careers within an 'employed' status are unlikely to be of relevance to all but a small minority. Even sustained employment, as suggested above, is also relatively rare unless there is sectoral complementarity, allowing for movement between work areas on a regular basis.

However, the area where a form of meaningful career can be seen is in relation to self-employment or the development of entrepreneurial employment. Opportunities to create one's own employment and, from this, a career, are open within an extreme island tourism as they are elsewhere and do form an attractive option, particularly in the absence of larger-scale operators. Such opportunities exist within resident communities of extreme island destinations but, in practice, are much more likely to be in evidence through the initiative of "incomers" (Tinsley & Lynch, 2001; Lynch, 2005). In the case of entrepreneurial activity, incoming is often driven by lifestyle considerations (Getz, Carlsen, & Morrison, 2003) whereby people from, generally, urban locations choose to relocate to more remote situations and to develop new careers in tourism after working lives in other sectors of the economy.

Conclusions

There is little doubt that the tourism sector in remote and extreme island destinations faces challenges and opportunities across a range of business criteria, notably marketing and operations. The operating features of the tourism sector, in terms of remoteness, access, size and, above all, seasonality, place tourism in a really challenging situation when competing with more standard but far less interesting destinations.

   This chapter has sought to illustrate how these contextual factors impact upon the effective management of the people who are required to deliver products and services across a wide range of business types in tourism. Each of these factors presents challenges (and, in some cases, opportunities), which need to be addressed by both the private sector operators and by public authorities responsible for economic development and education/training within extreme island destinations. Without such consideration, island locations of this kind will be unable to compete effectively on the international tourism stage.

References

Adler, A., & Adler, P. A. (2004). *Paradise labourers: Hotel work in the global economy.* Ithaca, NY: Cornell University Press.

Arnould, E. J., & Price, L. L. (1993). River magic: Extraordinary experience and the extended service experience. *Journal of Consumer Research, 20*(1), 24–45.

Baum, T. G. (1993). *Human resource issues in international tourism.* Oxford: Butterworth-Heinemann.

Baum, T. G. (1996). Tourism in Åland: A case study. *Progress in Tourism and Hospitality Research, 1/2,* 111–118.

Baum, T. G. (1997). Making or breaking the tourist experience: The role of human resource management. In: C. Ryan (Ed.), *Tourist experience: A new introduction* (pp. 92–111). London: Cassell.

Baum, T. G. (1999). Human resource management in tourism's small business sector: Policy dimensions. In: D. Lee-Ross (Ed.), *HRM in tourism and hospitality. International perspectives on small to medium-sized enterprises* (pp. 3–16). London: Cassell.

Baum, T. G. (2002). Skills and training for the hospitality sector: A review of issues. *Journal of Vocational Education and Training, 54*(3), 343–363.

Baum, T. G., & Conlin, M. (1994). Comprehensive human resource planning: An essential key to sustainable tourism in island settings. In: C. Cooper, & A. Lockwood (Eds), *Progress in tourism, recreation and hospitality management: Volume 6* (pp. 205–217). London: Wiley.

Baum, T. G., & Farquharson, L. (2000). Human resource management in Scotland: Responses to new political structures. In: M. Lefever, S. Hoffman, & C. Johnson (Eds), *International human resource management in the global hospitality industry* (pp. 283–302). East Lansing, MI: Educational Institute of the American Hotels & Motels Association.

Baum, T. G., & Hagen, L. (1999). Responses to seasonality: The experiences of peripheral destinations. *The International Journal of Tourism Research*, *5*(1), 1–14.

Baum, T. G., & Lundtorp, S. (2000). *Seasonality in tourism*. London: Elsevier.

Chan, J., & Baum, T. G. (2005). Examining ecotourists' experience in lower Kinabatangan, Sabah, Malaysia. *Proceedings of the APacCHRIE conference*, Kuala Lumpur.

Conlin, M., & Baum, T. G. (2003). Comprehensive human resource planning: An essential key to sustainable tourism in island settings. In: C. Cooper (Ed.), *Classic reviews in tourism* (pp. 185–201). Clevedon: Channel View Publications.

Getz, D., Carlsen, J., & Morrison, A. (2003). *The family business in tourism and hospitality*. Wallingford, Oxford: CABI.

Jithendran, K. J., & Baum, T. G. (2000). Human resource development and sustainability: The case of India. *International Journal of Tourism Research*, *2/6*, 403–436.

Keep, E., & Mayhew, K. (1999). *Paper 6: The leisure sector*. London: Skills Task Force Research Group, Department of Education and Employment.

Lynch, P. A. (2005). The commercial home enterprise and host: A United Kingdom perspective. *International Journal of Hospitality Management*, *23*(2), 255–271.

Riley, M. (1996). *Human resource management in the hospitality and tourism industry* (2nd ed.). Oxford: Butterworth-Heinemann.

Tinsley, R., & Lynch, A. (2001). Small tourism business networks and destination development. *International Journal of Hospitality Management*, *20*(4), 367–378.

Warhurst, C., Nickson, D., Witz, A., & Cullen, A. M. (2000). Aesthetic labour in interactive service work: Some case study evidence from the 'New Glasgow'. *Service Industries Journal*, *20*(3), 1–18.

Chapter 4

Seasonality Issues

Lee Jolliffe and Regena Farnsworth

Introducing Seasonality

Like many other destinations in peripheral areas, most of the world's extreme cold-water islands exhibit extreme seasonality in tourism. Their remote locations, cold climates and rugged topography have a profound influence on tourism demand. This situation leads to the creation of seasonal tourism economies in these respective locations. In general, this may be characterized by a low number of visitor arrivals over a distinct season or seasons, limited infrastructure for tourism or seasonal employment. Drawing from the salient seasonality literature and the experiences of the cold-water island cases in this text, this chapter examines extreme seasonality in tourism with a view to determine if seasonality should be embraced (accepted) or challenged (overcome) at these locations.

Butler (2001, p. 5) defines seasonality in tourism as: "a temporal imbalance in the phenomenon of tourism, which may be expressed in terms of dimensions of such elements as number of visitors, expenditure of visitors, traffic on highways and other forms of transportation, employment and admission to attractions". Jang (2004, p. 819) describes seasonality as a, "… cyclical pattern that more or less repeats itself each year". BarOn (1975, p. 2) concluded that some areas have a "... very strong high season with negligible forms of tourist activity during the rest of the year". To understand seasonality better, Lundtorp (2001) suggested examining fluctuations in tourism reflected in basic measures, such as number of visitors, not only on an annual basis, but also by month, week and day. Expenditure levels are also an important measure of seasonal demand (Nadal, Font, & Rossello, 2004).

According to Getz and Nilsson (2004, p. 18), while the concept of seasonality is widely recognized, "extreme seasonality remains a somewhat subjective and illusive concept". This is due to the fact that, while it can be approached as a statistical problem, the numbers do not necessarily reflect the implications for the destinations or the businesses (see also Duval, 2004). Descriptions of "extreme seasonality" rely on quantitative methods comparing tourist arrivals, bed-nights, and/or expenditures throughout the year, and classifying certain months as extreme if they deviate from the average by some predetermined amount. Locations may be classified as having extreme seasonality if more than 50% of all tourism activity occurred during one or two months of the year. In some locations, as much as 80% of tourism expenditures occur within a two-month period. Destinations with extreme seasonality can develop policies that attempt to mitigate the extremes of seasonality (Hagen, 1998; Baum & Hagen, 1999), and business owners can adopt either coping or combating strategies as they embrace or challenge the seasonal nature of tourism demand (Jolliffe & Farnsworth, 2003; Getz & Nilsson, 2003; Duval, 2004). Given these descriptions, most of the cold-water islands included in this text would be classified as experiencing extreme seasonality.

Seasonality in Tourism: Causes, Consequences, Responses

The basic causes of seasonal variations in demand (see Table 4.1) are divided into 'natural' — due to climate and geographical location, and 'institutional' — due to such events as statutory and school holidays (Butler, 2001). Seasonality in demand is also affected by the introduction of new tourism destinations and the differential pricing of tourism products (BarOn, 1975). Some destinations may exhibit special features best appreciated in particular seasons (Lundtorp, 2001). Vacationing has also depended on historic conventions such as seasonal working patterns and climatic condition adjustments like summer heat (Bender, Schumacher, & Stein, 2005).

When the consequences of seasonality are examined at the overall industry or policy level, seasonality is frequently described as a difficulty that must be overcome. Baum and Lundtorp (2001, p. 2) indicate that "Seasonality is widely seen as a 'problem' to be 'tackled' at a policy, marketing and operational level". Butler (2001, p. 5) indicates "Seasonality has frequently been viewed as a major problem for the tourism industry, and has been held responsible for creating or exacerbating a number of difficulties faced by the industry, including problems in gaining access to capital, in obtaining and holding full time staff, for low returns on investment causing subsequent high risk in operations, and for problems relating to peaking and overuse of facilities".

For tourism destinations, their management organizations and governments, seasonality in tourism demand is, therefore, a challenging policy issue. Where there is a single season, BarOn (1975, p. 49) provides advice for extending the season, suggesting:

> "introducing a second season in the spring, autumn or winter and possibly a third season in accordance with the climatic, cultural and religious circumstances of the country; providing activities which are not entirely dependent on the weather, such as conferences or festivals which can be timed outside of the main season, spa and health tourism; discouraging tourism in the high season".

Some destinations have attempted to address seasonality in tourism with policies aiming to extend or alter traditional tourism seasons. Typical responses include programmes to extend the season, such as that attempted in Prince Edward Island by subsidizing the wage costs for tourism establishments to stay open (Jolliffe & Farnsworth, 2003), and the hosting of festivals and events, as seen in North Atlantic islands (Hagen, 1998).

Table 4.1: Causes of seasonality in tourism.

Natural	Institutional
Temperature	Institutionalized holidays (religious, national, civic, school, work)
Rainfall, snowfall	Economic (economies, cost of access)
Hours of daylight	Government travel policies (transportation/safety/security/exchange rates/control of visitor flows, visas) access frequency (regulated schedules)
Geography (destination features, location)	Trends in tourism (adventure, leisure, culture)
Acts of nature (hurricanes, earthquakes, floods, draughts)	Government tourism policies (marketing of destination, availability and mobility of labour force, funds for development)

Source: Adapted from Jolliffe and Farnsworth (2003).

Recent research on seasonality (*e.g.* Duval, 2004; Getz & Nilsson, 2004; Jolliffe & Farnsworth, 2003; Goulding, Baum, & Morrison, 2005) has approached the subject from the perspective of the individual tourism business, concluding that seasonality is not intrinsically problematic at the business level. Duval's study of tourism-related businesses in the Central Otago region of New Zealand concluded that business owners recognize the seasonal nature of tourism in their region, and not all of them see seasonality as detrimental. "To some, seasonal fluctuations are a hindrance … [but] for others, seasonality is not an issue, or at the very least it is a welcome reprieve from busier peak seasons" (Duval, 2004, p. 336). Duval recommends that policy decisions and managerial procedures need to take into account how local businesses perceive seasonality. An important question to consider regarding seasonality is therefore: do the local tourism businesses view it as a problem to be tackled, or as a characteristic of the industry that suits their lifestyle?

Researching family businesses on the island of Bornholm, Denmark, Getz and Nilsson (2004) conclude that owners adopt strategies categorized as "coping" with or "combating" seasonality, with some businesses "capitulating" to it by terminating the business. Coping (or adapting to seasonality) is characterized by such actions as closing part of the year, reducing staff and/or seeking other sources of income, employment and/or self-employment. Combating seasonality involves such things as staying open all year, developing other tourist segments and/or exporting products. Duval (2004) and Getz and Nilsson (2004) recognize that whether seasonality is a problem or not is dependent on the perception of the business owner. They conclude that "for many owners, extreme seasonality was not a serious problem because they closed and did not worry about it, or had never intended their businesses to be open all year" (Getz & Nilsson, 2004, p. 25). Goulding et al. (2004) examine the relationships between tourism seasonality and the lifestyle motivations of small family businesses in Scotland. Tourism operators surveyed embraced the concept of seasonality with a range of reasons influencing the decision to operate seasonally including: the influence of other seasonal businesses, closure for holidays, rest and relaxation and personal/family commitments.

Findings and conclusions drawn by Duval (2004) as well as those of Getz and Nilsson (2004) and Goulding et al. (2004) seem congruent with Jolliffe and Farnsworth's (2003) proposed model of business responses to seasonality. They suggest that individual businesses may develop a strategy for dealing with seasonality that falls on a continuum ranging from "embracing" to "challenging" seasonality. Businesses that embrace seasonality are believed to appreciate the seasonal nature of their business and engage in business practices that fit best with the peaks and troughs of the industry. Those that challenge seasonality, on the other hand, engage in business practices that best fit a year-round business. Neither embracing nor challenging seasonality is seen as inherently more effective. Rather, what matters is whether business practices, in such areas as managing human resources and marketing tourism products, fit well with the business strategy of either embracing or challenging seasonality. Therefore, seasonality is not always viewed as a problem, particularly at the level of the individual business.

It is also recognized that seasonality can be positive, as a break in the visitor cycle can provide value to both physical and human resources within host communities (Baum & Hagen, 1999). Flognfeldt (2001) notes the ability of seasonality in tourism demand to present opportunities in rural destinations for tourism to be balanced with other activities (such as agriculture or teaching). Getz and Nilsson (2003, p. 28) observed a few double-occupation families among family businesses on Bornholm, performing entirely different work counter-cyclically. Saarinen (2003) notes tourism can contribute to maintaining local services in peripheral locations, thus countering political agendas that lead to a seasonal retrenchment or mothballing of services and high rates of labour out-migration. Goulding et al. (2004), Baum and Hagen (1999) and Flognfeldt (2001) argue that this seasonal trading may be advantageous to local economies, offering the small seasonal business owners a chance to rest and recover in preparation for the next season.

Seasonality in Tourism: Cold-Water Island Lessons

Some researchers recognize cold-water island destinations as having a propensity towards seasonality (Baum & Hagen, 1999; Baum & Lundtorp, 2001) with single tourism seasons most often dominating (Hagen, 1998). Others (BarOn, 1975; Butler, 1994; Saarinen, 2003) indicate that seasonality in tourism is more difficult to overcome in the peripheral areas of the north. It is not difficult to surmise that this observation could also apply to the peripheral areas of the south. For many of the islands profiled in this text, this single season is predicated by climate and location. The exercise of examining seasonality in tourism at these locations is hampered by the paucity of reliable data on tourism visitation, a thread running through most of the cases. The case of Iceland, with a well-developed tourism industry, skews both the interpretation of seasonality across the cases and the overall sample of predominately remote and little visited small and underdeveloped cold-water island tourism cases. There is also a lack of information, with the exception of Stewart Island, on the attitudes of local residents and business owners towards seasonality. These data, if available, could be usefully compared to previous enquiries (*e.g.* Duval, 2004; Getz & Nilsson, 2004; Goulding et al. 2004; Jolliffe & Farnsworth, 2003). Nonetheless, an analysis of the information available on cold-water islands discussed in this text allows some

interesting comparisons and reveals lessons about seasonality that should prove useful in
other contexts as well.

In northern Canada, both Banks and Baffin Islands are distinctly single season destinations.
Banks Island is at an early stage of tourism development, having a low population and receiving few visitors during the brief summer season. The author of this case indicates, "Weather
and daylight determine the seasonality of the industry". Furthermore, there is no standard
tourism infrastructure and there are no plans for winter tourism. Only several cruise ships have
stopped at the island. In contrast, Baffin Island is a more developed tourism destination, with
a short summer season, mainly focused on July and August and a growing number of cruise
visits. Baffin received an estimated 33,000 visits in 2002, 21% of these being tourists.
Community-based tourism has been adopted as a means to diversify the resource-based economy as well as information and communication technologies (ICTs) are noted as a tool to
shape and brand the destination. It is of note that at both Banks and Baffin Islands tourism
compliments resource-based economies and occupations. This may be a key factor in determining the sustainability of the seasonal tourism industry. Much like Banks Island, Nunivak
Island, Alaska with a small native population lacks the infrastructure for receiving significant
visitation. Nunivak has recently been part of a regional rural Alaska tourism infrastructure
assessment conducted by regional and state economic development agencies.

Nestled in the Atlantic Ocean, between North America and Europe, Iceland has developed a strong spring/summer tourist season with arrivals amounting to 278,000 in 2002
(WTO, 2005). Iceland demonstrates the level to which tourism in some other extreme
islands might rise, stretching the normal seasonal tendency. Nearby, Greenland is also
highly seasonal with most arrivals in July and August amounting to some 30,000 in 2003,
a seasonal pattern that includes significant cruise arrivals and is more reflective of the other
extreme island cases profiled in this volume.

In the northern hemisphere, on the other side of the ocean, tourism is developing somewhat differently at the small islands of Svalbard (Norway), the Luleå Archipelago
(Sweden) and the Solovetsky Archipelago (Russia). Seasonality in tourism is known to
affect employment patterns, and in some natural resource-based economies, a transition
from year round resource occupations to tourism can lead to the introduction of seasonal
tourism employment and sometimes to tourism replacing resource-based employment
(Saarinen, 2003). Such is the case with Svalbard where, before the decline of mining and
the ramping up of tourism, seasonal employment was unknown. At this location, 25% of
the workforce is now employed in tourism. At the Luleå Archipelago, ice has been adopted
as a competitive advantage (much like Iceland), with conferences and events on the ice
proposed as a method of creating demand for winter tourism. There is the possibility of
organizing specialized tours to extreme cold-water islands: such tours have the capacity to
increase visitation and augment visitor numbers. Appealing to higher-end tourists should
allow destinations that adopt this approach to benefit from a lower volume of tourism as
well as a higher level of spending and a longer length of stay. In the Solovetsky Islands,
however, authority structures (local administrative government, preservation and religious
agencies) conspire to preserve the historical and spiritual aura of the place, and therefore
clamp down on tourist numbers, reinforcing the seasonal nature of this destination.
Tourism here is clearly traditionally seasonal, with a short summer season and no interest
on the part of the various authorities in developing winter tourism.

In the southern hemisphere, the remote Falklands, Macquarie, Stewart and Chatham Islands all offer lessons in seasonal destination development. In the Falklands, restricted access is limiting the growth of tourism (34,000 arrivals in 2003), with most of the tourists being cruise passengers arriving seasonally from October until late March or early April (spring and summer in the southern hemisphere). It is possible the presence of the military on the island, as a clientele which is not "seasonally dependent", contributes to smoothing the demand for tourism services. Macquarie Island (Australia) receives few visitors (annual arrivals over the last decade average out at about 500) but has potential as a stopover for those on Antarctic cruises. However, this visitation would need to be planned so as not to threaten the fragile environment. At Stewart Island, with approximately 62,000 arrivals in 2002, there is evidence residents are concerned with the possible impacts of tourism growth. Surveyed on the perceived impact of establishing a new national park islanders note seasonality as a perceived cost, potentially creating a 'boom or bust' or 'feast or famine' situation. Respondents feared that local businesses would become dependent on park visitation and that it would be difficult for these small businesses to sustain themselves over the slow season. This view of the challenge of seasonality is also reflected in Duval's (2004) study of seasonal tourism operations in other areas of New Zealand. At the remotely located and sparsely inhabited Chatham Islands (New Zealand), the development of a local tourism industry is constrained by limited access as well as by co-management issues with local authorities and conservation entities. Islanders here are hoping to avoid the 'boom-bust' economic effect associated with single industries by pursuing a combination of aquaculture, agriculture and tourism development.

A distinct trend across the cases is the potential for cruise tourism, both to individual extreme island destinations and to island regions, such as the Artic and Antarctic. Such tourism is known to have both positive and negative impacts, to increase visitor arrivals and to slightly mitigate the extreme seasonality experienced by these destinations. Since most cruise programmes to these islands are at an early stage of development, planning for sustainable forms of visitation with limitations for environmental sustainability is essential. It is recognized that seasonality in cruise visits can lead to peak pressures on island infrastructures (Gössling, 2003) and can also lead to power imbalances between local authorities and businesses and transnational cruise lines (Lester & Weeden, 2004).

Another challenge to developing tourism beyond traditional seasons at the locations studied is multi-level governance — with provincial, local, federal and at times even international regulations and guidelines (as is the case with UNESCO World Heritage site status) affecting development. There is some evidence of local authorities working with non-governmental conservation agencies (as on Svalbard, Solovetsky and Stewart) on co-governance models. Since the conservation and preservation agenda is at the forefront, any policy development related to seasonality in tourism at these destinations will be closely linked to sustainability.

It is evident from the cases considered that for extreme-cold-water island destinations, their remote locations, cold climates and difficult access serve to control and dampen the demand for tourism. Some cases, such as that of Iceland and the Luleå Archipelago, indicate that it is possible to employ destination characteristics to increase the demand for tourism and to somewhat alter the nature of the single tourism season. It is observed that most of the locations in this text, with the exception of Iceland, are at a very early stage of development as tourism destinations, with small visitor numbers and as of yet limited physical change (Butler, 1999). As tourism develops at these remote island destinations, it is thus possible that the extreme nature of climate and geography may act as a natural control to the levels of visitation, thus predetermining highly seasonal forms of tourism.

Conclusion

Despite what other authors have indicated regarding seasonality as an obstacle (Baum & Lundtorp, 2001; Butler, 2001), we do not agree that seasonality is a problem: rather for the cold-water islands of the world profiled in this text seasonality in tourism is an asset. Our view has also been reflected in the seasonality literature (Goulding et al. 2004; Baum & Hagen, 1999; Flognfeldt, 2001). The destinations we reviewed are distinctly 'seasonal destinations', many having a single season. Extreme seasonality is a common characteristic of tourism at these destinations, that is most of the tourists arrive during a short season. Seasonality in tourism at these locations is a part of the destination image, which is a destination characteristic and as such is an asset instead of a problem. Therefore, our perspective is that embracing seasonality, rather than challenging it, is a good fit for most of these locations.

The locations profiled are for the most part at an early stage of tourism development where they can choose how their destinations can develop. Seasonality, as a positive, can help these societies to preserve their way of life. We note that factors of geography (climate), location, low populations and lack of infrastructure serve as barriers to development, controlling the nature of single season destinations. Some destinations may be able to slightly mitigate this single season, extreme seasonality situation by creating shoulder seasons that exploit remote locations and cold climate features such as ice, other destinations will choose not to, for example by stating 'no winter tourism'. Seasonality in tourism employment may be diminished by complimentary occupations conducted in the off season, such as teaching, farming, art and craft production. Finally, seasonality will contribute to the management, preservation and conservation of local environments and evidence of human settlement as well as the well being of communities in these remote island destinations.

The destinations profiled will need to develop a balanced view of seasonality in tourism. They may choose to accept the seasonal nature of their destinations. In order to better understand the nature of their own seasonality, they will need to collect longitudinal and reliable data on the demand for tourism. This information will be necessary if destinations choose to challenge seasonality. As BarOn (1975, p. 45) indicated, understanding seasonality in tourism at a destination can lead to the introduction of methods to spread demand and to consequently reduce losses. However, he also indicates that "The social and personal costs of this should be taken into account as a 'seasonal loss' even though they are difficult to quantify". Seasonality in tourism is a complex issue, and as shown by the insights from the cold-water island cases reviewed, the attitudes of local tourism operators and residents will also have to be taken into account as tourism grows. These extreme island destinations experiencing limited seasonal visitation could possibility act as laboratories for the continued study of seasonality: one of the most vexing policy issues in tourism, particularly in peripheral cold-climate environments (Baum & Lundtorp, 2001).

It is possible that, by accepting and working with seasonality, such and similar destinations can demonstrate that seasonality is not an inherent problem, but an asset to be valued by the local population and tourism industries alike and which can be marketed as a key destination attribute.

References

BarOn, R. V. (1975). *Seasonality in tourism.* London: The Economist Intelligence Unit Limited.

Baum T., & Hagen, L. (1999). Responses to seasonality in tourism: The experiences of peripheral destinations. *International Journal of Tourism Research, 1*(5), 299–312.

Baum, T., & Lundtorp, S. (Eds). (2001). *Seasonality in tourism.* Oxford: Pergamon.

Bender, O., Schumacher, K. D., & Stein, D. (2005). Measuring seasonality in central Europe's tourism: How and for what? *Proceedings of 10th international conference on information and communication technologies in urban planning and spatial development and impacts of ICT on physical space,* pp. 303–309, http://mmp-tk1.kosnet.com/corp/archiv/papers/2005/CORP2005_BENDER.pdf%20 (accessed 20/10/2005).

Butler, R. W. (1994). Seasonality in tourism: Issues and implications. In: A.V. Seaton (Ed.), *Tourism: The state of the art* (pp. 332–339). Chichester: Wiley.

Butler, R. W. (1999). Tourism: An evolutionary perspective. In: J. G. Nelson, R. W. Butler, & G. Wall (Eds.), *Tourism and sustainable development: Monitoring, planning, managing, decision making – a civic approach* (pp. 33–62). Waterloo: University of Waterloo.

Butler, R. W. (2001). Seasonality in tourism: Issues and implications. In: T.G. Baum, & S. Lundtorp (Eds), *Seasonality in tourism* (pp. 5–21). Oxford: Pergamon.

Duval, D. (2004). When buying into the business, we knew it was seasonal: Perceptions of seasonality in Central Otago, New Zealand. *International Journal of Tourism Research, 6*(5), 325–337.

Flognfeldt, T. (2001). Long-term positive adjustments to seasonality: Consequences of summer tourism in the Jotunheimen area, Norway. In: T.G. Baum, & S. Lundtorp (Eds), *Seasonality in tourism* (pp. 109–117). Oxford: Pergamon.

Getz, D., & Nilsson, P.-Å. (2004). Responses of family businesses to extreme seasonality in demand: The case of Bornholm, Denmark. *Tourism Management, 25*(1), 17–30.

Gössling, S. (2003). *Tourism and development in tropical islands: Political ecology perspectives.* Cheltenham: Edward Elgar.

Goulding, P. J., Baum, T. G., & Morrison, A. (2004). Seasonal trading and lifestyle motivation: Experiences of small tourism businesses in Scotland. *Journal of Quality Assurance in Hospitality and Tourism, 5*(2/3/4), 209–238.

Hagen, L. (1998). *Seasonality in tourism in the small islands of the North Atlantic.* Charlottetown, Prince Edward Island: Institute of Island Studies, University of Prince Edward Island.

Jang, S. (2004). Mitigating tourism seasonality: A quantitative approach. *Annals of Tourism Research, 31*(4), 819–836.

Jolliffe, L., & Farnsworth, R. (2003). Seasonality in tourism employment: Human resource challenges. *International Journal of Contemporary Hospitality Management, 15*(6), 312–316.

Lester, J., & Weeden, C. (2004). Stakeholders, the natural environment and the future of Caribbean cruise tourism. *International Journal of Tourism Research, 6*(1), 39–50.

Lundtorp, S. (2001). Measuring tourism seasonality. In: T.G. Baum, & S.Lundtorp (Eds). *Seasonality in tourism* (pp. 5–22). Oxford: Pergamon.

Nadal, J. R., Font, A. R., & Rossello, A. S. (2004). The economic determinants of seasonal patterns. *Annals of Tourism Research, 31*(3), 697–711.

Saarinen, J. (2003). The regional economics of tourism in Northern Finland: The socio-economic implications of recent tourism development and possibilities for regional development. *Scandinavian Journal of Hospitality and Tourism, 3*(2), 91–113.

World Tourism Organisation (WTO). (2005). *WTO tourism market trends: 2004*. Madrid: WTO.

SECTION II

ISLAND CASE STUDIES

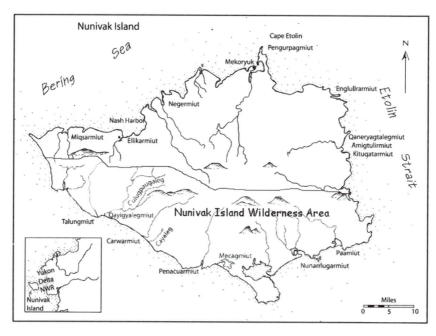

Image 2: Nunivak map.

Chapter 5

Nunivak Island, Alaska

Ted Berry

Introduction

Nunivak Island (population around 215) is located in the Bering Sea about 64 km off the coast of Southwest Alaska, USA (NPT, 2004a). It is about 885 km west of Anchorage and 241 km west of Bethel, the administration centre for the region. The island has a land area of 4210 km^2 (NPT, 2004b). At 60.39° North and −166.19° West, it is south of the Arctic Circle. The only village on the island is Mekoryuk on the North coast with 97% of residents being either full or part Cup'ig (*pronounced Choop-ig*) Eskimo (ADCCED, 2005a). Natives of Nunivak are also known as Nuniwarmiut, meaning the people of Nuniwar (Nunivak) island. Cup'ig translates as "The Real People" and is also the word used for their language. It differs from Yup'ik, the language used on the adjacent Yukon-Kuskokwim Delta (NPT, 2004a).

The surrounding ocean influences the climatic conditions on the island, making storms and fog more frequent than on the adjacent Yukon-Kuskokwim Delta. Average annual precipitation is 377 mm and snowfall is 1448 mm. Average February temperatures are −12°C and average summer temperatures are 9.4°C (Western Regional Climate Center, 2005). Winter temperatures can get as low as −40°C. A wind chill factor of −62°C is not unknown. As an indication of the locals' tolerance of these conditions, the school does not close until the wind chill reaches −39°C. At mid-winter there are 4 hours of daylight. During summer the reverse is true, giving plenty of daylight for outdoor activities. Even though the summer sun goes below the horizon, it never actually gets completely dark. Although the growing season is only about 3 months long, the protracted daylight hours mean that plant growth is rapid.

The southern half of the island, about 242,800 ha, is occupied by the Nunivak Island Wilderness Area and is managed as part of the 8,903,084 ha Yukon Delta National Wildlife Refuge by the United States Fish and Wildlife Service. The interior of the island contains a number of crater lakes, cinder cones and lava flows indicating that the island was formed through volcanic action. Mount Roberts, at 511 m, is the tallest peak on the island. Vegetation is almost exclusively tundra surrounded by rocky shores and lagoons containing eelgrass, an ideal feeding ground for migratory waterfowl. Large seabird colonies nest on cliffs along the western shoreline in addition to the large variety of migratory birds that visit the island. Sea mammals frequent the coastal region (Yukon Delta National Wildlife Refuge, 2005). About 4000 reindeer graze on a large plateau broken by a few peaks at 150–250 m in elevation. The animals were introduced in 1920 and are owned and managed by the local Native Corporation. In addition, there is a herd of about 530 musk-oxen managed by the Department of Fish and Game. These animals were introduced from Greenland in 1936 by the State of Alaska to replace Alaskan musk-oxen hunted to extinction 50 years previously. The intent was for the animals to breed on Nunivak before being re-introduced to other parts of the state. These animals can be hunted in small numbers each year, using permits issued via a lottery system (Alaska Department of Fish and Game, 2002, p. 3).

Historical and Cultural Overview

Cup'ig people have occupied Nunivak for over 2000 years and today, a federally recognized tribe is located in Mekoryuk. Up to the 1940s, the women and children on Nunivak lived in semi-subterranean sod houses while men lived in a '*kasigi*', or men's community house. The first known Westerner to visit Nunivak was the Russian, Captain Mikhail S. Vasilev of the Russian American Company, in 1821. Vasilev said there were 400 people living in some 16 villages on the Island. Oral history, and early visitors however, recorded that there were several villages and up to 700 people on the island subsisting on fish, seal, caribou, berries, and other local foods (Lantis, 1946, p. 161). In 1900 an epidemic wiped out the population, leaving only four families alive (TDX Corp., 2004).

In the 1930s, Jacob Kenick, an Eskimo missionary, built the Evangelical Covenant Church in Mekoryuk. The church banned all culturally related dancing, singing, mask-making, and similar activities. Despite the ban, the cultural spirit lived on in artifacts like the ivory and wooden masks, and reindeer beard dance fans that continued to be made for sale. The memory of traditional songs declined, but enough survived for a recent revival. Encouragement from the elders helped overcome the shame that people associated with such activities due to the ban imposed by the church. Far from being evil or ungodly, Eskimo dancing celebrated such things as success in providing food for the family or it was used to tell stories, to make people laugh or just to socialize (TDX Corp., 2004).

Nunivak people were also made to feel ashamed of their language (Drozda & Horner, 2002). However, in 2002 a major grant was awarded by the federal Department of Health and Human Services for Cup'ig language development and revival. Among other things the grant pays for materials and curriculum development for a Cup'ig language immersion program for grades K-3 at the Nuniwarmiut School in Mekoryuk (NPT, 2004c).

The 1950s and 1960s brought rapid socio-economic change to the islanders and their culture. An airstrip was built in 1957, making the island more accessible to outsiders and to goods and services from mainstream USA. During this period, the Territorial Guard was formed and men went to Fort Richardson near Anchorage for training. The school at Mekoryuk attracted families, making this the only permanent settlement. In addition, many families moved to Bethel to be near the high school, returning during late spring for fishing and sea mammal hunting. The City was incorporated in 1969 and a high school was constructed in 1978 (TDX Corp., 2004).

Subsistence activities are still a major part of the local economy. Most families have fish camps where salmon are cut, dried and/or smoked to help them through the winter. Reindeer, seal meat, seal oil, and other foods are also stored (ADCCED, 2005b). Native crafts include grass coil baskets, bowls, trays, dance fans, mats, and other grass artifacts traditionally produced by women.

Traditional Nunivak island clothes include those woven from quiviut (the soft under fur from musk-oxen) and Parkas made from suitable animal skins. To keep dry and warm fishermen and hunters often wore breathable waterproof boots made from sealskin (ivuciq) and seal intestine raincoats. Cup'ig men make spears and spear-throwers, ropes, nets, hooks, watertight containers, sleds, and boats from the natural resources of the land (Johnston, 1998).

Employers on the island include Bering Sea Reindeer Products Co., the school, the city, the village corporation, construction companies, service industries, and commercial fishing. Fifty-five residents hold commercial fishing permits, primarily for halibut, and herring roe (TDX Corp., 2004). Coastal Villages Seafood, Inc. processes halibut and salmon and is also an employer during the season. In addition, income is garnered from native crafts.

Tourism does not appear to be a significant part of the local economy. However, there are several licensed hunting guides and transporters on the island. Guide services for musk-oxen and reindeer hunting provide significant income for several families. In 2000, 77 residents were employed and the unemployment rate was 19.8%. The median household income was $30,833 with a *per capita* income of $11,957. In the same year, 21.9%, or approximately 47 residents, were living below the poverty level (TDX Corp., 2004). There is a 2% sales tax but no property taxes (ADCCED, 2005c).

Nunivak relies heavily on air transportation for passenger, mail, and cargo service. The State-owned, 914 metre-long, gravel runway allows year-round access but is only equipped for visual landings. Considering the island is prone to foggy weather, planes are often not able to land. The closest all-weather airport big enough to accommodate large passenger jets is 241 kilometers away at Bethel. For heavy goods such as oil and building materials, there is a barge from Bethel twice each summer. Boats, snow machines, and all terrain vehicles are used for travel within the Island (ADCCED, 2005c; Denali Commission, 2003, p. 5).

Organisations

Nunivak has a number of organisations, which could play a role in any tourism policy present or future; however, the City of Mekoryuk is not one. All elected members have resigned and been replaced with people selected by the Native corporation. In effect, the "city" only exists on paper in order to maintain existing Memorandums of Authority (MOAs) and enter into new ones. The Mekoryuk-based Native Corporation is called the Nunivak Island Mekoryuk Alaska Corporation (NIMA). It is a private Alaskan Native owned for-profit company organized under Alaska law pursuant to the 1971 Alaska Native Claims Settlement Act. Its mission is to pursue and develop economic opportunities to enhance shareholder standard of living through business diversification, professionalism, innovation, and respect for heritage and culture. It is committed to preserving the Cup'ig culture and traditions, and acknowledges the importance of protecting ancestral lands (NIMA, 2005).

In 2003, NIMA established the Nunivak Island Cultural Education and Adventures (NICEA) as a subsidiary company. A main focus is to re-establish a traditional seasonal camp at Ellikarrmiut (Nash Harbor) to provide a culturally rich, wilderness-based, educational environment for students to study indigenous culture and environment as well as the Western sciences. The organization aims to provide alternative education, wildlife viewing, and outdoor adventure-based activities such as hiking, backpacking, and kayaking. This will be done through its partnerships with the Alaskan Outdoor Center (AOC), Kuskokwim Campus of the University of Alaska Fairbanks (KUC), and the United States Fish and Wildlife Service (Nunivak Island Cultural Education and Adventures 2003; Don, 2005).

The AOC is based in Bethel, and is "committed to providing creative and challenging alternative-education experiences for rural Alaskans". In addition, the unit "strives to maintain a culturally relevant approach to curriculum development and encourages a high level of sport in all activities". The AOC also "promotes village-based economic development to support the growth and implementation of locally driven educational opportunity" (Alaskan Outdoor Center, 2005). The facility offers a number of courses; but one in particular that concerns Nunivak is run under the auspices of the KUC.

KUC is based in Bethel and conducts the Ellikarrmiut Summer Science Field Camp on Nunivak as part of the Science and Technology Academy's "Building Bridges" Initiative. The program is aimed at high school science and technology students in the Yukon-Kuskokwim Delta. It is held at Ellikarrmiut (Nash Harbor), in cooperation with a number of organizations including the United States Department of Agriculture, the National Science Foundation Tribal Colleges and Universities, the AOC, and NIMA (Summer Science Field Program, 2005).

The Camp program is designed to encourage Yukon-Kuskokwim Delta high school juniors and seniors to consider careers in Science and Technology in a way that is both hands-on and adventure-based. Participant selection is based partly on academic performance in school. The core curriculum is a blend of Western academic and the traditional subsistence sciences. Nunivak elders teach indigenous sciences, culture, survival skills, and activities such as skin boat building and reindeer herding. Cross-country backpacking and ocean kayak field excursions are integrated in the field curricula. Modern kayaks, hiking, and camping equipment and trained support staff are provided by the AOC (Summer Science Field Program, 2005).

Cruise West passengers also visit Ellikarrmiut, the locality used for the Summer Science Field Camp. Using medium-sized ships, the company has operated luxury cruises taking in Nunivak since 2003. In 2005 four cruises anchored off Ellikarrmiut (Nash Harbor), although one cruise could not land any passengers because of inclement weather. Visitors go ashore where a small number of locals from Mekoryuk, 64 kilometers away, offer opportunities to explore the surrounding hills as well as see, and buy, traditional crafts. Visitors may also get an insight into Cup'ig culture and traditions (Don, 2005).

Finally, anybody who has done any internet research on Nunivak would more than likely be familiar with the extensive information source at www.nunivak.org, the home page of Nuniwarmiut Piciryarata Tamaryalkuti Inc. (NPT). This private, nonprofit corporation's intention is to preserve and promote Cup'ig Eskimo cultural identity, especially among young people, by recording and passing on the knowledge of village elders. Goals include the development "of materials and programs which capture the imagination of our young people and instill a sense of pride in themselves and their Cup'ig heritage and Native language" (NPT, 2004d).

Tourism on Nunivak?

Nunivak islanders could, if they wished, cater for a broad spectrum of visitors. The island is remote, scenic, pristine, and ideal for activities such as sea kayaking, wilderness hiking, fishing, hunting, and wildlife viewing. The Cup'ig culture is unique and has much to offer. Tourists could sample Eskimo foods such as dried salmon strips, smoked and fresh salmon, native "ice cream" (a mixture of berries, sugar, and shortening), and "stink head" (fish head buried for some days before being eaten). Other common native foods include musk-oxen, reindeer, halibut, and various sea mammals such as seal in addition to ducks, geese, and other fowl. There are also more exotic foods such as "mouse food" (small roots stored underground by mice) and seal oil.

Relics of the past include the abandoned village of Ellikarrmiut (mentioned above) containing the remains of semi-subterranean sod houses and some "people-faced" stone heads made of round rocks. These are assumed to have been produced by the ancestors of the present day Cup'ig people. Nobody knows when, or why, they were carved (Kolerok, 1986).

Although no official figures exist, about 250 tourists came to Nunivak during the 2005 season. Notwithstanding the small number of people involved in tourism on the island, seven key individuals were identified and surveyed. Selection was based on their connection with the industry and their role in society. The survey consisted of 13 questions and was conducted over the phone. Respondents were located in Bethel, Mekoryuk, and Anchorage, Alaska.

The Magic Island "Lure" and "Special Interest", versus "General Interest" Tourism

Nunivak may be an island, but does it possess that magic island "lure" (Lockhart, 1997) that is often used to sell tropical island destinations? Survey respondents thought that being an island out in the Bering Sea would definitely help attract visitors. Language such as "special aura", "uniqueness", "isolation", and "different ecology from the neighboring mainland" was used to describe what it is about the island that attracts people.

Although the concept of "islandness" (Baum, 2000, p. 215) should not be overlooked, most respondents felt that the future of tourism on the island was in special interest groups such as adventure tourism and wildlife tours. Nevertheless, an estimated ninety percent of tourists in 2005 were cruise ship passengers who came for a few hours "just to have a look" at the island, the culture, geography, environment, and the like. The latter comments were those of a Cup'ig Eskimo who traveled the 64 km from Mekoryuk via small craft to attend to the visitors' needs. The cost of an ocean trip of that distance at over US$1.06 per litre for fuel is not insignificant and would have to be recouped before making any profit. On the occasion when adverse weather stopped passengers from coming ashore, he reported that he was able to board the cruise ship to give his "presentation".

Respondents who were also members of NICEA, the body responsible for promoting tourism, consider cruise passengers desirable and are working towards bringing more to the island. These visitors tend to be ecologically sensitive and do not interfere with the culture in any way as they do not go anywhere near the island's only permanent settlement. In addition they provide a modest income to a few people.

Is Mass Tourism Likely or Desirable on Nunivak, and what about the Problem of Access?

The concept of mass tourism on Nunivak was not considered by survey respondents to be a practical reality even if there were improvements to the airport to allow all-weather access or a longer runway to accommodate bigger planes. At present, mass tourism by air is not a possibility. Regardless, most respondents considered that mass tourism would be certain to cause negative effects on the environment, subsistence activities, and the Cup'ig culture, all three of which are top priorities for NIMA and NICEA. They indicated that no amount of economic gain could compensate for the loss of these resources.

Having almost lost their language and dance traditions because of the religious ban, it appears that islanders are justifiably not willing to risk losing anything else connected with their way of life. The majority opinion among people surveyed was that mass tourism would tend to dilute the culture and work against current efforts to revive certain aspects of it (*see above*). The prospect of mass tourism having a negative effect on the very things that people come to see and experience was not considered by any of the people surveyed. This is not surprising since generally, negative affects such as these do not occur until later in the tourism cycle (Butler, 1980, p. 8).

Most respondents were of the opinion that, as the majority of visitors arrived by ship, that is where promotional efforts should be concentrated. However, the question remains, if air access were to be improved, would more visitors be attracted? "Distance Decay" on Nunivak appears to be alive and well (Tobler, 1970).

Dependence on Outside Tourism Organizations and the Fickleness of Fashion

One of the most common themes in tourism research writings is dependency, characterized by loss of local control due to external ownership, importation of managerial expertise, and the leakage of profits back to a core region, usually an urban centre and often overseas (Oglethorpe, 1984; Keller, 1987, p. 20; Weaver, 1988, 1990, 1992). It is seen as a negative influence on tourism areas and is a feature of Butler's (1980, p. 8) 'development' stage.

Where dependency has been avoided, such as the island of Grand Cayman (Weaver, 1990), long-term stability is predicted for the tourism industry. Where the reverse is true, such as Antigua, external control has occurred and social, economic, and environmental stresses are building up and may lead to stagnation and decline (Weaver, 1990, p. 13). Locals are dissatisfied with tourism as much of the financial and economic gain does not reach a large section of the local economy (Weaver, 1988, p. 329).

The case of Nunivak is similar to Baunei (on the Italian island of Sardinia), where development is owned and controlled by the locals through a customary land ownership system, called a '*comune*', which still controls 90% of the land within the municipality. This system means non-locals find it difficult to get a foothold in the ownership and control of tourism facilities (McVeigh, 1992). On Nunivak, all land is controlled by either Cup'ig Eskimos or by the United States Fish and Wildlife Service. These groups work closely together and consequently all except two survey respondents thought that dependency and control by outside bodies was not likely.

When reminded that both major suppliers of tourists, the University and Cruise West, are owned and controlled from outside Nunivak, these respondents pointed out that NIMA has to approve all tourism. The two respondents who thought otherwise were both aware of cases where dependency and lack of local control has occurred. One elder said that he was afraid outside interests would establish accommodation and eating venues in Mekoryuk because local entrepreneurs do not appear to be interested. This would pave the way for some degree of outside control. He said that outside business people would point to the economic and employment advantages of investment and present a very convincing argument to local authorities.

Dependency is also associated with changes in fashion. When an oligopolistic group of outside agents or tour operators observes that an area is becoming less fashionable, they will tend to direct their clientele to other destinations. For regions that have become dependent on tourism income from a limited market source, the effects can be devastating. Often, there is no alternative market to turn to in the short-term as "dependent" destinations are apt to neglect effective market research because of reliance on outside agents and tour operators. Such was the case of Malta in the 1980s (Oglethorpe, 1984, p. 152).

Nunivak is a destination for special interest tourists and those seeking the novel and the authentic, with interests in natural environments and traditional cultures (e.g. MacCannell, 1989). It is safe to say that when it comes to choosing a destination, these travelers are not motivated by fashion. The destination either has what they are looking for or it does not.

Special interest destinations are not necessarily cold, or even islands. Places like Rome and Venice have unique, culturally related, attractions that are perennial. This is not to say that the popularity of such destinations is not subject to the effects of war, natural disasters, economic depressions, and the like. These types of destinations however, have a totally different competitive advantage over regions competing for a share of the leisure-oriented tourism market and are not necessarily subject to the same cycles or market forces (Berry, 2001, Section 1.2).

Potential Conflict between Tourism and Cup'ig Eskimos?

Resentment towards visitors does not generally start to appear until the tourism cycle is much more advanced than it is on Nunivak (Butler, 1980, p. 8). Nonetheless, survey results showed that, in relation to hunting, some local people feel resentment towards outside hunters for taking their animals, even though there is a government controlled tag system. Respondents did however, qualify their answers by saying that negative feelings towards tourists would not exist as long as there is no interference in subsistence activities and no damage to historical sites. Hunting could be considered by some people to be interference in locals' subsistence needs. If Nunivak is to have sustainable tourism, it is essential that land use conflicts such as this be avoided (Latimer, 1985).

Conclusion

Nunivak is at a very early stage of its tourism development. In terms of Butler's (1980) Tourism Area Life Cycle (TALC), most of the characteristics of the first 'exploration' stage appear to be present. Tourism on Nunivak is characterized by the presence of a few adventurous tourists who are attracted to the area because of its unique and different natural and cultural attractions (Butler, 1980, p. 7). Permanent tourism facilities do not exist and what contact there is with the locals is deemed to be a positive experience. In addition, the economic return from tourism to the island economy appears to be insignificant at this stage. The one deviation from the model is that contact with locals is low rather than high because NICEA policy directs tourists to Ellikarrmiut instead of the village of Mekoryuk.

The deviation from the TALC model at this early stage shows that local decision makers are willing to make policies to guide tourism development in the region. If this willingness to direct the course of the industry continues over time and the right decisions are made, the Nunivak TALC may avoid some of the less desirable features associated with the model. These include dependency and all its associated problems, conflict between locals and tourists, and eventual decline.

Although it is very early days, the stage is set for an active tourism industry given appropriate infrastructure. Tourism is actively pursued by the leading policy making bodies (NIMA and NICEA) and is considered desirable for the island on economic grounds as a supplement to existing income generating activities. Policies and plans exist regarding groups of tourists and even for individuals coming to do specific activities such as hunting, backpacking, and kayaking. A tourism strategy to encourage educational, cultural, and adventure tourism does exist but most people surveyed expect industry growth to be slow. According to one respondent, "tourism is coming and there is nothing we can do to stop it". He said that the island has a lot to offer and people will want to come "to have a look".

As mentioned above, for any significant long-term increase in tourism activity, airport access will have to be improved to allow for bigger planes and all-weather landing. Most respondents however, thought such improvements unnecessary at this stage even if the state offered funding. Notwithstanding, if Nunivak decision makers do decide at some future date that airport improvements are necessary, is there enough influence in the corridors of power to secure the funding or is the island dismissed as a political backwater (Baldacchino, editorial introduction to this volume)? There are numerous similar airstrips on the adjacent Yukon-Kuskokwim Delta serving much larger populations; so it is conceivable that funding would go to those villages before Nunivak.

Most respondents were of the opinion that the island was not well represented in the corridors of power but they did not think that Nunivak was dismissed as an insignificant backwater. One respondent complained that the island did not even have a badly needed weather station for Bering Sea fishing boats so he didn't hold out much hope for an all weather landing system at the airport. Generally it was felt that the US Department of Fish and Game was an important player in the island's political picture through its management of the Wilderness Area covering half the island. Realistically, if Nunivak seriously wishes to attract more than a few hundred tourists annually, it may have to plan to find its own infrastructure funding rather than wait for state or federal governments, as in the case of

Cairns, Australia (Berry, 2001, p. 4). The alterative is to continue to cater mainly for cruise passengers who stay aboard ship and have limited spending on shore. Other tourists will need to be on a flexible schedule in case they get "weathered in".

Acknowledgments

I am grateful for the cooperation of a number of people who kindly gave their time to talk with me about Nunivak and issues surrounding tourism on the island. In particular I would like to thank; Jobe Weston, Chairman, Ceñaliulriit Coastal Resource Service Area (covering the Yukon-Kuskokwim Delta); Abe David, transporter/guide for musk-oxen hunts; Wayne Don, Nunivak Island Mekoryuk Alaska Corporation (NIMA) board member (treasurer) and member of Nunivak Island Cultural Education and Adventures LLC (NICEA) Board of Advisors; Dr Corkeron of Kuskokwim Campus of the University of Alaska, Fairbanks (KUC); Martin Leonard III of the Alaska Outdoor Center and KUC; Terry Don, NIMA Vice Chairman and NICEA Board of Advisors; Kevin McCalla, site administrator, Nuniwarmiut School, Mekoryuk, Nunivak Island. I would also like to thank Kevin McCalla, Amelia Savinova and Pam Lau for generously giving their time and expertise to proofread the chapter.

References

Alaska Department of Commerce, Community and Economic Development (ADCCED). (2005a). Bethel census area: Tourism. Juneau. www.commerce.state.ak.us/dca/AEIS/AEISMainFrame.cfm? CensusArea=Bethel&Industry=Tourism&IndexItem=TourismOverview (accessed 29/09/2005).
Alaska Department of Commerce, Community and Economic Development (ADCCED). (2005b). Developing Alaskan rural tourism: Yukon Kuskokwim. Delta. Juneau. www.dced.state.ak.us/oed/dart/yukon_kusko.htm (accessed 29/09/2005).
Alaska Department of Commerce, Community and Economic Development (ADCCED). (2005c). Community database online. Juneau. www.commerce.state.ak.us/dca/AEIS/AEISMainFrame.cfm? CensusArea=Bethel&Industry=Maps&IndexItem=CensusMap (accessed 29/09/2005).
Alaska Department of Fish and Game. (2002). Muskox annual survey and performance report: Federal aid annual performance report. Juneau. www.wc.adfg.state.ak.us/pubs/techpubs/federal_aid/survey_inven/mus03perf.pdf (accessed 29/09/2005).
Alaskan Outdoor Center. (2005). www.alaskanoutdoorcenter.org (accessed 29/09/2005).
Baum, T. G. (2000). Tourism and cold water islands in the North Atlantic. In: G. Baldacchino, & D. Milne (Eds), *Lessons from the political economy of small islands: The resourcefulness of jurisdiction* (pp. 214–229). Basingstoke, Macmillan & New York, St Martin's Press.
Berry, E. N. (2001). *An Application of Butler's (1980) tourist area life cycle theory to the Cairns region, Australia, 1876 to 1998.* Unpublished doctoral dissertation, Tropical Environment and Geography, James Cook University, Cairns Campus. www.geocities.com/tedberry_aus/tourismarealifecycle.html (accessed 29/09/2005).
Butler, R. W. (1980). The concept of a tourism area cycle of evolution: Implications for management resources. *The Canadian Geographer, 24*(1), 5–16.

Denali Commission. (2003). Alaska primary care Mekoryuk health clinic: Facility assessment and inventory survey report, Juneau.

Don, T. (2005). Nunivak island offers cultural experience. www.geocities.com/qayaq_alaska/nicea_deltadisc_article.pdf (accessed 29/09/2005).

Drozda, R. & Horner, T. (2002). Qusngim Kevga Reindeer Messenger Festival. www.nunivak.org/qusngim/qksmith.htm (accessed 29/09/2005).

Emily Johnston Homepage. (1998). www.alaska.net/%7Egwjnota/html/Emilys.htm (accessed 29/09/2005).

Keller, P. C. (1987). Stages of peripheral tourism development: Canada's Northwest territories. *Tourism Management, 8*(1), 20–32.

Kolerok, R. (1986). Tape number 86NUN027. Bureau of Indian Affairs, ANCSA program office: Anchorage, Alaska.

Lantis, M. (1946). The social culture of the Nunivak Eskimo. *Transactions of the American Philosophical Society 35*(3), 153–323.

Latimer, H. (1985). Developing island economics: Tourism vs agriculture. *Tourism Management, 6*(1), 32–42.

Lockhart, D. G. (1997). Tourism and islands: An overview. In: D. G. Lockhart, & D. Drakakis-Smith (Eds), *Island tourism: Trends and prospects* (pp. 3–20), London, Pinter.

MacCannell, D. (1989). *The tourist: A new theory of the leisure class*, revised edition. New York: Schocken Books.

McVeigh, C. (1992). *Tourism and development in highland Sardinia: An economic and socio-cultural impact study of tourism in Baunei.* Unpublished doctoral dissertation. Microfiche, McGill University, Montreal.

Nunivak Island Cultural Education and Adventures (2003). Available at: www.nimacorporation.com/NICEALLC.htm (accessed 29/09/2005).

Nunivak Island Mekoryuk Alaska (NIMA) Corporation (2005). About us. http://www.nimacorporation.com/about%20us.htm (accessed 29/09/2005).

Nuniwarmiut Piciryarata Tamaryalkuti Inc. (NPT) (2004a). We Are Cup'it. www.nunivak.org/people.html (accessed 29/09/2005).

Nuniwarmiut Piciryarata Tamaryalkuti Inc. (NPT). (2004b). Geographic facts and figures. www.nunivak.org/geography/facts_figs.htm (accessed 29/09/2005).

Nuniwarmiut Piciryarata Tamaryalkuti Inc. (NPT) (2004c). Press release: ANA language grant II. www.nunivak.org/language/ANAIIpress.htm (accessed 29/09/2005).

Nuniwarmiut Piciryarata Tamaryalkuti Inc. (NPT). (2004d). Mission statement. www.nunivak.org/mission.html (accessed 29/09/2005).

Oglethorpe, M. K. (1984). Tourism in Malta: A crisis of dependence. *Leisure Studies 3*(1), 147–61.

Summer Science Field Program Kuskokwim Campus, University of Alaska Fairbanks: http://fc.bethel.uaf.edu/~summer_science/ (accessed 29/09/2005).

Tanadgusix Native Village Corporation (TDX, Corp.). (2004). Saint Paul, Alaska. www.beringsea.com/ (accessed 29/09/2005).

Tobler, W. (1970). A computer movie, *Economic Geography 46*(2), 234–240.

Weaver, D. B. (1988). The evolution of a 'Plantation' tourism landscape on the Caribbean island of Antigua. *Tijdschrift Voor Economische en Sociale Geografie 69*(3), 19–31.

Weaver, D. B. (1990). Grand Cayman island and the resort cycle concept. *Journal of Travel Research 29*(2), 9–15.

Weaver, D. B. (1992). Tourism and the functional transformation of the Antiguan landscape. In: A. M. Conny (Ed.), *Spatial Implications of Tourism* (pp. 161–175). Groningen, The Netherlands: Geographical Perspectives.

Western Regional Climate Center. (2005). Mekoryuk, Alaska. www.wrcc.dri.edu/cgi-bin/cliMAIN.pl? akmeko (accessed 29/09/2005).

Yukon Delta National Wildlife Refuge (2005). Wild lands, Bethel. http://alaska.fws.gov/internettv/ nwrtv/yukondeltatv/wildlands.htm (accessed 29/09/2005).

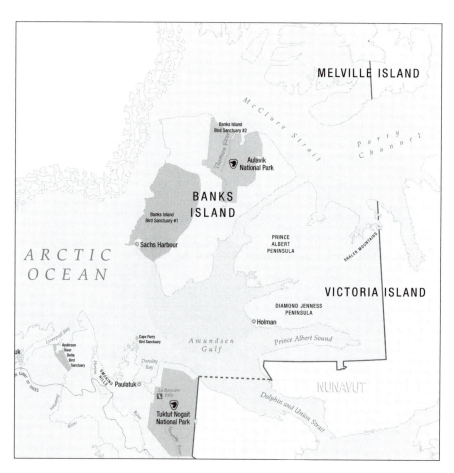

Image 3: Banks Island map.

Chapter 6

Banks Island, Northwest Territories, Canada

Sarah Marsh and Suzanne de la Barre

Introduction

Banks Island is located just north of the 70th parallel in the Northwest Territories of Canada. It is the westernmost island of the Canadian Arctic Archipelago, and is about 400 km from north to south and 200 km from east to west. The island measures 67,340 km^2, with elevations ranging from sea level to just over 600 m. Although it is Canada's fifth largest island, it is home to only one village, Sachs Harbour: the northernmost community in the Northwest Territories.

According to Butler (2002), tourism in frontier/peripheral areas is characteristically small scale, and is consumptive in form, drawing on the natural resources of the region, for instance wildlife and hunting. Moreover, it is elite in nature and usually attracts foreign rather than domestic travellers. This is an accurate description that summarizes tourism on Banks Island. While tourism is occurring, it is not the 'boom' often associated with the industry elsewhere, notably other — warm water — island destinations. The economy on Banks Island is primarily based on hunting and trapping, and tourism does not appear to be a high revenue generator at this time (Legislative Assembly of the Northwest Territories, 2005). While Parks Canada and the Banks Island Hunters and Trappers Association record visitor numbers, the economic impact of these visits has not yet been calculated. In addition, because there has not been an influx of tourists to the island and standard tourism infrastructure has not been developed, the industry does not appear to be detrimental to the integrity of the island's environmental or cultural life. Nonetheless, the apparent lack of impacts must be assessed taking into consideration the particular fragility island environments: because of their insularity, island ecosystems are fragile and vulnerable to impacts caused by tourists (Briguglio & Briguglio, 2002).

Worldwide, regions and countries have often developed sustainable tourism management plans *after* mass tourism has occurred and damage has already been inflicted on the environment (García-Falcón & Medina-Muñoz, 1999; Diamantis, 2000). Banks Island presents a particularly compelling case study given the combined potential for increased tourism and the lack of a sustainable tourism management plan. Furthermore, sustainable

Extreme Tourism: Lessons from the World's Cold Water Islands
Copyright © 2006 by Elsevier Ltd.
All rights of reproduction in any form reserved
ISBN: 0-08-044656-6

tourism discussions about Banks Island are exacerbated by current documentation on the effects of climate change. Hassol (2004) for instance claims that human induced changes in the Arctic climate are the most significant on earth. The fragility of the ecosystem on Banks Island and the anticipated changes resulting from climate change alone may be the cause for a sustainable tourism management strategy.

This case study will examine the current tourism development context on Banks Island and discuss some issues pertaining to sustainable tourism practices. The case study will highlight, how a sustainable tourism strategy could proactively address problems or threats associated with increased tourism on Banks Island. An introduction to the socio-cultural and environmental situation on Banks Island will introduce the tourism context, and provide the background necessary for the discussion. Semi-structured interviews were conducted with residents of Banks Island for the purposes of this case study. In addition, government publications, NWT tourism promotional material and government reports and studies were used to gain insight into tourism operations, limitations and considerations on the island.

People, Culture and Economy

While the Thule people inhabited the island between 1000 and 1600 AD, it is believed that the Inuvialuit, Inuit people descended from the Thule, did not establish permanent residence on Banks Island until 1929 when three families built their homes (Outcrop Ltd., 1990). Prior to the Inuvialuit settlement, Europeans spotted the island in 1820 and wintered at Mercy Bay in the 1850's (*ibid.*). Scientific and military exploration of the island occurred a 100 years later in the 1950's (Canadian Museum of Civilization Corporation, 2003).

In 2000, there were 153 people residing in Sachs Harbour, 89% of the people were Inuvialuit and 11% were non-aboriginals (Legislative Assembly of the Northwest Territories, 2005). The low population continues to create challenges in terms of the island's political profile, its cost of living and its infrastructural development. However, a low population also creates advantages. For instance, compared to other northern communities, the small population has enabled the people of Banks Island to continue living cooperatively off the land, and to maintain relatively self-sufficient lifestyles harvesting muskoxen, caribou, polar bears, whales and seals (Outcrop Ltd., 1990; Western Arctic Handbook Committee (WAHC), 2002a).

While oil and gas exploration continues in the Beaufort Sea, trapping and hunting remain the major industries in the region, with tourism a distant third (Legislative Assembly of the Northwest Territories, 2005). In 2002/2003, there were 38,000 leisure visitors to the Northwest Territories accounting for $41.5 million US in spending (Trim & Zieba, 2004). Annual tourism spending on Banks Island accounts for 1–2% of total territorial spending, but the amount of money actually left on the island is unknown. The hunting sector represents 3% of the Northwest Territories' annual leisure visitation, but generates 37% of total leisure tourism spending (*ibid.*).

Aboriginal self-government is being negotiated in the Beaufort-Delta region, which includes Banks Island. The Inuvialuit and Gwich'in communities are attempting to regain self-reliance in order to protect their culture and languages, and to plan their own futures.

The federal and territorial governments support this initiative, and are currently negotiating the endeavour with the residents. The Beaufort-Delta Self-Government Office (2003) believes that acquiring self-government will enable the citizens to approve constitutions and make decisions specific to their culture and society. The Northwest Territories does not utilize the standard system of political parties used in most other Canadian provinces and territories; instead, the region operates under consensus style governance similar to traditional styles of governance and leadership common to the Aboriginal cultures of the Northwest Territories.

Environmental Characteristics

Banks Island is characterized by its unpredictable weather and its strong winds coming off the Arctic Ocean. Summers are brief, bright and cool, lasting from late-June to mid-August with average temperatures of 6.2°C in July; while the winter season is long and dry, with mean January temperatures of −29.9°C (WAHC, 2002b). The island receives 24 h of daylight for over two months each summer, and "Polar Nights," when the sun stays below the horizon, occur between mid-November and mid-January (WAHC, 2002a,b).

Although the island is above tree line, it has the richest vegetation in the region, and the uplands of the area are home to polar desert and semi-desert plant communities (Canadian Heritage and Parks Canada, 2004). Dwarf shrubs, sedges, grasses and 210 different flowering plant species cover the Arctic tundra, and during the summer months, wet meadows cover much of the land (WAHC, 2002a). The Arctic Ocean around Banks Island is home to beluga whales, bowhead whales, grey whales, walruses, bearded seals and ringed seals. Wolves, Arctic foxes, polar bears, Peary caribou and muskoxen occupy the island. Many bird species, including Brant geese, tundra swans and Sandhill cranes, migrate to or permanently reside on Banks Island.

Aulavik National Park encompasses more than 12,000 km^2 of land at the northern end of Banks Island. The Thomsen River winds its way through the park and is the northernmost navigable river in North America. The Peary caribou and the highest density of muskoxen in the world can be found within the park boundaries. There are also two bird sanctuaries, established to protect the nesting and moulting grounds of migrating bird species. The sites attract approximately 10,000 black Brant geese and 500,000 lesser snow geese annually (WAHC, 2002a).

An imminent and growing environmental concern in the Arctic generally is climate change. According to the *Arctic Climate Impact Assessment*, the average temperature in the Canadian Arctic has increased 1–2°C over the past 50 years and is expected to increase 3–5°C by 2090, which will cause melting of the ice around Banks Island. Higher temperatures and less sea ice have a number of implications on the Arctic environment including easier access through the Northwest Passage for freight and cruise ships, poor survival conditions for muskoxen and polar bears and thawing permafrost (Hassol, 2004).

Climate change is already impacting bird migration to Banks Island; studies have shown that a warmer climate is contributing to the northward extension of some species and new arrivals of species typically found in the south (WAHC, 2002b). Similarly, adverse snow conditions resulting from global warming are expected to limit the foraging abilities of muskoxen, ultimately decreasing population size (Hassol, 2004). Polar bears will also be negatively affected by the anticipated shortened sea ice season. Since animal populations are expected to decrease with current climate change forecasts, existing sport hunting practices may have to be altered to ensure stable animal populations in the future.

Positioning Banks Island Tourism

Banks Island is primarily promoted to naturalists and sport hunters. Its marketing strategies overwhelmingly reflect these two niche markets. In one of these strategies, Banks Island has been billed as "an Arctic Garden of Eden" and "an oasis and refuge for both flora and fauna" (Equinox Expeditions, 2005; The Great Canadian Adventure Company, 2005). Apart from key references to the Arctic, this promotional strategy conjures images of natural beauty and seclusion that can make it sound like any typical warm water destination. Photographs accurately reflect the uniqueness of the Arctic as a tourism destination by highlighting the rolling tundra landscapes, beautiful wildflowers and birds and animals like hares, foxes, muskoxen and polar bears. However, the presence of humans and their built environments are markedly absent as people and buildings are not often included in the advertising materials. In this sense, Banks Island may provide an apposite example for what Milne, Grekin, and Woodley (1998, p. 103) have identified as the need for peripheral destinations to create elaborate fantasies in "unreal worlds" that offer "an opportunity to get away from the sites of everyday routine and into the extraordinary". Tourism, they claim, especially in remote areas, uses nature as an oppositional force to everyday urban life.

Shields presents the "idea of North" in his 1991 essay. He claims that, "for most English-speaking Canadians, the 'North' is not just a factual geographical region but also an imaginary zone: a frontier, a wilderness, an empty 'space'" (1991; p. 165). Heinimann adds that, "the role of the imagination in defining the North is more important than for any other region in Canada" (1993; p. 135). Milne et al. (1998) discuss some of these issues in terms of how the "idea of North" is promoted for tourism purposes, and how, with images of lost wilderness and frontier landscapes, it captures the imagination of audiences beyond Canada (Cavell, 2002).

The competing marketing strategy offers literature and marketing campaigns that promote Banks Island as a dangerous but highly rewarding destination: "this is, by far, the toughest hunt on earth and is not for the weak at heart" and "if you like to mix your hunting adventure with a chance to sharpen your survival skills, the western High Arctic is the place to be" (Alaska Hunting Safaris, 2003; NWT Arctic Tourism, 2003a). Here, the images used exploit the "idea of North" and show proud hunters alone with their trophy animal in the barren landscapes that have come to symbolize the ever-enduring romantic tropes of adversity and conquest. In fact, it is likely that the isolation portrayed is integral to closing the sale for a hunting trip to the island. The myths and discourses that associate Banks Island with either a natural paradise to escape to, or a frontier still available to conquer, have had varying results in terms of increasing the number of tourists who visit the island: while the images may attract some tourists, they inevitably deter others.

Specialized and direct marketing and promotion of Banks Island as a tourism destination have not been pursued. However, each year, two pan-territorial travel brochures are developed by the territory's tourism marketing agency, publishing information on the single guesthouse, the national park and big game hunts on the island. Independent crews from Japan, Britain and France have also produced promotions for Banks Island, documenting the Inuvialuit way of life and capturing island wildlife images (personal communications, 2004). Books about history, nature, the Arctic and travel in the north have also been published, including *Canada's Western Arctic including the Dempster Highway* (2002) and *Natural History of the Western Arctic* (2002).

Although there are some similarities between cold and warm water destinations, the risks associated with isolation and distance from civilization and amenities like hospitals put Banks Island tourists in a different destination category than warm water ones. The potential hazards of travelling to the island act as a system to regulate tourism flow. In this sense, perhaps the defining difference distinguishing Banks Island tourists from warm water tourists is the realization of potential risk. Visitors to the island usually understand the nature of uncontrollable elements in the Arctic including life threatening weather conditions, wild animals and insects (Lutra Associates Ltd., 1990).

Banks Island Tourists

Butler (2002) suggests that Canadian Arctic regions have the novel appeal of the Inuit people and rare animal species, as well as the seclusion necessary to interest certain tourists. A tourism study in 1990 confirms this is the case for Banks Island (Lutra Associates Ltd., 1990). It stated that people visiting the island are seeking isolated, unspoiled destinations. These visitors are hoping to escape their busy lives and experience the remoteness and uniqueness of the north, while not causing damage to the island or the local culture (Lutra Associates Ltd., 1990).

The untouched Arctic environment and big game species are prime motivators for tourists to Banks Island. The island escaped glaciation during the last Ice Age, which has translated into a landscape and vegetation variety different from the surrounding islands. The tundra landscape, the array of wildflowers, and the navigable terrain and rivers attract naturalists. Meanwhile, the potential of hunting a trophy muskoxen or polar bear appeals to dedicated sport hunters. Both types of visitors are typically knowledgeable about the island's flora and fauna, are experienced in their chosen travel activities, and have a great deal of respect for local residents, their way of life and their land (Lutra Associates Ltd., 1990). Visitors to Banks Island are also known to research and prepare well for their trips due to the extreme conditions and lack of typical tourism infrastructure and amenities (personal communications, 2004).

Naturalist visitors travel to the island in June, July and August, with hunters arriving in the spring and fall. Weather and daylight play a significant role in determining the seasonality of the industry. There are usually no tourists during the winter months when temperatures are at their lowest and during Polar Nights. Although Polar Nights are a unique phenomenon, they have not yet been marketed and tourists have not planned trips to Banks Island to experience them.

Naturalists

According to the 1990 tourism study, the naturalists attracted to Banks Island include equal number of men and women who are adventurous between the age group of 25 and 44 years with some university education, and are in professional/managerial positions or are self-employed (Lutra Associates Ltd., 1990). These tourists are relatively affluent, earning upper-middle or high household incomes; the upper-middle income earners perceive their trip to Banks Island as a "once in a lifetime experience," while high income earners typically become repeat visitors. The naturalists frequently travel internationally and feel that money spent on vacations is money well invested. Some naturalists prefer to travel with a guide, allowing a professional to plan the trip, while other, more self-sufficient or experienced travellers, prefer the challenges of travelling without a guide (Lutra Associates Ltd., 1990; personal communications, 2004).

Naturalist-tourists visit Aulavik National Park and the bird sanctuaries on Banks Island. According to the National Parks office in Sachs Harbour, approximately 20–40 people visit Aulavik National Park annually (personal communications, 2004). While in the park, travellers hike, partake in bird and wildlife viewing, paddle the Thomsen River and explore the area. Unlike sport hunters, visitors can canoe, kayak or raft down the Thomsen River with or without guides, and are invited by Banks Island residents to explore, but not disturb, the historic and archaeological sites in the park (personal communications, 2004). Residents feel it is important for visitors to learn about the culture while respecting and appreciating artefacts and ancient structures found throughout the park (personal communications, 2004). Bird sanctuary visitors require a permit and access may be restricted, depending on the time of year (WAHC, 2002a); however, people can bird-watch almost anywhere on the island. Bird watching begins in early June and lasts until the end of July.

Sport Hunters

Sport hunting is a consumptive tourism activity and is known to promote physical, psychological, social and emotional benefits (Daigle, Hrubes, & Ajzen, 2002). Sport hunters visiting the island are typically males aged 35–65 years who share many of the same characteristics as naturalists coming to the area (Lutra Associates Ltd., 1990). They are high-school graduates, have a high household income and are willing to travel long distances to hunt a variety of species. The majority of hunters are members of clubs or associations where they share information about various aspects of hunting and their hunting trips. This group enjoys new challenges and will travel long distances to hunt different species. According to one resident business operator, some visitors are seeking a "once in a lifetime experience" hunting excursion, those with higher incomes become enthusiastic repeat visitors (personal communications, 2004).

Each year approximately 40 sport hunters come to Banks Island in search of two trophy species: muskoxen and polar bears. The muskoxen and polar bears on Banks Island are well known within the sport hunting industry, and are highly sought after because of their good health and size (NWT Arctic Tourism, 2003a). Muskoxen can be hunted between mid-August and the end of April, while polar bears between October and the end of May. In 2003, approximately 30 muskoxen licenses and four polar bear licenses were sold to tourists on Banks Island (personal communications, 2004). Regulations require sport hunters to hire a local guide to hunt on Banks Island (NWT Arctic Tourism, 2003a). Guides often arrange, or assist in arranging, accommodation and transportation on the island, as well as the logistics of the hunting excursion (personal communications, 2004).

The impacts of reduced sport hunting opportunities on tourism on Banks Island due to climate change are unknown. Nonetheless, it can be speculated that there could be considerable economic losses. Conversely, if there are reduced number of polar bears or muskoxen available to hunt, and the government limits the number of licenses available, the demand for the licenses may increase, allowing hunting guides to inflate the amount of money charged for a hunt, thus a potential positive economic impact may be realized. Weighed against the negative impacts of climate change however, this seems an unlikely means to an end.

Tourism Infrastructure

Banks Island does not have a well-developed tourism infrastructure — there are no restaurants, visitors' centres, and, with the exception of one locally owned 4-bedroom guesthouse, there are no hotels. Thawing permafrost will impact buildings and infrastructure on Banks Island. Hassol (2004) predicts that melting permafrost and slope instability will plague the central Canadian Arctic. Buildings in Sachs Harbour may begin collapsing or sliding on unstable slopes as a result of forecasted and existing climate changes. Establishing tourism infrastructure like hotels, restaurants and sewage systems will be negatively impacted by these changes. As such, residents play, and may be required to continue to play, a critical role in the provision of basic tourist services. Currently, residents are often called upon to offer a bed to sleep in; they generously share traditional clothing and meals, and a taste of the Inuvialuit culture within their homes. Most travellers are prepared to camp and do not require this support from the community. However, others rely heavily on the services offered by residents. Similarly, while on the island, various modes of transportation are utilized and often rely on the generosity of locals. During the winter hunting season, guides and guests travel by snowmobile and sled, or by dogsled. During the summer, visitors can drive all-terrain vehicles and trucks, although roads outside of Sachs Harbour are limited. One business rents trucks, but all-terrain vehicles and snowmobiles must be rented or borrowed from community residents.

In the 1990 Banks Island tourism study, residents were contacted by telephone and asked questions pertaining to tourism and Banks Island (Lutra Associates Ltd., 1990). One resident noted that tourism was not just valued by the visitors; he claimed that in a small community, it is exciting and refreshing to meet new people and learn about different parts of the world. Tourism also gives the Inuvialuit a chance to showcase their culture to educate guests about the Arctic way of life. The Inuvialuit people of Sachs Harbour maintain many traditional activities including carving, muskoxen wool processing, northern games and story telling which are shared with the guests staying on the island. The lack of infrastructure on the island currently necessitates that tourists rely in significant ways upon the generosity of the Inuvialuit residents, and interact closely with them. Through this interaction, tourists learn more about the local culture and locals learn from the visitors and have an opportunity to interact with new people. Increasing the number of tourists to the island without addressing the infrastructure issues means that locals would be required to host more tourists in the same way they host the current few. It is very likely that such an expectation would not be sustainable. Increasing the infrastructure on the other hand could detrimentally affect current traditional lifestyles and the environment.

Access issues also challenge the Banks Island tourism development context. The island is mainly accessible by air, although two cruise ships have stopped on the island when ice conditions allowed, permitting up to 90 passengers to explore the coastline. However, generally speaking, water access to the island is dependant on ice floes — a flat mass of floating sea ice, which have prevented ships' access in the past. To manage access and usage, Parks Canada Aircraft Landing Permits are required to land within Aulavik National Park. Visitors can travel by airplane or helicopter to a variety of gravel, grass or sandbar landing strips throughout the island; however, fees for air travel in the Western Arctic are typically higher than similar flights in other regions. In 1990, round-trip air charters from Inuvik to the Thomsen River cost US$14,964, or US$2494 per person with six travellers (Lutra Associates Ltd., 1990). Scheduled flights from Inuvik to Sachs Harbour occur twice weekly, and flights to other areas on the island are typically chartered from the mainland. Some residents who want to increase the number of tourists who visit the island feel that the cost (US$1457 return) of flying into Sachs Harbour from Inuvik is expensive and deters tourists from making the trip. On the other hand, the high travel expense assures that only a few affluent tourists make the journey. The latter strategy requires a steady and reliable affluent pool from which to draw upon; not to mention an undisturbed product to promote. This conundrum may threaten the economic sustainability of the island's tourism industry. It also points to the need for research that can more effectively determine what other types of tourists, and how many of them, and under what conditions, can benefit Banks Island in a sustainable and manageable manner.

Community Benefits of Tourism

Unlike sport hunters, hikers and canoeists are not required to book a guide. Nonetheless, when naturalists do book a guide, they do so through the only company licensed to take tourists on naturalist excursions in Aulavik National Park; the company is located in Alberta, Canada and typically makes one trip each year (personal communications, 2005). Their guides are not local and often travel with the guests to the island. Almost all revenue from the guided trips remains with the Alberta-based company. In 2004, the company brought one group to the island for a canoe trip on the Thomsen River and during the visit, the guide estimates that guests spent about US$760 on crafts and books, and US$115 on groceries in Sachs Harbour (personal communications, 2005). The guests did not require local accommodation, and hired a company based in Inuvik for their flight to the island and to Aulavik National Park.

Banks Island Big Game Hunts (BGH) is a community-owned business and the only guiding service on the island. Sport hunters travelling to the island for a big game hunt are required to book with BGH through one of the two American booking agencies. The booking agency contacts BGH to arrange a guide for their guest; a rotation system is in place to ensure all guides have an equal opportunity for employment. BGH charges US$2850 to hunt a muskox, and US$18,500 to hunt a polar bear (NWT Arctic Tourism, 2003b). Hunting fees include accommodation and meals while on the hunting excursion, but do not include airfare, shipping, accommodation or food costs while in Sachs Harbour (*ibid.*). As a result, polar bear and muskoxen hunts are the most significant tourism economic generators on the island. It appears as though a large portion of the revenue generated through hunting trips remains in Sachs Harbour, while the remainder is retained by the booking agency in the United States (personal communications, 2004). Island residents recently held a vote to decide whether guides should be allowed to book their own clients without utilizing the community-owned guiding agency. Initially residents felt that allowing the hunting guides to work independently from BGH would be detrimental to the hunting industry on the island, but with more discussion they voted in favour of allowing the guides to promote themselves and contract out their guiding services directly to guests (personal communications, 2005). The impact this decision will have on the community and the hunting industry is unknown; however, it has been speculated that this change will benefit the island and allow more dedicated guides to work directly with clients (personal communications, 2005).

The difficulties associated with 'leakage' — where economic benefits leave or never reach the community — from external guiding operations that bring in guides for tourism purposes, are well documented in the tourism literature (Honey, 1999; McLaren, 1998; Milne et al., 1998). So, while polar bear and muskoxen hunts are the most significant tourism economic generators on the island, it remains unclear how much money generated actually stays in the community. Furthermore, by not using local resources, not only is there economic leakage, but also local cultural traditions and environmental concerns, among other things, are less likely to be understood by tourists in ways that can help mitigate the potential negative impacts of tourism. For instance, Banks Island residents feel it is important for visitors to learn about the culture while respecting and appreciating artefacts and ancient structures found throughout the park (Lutra Associates Ltd., 1990). Not using local guides means that an important learning opportunity has been lost, and that negative impacts from tourism might ensue. Independent "naturalist" travellers to Banks Island appear respectful of the culture and knowledgeable about how to travel in this type of fragile environment (*ibid.*). However, while this may currently be to the advantage of the island, increasing the number of tourists to Banks Island might also increase the number of tourists who do not educate themselves about the island, its environment and its culture. Moreover, as Milne et al. (1998, p. 108) observed: "tour operators do not always take a proactive approach in educating their clients about the realities of Arctic life". For all these reasons, increasing the capacity of local guides for economic benefits and educational purposes should therefore be contemplated as part of an overall strategy for sustainable tourism management.

Capacity building however does necessitate training — and training can, and perhaps in peripheral and remote areas we might say 'should' — be considered a 'planned for' community benefit of tourism. The challenge, however is that, in as much as the infrastructure can keep tourists away from Banks Island given the high expense of getting there, this same infrastructure can be prohibitive to training opportunities. In this sense, 'access' issues on Banks Island encompass a variety of questions that can have significant and far-reaching impacts. When combined with issues of 'scale' they make a compelling case for the need for strategic sustainable tourism planning. 'Scale' refers to what may likely be the relatively small number of tourists that would be ideal for the 'carrying capacity' of the island. A carrying capacity policy can provide insight into the ideal number of tourists a destination can handle while still maximizing economic benefits before negative tourism impacts become increasingly inevitable. Access, carrying capacity and community benefits are all linked and should be considered inherently part of an overall sustainable management plan.

Tourism Planning and Development

The tourism mandate of the Northwest Territories' government states that the tourism industry should grow to 45,000 non-resident leisure tourists by 2008. Concomitantly, it stipulates that the sustainability of the environment and northern way of life is paramount (Government of the Northwest Territories, 2003). In 1992, the community of Sachs Harbour developed a Conservation Plan for renewable resources on Banks Island. Eight guidelines were created to encourage tourism while "maintaining the environment and cultural lifestyles" (Community of Sachs Harbour, 1992, p. 54). The guidelines were not specific, but suggested restricting the number of tourism operators, visitors to the island, and flights to the island; it also presented wildlife considerations and protection of heritage resources. The document implies that the community has made efforts to manage the tourism industry. Unfortunately, there is currently no documentation addressing whether the guidelines have been effectively implemented.

The territorial government is not solely responsible for tourism development, but significant funding, resources and personnel are supported for the purpose of tourism development. The high costs of starting a business in Sachs Harbour or on Banks Island and the small number of tourists are thought to be the major constraints limiting business development. Tourism research has been limited to the 1990 study, and the community renewable resource plan that was written in 1992. In effect, Banks Island does not appear to be of much political interest territorially or nationally. This creates both challenges and opportunities to tourism development. On the one hand, the studies' recommendations are not enforced or acted upon, and the lack of current research regarding the economy, tourism and other government issues in the region limit the growth of the island's tourism industry, as well as its planned potential to be sustainable and provide benefits to Island residents. However, such a vacuum of political interest from 'the centre' could provide significant opportunities for the local population to direct its own tourism development. Local control and self-government, along with government support for self-determination and local control over tourism resources, are strategies that can help to mitigate tourism's impact on vulnerable regions (McLaren, 1999; Richards & Hall, 2000). Indeed, they are inherent principles for sustainable tourism (Nelson, Butler, & Wall, 1999).

Conclusion

Banks Island presents a unique tourism opportunity for visitors who are seeking experiences in remote, exotic, northern and natural environments. Tourism development on

Banks Island enjoys a slow and steady pace. Small numbers of naturalists and sport hunters visit the island each year and learn about wildlife, the Arctic, and Inuvialuit culture while participating in their chosen activities. While no studies exist to support the claim, it would appear that, to date, visitors to Banks Island have had a relatively low impact on both socio-cultural and environmental features. The increasing effects of climate change however may significantly alter the environment that originally motivated travellers to this island destination. Indeed, it threatens to challenge tourism development in a variety of other ways, including the possibility for further infrastructure development.

A sustainable tourism development and management plan that takes into account the impacts of climate change is both timely and appropriate. Moreover, economic, cultural and social benefits could be increased and managed through careful tourism planning. An emphasis on increasing community ownership and involvement in tourism by residents could be strived for by increasing local opportunities for tour guiding and other businesses; these strategies might be particularly effective if they were supported by policy or other similar mechanisms. Importantly, government structures currently exist, for instance through self-government initiatives, that can facilitate and maintain community ownership of tourism resources.

References

Alaska Hunting Safaris. (2003). *Experience an Arctic hunting adventure: Canada's Northwest Territories polar bear.* http://www.polarbearhunting.net (accessed 20/10/2005).

Beaufort-Delta Self-Government Office. (2003). *Strength through Partnership.* http://www.selfgov. org (accessed 20/10/2005).

Briguglio, L., & Briguglio, M. (2002). Sustainable tourism in small islands: The case of Malta. In: F. di Castri, & V. Balaji (Eds), *Tourism, biodiversity and information* (pp. 169–184). Leiden: Blackhuys Publishers.

Butler, R. (2002). The development of tourism in frontier regions: Issues and approaches. In: S. Krakover, & Y. Gradus (Eds), *Tourism in frontier areas* (pp. 3–19). Lanham: Lexington Books.

Canadian Heritage and Parks Canada. (2004). *Aulavik National Park interim management guidelines.* http://www.pc.gc.ca/pn-np/nt/aulavik/docs/plan1/sec6/index_e.asp (accessed 20/10/2005).

Canadian Museum of Civilization Corporation. (2003). *Northern people, northern knowledge: The story of the Canadian expedition: 1913–1918.* http://search.civilization.ca/dwesearch.asp?show Doc=47632&page=1&resultsetToken=IKT000032327.1130012076&Lang=en&docType (accessed 20/10/2005).

Cavell, J. (2002). The second frontier: The north in English-Canadian historical writing. *Canadian Historical Review, 83*(3), 364–389.

Community of Sachs Harbour. (1992). *Sachs Harbour community conservation plan.*

Daigle, J., Hrubes, D., & Ajzen, I. (2002). A comparative study of beliefs, attitudes and values among hunters, wildlife viewers, and other outdoor recreationists. *Human Dimensions of Wildlife, 7*(1), 1–19.

Diamantis, D. (2000). Ecotourism and sustainability in Mediterranean Islands. *Thunderbird International Business Review, 42*(4), 427–443.

Equinox Expeditions. (2005). *Thomsen River Canoeing: Land of the Muskox.* http://www.equinoxexpeditions.com/aulavik.html (accessed 20/10/2005).

García-Falcón, J., & Medina-Muñoz, D. (1999). Sustainable tourism development in islands: A case study of Gran Canaria. *Business Strategy and the Environment, 8*(6), 336–357.

Government of the Northwest Territories. (2003). *Northwest Territories tourism strategy* (pp. 1–12).

Hassol, S. J. (2004). *Impacts of a warming Arctic: Arctic climate impact assessment.* Cambridge: Cambridge University Press.

Heinimann, D. (1993). Latitude rising: Historical continuity in Canadian Nordicity. *Journal of Canadian Studies, 28*(3), 134–139.

Honey, M. (1999). *Ecotourism and sustainable development: Who owns paradise?* Washington DC: Island Press.

Legislative Assembly of the Northwest Territories. (2005). *Community profile: Sachs Harbour.* Retrieved from www.assembly.gov.nt.ca/VisitorInfo/NWTMapandHistory/SachsHarbour.html (accessed 20/10/2005).

Lutra Associates Ltd. (1990). *Banks Island tourism study* (pp. 1–83).

McLaren, D. (1998). *Rethinking tourism and ecotravel.* West Hartford, CT: Kumarian Press.

Milne, S., Grekin, J., & Woodley, S. (1998). Tourism and the construction of place in Canada's Eastern Arctic. In: G. Ringer (Ed.), *Destinations: Cultural landscapes and tourism* (pp. 101–120). London: Routledge.

Nelson, J. G., Butler, R., & Wall, G. (Eds). (1999). *Tourism and sustainable development: Monitoring, planning, managing, decision making: A civic approach.* Department of Geography, Publication Series No. 52. Heritage Resources Centre, Joint Publication No. 2 (2nd ed.). Waterloo, Ontario: University of Waterloo.

NWT Arctic Tourism. (2003a). *2004 guide to hunting and fishing in Canada's Northwest Territories* [Brochure]. Yellowknife.

NWT Arctic Tourism. (2003b). *2004 explorer's guide* [Brochure]. Yellowknife.

Outcrop Ltd. (1990). *Northwest Territories data book 1990/91: The complete information guide to the Northwest Territories and its communities.* Yellowknife.

Richards, G., & Hall, D. (2000). *Tourism and sustainable community development.* London: Routledge.

Shields, R. (1991). The true north strong and free. In: *Places on the margin: Alternative geographies of modernity.* London: Routledge.

The Great Canadian Adventure Company. (2005). *Kayaking the Thomsen River on Banks Island.* Retrieved from http://www.adventures.com/gasnet/1534-2.htm (accessed 20/10/2005).

Trim, S., & Zieba, R. (2004). Resources, Wildlife and Economic Development Paper presented at NWT Arctic Tourism conference.

Western Arctic Handbook Committee. (2002a). *Canada's Western Arctic including the Dempster Highway.* Inuvik: Western Arctic Handbook Committee.

Western Arctic Handbook Committee. (2002b). *Natural history of the Western Arctic.* Inuvik: Western Arctic Handbook Committee.

Image 4: Baffin + Nunavut map.

Chapter 7

Baffin Island, Nunavut, Canada

Simon Milne

Introduction

The Inuit of Canada's Baffin Island face a number of important challenges in their attempts to gain greater control over their economic destiny. The physical realities of the region, including its isolation, limited population base and harsh climate, largely preclude the growth of commercial agriculture and manufacturing. As a result, most attention has been focused on the exploitation of the region's diverse natural resource base. These resources have, however, created few sustainable, down-stream linkages with the local economy and generated little in the way of technology-transfer and local employment (GNWT, 1997; Vail & Clinton, 2002). The reliance on resource exploitation and external markets has left the region with a legacy of a 'boom and bust' economy that is highly vulnerable to the vagaries of international demand (Pretes & Robinson, 1989). Pressures on the economy have also come from somewhat unexpected quarters, for example international legislation banning the trade of seal pelts had a major impact on communities in the early 1980s. The value of fur harvesting in the region fell from almost C$1m in 1980 to C$82,000 by 1988 when the Greenpeace-inspired ban was well established. These changes created profound economic dislocation in several hamlets (Wenzel, 1989, 1991).

In an attempt to diversify community economic structures and reduce levels of direct economic dependence on the public sector, the Government of the Northwest Territories (GNWT) in conjunction with the region's hamlets, has been actively developing and promoting tourism in recent decades (Corliss, 1999). In the early 1980s a formal 'community based' tourism policy was established (GNWT, 1983; Marshall, Macklin & Monaghan Ltd., 1982; Anderson, 1991; Hinch & Swinnerton, 1993). The overarching goal of the strategy is to develop an industry that is substantially planned, owned and operated by Inuit and Northern residents and which reflects community aspirations. The government favors the development of non-consumptive 'ecotourism': focusing on adventure (hiking, kayaking), naturalist (wildlife viewing), and arts/culture tours (Hamley, 1991; Hamilton, 1993; Addison, 1996). The guiding principles for the industry's future are as follows.

- Development must be consistent with the abilities and aspirations of the host communities; it must respect northern cultures, expectations and lifestyles,
- Development must be sustainable with the use of today's resources and not compromise their use by future generations; it should be designed to yield maximum economic benefits for residents,
- Tourism should be well distributed between communities, to facilitate this, government support will be given to small and medium-sized communities,
- Development will recognize and respect the spirit and intent of all aboriginal land claims,
- Major tourism initiatives will embody extensive community and industry participation in the planning process,
- The private sector should take the lead in developing a viable tourism industry. Government provides financial incentives and public infrastructure support and will encourage and support the private sector in the marketing arena (GNWT, 1990, pp. 13–15).

This paper examines the role that information and communication technologies (ICT) can potentially play in influencing the shape and nature of local economic development and the attainment of these guiding principles. It is argued that elements of the emerging field of community informatics (CI) can add an important dimension to our attempts to cope with the complex issues that characterize the tourism and development nexus in Baffin Island, particularly issues relating to the ability of local people to highlight, 'sell' and also maintain and strengthen their unique local identity in the face of globalising pressures.

Baffin Island and Nunavut Tourism

Baffin Island is found in the North East of the Canadian Territory of Nunavut, a jurisdiction carved out from the former Northwest Territories in 1999. The land is only sparsely vegetated and underlain by continuous permafrost. The physical landscape includes mountain ranges of up to 3000 m, fjords, glaciers and lowlands. Most Inuit lives are a mix of traditional and modern lifestyles. Subsistence hunting continues to play a major role in the domestic economy and cultural survival of the people (Hicks & White, 1998). The population is projected to rise to 17,000 by 2006; with people living in 13 communities that each comprise, with the exception of Nunavut's capital Iqaluit, between 500 and 1500 people. The island's population is young, with 55% of Baffin Island Inuit aged under 25 (Corliss, 1999; Vail & Clinton, 2002).

The creation of the territorial government is enabling the people of Nunavut to take charge of their own destiny. However, there is a long way to go before Nunavut can reach its goal of economic self-sufficiency (Hicks & White, 2001). Average incomes are low; many people need more education; unemployment is high; transportation costs are high; and as a result, the cost of living is 1.6–3 times higher than in southern Canada (DIAND, 2002).

Hunting, trapping and fishing continue to play an important role in the economy. In most communities, people still rely on traditional foods like caribou, arctic char and seal as primary foods. The people of Nunavut are also famous for arts and crafts. Inuit carvings in soapstone, whalebone and ivory, along with prints and tapestries by well-known Inuit artists sell for thousands of dollars. An estimated 30 percent of Inuit derive some income from arts and crafts. The public sector is also an important source of employment with the Government of Canada investing up to C$40 million to help recruit and train Inuit employees for the Nunavut public service (DIAND, 2002).

In the 1980s, millions of dollars flowed into tourism development in Nunavut through the Canada-Northwest Territories Economic Development Agreement. Advice on licensing, guide-training, marketing and business issues was provided by regional employees of the old Department of Economic Development. Tourism became a centerpiece of the region's economic development policy (Corliss, 1999; Bell, 2003).

In the early 1990s, economic development agreements came to a halt and the territorial government slashed its budget and reorganized the old Department of Economic Development. In 1996, Nunavut Tourism was created out of the old NWT Tourism Industry Association with just one employee and a marketing budget of only C$20,000. The Nunavut Land Claims Agreement also included the establishment of three new national parks, which have become a major tourist attraction for the region (Corliss, 1999; Bell, 2003).

After 2001–2002, Nunavut Tourism's budget was increased by about C$1m a year, enough to pay for a modest advertising campaign and to develop a Nunavut 'brand'. In 2002–2003, Nunavut Tourism received about C$2.3m from the territorial government to deliver tourism programs. Another C$1.5m was for capital improvements to parks and visitor centres. Nunavut Tourism has recently been part of an interagency task force on tourism development, which brings together representatives from organizations such as the Government of Nunavut, Parks Canada, Department of Indian Affairs and Northern Development (DIAND), Nunavut Tunngavik Inc and Heritage Canada (Northern News Services, 2003).

Any discussion of the development of the tourism industry is influenced by the sporadic nature and often questionable quality of tourism statistics (Bell, 2003). It is estimated that 33,000 people visited Nunavut in 2000. About 21 percent of these were vacationers. The unspoiled beauty of parks and the chance to experience Inuit culture are major attractions. Business travel has always been an important sector and it is estimated that nearly three quarters of all travelers visit the region for professional reasons. Iqaluit's increased importance as a political center has played an important role in maintaining this flow.

Tourism is estimated to be worth C$30m a year in Nunavut, making it one of the territory's largest economic sectors. The average tourist spends about $1900 in total, excluding pre-paid costs, which are difficult to quantify (Vail & Clinton, 2002; Nunavut Tourism, 1998). There are estimated to be over 120 tourism operators in Nunavut. Tour operators, outfitters and accommodation providers dominate the sector, with restaurants and galleries also playing an important role. Fifty-eight hotels and bed and breakfasts offer nearly 750 beds, though many of these are taken by workers on extended visits Although accurate information on the number of employees is not available it is estimated that the Nunavut tourism and parks industry alone employs 500 people on a full-time equivalent basis (Vail & Clinton, 2002).

The main tourist season is July and August, with some visitors also arriving in June and September. Past research has revealed that visitors to Baffin Island are relatively affluent, and well educated compared to the general Canadian populace (Milne, Tarbotton, Woodley, & Wenzel, 1997; GNWT, 1996). Most independent tourists are from Canada, usually originating from Ontario or Quebec. The largest foreign group come from the United States and many travel on small, expert-led packages that characterize the region.

While 'consumptive' forms of tourism, such as sports hunting and fishing, have long been part of the region's tourist industry, government policy has assisted non-consumptive tourism (GNWT, 1993; Vail & Clinton, 2002), such as soft adventure (hiking, kayaking), wildlife viewing and arts/cultural tours. The bulk of travelers arrive by plane through Iqaluit. Cruise ship visits have also grown in number in recent years, taking tourists to a range of outlying communities in addition to the capital — including Pond Inlet, Cape Dorset, Kimmirut and Pangnirtung (Woodley, 1999; Grekin & Milne, 1996; Vail & Clinton, 2002). The number of cruises is likely to increase in the future and with it, the demand for tourism products such as, town tours, cultural performances and arts and crafts sales.

Those who market the Baffin Region rely on an array of channels to distribute their products. Limited marketing budgets necessitate careful targeting of funds. In this respect it is interesting to note that word of mouth and the Internet were the two most important sources of information about the Baffin region, particularly among independent tourists even in the early days of the technology's uptake (Milne et al., 1997; GNWT, 1996).

Industry Development Issues

A number of key issues have been raised in past research on the Baffin and Nunavut tourism industry, including a lack of investment in infrastructure, parks and other visitor facilities; relatively high transportation costs faced by visitors to the North and the need for training in the hospitality industry (Anderson, 1991; Vail & Clinton, 2002). Research in the 1990s highlighted other subtle, yet pervasive themes that also have a major influence on the development of a high yield sustainable tourism industry.

Cultural Interaction

Past community-based studies have revealed that local Inuit favor tourism to other industries and prefer to receive tourists who have an interest in local culture and hunting. There is less interest in adventure travelers or what local people sometimes refer to as 'Greenpeace' tourists. The latter are seen as visitors who want to experience the natural environment but have little interest in interacting with communities or learning about the Inuit people's relationship with the natural resources of the region (see Nickels, Milne, & Wenzel, 1991; Milne, Ward, & Wenzel, 1995; Grekin & Milne, 1996). This may be due to the lack of desire to witness local cultural traditions, such as hunting, rather than a lack of respect for Inuit culture, as one elderly female tourist mentioned (Milne et al., 1997)

> Although I understand the native peoples of the North must hunt to live, I don't care to witness it. It is something I put up with when I visit.

Whatever the motivations for this tourist behavior, there are concerns that these tourists may go straight into the 'wilderness' and not interact much with the Inuit. A potential outcome of this is that they may misunderstand certain experiences and spread 'false rumors' (Grekin & Milne, 1996).

Earlier visitor-satisfaction studies show that although visitors enjoy their experience, there is some lack of satisfaction with the opportunity to sample country foods, to meet carvers or to have any contact with residents (Reimer, 1989; Reimer & Dialla, 1992). Even when tourists seek out the tourism experience preferred by local Inuit, it may at times not be accessible because of lack of resources, high cost or mistrust. One such independent traveler (Milne et al., 1997) was 'very dissatisfied with the cultural experience' because

> I would have liked to hear some Inuit throat singing, to learn more about how they hunt, and use the seal products, etc., but the opportunities never arose. I would have loved to meet the elders, and hear their stories, but again, short of barging into their meetings, how do you meet them? … the educational programs aren't in place. The ones that are, are too expensive.

Another group of three tourists who visited Pond Inlet in 1993 made specific mention of their unfulfilled desire to view hunting and identified a possible explanation (Grekin, 1994)

> We quickly realized that tourists were regarded as Greenpeace members. We asked several times to join a seal hunt but noticed lots of reluctance and got negative answers. … I regret this fact. It would have been very interesting for us.

The challenges posed by this cultural interaction were also highlighted by a Canadian geologist from New Brunswick who, upon visiting Nanisivik, was shocked by the apparent total disregard of the northerners for the environment and for conservation of the natural resources (polar bear, narwhal, seal).

Yield

Linkages between tourism and the rest of the economy can be developed further (Milne et al., 1997; Nunavut Tourism, 1998; Vail & Clinton, 2002). Such linkage formation will enhance the downstream benefits associated with the sector. The most significant area of visitor expenditure is arts and crafts, which amounts to 30 percent of average daily expenditure of independent tourists. Handicrafts tend to be high-end items, often costing several hundred dollars a piece. Tourists associate carvings in particular with Inuit, thus compelling a high proportion of tourists to make such purchases (Blundell, 1993). If made in local communities, these purchases have been shown to have a very positive impact on local economic structures and to add positively to the visitor experience (Milne et al., 1995). Unfortunately many visitors find it difficult to buy art at the local level, especially directly from artists, and therefore an opportunity to maximize yield is foregone.

Meals account for a substantial proportion of visitor expenditure. The degree, to which the food supplies required by hotels, restaurants and supermarkets are local in origin (as opposed to being imported), will have a significant effect on tourism's economic benefits for the host region (GNWT, 1990). An early tourist survey (Acres, 1988) indicated that over 70 percent of respondents had tried arctic char and nearly 50 percent had sampled caribou. Seal, Baffin shrimp, scallops and Greenland halibut (turbot) were sampled by a minority. The results of more recent studies similarly identify arctic char and caribou as the most commonly consumed local foods (GNWT, 1996; Milne et al., 1997). These results indicate that there is demand for local food supplies and the potential to maximize yield in this category of visitor expenditure.

A Role for Information Technology

Yield and the cultural experiences of both visitors and Inuit will be influenced by the way in which products and experiences are commoditized and marketed (Milne, Grekin, Woodley, & Wenzel, 1998). They will be shaped by people's broader pre-arrival perception of a destination — shaping that is done through media, word of mouth and a number of other influences including: film, radio, television, magazines and books. Public perceptions of the Inuit have shifted over the years from the 'happy Eskimo' and 'noble savage' to more recent notions of a people struggling to come to terms with high youth suicide rates and dependent economic structures. Indeed Brody (1975, p. 86) has observed that Inuit are criticized both for not being 'White enough' as well as for not living up to the Whites' idea of 'perfect Eskimoness'. Milne et al. (1998) argue that Inuit communities have had relatively limited ability to portray themselves to the outside world. Media, tourism brochures and marketing campaigns have thus far tended to emphasize wildlife, wilderness and landscape over people and culture. Studies have also highlighted the region's lack of representation on mainstream global distribution systems (Milne & Grekin, 1992).

Commentators are arguing that the Internet provides an opportunity for Inuit communities to exert greater control, not only over their economic destiny but also over their self-representation, possibly helping to recreate or relaunch a faithful 'Inuit' brand (Milne et al., 1998; Mason & Milne, 2002, pp. 307–308). There is a great rush among tourism destinations to be part of the network age, and high hopes are held that digital technologies will lead to improved industry performance and, in some cases, greater participation in tourism planning (Ghose, 2001; Milne & Ewing, 2004). Some argue, however, that ICT may be of little use to relatively marginalized populations and small businesses, and may actually widen the inequalities between rich and poor unless appropriate policy instruments are developed (see Castells, 2000).

There is a growing interest in the potential of the Internet to enhance access to, and the shaping of, information by communities and businesses. Commentators argue that the Internet can strengthen business relationships, establish and build networks and communities (both virtual and real), and drive visionary strategy development (Surman & Wershler-Henry, 2001; Kenny, 2002). Some argue that ICT, and particularly the Internet, may provide an important tool in attempts to maximize tourism's benefits for communities and 'level the playing field' for smaller tourism firms and community-based experiences/products (Buhalis, 2000; Mason & Milne, 2002; Levinson & Milne, 2004).

The Internet has several key features that make it an important potential alternative to traditional methods of tourism-related information dissemination in the Baffin Region (Mason & Milne, 2002). Websites are flexible, their images and text can be changed easily. There are cost savings in distribution, service, marketing and promotion with such sites and the profile of Internet users (higher income, more educated) is of interest to communities seeking to attract high-yield travelers. Websites also have the potential to reflect community aspirations more effectively than many traditional marketing approaches.

The process of developing a destination website (portal) can, potentially, be an effective way to foster cooperation and networking between players in the local tourism scene (Mason & Milne, 2002). It is also relatively easy to build tourism-related portals that link into other sectors of the economy — maximizing opportunities for economic linkage creation. It is this potential ability of the Internet to foster cooperation and community that has links to the emerging discipline of CI. CI focuses on the design and delivery of technological applications to enhance community development, and improve the lives of residents (Gurstein, 2000). CI literature focuses on five key areas in which ICT can enhance community quality of life (O'Neil, 2002)

- the promotion of strong democracy and participation in planning processes;
- the development of social capital;
- the empowerment of individuals, especially marginalized groups;
- the strengthening of community and 'sense of place'; and
- the creation of sustainable community economic development opportunities.

The role of the Internet as a marketing tool is vital to the tourism industry in the region (Milne et al., 1997; Nunavut Tourism, 1998) and Internet development in the region has reflected many of the key dimensions of community informatics. We now explore the development and content of the Baffin region's tourism-web presence in the late 1990s.

Baffin Tourism and the Internet

In November 1994, a symposium called 'Connecting the North' was organized to discuss the best options available for communities to link into the Internet and since that time the presence of Canada's Arctic on this global communication medium has grown significantly (Mason & Milne, 2002). Many of these sites — such as www.nunavut.com and www.gov.nu.ca — exist predominantly for inter-community contact and governance purposes. They do however contain tourism sections and links, as well as insights on Inuit life and the local landscape, which directly and indirectly shape tourist perceptions (Milne & Mason, 2002). Early tourism websites, such as a now defunct NWT Virtual Explorers' Guide, offered a variety of information and tour options. In addition, the site offered access to information on the history of the land, vacation planning, different types of tours, parks and contacts for Western and Eastern tourism operators.

In the late 1990s, the Nunavut handbook (www.arctic-travel.com) that had become a major resource for travelers to Baffin Island was placed on the Internet in conjunction with www.nunavut.com. Immediately it became possible to add a 'community' touch to the marketing material through local-content development and design input. While virtual tours and photo galleries provided plenty of the usual imagery of polar bears and tundra, the site also featured and marketed what visitors felt was most missing from their travel experience, a chance to learn about local people and their way of life. The site also made it clear from the outset that Inuit life is indeed shaped by the land and that although the hunting of wildlife may be offensive to some tourists, it is an integral part of daily life in Baffin communities.

The site also pulled no punches about the difficulties involved in traveling to the region. It is, after all, unlikely that any infrastructure development will ever make Baffin Island easy to reach. A community member's first person account of flying in to Pangnirtung makes it very clear that you need to be able to stomach small planes and airstrips if you intend to travel within the island

> The plane begins its descent and I try to reassure myself that the mountains in front of me are scenery, not obstacles. Dwarfing both the aircraft and the town site below, it makes me realize how small I really am. That uncomfortable feeling resurfaces a few minutes later, when it appears that the pilot is about to land on one of Pangnirtung's few straight streets. Dirt roadway turns to gravel runway at the last second though, and we touch down. (Former Pangnirtung Community Web-Page 2000)

The extent to which these early initiatives have actually succeeded in enhancing visitor experience and yield is impossible to judge without regular research on the performance of the industry. Nevertheless, it appears that some of the early progress made by the Nunavut and arctic-travel sites has been turned back. Thus www.arctic-travel.com has reverted to an advertising platform for the Nunavut Guidebook. Meanwhile, the Nunavut Tourism site www.nunavuttourism.com is a new, well-designed and technically competent site, which offers a comprehensive array of product options. Sadly, however, it lacks the stories, local content and direct linkage to cultural tourism of the previous sites.

Conclusion

While tourism has great potential to provide a stable and sustainable source of economic development for Inuit communities, it is clear that the industry faces some important challenges (Bell, 2003; Vail & Clinton, 2002). The industry can do more to both improve its economic yield and provide richer cultural experiences for both the visitor and residents. Inuit would like to see more tourists who have an interest in local culture and also, in some cases, hunting. Residents want visitors who accept local norms and want to meet people, and not just see wildlife; they do not want mass tourism, but appropriate community tourism. The Internet appears to offer considerable potential to achieve these goals. It represents a vehicle for the Inuit of Baffin Island to provide their own interpretation of the Arctic landscape and of their own lives to potential tourists. The fact that Nunavut is a jurisdiction (and the world's largest for indigenous people) means that the Inuit political self-determination can contribute strongly to a just and self-determined tourism policy and marketing. The highly educated, high-income profile of visitors to the region (see Milne et al., 1998) makes it extremely likely that many visitors will have access to the Internet and will be receptive to local content and information.

The Internet, however, does not provide a total solution. Cost and technological barriers remain important impediments to peripheral regions that are attempting to reach and influence the market place through this new distribution technology (Milne et al., 1998). At the same time, it is important that communities and locals have direct input into the web-site development process; otherwise they run the risk of again placing the construction of 'place' in the hands of outsiders (Mason & Milne, 2002). Such developments must revolve around technology transfer and the provision of suitably trained human resources (Hull & Milne, 2004).

There are no clear answers about whether information technology, and the related field of community informatics, can enhance the tourism development process in Baffin Island. There is also uncertainty as to what the Internet means for today's citizens wanting to engage more fully in tourism development processes, both in terms of planning and ownership (Milne & Ewing, 2004). Whatever the outcomes to these uncertainties, it is clear that the impacts of information technologies on the perception, consumption and construction of tourism spaces need to be understood so that they can be better harnessed in order to develop the potential of the Baffin Island and Nunavut tourism industries. ICT can provide local people real input into the commodification of resources for tourist consumption, enabling an appropriate response to the changing spatial patterns of international tourism, and thus a stronger influence into their own economic and cultural destiny.

References

Acres International. (1988). *Baffin visitors survey*. Acres International, Vancouver.

Addison, L. (1996). An approach to community-based planning in the Baffin Region, Canada's Far North. In: L.C. Harrison, & W. Husband (Eds), *Practising responsible tourism: International case studies in tourism planning, policy and development*. (pp. 296–312). New York: Wiley.

Anderson, M.J. (1991). Problems with tourism development in Canada's Eastern Arctic. *Tourism Management*, *12*(3), 209–220.

Bell, J. (2003). Neglected tourism industry seeks new lease on life. www.nunatsiaq.com/archives/31128/news/nunavut/31128_01.html (accessed 20/10/2005).

Blundell, V. (1993). Aboriginal empowerment and souvenir trade in Canada. *Annals of Tourism Research*, *20*(1), 64–87.

Brody, H. (1975). *The people's land: Eskimos and Whites in the Eastern Arctic*. Harmondsworth: Penguin.

Buhalis, D. (2000). Tourism and information technologies: Past, present and future. *Tourism Recreation Research*, *25*(1), 41–58.

Castells, M. (2000). *The rise of the network society* (2nd ed.). Oxford: Blackwell.

Corliss, G. (1999). *Community-based tourism planning and policy: The case of the Baffin Region, Nunavut*. Unpublished MA dissertation. Department of Geography, McGill University, Montreal.

Department of Indian and Northern Development. (2002). *The Nunavut economy challenge and potential*. Ottawa: Government of Canada.

Ghose, R. (2001). Use of Information Technology for community empowerment: Transforming GIS into community information systems. *Transactions in GIS*, *5*(2), 141–163.

Government of the Northwest Territories. (1983). *Community based tourism: A strategy for the Northwest Territories tourism industry*. Yellowknife: Department of Economic Development and Tourism.

Government of the Northwest Territories. (1990). *Building on strengths: A community-based approach.* Yellowknife: Department of Economic Development and Tourism.

Government of the Northwest Territories. (1993). *Marketing strategy: Baffin region 1993 to 1995.* Iqaluit: Department of Economic Development and Tourism.

Government of the Northwest Territories. (1996). *Tourists visiting Nunavut: A profile.* Iqaluit: Department of Policy, Planning and Human Resources.

Government of the Northwest Territories. (1997). *Northwest territories economic framework.* Yellowknife: Department of Resources, Wildlife and Economic Development.

Grekin, J. (1994). *Understanding the community-level impacts of tourism: The case of Pond Inlet, NWT.* Unpublished MA dissertation. McGill University, Montreal.

Grekin, J., & Milne, S. (1996). Community-based tourism: The experience of Pond Inlet. In: R.W. Butler, & T. Hinch (Eds), *Tourism and native peoples* (pp. 76–106). London: Thomson International.

Gurstein, M. (2000). Community informatics: Enabling community uses of information and communications technology. In: M. Gurstein (Ed.), *Community informatics: Enabling community uses of information and communications technologies* (pp. 1–31). London: Idea Group.

Hamilton, R.W. (1993). *The Baffin handbook: Travelling in Canada's Eastern Arctic.* Iqaluit: Nortext Publishing Corporation.

Hamley, W. (1991). Tourism in the Northwest Territories. *Geographical Review, 81*(4), 389–399.

Hicks, J., & White, G. (2001). Nunavut: Inuit self-determination through a land claim and public government?. In: K. Brownsey, & M. Howlett (Eds), *The provincial state: Politics in the provinces and territories* (2nd ed.). Pererborough, Ontario: Broadview Press (Chapter 14).

Hinch, T.D., & Swinnerton, G.S. (1993). Tourism and Canada's North-West territories: issues and prospects. *Tourism Recreation Research, 18*(2), 23–31.

Hull, J., & Milne, S. (2004). IT and tourism in Labrador: Where two highways meet, *Proceedings of the tourism state of the Art conference, Glasgow,* July (CD).

Kenny, C. (2002). Information and communication technologies for direct poverty alleviation. *Development Policy Review, 20*(2), 141–157.

Levinson, J., & Milne, S. (2004). From brochures to the Internet: Tourism, marketing & development in the Cook Islands. *Journal of Pacific Studies, 26*(1–2), 175–198.

Marshall, Macklin & Monaghan Ltd. (1982). *Baffin region tourism planning project: Regional tourism strategy.* Iqaluit: Prepared for the Department of Economic Development and Tourism.

Mason, D., & Milne, S. (2002). E-Commerce and community tourism. In: P.C. Palvia, S.C. Palvia, & E.M. Roche (Eds), *Global information technology and electronic commerce: Issues for the new millennium* (pp. 294–310). Marietta, GA: Ivy League Publishing Limited.

Milne, S., & Ewing, G. (2004). Community participation in Caribbean tourism: Problems and prospects. In: D. Duval (Ed.), *Tourism in the Caribbean: Trends, development, prospects* (pp. 335–358). London: Routledge.

Milne, S., & Grekin, J. (1992). Travel agents as information brokers: The case of the Baffin region, Northwest Territories. *Operational Geographer, 10*(3), 11–15.

Milne, S., Grekin, J., Woodley, S., & Wenzel, G. (1998). Tourism and the construction of place in Canada's Eastern Arctic. In: G. Ringer (Ed.), *Destinations: Tourism and the construction of place* (pp. 101–120). London: Routledge.

Milne, S., Tarbotton, R., Woodley, S., & Wenzel, G. (1997). *Tourists to the Baffin region: 1992 and 1993 profiles.* McGill Tourism Research Group, Industry Report No. 11, Department of Geography, McGill University, Montreal.

Milne, S., Ward, S., & Wenzel, G. (1995). Linking tourism and art in Canada's Eastern Arctic: The case of Cape Dorset. *Polar Record, 31*(176), 125–136.

Nickels, S., Milne, S., & Wenzel, G. (1991). Inuit perceptions of tourism development: The case of Clyde River, Baffin Island, NWT. *Inuit Studies, 1591,* 157–169.

Northern News Services. (2003). *Tourism big earner for Nunavut: Territory sprucing up image for adventurous travellers.* www.nnsl.com/ops/tournuna.html (accessed 20/10/2005).

Nunavut Tourism. (1998). *The impact of tourism on the Nunavut Economy.* Iqaluit: Nunavut Tourism.

O'Neil, D. (2002). Assessing community informatics: A review of methodological approaches for evaluating community networks and community technology centres. *Internet Research: Electronic Networking Applications and Policy, 12*(1), 76–102.

Pretes, M., & Robinson, M. (1989). Beyond boom and bust: A strategy for sustainable development in the North. *Polar Record, 25*(1), 115–120.

Reimer, G. (1989). *Resident attitudes towards tourism development in Pangnirtung, Northwest Territories.* Final Report on a Research Project Funded by the Northern Scientific Training Program. Hamilton: McMaster University.

Reimer, G., & Dialla, A. (1992). *Community based tourism development in Pangnirtung, Northwest Territories: Looking back and looking ahead.* Iqaluit: Department of Economic Development and Tourism.

Surman, M., & Wershler-Henry, D. (2001). *Commonspace: Beyond virtual community.* London: FT.com (Financial Times/Pearson).

Vail, S., & Clinton, G. (2002). *Nunavut economic outlook May 2001: An examination of the Nunavut economy.* The conference board of Canada, economic services group. Retrieved from www.cbsc.org/nunavut/english/pdf/NunavutENGLISH.pdf (accessed 20.10.2005).

Wenzel, G. (1989). Sealing at Clyde river, NWT: A discussion of Inuit economy. *Inuit Studies, 13*(1), 3–22.

Wenzel, G. (1991). *Animal rights, human rights.* Toronto: University of Toronto Press.

Woodley, S. (1999). *Community-based tourism in Kimmirut, Baffin Island, Nunavut: Regional versus local attitudes.* Unpublished MA dissertation. Department of Geography, McGill University, Montreal.

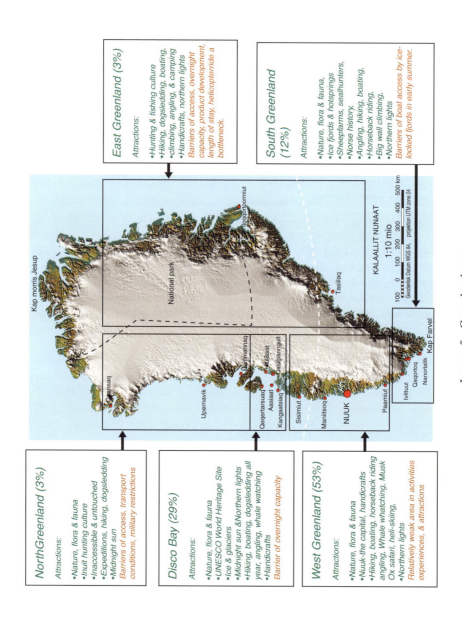

North Greenland (3%)

Attractions:

- Nature, flora & fauna
- Inuit hunting culture
- Inaccessible & untouched
- Expeditions, hiking, dogsledding
- Midnight sun

Barriers of access, transport conditions, military restrictions

Disco Bay (29%)

Attractions:

- Nature, flora & fauna
- UNESCO World Heritage Site
- Ice & glaciers
- Midnight sun &Northern lights
- Hiking, boating, dogsledding all year, angling, whale watching
- Handicrafts

Barrier of overnight capacity

West Greenland (53%)

Attractions:

- Nature, flora & fauna
- Nuuk-the capital, handicrafts
- Hiking, boating, horseback riding angling, Whale whatching, Musk Ox safari, heli-skiing,
- Northern lights

Relatively weak area in activities experiences, & attractions

East Greenland (3%)

Attractions:

- Hunting & fishing culture
- Hiking, dogsledding, boating, climbing, angling, & camping
- Handicrafts, northern lights

Barriers of access, overnight capacity, product development, length of stay, helicopterride a bottleneck.

South Greenland (12%)

Attractions:

- Nature, flora & fauna,
- Ice fjords & hotsprings
- Sheepfarms, sealhunters,
- Norse history,
- Angling, hiking, boating,
- Horseback riding,
- Big wall climbing,
- Northern lights

Barriers of boat access by ice-locked fjords in early summer.

Image 5: Greenland map.

(Reproduced with permission from Kort and Matrikelstyrelsen.)

Chapter 8

Greenland/Kalaallit Nunaat

Berit C. Kaae

Introduction

Greenland, Kalaallit Nunaat is a North Atlantic country with an up to-3-km thick inland ice sheet, leaving 410,449 km^2 of ice-free coastal lands (Statistics Greenland, 2002). Although the world's largest island, Greenland has a population of only 56,854 (Statistics Greenland, 2004a) with 88% being Inuit and 12% being Danes and other nationalities. As a relatively remote cold-water destination, tourism has only become a significant societal factor in Greenland since the 1990s.

Cruise ships carrying tourists from the United States and France have been observed in Greenland as early as the 1930s. But organized tourist travel to Greenland only began in 1959 with flights from Copenhagen and one-day tourist flights from Iceland (Thalund, 2000). From around 500 tourists in 1960 (Ministeriet for Grønland, 1973), the number of tourists visiting Greenland remained quite low: in 1992, some 3500 tourists visited Greenland (Greenland Tourism, 2001).

In 1991, tourism became one of three key issues in a commercial development strategy established by the Greenlandic Home Rule Government. The intentions were to diversify the economy by supplementing income from the declining fishing industry with incomes from minerals and tourism. Substantial public funds were allocated to tourism development. Consequently, Greenland has now become an emerging tourist destination. Tourism has grown steadily and substantially since the early 1990s from around 4000 tourists in 1993 to over 34,000 tourist arrivals in 2001 (Statistics Greenland, 2002). After a slight drop to 27,603 in 2002 — most likely owing to the worldwide tourism decline and security concerns associated with 9/11 — the numbers have increased again to just below 30,000 in 2003 (Statistics Greenland, 2004b).

Most tourists in Greenland (84%) come from Scandinavia — primarily Denmark; 7% come from other Northern European countries; 5% from Southern or Central Europe; while a trickle come from non-European countries — primarily 2% from North America (Statistics Greenland, 2004b). Just below half of the tourists (45%) are on holiday, one-fourth are on business trips (25%), 18% are primarily visiting family and friends, while the remaining come to study (4%), attend conferences or seminars (3%), or participate in other activities (5%) (Statistics Greenland, 2004b). On average, tourists stay for 14.9 days and this has increased slightly over the past 5 years (Table 8.1); however, mean length of stay varies with the season and purpose of the visit.

Tourists primarily stay overnight in hotels (37%), private homes (31%) and in youth or sailor hostels (16%), while 6% stay in tents, 3% in cruise ships, 6% on boats and 1% in huts or sheep farms (Statistics Greenland, 2004b). The overnight capacity varies throughout the year but has increased slightly in the peak season since counts started in 2000 (Table 8.1). In 2003, Greenland had 186, 187 registered overnight stays by tourists (Statistics Greenland, 2004c).

Owing to climatic conditions, Greenland tourism is highly seasonal with most tourists arriving in July and August: just below 6000 tourists visited in July 2003 while around 1500 tourists visited Greenland during each of the winter months (Statistics Greenland, 2004b).

Greenland Tourism divides the island into four tourist regions; though, statistically, North Greenland is subdivided into the popular Disco Bay area and remote North Greenland. Each tourist region offers a variety of attractions and activities, all of which tend to focus strongly on nature qualities. The mid-region in Western Greenland where the capital Nuuk is located receives 53% of all tourists coming to Greenland; but only a third are vacation tourists (Statistics Greenland, 2004b). The Disco Bay area is visited by 29% of all tourists, of which over three-fifths (62%) are vacation tourists. As the area received status as a world heritage site in 2004, more tourists may be expected in the future. Southern Greenland with its milder climate and Norse heritage is also popular, receiving 12% of all tourists with close to half of these (52%) being vacationers. Only few tourists go to the remote North Greenland (3%). The sparsely populated East Greenland receives only few tourists (3%), mostly by cruise ships or on one-day tours from Iceland.

Tourism Activities

Tourism in Greenland is strongly linked to nature and culture. Nature experiences are oriented towards ice and snow, flora and fauna, hiking and camping, seeing the midnight sun or the northern lights, dog sledding, sailing along the coast on ferries or cruise ships,

Table 8.1: Tourist arrival statistics in Greenland during peak season (July): 1999–2003.

Greenland	Gross tourist arrivals	Tourist arrivals in peak month (July/August)	Average length of stay (days)	Number of tourist beds (July)
1999	26,410	5537	14.2	Not available
2000	31,331	5949	14.4	2103
2001	32,558	6077	14.4	2251
2002	27,603	5108	14.9	2210
2003	29,712	5832	14.9	2437

Source: Statistics Greenland (2002, 2004b,d), Greenland Tourism (2004).

angling and whale watching. It also involves more specialized activities such as rock climbing, mountain biking, kayaking, ice golf, heli-skiing, adventure racing, Polar Circle marathon running and other sport events. Cultural experiences include viewing the historic remains of the early Inuit and Norse cultures as well as experiencing present-day culture. This double focus on nature and culture is strongly reflected in printed or internet-based marketing material (Greenland Tourism, 2004b–h).

Accessibility

Greenland is accessible either by air or cruise ship. Following the basic geographic distance-decay concept (Pearce, 1989), the volume of tourist traffic to and particularly within Greenland decreases with distance away from the generating areas, with the notable exception of Denmark. There are 5–10 weekly connections from Copenhagen to Kangerlussuaq in West Greenland and Narsarsuaq in South Greenland, with connecting flights to Nuuk and other towns. Within Greenland, transportation is by air or coastal ferries while roads are only local. Greenland has a total of 12 airports, 5 heliports and 42 helistops in smaller villages (Greenland Tourism, 2004a). Air Iceland has three weekly connections from Keflavik in Iceland to Kulusuk in East Greenland and onwards to Kangerlussuaq and Nuuk. Although Air Greenland operates most flights, accessibility and operators to Greenland are expanding. As from summer 2005, Air Iceland operates two weekly flights between Iceland and Narsarsuaq in South Greenland (Greenland Tourism, 2004g); the Great Canadian Travel Company operates two charter flights weekly between Iqaluit in Nunavut and Aasiaat in North Greenland with connection to and from Ottawa and Montreal; and a weekly charter flight links Frankfurt to Kangerlussuaq via Keflavik in Iceland (Greenland Tourism, 2004g).

Accessibility — both external and internal — is a key issue in Greenland's development, and depends primarily on infrastructure and prices. The mountainous coastal terrain limits the length of airport runways and only allows for smaller planes. Several plans to expand runways to provide direct access for larger planes to the capital Nuuk and other towns are often discussed; but the infrastructure expansions are very expensive, creating a barrier to tourism. In a few cases, plans to increase infrastructure collide with tourism interests: one example being a plan to establish a road on the 160 km corridor from Kangerlussuaq airport to the coastal town of Sisimiut, conflicting with this area being a popular hiking and dog sledding area for tourists.

Price severely modifies the distance-decay curve of tourism flows to Greenland. Travel to Greenland is notoriously expensive, as is the case in most Arctic regions (Smith, 1996). Greenland is overflown by most of the transatlantic jet routes between cities in Europe and those in North America (Smith, 1996). But the airfare to Greenland is several times higher than these flights, even though the latter would typically traverse twice or three times the distance (Air Greenland, 2004).

Apart from physical access, market access is a key issue (Pearce, 1989). Distances and the 4 to 5-hour travel time to Greenland from the main markets of Denmark and neighbouring countries are not seen as limiting factors. Greenland is within almost equal proximity to industrialized and urbanized countries as many popular warm-water destinations. Greenland Tourism is making efforts to diversify Greenland's tourist markets.

A high dependency on a few transport providers makes tourism in Greenland vulnerable to market changes. Airlines and shipping firms often make decisions in the best interest of their shareholders and it may be difficult to influence the corporate level decision-making of these firms (Smith, 1996). In Greenland, however, the airline is largely governmentally controlled with the main share holders being Greenland Home Rule (37.5%), Scandinavian Airlines (37.5%) and the Danish Government (25%) (Air Greenland, 2004).

In contrast, cruise lines are commercially owned and driven. Greenland is increasingly becoming part of cruise ship itineraries in the North Atlantic: moorings have expanded from 28 in 1994 to 167 in 2003, with a total of 9993 registered cruise-ship passengers (Greenland Tourism, 2004a). Cruise tourism has a different pattern than land-based tourism and affects more remote coastline communities and archaeological sites. Since 2003, a head tax provides governmental income from cruise tourism (Greenland Tourism, 2004a), while the benefits to local communities from cruise tourism appear to be limited. Again, this trend is reflected in other Arctic regions (Smith, 1996).

While price, infrastructure and climate negatively modify the distance decay curve of tourism flows to Greenland, close historic and administrative links to Denmark modify it positively. Overall, access barriers are often perceived as problems in relation to the intentions of tourism policies for expanding tourism; yet, at the same time, barriers prevent a descent into mass tourism: Greenland has attracted fewer but wealthier tourists than most comparable island destinations.

Nature

Tourist images of Greenland are strongly linked to the natural and environmental qualities of a pristine Arctic wilderness with unique landscapes, ice formations, wildlife and plant communities that are highly appealing to tourists. Traditionally, Arctic nature suggests images of immense expanses of untrammelled, clean nature (Kaltenborn, 1996). Nature in Greenland includes a number of habitats closely adapted to the high, low and sub-Arctic conditions and these are generally more sensitive than habitats in temperate areas owing to slow regeneration in the short growth season. Although Greenland has a low population density, the use of natural resources is a key factor in Greenlandic society and is increasingly affecting sensitive nature areas (Due & Ingerslev, 2000). Furthermore, most protected land is located in the sparsely populated and rarely visited high Arctic; in contrast with low and sub-Arctic zones, where most impacts from recreation and tourism as well as hunting, fishing, agriculture and mineral extraction take place, and, therefore, enjoys less protection (Due & Ingerslev, 2000).

While the world's largest national park in North East Greenland is only accessible with special permits, the popular tourist area of Ilulissat Icefjord (40,240 ha) was declared a UNESCO World Heritage Site in 2004 (UNESCO, 2004). The icefjord is located on the west coast of Greenland, 250 km north of the Arctic Circle and it is the sea mouth of Sermeq Kujalleq, one of the fastest (19 m/per day) and most active glaciers in the world. Its annual calving amounts to over 35 km^3, which is more than any other glacier outside Antarctica. The Ilulissat Icefjord offers both scientists and visitors easy access for close view of the calving glacier front and the ice-filled fjord. The wild and highly scenic combination of rock, ice and sea, along with the dramatic sounds produced by the moving ice, combine to present a truly memorable natural spectacle (UNESCO, 2004). The region is already a popular tourist area, and the status as World Heritage Site is likely to attract still more visitors.

The impacts from tourists on nature and culture in Greenland remain largely unexplored. However, an ongoing inter-Nordic project involving Greenland, Iceland and Svalbard aims at mapping the environmental impacts of the Arctic tourism industry and thereafter to suggest means of implementing more sustainable forms of tourism. In Greenland, the project involves two destinations: Ilulissat and Ammassalik. Initial results indicate that impacts on nature originate as much from local residents as from tourists and that visual pollution (eyesores) greatly influences tourist perceptions and the quality of their experience. Consequently, the project has initiated the removal of offending visuals in Ilulissat (Nordic Council of Ministers, 2001).

The transition of Inuit culture also influences the use and perception of natural resources in Greenland. While traditional Inuit culture has a deep respect of nature and use only the resources needed for sustainable living, Hansen (2001) suggests that this has severely changed: now over-hunting and wasteful use of natural resources are taking place, which may deplete the Greenlandic fauna in a few decades. A status report on biodiversity of Arctic flora and fauna by CAFF (Conservation of Arctic Flora and Fauna, 2001) also takes a pessimistic view on the future of Arctic ecosystems. It points to the external threats from global warming, introduction and invasion of non-endemic species, and pollution from industry and cars, which accumulates in the Arctic environments.

Still, most of these latent threats are not directly visible, and to tourists Greenland continues to symbolize 'pure nature'. An increased interest in exotic 'green' destinations and in environmental awareness, both by the general public and among tourists (Kaltenborn, 1996) may contribute to increasing tourism in Greenland. As concerns over the modern industrial development and the global resource situation become more significant to the Western public, interest in unspoiled nature is increasing as a response to recognizing it as a scarce good (Kaltenborn, 1996).

Climatic Conditions and Change

The island of Greenland stretches 2700 km over three climatic zones from high Arctic climate in the north through low Arctic to relative mild sub-Arctic climates in the south, providing a wide variety of terrestrial and aquatic ecosystems. The Arctic climate with the inland ice cap, glaciers and icebergs is a main attraction factor in tourism. However, most tourists prefer to visit during the milder summer months. The Arctic climate poses an additional barrier to tourism since the season is short and transportation by boats and planes is affected by ice-choked or ice-locked waters, strong winds, snow, ice and fog. The northern location also creates attractions such as the midnight sun in the summer season and the Northern Lights (*aurora borealis*) during seasons with darkness.

The Arctic is very sensitive to climate changes resulting from global warming as temperatures rise faster there. Effects are also beginning to show in Greenland where the inland ice sheet has declined by 16% over the last 25 years (ACIA, 2004). The Arctic

Climate Impact Assessment conducted by an international team of 300 scientists has predicted increasing temperatures, changes in atmospheric and oceanic circulation patterns, raising sea levels and wider variations in precipitation. The Arctic is also likely to experience changes in vegetation, shifts in animal species, coastal impacts, changes in marine transportation, thawing of permafrost, ultraviolet radiation and effects on the indigenous communities. In terms of tourism, the decline in summer ice is likely to expand the navigable waters and lengthen the summer navigation season leading to an expansion of tourism (ACIA, 2004). Rising temperatures will affect the habitats of different species including a decline in trout and other freshwater fish, hereby impacting sport fishing and tourism (ACIA, 2004).

The effects of global warming on the natural environment and on local communities may indirectly impact tourism. If key attractions such as glaciers and ice melt away, wildlife changes to other species and local communities become too affected, tourism may decline. In fact, it may appear ironic but, if Greenland ends up living up to its name, tourism is likely to decline severely.

Cultural Resources in Greenland

Greenland's cultural resources and some of its most interesting tourism attractions

Greenland has been inhabited on and off for the past 4500 years (Grønnow, 2000). The earliest known residents were the Inuit who originated from Central Asia and arrived in Greenland via Alaska and Canada some 6–7 millennia ago. The so-called Saqqaq and Dorset immigrant waves followed. This latter culture used iron from meteorites and traded copper with groups in Canada (Grønnow, 2000). The last major wave of immigration by the Thule Culture took place from Canada around 1200 AD (Gulløv, 2000). This is the origin of the current Inuit population. This culture was based on hunting and fishing, following the seasonal migrations of animals to ensure adequate supplies for long winters in more permanent settlements. Hunting tools became highly developed during this period and larger boats, kayaks and dog sleds provided this culture with higher mobility (Gulløv, 2000). Most of the pre-historic remains seen in Greenland today originate from the Thule Culture.

Around 985 AD, an immigration of Norse farmers from Iceland took place led by Eric the Red. The Norse immigrants settled in the fjords of Southern Greenland near Nuuk and lived from farming, hunting and fishing (Arneborg, 2000). Erik's son, Leif den Lykkelige (Leif the Happy) introduced Christianity in Greenland and several churches were constructed. Today, Norse ruins and building reconstructions are among the tourist attractions. Sometime after 1408, the Norse settlers disappeared, possibly because of climatic changes. In 1721, Norwegian priest Hans Egede arrived in Greenland in search of the Norse settlers but, when unsuccessful, he started to preach among the Inuit and to establish trade posts. This initiated a process of colonization, which made Greenland a frontier of cultural and natural scientific exploration and expeditions. Meanwhile, Danish sovereignty had been established in the 1600s. In 1953, Greenland became an equal member of the Danish Kingdom and in 1979 the Greenlandic Home Rule Government was established. The strong ties to Denmark are reflected in the majority of tourists to Greenland still coming from Denmark.

Many of the cultural remains from the various pre-historic and historic periods in Greenland, as well as present-day culture, are now part of the tourism product in Greenland. Images of Greenland start forming at early ages among Danish children, since they are led to believe that Greenland is the home of Julemanden (the Danish Santa). The tourist office in Nuuk has a giant mailbox and a service replying to letters to Julemanden.

Culturally, tourism may help preserve and even revive some cultural aspects in Greenlandic society undergoing many transitions owing to factors beyond tourism. Examples would include maintaining traditional dog sledding rather than snowmobiling. However, alongside these traditional attributes, tourism brochures also emphasize Greenland's modern aspects and services.

Tourists and Travel Motives

Tourism is motivated by the search for certain psychological or intrinsic rewards, either personal or interpersonal (Isa-Ahola, 1982). Furthermore, these pull-factors are combined with push-factor motives of escaping the everyday environment. In his theory of ritual inversion, Graburn (1983) suggests that tourists seek out travel experiences that differ from their normal life but that each kind of tourism is characterized by the selection of only a few key reversals. The sense of difference from one's normal situation is also mentioned as a key attractor by Conlin and Baum (1995) and by Butler (1993).

Moreover, tourists have different psychological profiles. Plog (1974, 1987) places these profiles on a continuum ranging from anxious, self-inhibited, non-adventurous *psycho-centric* tourists seeking the safety of the predictable, through *mid-centric* to self-confident, outgoing and curious *allocentric* tourists seeking risk and adventure. The tourist 'types' described by Cohen (1972, 1979) and others (Smith, 1977; Elands & Lengkeek, 2000) represent various combinations of psychological profiles, motives and types of reversals from home environments. Greenland is still at the relatively early stages of tourism development in relation to Butler's (1980) destination life cycle model and tourism advertisements are more likely to appeal to the more adventure-seeking segment of the mid-centrics. The true allocentric adventurers or 'explorers' will find their own way as Greenland provides excellent opportunities for extreme sports and adventure tourism activities such as rock climbing or crossing the Inland Ice. Generally, the tourists in Greenland have tendencies towards the 'explorer' end of the Cohen typology spectrum, while the high comfort tourists are under-represented. However, Greenland also attracts golf tourists playing on the inland ice and an increasing number of cruise tourists.

The Travel Career Ladder implies that the motivation of tourists changes over time as they become more experienced (Pearce, 1988, 1991; WTO, 1997). Tourists in Greenland tend to be older with the 50–59 year age group predominating (Statistics Greenland, 2004b). Over 40% of the tourists are 50 years or older. Possibly, experienced warm-water tourists become more interested in cold-water destinations over time, as warm water loses its novelty as a reversal.

To tourists, Greenland represents key reversals, with the Arctic climate, ice and snow contrasting with usually temperate home environments; a vast rugged wilderness landscape contrasting with the groomed landscape of small-scale or intensive farmland and a remoteness contrasting with the high population density and high accessibility of urban clusters. As in other Arctic regions, the high degree of naturalness — the absence of human impacts and disturbances (such as roads, settlements and artefacts) and numerous views of scenic mountains, glaciers and sea are highly valued salient characteristics (Kaltenborn, 1996).

Another key reversal is the indigenous Inuit culture that (at least in the mind of tourists) is closely linked to nature and contrasts with the more technological and nature-detached culture of industrialized societies. But the close ties with Denmark also provide some socio-cultural similarities (such as language and currency). Visiting Greenland may also to some extent express *individuality* as a contrast to the mainstream sunlust; the high prices add to the feeling of an exclusive experience. Visits are also linked to *initiation* in the sense of being described as a 'once in a lifetime experience', representing a 'rite of passage' building on the myth of hardship endured by the early explorers. Greenland Tourism markets Greenland as offering 'experiences from a completely different world', thereby focusing on the reversals.

Contrasting its warm-water cousin of the many S's (sun, sea, sand, surf, sex, etc.), Greenland may be the land of the many I's: ice, icebergs, icefjords, indigenous Inuits, inaccessibility, initiation, island isolation and individuality. This may appeal to certain segments of travellers, but the existence of a specific 'cold-water tourist' cannot as yet be confirmed. There is as yet not enough systematic knowledge about the tourists, their travel patterns, motives and experiences. Greenland may be just a diversion from the warm-water destinations of the current North European tourism market. However, as new tourist markets develop in warm-water regions, the cold climate and its unique ice and snow experiences may become key reversals attracting new affluent tourist segments. As a post-modern phenomenon, global forces such as changes in the international economy, demographic patterns, more affluent tourists, global tourism patterns with significant shifts towards more travel in fragile areas and changes in norms and value systems (Kaltenborn, 1996) are likely to influence and perhaps increase tourism to Greenland.

Vulnerability

But: increase it by how much? Isolated islands are often characterized as more vulnerable as tourism tends to be more pervasive in its economic, socio-cultural and environmental impacts than on mainland destinations (Conlin & Baum, 1995). As such, Greenland is quite vulnerable to impacts from tourism environmentally, socio-culturally and economically. Although the world's largest island in size, the areas along the Greenlandic coast not covered by the permanent ice sheet are relatively small and the ecosystems are fragile. With a dispersed population of only 56,854 living in 18 towns and 59 smaller settlements, the socio-cultural impact of over 30,000 tourists per year provides both opportunities and risks.

As a small economy, Greenland tourism is highly vulnerable to fluctuations in tourism flows and to changes in infrastructure development and access. Tourism in Greenland is highly dependent on infrastructure development and on the policies and practices of single facilities and operators. One example is cruise-ship tourism where large numbers of tourists make short-term visits to small towns, settlements or archaeological sites. Here, impact depends crucially on how these visits are prepared, carried out and how well informed and aware the tourists are of the ecological and socio-cultural vulnerability of the visited areas (see Thomson & Thomson, this volume).

Tourism policies and strategies in Greenland are based on the intentions of ecological, socio-cultural and economic sustainability (Greenland Tourism, 2003) but the operational-ization of these objectives is as difficult in Greenland as in other countries. A few hotels participate in environmental labelling schemes. Tourism may be a catalyst in clean-up efforts by the local communities in Greenland where a sometimes low awareness of litter and other eyesores is confronted with the high expectations held by tourists of a pristine Arctic wilderness and a local population living in harmony with nature. These contrasting value systems are both an attractor and a barrier in tourism.

Growth Patterns and Future Trends

The development of tourism in Greenland has not been random and uncontrolled as expe-rienced in many warm-water destinations. As an expensive cold-water destination, the tourism industry faces the challenge of attracting tourists and creating growth. Greenland has had a tourism board since 1991 and the intention of the first Greenlandic tourism plan was to increase tourism to 35,000 tourists by year 2005, each with an expenditure of 15,000 DKK (approx. US$ 1800), creating 2200–2500 full-time jobs in tourism, 1000–1500 other full time jobs outside the sector and to generate local revenues of 500 million DKK (US$ 42 million). Finally, any such development had to be environmentally and culturally responsible. Though it was later realized that the expenditure and multiplier effects had been too ambitious, the expected benefits were not adjusted and instead the desired annual tourist numbers were upgraded to 61,000 by year 2005 (Lyck, 1998).

While the originally intended number of tourists has almost been met, the expected income and job generating effects have been smaller than expected. However, tourism does contribute significantly to the economy. The tourism strategy plan 2003–2005 (Greenland Tourism, 2003) represents a shift — in focus towards sustainable tourism development – environmentally, economically, and socially –, capacity building and alliances. Some local activities focus on an improved coordination of infrastructure, an enhanced cooperation among destinations, and on advising, marketing, documentation and education in tourism. Within the tourism policy framework, local staff are being trained to work in tourism and a number of manuals have been established. A network of licensed outfitters has successfully been built up: each year, additional courses and seminars are arranged by Greenland Tourism in order to develop skills among outfitters (Greenland Tourism, 2004a,g).

Generally, tourism in Greenland has not been the victim of a boom-and-bust mentality in the sense of rapid growth and overexploitation to make a quick profit and then move on. On the contrary, efforts to attract more tourists have in some cases been so difficult com-pared to the investments that the bust has come without a boom. Several prospective pro-jects have not proved feasible owing to such factors as difficulty of access, high prices and investment costs, constraints of seasonality and climatic conditions.

The high prices and difficulty of access currently function as a growth control mecha-nism, excluding mass tourism. This provides some control over the growth on land; but, if accessibility was improved, this would change. A less controllable growth pattern is related to the increase of cruise-ship tourism in Greenland. Both the size and number of boats are increasing and the short visits may cause high impacts even in remote locations.

Conclusion

Greenland is an emerging destination in extreme cold water. The slow growth in the industry has limited its impact and allowed for policy adjustments and a steady professionalization of the industry. Tourism strategies have been developed based on stated intentions of environmental, socio-cultural and economic sustainability. The focus of the plans is on the promotion of tourism, networking within industry structures, the upgrading of human resource skills and the education of and close cooperation with local outfitters and communities.

   In this context, not enough attention has yet been given to the complex interactions of tourism management, wilderness protection and economic development. Tourism management is fundamentally a competition over control and allocation of values and resources (Kaltenborn, 1996), and increased cooperation with nature managers is highly relevant: as in the case of the new World Heritage Site of Ilulissat Icefjord where nature protection and tourism just *have* to balance. More detailed insights are also needed on tourist activities, motives, experiences and outcomes from travels in Greenland in order to foster a deeper understanding of their interests and needs. This may also clarify the possible existence of a certain type of 'cold-water' tourist. Detailed studies of the actual benefits and impacts of tourism are also needed to better appreciate how Greenlandic society can best optimize the benefits and minimize the negative impact of this emerging industry. Examples from other cold-water islands should inspire this process.

References

Arctic Climate Impact Assessment (ACIA). (2004). *Impacts of a warming Arctic.* Cambridge: Cambridge University Press. www.amap.no/acia/index.html (accessed 20/10/2005).

Air Greenland (2004). *Årsrapport 2003.* www.airgreenland.gl/editor/download/2003aarsrapport_dk.pdf (accessed 20/10/2005).

Arneborg, J. (2000). 'Nordboerne'. In: B. H. Jakobsen, J. Bøchner, N. Nielsen, R. Guttersen, O. Humlum, & E. Jensen (Eds), *Topografisk atlas Grønland* (pp. 54–55). Copenhagen: Det Kongelige Danske Geografiske Selskab og Kort & Matrikelstyrelsen.

Butler, R. W. (1980). The concept of a tourist area-cycle of evolution: Implications for the management of resources. *Canadian Geographic, 14*(1), 5–12.

Butler, R. W. (1993). Tourism development in small islands. In: D. G. Lockhart, D. Drakakis-Smith, & J. A. Schembri (Eds), *The development process in small island states* (pp. 71–91). London: Routledge.

Cohen, E. (1972). Towards a sociology of international tourism. *Social Research, 39*(1), 164–182.

Cohen, E. (1979). A phenomenology of tourist experiences. *Sociology, 13* (2), 179–202.

Conlin, M. V., & Baum, T. G. (Eds). (1995). *Island tourism: Management principles & practice.* New York: Wiley.

Conservation of Arctic Flora and Fauna (CAFF). (2001). *Arctic flora and fauna: Status and conservation.* Helsinki: Edita. www.caff.is/sidur/sidur.asp?id=18&menu=docs (accessed 20/10/2005).

Due, R., & Ingerslev, T. (Eds). (2000). *Naturbeskyttelse i Grønland*. Technical Report no. 29, Grønlands Naturinstitut. www.natur.gl/dokument/Følsomme%20områder.pdf (accessed 20/10/2005).

Elands, B., & Lengkeek, J. (2000). *Typical tourists: Research into the theoretical and methodological foundations of a typology of tourism and recreation experiences*. Mansholt Studies No. 21. The Netherlands: Wageningen.

Graburn, N. H. H. (1983). The anthropology of tourism. *Annals of Tourism Research*, *10*(1), 9–33.

Greenland Tourism. (2001). Estimates of number of tourists to Greenland: 1993–2000. www.statgreen.gl (accessed 20/10/2005).

Greenland Tourism. (2003). *Tre vigtig år — oplæg til strategi og handling for turismen i Grønland 2003–2005* (28pp.).

Greenland Tourism. (2004a). *Årsrapport 2003*. (25pp.).

Greenland Tourism. (2004b). *Greenland — 2,175,600 km² of pure adventure*. Main brochure, 23pp. http://www.greenland.com/Tools/Download_Center/ (accessed 20/10/2005).

Greenland Tourism. (2004c). *Nordgrønland — oplevelser af en helt anden verden* (16pp.).

Greenland Tourism. (2004d). *Vestgrønland — oplevelser af en helt anden verden* (16pp.).

Greenland Tourism. (2004e). *Sydgrønland — oplevelser af en helt anden verden* (16pp.).

Greenland Tourism. (2004f). *Østgrønland — oplevelser af en helt anden verden* (8pp.).

Greenland Tourism. (2004g). www.greenland.com

Greenland Tourism. (2004h). www.visitgreenland.dk

Grønnow, B. (2000). 'Palæo-eskimoerne: De første Mennesker i Grønland'. In: B. H. Jakobsen, J. Bøchner, N. Nielsen, R. Guttersen, O. Humlum, & E. Jensen (Eds), *Topografisk atlas Grønland* (pp. 46–51). Copenhagen: Det Kongelige Danske Geografiske Selskab og Kort & Matrikelstyrelsen.

Gulløv, H. C. (2000). Thulekulturen. In: B. H. Jakobsen, J. Bøchner, N. Nielsen, R. Guttersen, O. Humlum, & E. Jensen (Eds.). *Topografisk Atlas Grønland* (pp. 52–53). Copenhagen: Det Kongelige Danske Geografiske Selskab og Kort & Matrikelstyrelsen.

Hansen, K. (2001). Til den bitre ende. *Polarfronten*, 2, 15.

Isa-Ahola, S. (1982). Towards a social psychological theory of tourism motivation: A rejoinder. *Annals of Tourism Research*, *9*(2), 256–61.

Kaltenborn, B. P. (1996). Tourism in Svalbard: Planned management or the art of stumbling through? In: M. F. Price (Ed.), *People and tourism in fragile environments* (pp. 89–108). New York: Wiley.

Lyck, L. (Ed.). (1998). *Turismestrategi og — udvikling i Grønland*. Copenhagen: Nordic Press.

Ministeriet for Grønland. (1973). *Turisme i Grønland*. Betænkning 700, 134 pp.

Nordic Council of Ministers. (2001). *Towards a sustainable Nordic tourism*. TemaNord 2001 p. 546. Copenhagen: Nordic Council of Ministers.

Pearce, D. (1989). *Tourism development* (2nd ed.). Oxford: Longman.

Pearce, P. L. (1988). *The Ulysses factor: Evaluating visitors in tourist settings*. New York: Springer-Verlag.

Pearce, P. L. (1991). Fundamentals in tourist motivation. In: D. G. Pearce, & R. W. Sutter (Eds), *Tourism research: Critiques and challenges* (pp. 113–124). London: Routledge.

Plog, S. (1987). Understanding psychographics in tourism research. In: J. R. B. Ritchis, & C. Goeldner (Eds), *Travel tourism and hospitality research* (pp. 203–214). New York: Wiley.

Plog S. C. (1974). Why destination areas rise and fall in popularity. *Cornell Hotel Restaurant and Administration Quarterly*, *55*(8), 13–16.

Smith, V. L. (1977). *Hosts and guests: The anthropology of tourism*. Philadelphia: University of Pennsylvania Press.

Smith, V. L. (1996). The Inuit as hosts: Heritage and wilderness tourism in Nunavut. In: M. F. Price (Ed.), *People and tourism in fragile environments* (pp. 33–50). New York: Wiley.

Statistics Greenland. (2002). Flypassagerstatistikken 2001. *Turisme 2002*, Vol. 2. www.statgreen.gl/dk/publ/turisme/02-1fly.pdf (accessed 20/10/2005).

Statistics Greenland. (2004a). *Nøgletal*. www.statgreen.gl/ (accessed 20/10/2005).

Statistics Greenland. (2004b). Flypassagerstatistikken 2003. *Turisme 2004*, Vol. 1. www.statgreen.gl/ dk/publ/turisme/04-1fly.pdf (accessed 20/10/2005).

Statistics Greenland. (2004c). Overnatningsstatistikken 2003. *Turisme 2004*, Vol. 2. www.statgreen.gl/ dk/publ/turisme/04-1hot.pdf (accessed 20/10/2005).

Statistics Greenland. (2004d). *Special data extracts on average length of stay, peak month visitation, bed capacity and previous visits*. Analysis by Josef Kajangmat.

Thalund, S. (2000). 'Moderne Turisme i Sisimiut'. In: B. H. Jakobsen, J. Bøchner, N. Nielsen, R. Guttersen, O. Humlum, & E. Jensen (Eds), *Topografisk atlas Grønland* (pp. 236–237). Copenhagen: Det Kongelige Danske Geografiske Selskab og Kort & Matrikelstyrelsen.

UNESCO World Heritage Centre. (2004). *World Heritage list: Ilulissat Icefjord* http://whc.unesco.org (accessed 20/10/2005).

World Tourism Organization (WTO). (1997). *International tourism: A global perspective*. Madrid, Spain: WTO.

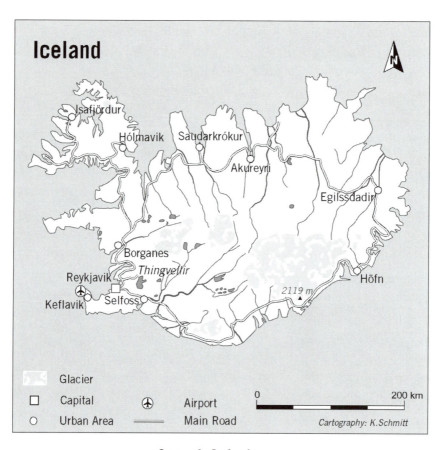

Image 6: Iceland map.

Chapter 9

Iceland

Stefan Gössling

Just Another (Cold) Island?

> Tourist attractions: Iceland's main attraction is its scenery, particularly during late spring and summer. The rugged landscape includes geysers and hot springs in various parts of the country and numerous waterfalls streaming from the glaciers and volcanic fields. The major historic site, now a national park, is Thingvellir, where the world's first parliament convened. Outdoor activities, including camping, hiking, skiing, and horseback riding, are popular. Although Icelandic horses are smaller than others, they are held in high esteem because of their unique abilities in performing different types of trots and are exported worldwide. Golf courses are available throughout the country and international tournaments are held. River-rafting also is commercially available in a few places. Fly fishing for Atlantic salmon and various types of trout has been an important part of the tourism industry for decades, but licenses cost $3,000/person per day. Hunting is increasingly popular, mostly for geese, ptarmigan, reindeer, fox, and ducks. (US Department of State, 1997, p. 14).

This largely persists as the image of Iceland: a cold water island on the Atlantic periphery, as 'close' to North America as to Europe. The island is particularly attractive in "late spring and summer"; but then, the average temperature in July is 11°C. What, one wonders, can justify a trip to Europe's expensive north-western outpost?

Icelandic tourism illustrates how fast such an industry can grow in a small economy: international tourist arrivals jumped from 142,000 in 1990 to 278,000 in 2002 (World Tourism Organization (WTO), 2005). Tourism generated receipts of € 264 million in 2002, or € 950 per tourist. Growth in receipts from tourism grew at a staggering 11.7% per year in the period 1995–2000. Clearly, Iceland is a high-price destination: transport and food prices are well above those in most other European countries. This is also true for accommodation, with few opportunities to stay anywhere for less than € 80 per room per night. In summary, there is a considerable paradox: a cold water island with few truly unique sites, unfavourable weather conditions, very high prices and a two-month main 'season' that has, in terms of tourist arrival growth rates, turned into Europe's premier destination. This phenomenon begs explanation.

Cold-Water Island Fascination

Baum (1997, p. 25) conceptualized the fascination of cold-water islands in the North Atlantic in terms of 10 attributes: remoteness; small, discrete size; across the sea but not too far; different but familiar; slower pace, back a bit in time; common heritage; distinct culture and language; wilderness environment; water-focused society; and distinctive niche attractions. All these characteristics apply to Iceland. Overall, there might be just one aspect in Baum's list that only partially fits Iceland: the notion of being "a bit back in time". The general feature might rather be that of a highly vibrant, flexible society and economy, punctually coexisting with traditional lifestyles (e.g. sheep farming) in rural areas.

Baum's 'fascination factors' hardly explain the island's great appeal to tourists. Rather, the Iceland appeal is built on 'extremes' in terms of uniqueness, location and contrast, which are the foundation for the social construction of what is here termed the "myth of Iceland".

Extremes

Cold-water islands are usually extreme by their very nature — their degree of isolation, economic dependence on one main industry, relative inaccessibility and harsh living conditions are just a few examples. Iceland is no exception, and the tourist image of Iceland is consequently expressed in terms of "far North", "inaccessible", "wild", "rugged" or "isolated" (interviews, July 2004). Iceland may even be perceived as particularly extreme, which might be explained by the omni-presence of extremes in all spheres, including the environment, society, culture, economy and technology.

Environment

The very name "Ice-land" is the anti-thesis of hospitality. Indeed, as opposed to "Greenland", a far colder island that received its name also with the purpose to attract settlers, "Iceland" was named by one of the first visitors, Flóki Vilgerdarson, a Viking who attempted to settle on the island, but had to leave again because environmental conditions were too harsh. Frustrated, he called the land "Iceland" (Hjálmarsson, 1994). Indeed, about 12% of Iceland's terrestrial area of 103,000 km^2 is covered by glaciers, 54% by rugged terrain, 11% by lava and 4% by sand. The extremeness of the environment is also expressed in the landscapes encountered: glaciers intermingle with volcanoes, geysers, sulphur springs and bizarre lava-streams. Many roads are inaccessible except for off-road vehicles and only some of these are paved and accessible all the year round. Accordingly, snowmobiles (in winter) and jeeps are the preferred means of transport in many parts of the country, even for tourist activities. The vast majority of Iceland is of volcanic origin and, in geological terms, very young. With an age of 20 million years, and — in some places — less than 40 years (the islet of Surtsey came into existence from 1963–1967), Iceland is often portrayed as still being in the process of creation. Tourists may in some areas even have the feeling of witnessing the "birth of the Earth". The natural environment also makes a number of rather unusual activities possible, such as dog sledding on glaciers or bathing in craters. Even its fauna is an important part of the tourism product of Iceland. For example, whales come very close to the island, and whale watching has become an increasingly popular tourist experience, with some 72,000 tourists participating in this activity in 2003, 20% of these stating that whale watching was the main reason for them to visit Iceland (Oddsson, 2004). Whale watching contributed an estimated US$25 million to Iceland's economy. Trout and salmon fishing is another popular tourist activity. Day licences for Icelandic rivers and lakes are rather costly at US$35–130 per rod for trout and even more for salmon (www.angling.is). As the guidebook warns: "a licence to catch salmon is extremely expensive. Add the price of a guide, equipment and transportation and you have some of the most costly angling imaginable" (Mead, 2004, p. 37).

Society and Culture

Iceland's society and culture cannot be understood without considering the island's history. The first people to discover Iceland were Irish monks, who were seemingly impressed by the island, reporting that, in summer, it was possible to still pick fleas at midnight because the sun would not set (Hjálmarsson, 1994). Permanently settled by Norwegian Vikings from 874 onwards, the island grew rapidly in population, reaching 60,000 by AD 930 when a parliament (The *Althing*) was established, mostly to dispense justice. However, as the *Althing* only had legislative and judicative power, there were no opportunities to punish offenders of the law in their absence. Executive power was given to the accuser, who had the right to punish the condemned or to seek compensation. During this time, and up to AD 1100, most of the Icelandic *sagas* came into existence, stories of offence and revenge, seeking to "record their heroes' great achievements and to glorify the virtues of courage, pride, and honour" (US Department of State, 1997). Murderers sometimes had to leave Iceland. This was, for instance, the reason for Eiríkur Thorvaldsson, known as Eric the Red, to leave Iceland and to settle in Greenland, from where his son Leifur Eiríksson made the journey to North America, possibly around the year 1000. It is clear that this period is of great importance for today's image of Iceland, which often refers to the island's Viking past, a period of exploration and adventure, of outlaws and brave men.

For most of its early history (930–1262), Iceland remained independent, but came afterwards under the rule of Norway and later Denmark (Hjálmarsson, 1994). During these centuries, Iceland was usually seen as an outpost of these countries, a hinterland that could be economically exploited. Iceland impoverished subsequently and famine spread in the late 19th century when several years of bad harvests coincided with the violent eruption of the Askja volcano in 1875 and a number of earthquakes in 1896. Between 1870 and 1914, 10,000–20,000 Icelanders emigrated to Canada and the USA. Securing home rule in 1918, it was only in 1944, during the entanglements of World War II, that Iceland could declare itself independent from Denmark. Since then, the country has been prospering, and the CIA World Factbook states: "Literacy, longevity, income, and social cohesion are first-rate by world standards" (CIA, 2005).

The notion of a unique and somehow different society is nevertheless maintained. This is well exemplified by the Icelandic language, which is said to still be similar to the Vikings'. It maintains the old Nordic system of passing on the father's first name to the child, which becomes its last name ("son/daughter of"). Likewise, glamorous artists such as Björk have greatly influenced the perception of Iceland, and tourists visiting the country might also experience a number of "extreme" habits. Note, for instance, Mealer's (2001) recommendation to "stop in one of the few fishing villages and sample some of Iceland's traditional cuisine: ram's testicle, or pungent cubes of shark meat that have been buried in the sand and left to rot; then erase the memory with a shot of brennivin, a native schnapps known as Black Death".

Finally, the image of the post-Viking society is also maintained through famous writers such as Nobel Laureate Halldór Laxness, whose novels of ancient times are often characterized by great brutality. The image of the Viking relative is thus somehow part of tourist perceptions.

Economy and Technology

With an estimated 2005 population of just 296,737 (CIA, 2005), Iceland has, within a few decades, turned from one of the laggard into one of the leading economies in Europe: the country is number 7 on the Forbes-list of the most competitive economies in the world (Forbes, 2005); has an enviably low unemployment rate of 3.1%; and a *per capita* GDP (purchasing power parity) of US$31,900 in 2004 (CIA, 2005).

The importance of technology is visible everywhere in Iceland. Jeeps (often large "super jeeps") are an expression of technological superiority and a constant reminder of the extreme character of the environment. Iceland is also known for its vast energy resources, including hydropower and geothermal power. Their potential is such that comparably low energy prices can be guaranteed and the island has managed to attract energy-intense industries such as aluminium and ferro-silicon plants. In Reykjavik, the availability of cheap energy has made city-planners introduce heated streets to make the winter servicing of roads unnecessary. Some geothermal power stations are open for visitors, and the power plant at Nesjavellir close to Reykjavik is visited "by thousands of tourists each year" (information booklet Nesjavellir). Through guided tours, the plant is presented as an example of Icelandic engineering skills and technological achievement. Another example is the Blue Lagoon, an exclusive wellness spa using the "waste water" from an adjacent geothermal power plant and one of the main tourist attractions of Iceland.

Iceland appeared in the world media in 1998 when an Act was passed to set up a Health Sector Database (HSD), a pioneering database which includes all (meaning present, future and past) medical records of the entire population of Iceland (Mannvernd, 2005), with a view to help identify genetic traits and inherited diseases. This, in turn, would help to design drugs (Hlodan, 2000). The rights to use the database were granted to a biopharmaceutical company, DeCode, which describes its goal as the "development of new, more effective drugs based upon gene discovery work in some 50 common diseases" (DeCode

Genetics, 2005). The initiative sparked strong criticism; however, fundamental questions raised focused on privacy, intellectual property rights and the ethical limits of science and capitalism, putting Iceland at the forefront of international ethics debates (e.g. Lewontin, 1999; Mannvernd, 2005).

Another example in the technology sphere is the portrayal of Iceland as an emerging hydrogen-society, designing the cutting edge of energy technology. The world's media has been closely following this process, as the era of fossil fuels might see its end with the depletion of oil resources. Hence, Iceland has been in the spotlight of discourses on sustainable energy futures, even though it has frequently been overlooked that few other countries will have the electricity resources needed to produce hydrogen; likewise, technical problems are still substantial (e.g. Ministry of Industry and Commerce, 2005). Still, discussions on the hydrogen era are vivid, and add another example to the list of environmental, social, economic and technical extremes vividly discussed in and outside Iceland.

The Creation of a Myth

An analysis of the Icelandic Tourist Board's marketing strategy reveals a focus on four areas: the geographical distribution of tourists all over the island; the development of new tourism products; the development of a city break market to overcome the short season; and the focus on new markets in Asia to attract new tourist groups. Geographical distribution has the main purpose of involving all regions in tourism, and to reduce crowding effects at popular sites. Often, this goes along with the development of new products. For example, the historic site of Thingvellir is now marketed as a "must dive experience" (Iceland Review, 2005). City-break tourism, often sold in weekend packages, and special interest tourism, for example addressing young tourist groups mainly coming for a party holiday, are strategies with the main aim to overcome the short summer season. Furthermore, there are attempts to open up new markets (e.g. in Asia) and to develop business tourism (incentive tourism, conferences). While these strategies can be seen as *mechanisms* of marketing, they cannot explain *how* demand is created: *why* do tourists favour Iceland over other destinations?

It is clear that, given its small size and population, its environment and technological progress, Iceland is a nation that can be understood as "extreme". Extremes alone, however, do not create the "myth" of a destination. What is understood here, as the "myth of Iceland" is the social construction of a destination that weaves together environmental, social, economic, technological and political spheres into a larger semantic construction that is detached from fact. As will be argued, Iceland conjures magic in a deconstructivist human age, something that seems to have great appeal to tourists. This magic is both a result of a conscious process of marketing Iceland's extremes and a self-reinforcing, unplanned process of media coverage and word-of-mouth, inter-tourist communication channels. The "myth" is thus a complex phenomenon including marketing efforts and unplanned socio-cultural reproduction processes. On a more proximate level, the emergence of Iceland as a destination is facilitated by the emergence of a societal trend towards explorative, challenging and adventurous vacations (Swarbrooke, Beard, Leckie, & Pomfret, 2003).

The Image of Iceland

Given the image of tropical islands — the allure of warm climates, clear waters, hospitality and good food, which seem to have great appeal to a majority of leisure tourists (cf. WTO, 2005) — Iceland could almost be considered as an anti-place. In most respects, it is the counter-image of a tropical island: air and water temperatures are significantly lower, there are often strong winds blowing, and even in summer tourists will need a sweater and coat most of the time. In some areas, such as the Southwest, precipitation is above 2000 mm per year and rain rather a norm. Beaches in Iceland are black, and strolling along the coast one is more likely to come across whalebones than seashells. Low water temperatures, high waves and inaccessible coastlines generally prohibit bathing in the ocean. There is also comparably little vegetation in Iceland, and rock formations often have blackish, yellowish or brownish colours. Food, one of the main elements of vacations in the tropics, is generally restricted to a few dishes. For breakfast, most hotels offer traditional pickled sill, and it is not unusual that cod liver oil is on offer. Given Iceland's vast nature, climatic conditions and tourist attractions, the island invites to explore, contrasting tropical islands that put strong emphasis on relaxation and recovery.

An analysis of information material on display in the tourist information in Reykjavik, including advertisement by private companies and official material issued by the Icelandic Tourist Board, reveals that the image of a cold, peripheral, and "different" destination is re-enforced. Basically, there is a clear distinction between information material on the city of Reykjavik and the rest of Iceland. Reykjavik, Cultural City of Europe 2000, portrays itself as a modern, vibrant metropolis. Accordingly, the city is a gateway for adventure tourists, but also attracts predominantly young "party tourists", business travellers and incentive travel groups. In its information brochures, the city puts a focus on culture, including a multitude of art museums, galleries and exhibitions often presenting world-renowned artists. However, many of these exhibitions can also be said to be on the edge of art, or, in citing the introduction to a Paul McCarthy and Jason Rhoades exhibition from the 2004 event calendar: "testing the boundaries of conventional artistic practice and aesthetics". For instance, in July 2004, the monthly guide *What's on in Reykjavik* depicted a naked, one-legged man with a pig in his arm, announcing the photo-exhibition *The Life of Albert*. The year 2004 also saw the public photo-exhibition *Icelanders* in the centre of Reykjavik. Presenting "people from all over the island", the exhibition of 'small boat fishermen', 'tourist farmers', 'fox hunters' and 'rock collectors' turned the unconventional into the normal. What is said to represent Iceland is a collection of extreme living and extreme lifestyles at the far edge of society, supporting the notion that Icelanders and Iceland are out of this world. However, information materials focusing on Reykjavik also have a strong focus on consumerism, including shopping malls and, recently, *cuisine*, with a great number of exclusive and illusive restaurants being represented. Even though the focus of information booklets and brochures is clearly on culture, the unique character of the island's 'nature' is also part of the city image, for example by inviting tourists to visit the 'thermal beach' in the Southwest of Reykjavik city, where hot water is flowing into the sea. Overall, the impression remains that Reykjavik wants to market itself as a somewhat unusual, different and 'hip' place.

As for the 'rest of Iceland', pictures mostly depict landscape views, often aerial, ice formations, snow scooters, dogsleds, super jeeps, Northern lights, waterfalls, horses and whales. People shown usually wear sweaters or coats, often raincoats. Headlines read "Living on a volcano", "Whale-watching voyages", "Super jeeps", "Glacier experience" or "White, wild and wonderful". Moreover, these extremes are presented in contrasts, such as fire and ice, heaven and hell, modern and traditional. For instance, in close relation to Christian mythology, pictures of Iceland frequently take up the 'heaven and hell' motif. Heaven is symbolized by blue colours, such as any kind of ice, wide skies, but even the Blue Lagoon with its milky blue waters. The motif is contrasted with the insinuated existence of hell, symbolized through lava eruptions and black rock formations, which can be found in Icelandic mythology but also in contemporary information brochures, postcards and 'volcano-shows'. These refer to the existence of hell as a place of 'eternal fire' deep in the Earth, inhabited by damned souls: one of the main pillars of Christian mythology. The references to hell are even more evocative when visualized by hot steam eruptions and accompanied by the putrid smell of sulphur. In today's marketing of Iceland, the hell motif is sometimes used, as exemplified by one advertisement campaign for glacier tours: "We don't know about hell, but heaven froze over ages ago" (Gianatasio, 1998).

Ancient stories and beliefs; witchcraft, sorcery and magic are now also used to create new tourist sights, ultimately re-enforcing 'the myth'. Recently, a museum on witchcraft and magic was opened in Holmavik in the Westfjords, presenting material on the witch-hunts in the 17th century and dark stories of ancient Icelandic origin, which are illustrated with skulls, bones and a dead man's lower body. The latter exhibit is described as: "[...] the Nábrók, trousers made from the skin of a dead man's lower body, and when worn by the sorcerer, money would collect in the corpse's scrotum". Obviously, the museum is bound to impress. Far more important for the broad majority of tourists is the magic presented in Icelandic elf, troll and fairy tales. Books about 'Myths and Monsters' (Tryggvadóttir, 2002) can be found in any bookstore and 'hidden people' are referred to in various contexts. One guesthouse in Reykjavik, for instance, displays the following text in a frame on the wall: "When I was a child, I played with elf children and it often happened that I got to eat with them. The food was always delicious and light in colour. [...] I know that elves don't drink coffee while hidden people do, since the hidden people's food is more like ours, the humans" (signed with the name of the author, translated by two guests). The Icelander owning the guesthouse will inform any interested visitor that Icelanders are told stories about elves from early childhood, and that Elves are part of Nature for Icelanders. Elves might actually be the best example for a myth that reproduces itself, as there is no official marketing taking up the 'hidden people'. Despite this, a google search for 'elves' and 'Iceland' yielded more than 80,000 hits (May 2005). Several of the links refer to the "fact" that Icelanders believe in hidden people.

There is even an Elf School in Reykjavik, which was recently portrayed in Scanorama, the magazine published by Scandinavian Airlines. The magazine presents an account of the school and some statistics, claiming that a 2000-survey by an Icelandic newspaper revealed that 54% of all Icelanders believed in nature beings, in contrast to 1.8% in Sweden or 2.5% in Germany. The author of the article also took part in a tour around Reykjavik. He reports:

> Next to a car wreck, behind some office buildings, lies a rock officially pro-
> tected by the city. This is the site of the big chicken strike of 1941. At the
> time, the owners of the chicken farm decided to blow up a rock that was in
> their way. Following the decision, 800 hens stopped laying eggs. Two
> weeks later the chicken farm had gone from producing 550 eggs a day to
> none. The owners scratched their heads. This went on for a couple of
> months before someone pointed out that the rock might be the source of the
> problem. So the owners gave it a shot and decided not to blow the rock.
> Sure enough the hens started laying eggs again. They had gone on strike on
> behalf of the hidden people […] (Lundh, 2004).

Finally, the representation of Iceland in novels and movies might explain part of the myth. Famous books include, for example, Jules Verne's *Journey to the Centre of the Earth* (1864). In the book, Snæfellsjökull, a glacier in the Northwest of Iceland, is the starting point for the expedition. The book has also shaped the image of Icelanders as straight, honest and trustable persons. A less-known fact is that even the *Lord of the Rings* by J. R. R. Tolkien was based on Icelandic sagas (FAZ, 2004). Among the movies shaping the myth of Iceland is the James Bond film *Die another day*. The movie takes place in Iceland, and the representation of the island is literal: the only thing shown of the country is *ice*, except, in one short sequence, a paved road. More recently, even scenes for the new Batman movie were filmed in Iceland, also presenting the image of a dark, rainy, cold country.

The only exception to this general pattern of exploration and adventure elements is the omni-presence of geothermal pools in information materials, notably the Blue Lagoon. Pools seem of importance, as they add an element of relaxation, complementing Iceland's tourism product by offering opportunities for recovery and relaxation. However, the general image represented is that of a cold, unusual, majestic country, which is also the image reflected in books on Iceland, including titles such as "Lost in Iceland", "Magic of Iceland", "Wonders of Iceland", "Colours of Iceland" or "Land of Light". The myth is re-enforced by reference to this island's past — accordingly, horses are "Viking horses", the local beer is named "Viking" and the vodka *Eldurís* ("Fire-ice"). Danger signs in many places enforce the notion of adventure and remnants of extreme events remind of the forces of nature. For example, huge parts of bent steel put up along the road recall the 1996 eruption under the glacier Vatnajökull, which caused a major flood that washed away part of the ring road and its bridges.

Social Reproduction Processes

It has been shown that Iceland seeks to market itself as an 'extreme' and 'different' destination through the transformation of its history, culture, and nature into elements of 'magic'. As shown above, this process is facilitated by global media, which has an important role in maintaining and shaping the image of Iceland. Iceland seems to even attract an increasing number of media representatives in search of stories from the 'far side of life'. This usually results in exaggerated stories:

[…] Twelve hundred years ago, this North Atlantic Island was settled by the outcasts of Viking civilisation. The baddest of the bad. The weirdest of the weird. People like Eric the Red who were so radical, so violent, so off-the-wall, they were judged unfit for what was already a pretty wild society (Yogerst, 2003).

However, the tourists themselves also shape the image of a 'different' destination through inter-tourist communication channels that maintain and re-enforce the myth. For example, Alkimou (2004) studied tourist associations with Iceland and found that the broad majority of attributes mentioned fell into the categories 'nature' and 'different'. More specifically, tourists referred to fire, lava, volcanoes, glaciers and ice, geysers, geothermal sources, waterfalls, northern lights, or weather-related aspects (cold, rainy). Interestingly, even phenomena otherwise perceived as negative, such as rain, seem to become important elements of a vacation in Iceland, for example, occasional rain might then become part of the overall — anticipated — experience and is *not* perceived as unpleasant. Interviews conducted by the author in July 2004 also revealed that tourist perceptions vary widely depending on the sights visited. For example, tourists associated scenic landscape views with "beautiful", snowmobile rides as "challenging" or the experience of smouldering, barren lands at Mount Krafla as "war-like". Likewise, many tourists visiting a field of hot sulphur springs did very obviously *not* enjoy this experience due to the intense smell; however, it is likely that this visit will later on turn into one of the most memorable experiences that will be shared with friends or with other tourists. As in other studies (e.g. Kane & Zink, 2004), tourists were observed to discuss their experiences. This might have at least two purposes: first, there might be a psychological need to work up experiences, which can be done by sharing these. Second, discussions also create common Iceland adventurer identities, as tourist activities in cold-water islands seem to represent "serious leisure" (*ibid.*) activities. The rather informal character of tourism in Iceland, with few four-star hotels and a wide variety of guesthouses, facilitates inter-tourist communication channels. In conclusion, word-of-mouth communication channels seem of great importance in the creation of the "myth" of Iceland, which is indirectly supported by Alkimou's (2004) finding that 29% of all tourists had visited Iceland as a result of recommendations by friends or relatives (*n*=139; interviews were conducted during off-season).

Adventure Tourism

An increasing number of tourists expect "physical and emotional rewards" (Pigram & Jenkin, 1999, p. 6) from leisure activities, and self-fulfilment and re-affirmation of identity are increasingly part of the tourist experience (Craik, 1997). In consequence, tourism is increasingly evaluated in terms of being rewarding, enriching, adventuresome and/or a learning experience (Zeppel & Hall, 1992). Adventure tourism has a number of core characteristics, including uncertain outcomes of the vacation, danger and risk, challenge, anticipated rewards, novelty, stimulation and excitement, escapism and separation, exploration and discovery, absorption and focus, contrasting emotions (Swarbrooke et al., 2003, p. 9), and does thus address these emerging tourist expectations. Iceland, in turn, meets the core characteristics of adventure tourism, and, moreover, the island is in the position to appeal to a mass adventure market, as most of these attributes are on the soft adventure spectrum side. For example, danger, risk and challenge are calculated, and there is a minimum probability of a serious accident in Iceland. Hence, danger and risk might rather exist in the imagination of the tourists, and the challenge posed by the vacation is a perceptual one. Ultimately, the expectation of challenges, danger and risks is a means of re-producing the myth of the adventure island, as imagined risks become real ones in the perception of the tourists, while rewards of exploration and adventure are anticipated. Even other characteristics of adventure tourism fit rather well the image of Iceland — for instance, escapism and separation are almost self-evident elements of island-tourism, as their physical borders (being surrounded by water) also constitute mental borders and the feeling of being separated.

As Cater (2003) suggests, adventure tourism is based on deep, embodied experiences, which, in the context of Iceland, could be understood as experiences addressing all senses. Accordingly, expressions of risk, challenge and danger are not just visual, including smouldering volcano-landscapes, danger signs and super jeeps, but also opportunities to feel, hear, taste and smell. For instance, one can touch the ground in many places and feel the heat of the volcanic underground. Ripples in the road make cars bump. Sulphur springs cause smells that make the existence of hell quite plausible, and even tap water has a light sulphur smell to it. It is also possible to taste fermented shark, cod liver oil, puffin or other unusual food. Geysers and hot springs cause steam eruptions that fill the air with hissing sounds. There are thundering waterfalls, the cries of seagulls, or … complete silence. Altogether, these might sum up to deep, embodied, multi-sensorial experiences.

Adventure tourism usually takes place outdoors, but it can also contain cultural elements (cf. Swarbrooke et al., 2003). In Iceland, these include for instance the Viking past, stories of elves and hidden people, magic and witchcraft. Overall, adventure tourism thus meets the demands of what Poon (1993) termed the "new tourists": these are more heterogeneous, have travel experience, are no longer interested in 'warm' destinations, do not only travel to escape routine and home life, and feel secure even when travelling alone. Self-fulfilment and deep experiences seem an important travel motive for these tourists, and, as Swarbrooke et al. (2003) have pointed out, growth in this market is substantial.

The 'Myth' and its Future

The chapter has sought to show how Iceland's destination image is on the one hand created by various actors, including official marketing by the Icelandic Tourist Board, tour operators and other companies, and on the other hand by the media and tourists. Ultimately, these processes create the myth of a 'different' destination.

Figure 9.1 shows that the myth of Iceland is created through two processes: 'official' marketing by the Icelandic Tourist Board and private companies, as well as media and tourist communication channels. To which extent is the image of Iceland a result of the two processes? Hall once suggested that: "you cannot create destinations, destinations create themselves" (C. Michael Hall, lecture at Campus Helsingborg, Sweden, November 2004). Iceland might in fact support this hypothesis. Looking at official marketing materials, it is clear that extremes are frequently presented and the 'different' character of the island is

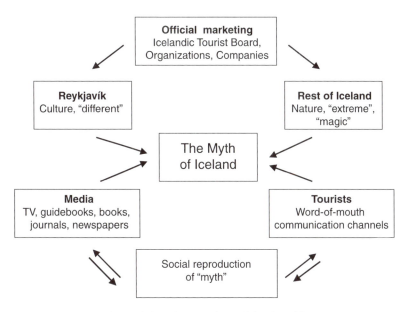

Figure 9.1: The creation of the 'myth'.

also pointed out. However, the notion of 'magic' seems to mainly come into existence through media and word-of-mouth communication channels; processes that ultimately seem self-reinforcing: knowing that there is magic, extremeness and difference, one might look out for these and pre-suppose their existence.

Iceland has turned into a successful adventure tourism destination with rapidly increasing tourist arrival numbers. The notion of magic and deep experiences, and opportunities for adventure and exploration do explain increasing tourist numbers, but there still seems a considerable cost-benefit paradox given Iceland's high prices and generally basic tourist infrastructure. One possible avenue to understanding this phenomenon might be the economic concept of Veblen-effects (Clarke et al., 2003), that is, consumer preferences to buy products as a direct function of their high price. In other words, high prices add an element of exclusiveness to the Icelandic tourism product. This is of importance, as Iceland might be in the position to attract a certain tourist clientele that could be characterized as wealthy, interested in culture and nature, and indifferent to the generally low standard of accommodation offered (most hotels are 2–3 stars). Simultaneously, it might limit the potential market for Iceland and result in *relatively* slow growth that gives the Icelanders a chance to adopt to socio-economic change. So far, however, no debates seem to exist in Iceland that challenge or question rapid tourism development.

Where is Iceland to go from here? Less than two decades ago, the island has been a rather unknown destination on the periphery of Europe, a place that has at best been described as moderately interesting for tourism. In the past decades, it has turned from a peripheral cold-water island into a centre between the European and American continents (a geographic feature well exploited by the profitable national airline, Icelandair). Iceland could, in comparison to classic warm-water island destinations, be considered as an anti-place, but it has managed to turn this into the very source of its attraction. Will the myth last? Clearly, Iceland has changed character, turning from a small-scale nature-based adventure tourism destination into a soft adventure mass destination. The introduction of a low-fare carrier, Iceland Express, has created more connections at substantially lower prices. This, together with an increasing number of cruise ships calling in Reykjavik, has greatly increased visitor numbers, often day- or weekend visitors. In the future, the balance between soft and hard adventure tourism might be difficult to maintain, particularly with massive tourist arrivals from China, as planned by the Icelandic Tourist Board. In guidebooks one can already read that: "on weekends in July–August, popular spots like Skaftafell can become uncomfortably crowded" (Mead, 2002, p. 113), and in interviews tourists express their disappointment that "wherever you come there are already three tourist busses". Indeed, the tourist industry already markets other, still more remote, destinations, such as Greenland. This could, in accordance with Zurich's (1992) model of gateway hierarchies, be interpreted as a shift towards a new periphery frontier and imply that the deconstruction of the 'myth' is already underway.

Acknowledgments

I am thankful for valuable discussions with Areti Alkimou, and I owe many Icelanders for their openness and the time they have spent talking to me. Special thanks for comments and discussions to Meike, Monika and Siegfried.

References

Alkimou, A. (2004). Aspekte der Fremdenverkehrsplanung auf Island. Destinationenmarketing und Imageanalyse. Zulassungsarbeit im Rahmen der Staatsexamensprüfung für das Lehramt in Gymnasien. Institut für Kulturgeographie der Universität Freiburg. [Aspects of tourism planning in Iceland. Destination marketing and image analysis. Dept. of Cultural Geography, Freiburg University, Germany).]

Baum, T. G. (1997). The fascination of islands: A tourist perspective. In: D. G. Lockhart, & D. Drakakis-Smith (Eds), *Island tourism: Trends and prospects* (pp. 21–35). London: Pinter.

Cater, C. (2003). Tourism on the edge; the search for embodied experiences in adventure. Presented at the 11th nordic conference on tourism and hospitality, Stavanger, Norway.

CIA. (2005). *The world factbook: Iceland*. Washington, DC: Central Intelligence Agency. www.cia.gov/cia/publications/factbook/geos/ic.html (accessed 20/10/2005).

Clarke, D. B., Doel, M. A., & Housiaux, K. M. L. (2003). *The consumption reader*. London: Routledge.

Craik, J. (1997). The culture of tourism. In: C. Rojek, & J. Urry (Eds), *Touring cultures: Transformations of travel and theory* (pp. 134–136). London: Routledge.

DeCode Genetics. (2005). www.decodegenetics.com/ (accessed 20/10/2005).

FAZ (Frankfurter Allgemeine Zeitung). (2004). Jenseits von Mordor. [Beyond Mordor.], Reiseblatt 15th January, p. 5.

Forbes. (2005). Finland tops competitiveness index – again. Available at: http://www.forbes.com/business/2005/09/28/wef-gci-finland-cx_pm_0928gci2005.html (accessed 02-01-2006).

Gianatasio, D. (1998). Allen & Gerritsen enters travel, tourism arena with campaign for Iceland adventure company. *Adweek,* 13th April, p. 5.

Hjálmarsson, J. R. (1994). Die geschichte Islands. *Iceland review.* Iceland: Reykjavik.

Hlodan, O. (2000). For sale: Iceland's genetic history. www.actionbioscience.org/genomic/hlodan.html.

Iceland Review. (2005). *Diving thingvellir.* www.icelandreview.com (accessed 20/10/2005).

Kane, M. J., & Zink, R. (2004). Package adventure tours: Markers in serious leisure careers. *Leisure Studies, 23*(4), 329–345.

Lewontin, R. C. (1999). People are not commodities. *The New York Times,* 23rd January www.mannvernd.is/english/articles/lewontin.NYtimes.html (accessed 20/10/2005).

Lundh, S. (2004). Elves. *Scandinavian airlines magazine,* December 2004/January 2005, pp. 68–71.

Mannvernd. (2005). Website of the Association of Icelanders for Ethics in Science and Medicine. www.mannvernd.is/english/ (accessed 20/10/2005).

Mead, R. (2002). *Iceland.* London: New Holland Publishers.

Mealer, B. (2001). Summer in the States: When all else fails, there's always Iceland. The last, best place on earth. Esquire, 1 May 2001. Available at: www.esquire.com (accessed 02-01-2006).

Ministry of Industry and Commerce. (2005). *Energy in Iceland. Domestic energy resources.* http://eng.idnadarraduneyti.is/ministries/homepage//nr/1170 (accessed 20/10/2005).

Oddsson, G. (2004). The economic impact of whale watching in Iceland: 2003. *Icewhale.* Husavik, Iceland: The Icelandic Whale Watching Association.

Pigram, J., & Jenkin, J. M. (1999). *Outdoor recreation management.* London: Routledge.

Poon, A. (1993). *Tourism, technology and competitive strategies.* Wallingford: CABI.

Swarbrooke, J., Beard, C., Leckie, S., & Pomfret, G. (2003). *Adventuretourism: The new frontier.* Amsterdam: Butterworth Heinemann.

Tryggvadóttir, G. (2002). *Myths and monsters in Icelandic folktales.* Reykjavik: Salka.

US Department of State. (1997). *Iceland.* background notes on countries of the world. www.state.gov/r/pa/ei/bgn/3396.htm (accessed 20/10/2005).

Verne, J. (1864). *Journey to the centre of the Earth.* London: Penguin Books.

World Tourism Organization (WTO). (2005). *WTO tourism market trends: 2004.* Madrid, Spain: WTO.

Yogerst, J. (2003). Chillin'. In Iceland, you can hang out with history. *The union tribune,* 9 November. www.signonsandiego.com/travel/031109iceland.html (accessed 20/10/(2005).

Zeppel, H., & Hall, C. M. (1992). Arts and heritage tourism. In: B. Weiler, & C. M. Hall (Eds), *Special interest tourism* (pp. 47–68). London: Belhaven Press.

Zurich, D. N. (1992). Adventure travel and sustainable tourism in the peripheral economy of Nepal. *Annals of the Association of American Geographers. 82*(4), 608–628.

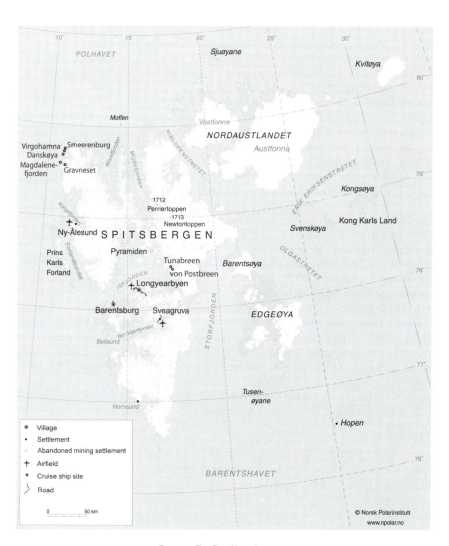

Image 7: Svalbard map.

Chapter 10

Svalbard, Norway

Arvid Viken

Introduction

This chapter deals with tourism in the context of the archipelago of Svalbard, internationally better known as Spitsbergen, which is actually the name of its largest island. Longyearbyen, the main town, is situated 958 km north of Tromsø on the Norwegian mainland. For almost 150 years, people have been travelling to Svalbard for recreational and adventure purposes. During most of the 20th century, Svalbard was primarily a destination for cruise ships, but over the last decade a land-based tourism industry has emerged, welcomed and partly stimulated by the Norwegian authorities. Since nature on these islands is harsh but vulnerable, environmental considerations are vital in the context of local policies and management systems, especially for tourism operations and strategies.

The tourist experiences offered on Svalbard are all related to nature. The scenery is magnificent, and there are special things to see: glaciers, icebergs, Arctic wildlife and heritage related to an exciting history of exploration and exploitation. The major tourist activities in wintertime are to go on day-trips skiing, snowmobiling or dog-sledging, though longer, multi-day tours are also available. The snowmobile tours, the most popular winter activity, take travellers through spectacular valleys to Barentsburg, or to the Tuna and Von Post glaciers in the Temple Fjord, at the most 60 km from Longyearbyen. It has recently also become possible to stay overnight on a boat that is located in a frozen fjord. In summer, the major tourist activities are day-trips by boats, longer-lasting cruises and hiking tours, or else to stay in Longyearbyen, where there is a wide choice of day-activities. Many tourists hope to get a glimpse of the polar bear, but most of them fail. The polar bear follows the edge of the ice shield and is normally far from the tourist tracks. However, there is always a slim chance — or risk — to come across the animal. Away from the ice (and seals) this is a hungry and dangerous creature. To track the bear is forbidden, and polar bear safaris are not offered.

This chapter will present Svalbard and its tourism industry, followed by a description of the transformations of the main town, Longyearbyen, from a mining community to a tourist destination. Next is a short description of tourist profiles and a discussion of cruise tourism. A review of the state of the environment is followed by a discussion of the management system and its overhaul in view of current trends towards governance practices. By way of concluding, it is argued that Svalbard has not only been quickly conquered by tourism, but also by a, more or less all-encompassing, governance system.

Svalbard

Svalbard is located in the Arctic Sea. It is one of the northernmost inhabited places on the Earth, stretching from the 74th to the 81st degree of latitude. The archipelago covers a land area of 61,229 km², with a coastline that is over 3500 km long. The climate is cold but, thanks to the Gulf Stream, not as cold as many other locations in the north. The average air temperature is +6°C in summer, −14°C in winter. The sea temperature hovers between 1 and +4°C. In the winter, the sea is normally frozen.

Svalbard was 'discovered' by the Dutchman Willem Barents in 1596. At first, the islands and the surrounding ocean were heavily exploited for industrial purposes, pride of place going to whale hunting undertaken in turn by the Dutch, English and Russians. Norway, then still part of Denmark, first settled the islands towards the end of the 18th century. Norwegians were at first involved in trapping polar bear, fox, seal and walrus, but eventually became more involved in coal mining, which was established with the support of English and American firms (Arlov, 1996).

It was only in 1920, in the diplomatic aftermath to the First World War, that an international treaty assigned sovereignty over the Svalbard Islands to Norway. However, the treaty also declared that all signatory parties should have equal rights to industrial development on the islands as long as they follow Norwegian law. The Russians have been the keenest to exercise this option.

The main and only authority on the islands is the Governor of Svalbard who represents the Norwegian State for all intents and purposes. Since the 1990s, the Governor's office has been granted new functions and has expanded its activities significantly. Thus, there is a double meaning to the term Governor of Svalbard today: it is the title of the highest ranking representative of the Norwegian authorities on the islands, as well as a public institution with 25–30 staff members.

Before the late 1980s, Longyearbyen was a typical 'company town' where most public services were provided by the mining company. The one key difference is that there were no residents; only miners with temporary jobs and in temporary lodging. The responsibility for public services was then taken over by *Svalbard Samfunnsdrift* (Svalbard Societal Services), a state agency. Since 2000, there has also been an elected assembly, *Longyearbyen Lokalstyre* (Longyearbyen Community Council) that takes decisions in societal matters and has taken over the formal ownership of Svalbard Societal Services.

The political turn-around in 1990 was related to a need for a broader industrial platform than coal mining that for the time being was heavily subsidised and politically controversial (Ministry of Industrial Affairs, 1990). An important prerequisite for more diverse industrial activities was to create a 'normal', permanent community in Longyearbyen with family life and diverse social activities. The 'normalisation' required the development of different types of private and public services, and opportunities for research, education, different service industries and tourism were stimulated. Along with the changes in the industrial platform Longyearbyen has gone through an extensive process of modernisation. However, the society is not totally 'normalised': the archipelago is an economic free-zone, without customs duties, without value-added tax and with very low rates of income tax. The infrastructure and construction works are technologically very advanced and expensive, as is also the case with housing. Most people do not own property but rent their apartment or house from their employer. The demographic structure has also changed dramatically: there still is a high turnover of workers, while tourism has largely created seasonal employment that was completely unknown before.

All settlements on Svalbard are and have always been temporary, since there is no indigenous population on the islands. As at 2004, there are two main settlements, the Norwegian town and capital of Longyearbyen with around 1750 inhabitants, and the Russian town of Barentsburg with around 800 people. Svea is the main mining site today, but almost everybody who works there commutes from Longyearbyen. In addition, there is one Polish and two other Norwegian settlements with very few people, along with a small number of trappers and adventurers scattered around the islands. For the Russians, mining is the main industry and remains a profitable business.

Svalbard Tourism in the Past

Tourism on Svalbard dates back to the mid-19th century (Arlov, 1996; Elstad, 2004). The exploration of the polar areas gave publicity to the Arctic (Riffenburgh, 1993), and people became aware of Svalbard. A few also followed in the wake of the explorers as the pioneer tourists in the area, first on private yachts in the 1850s, followed by cruiseships from the 1870s. Among the early 20th century cruise tourists to Svalbard was John Munroe Longyear, an American businessperson who eventually set up Arctic Coal, a mining firm: he has given his name to the main town. Cruise ships have since the late 1800s provided the bulk of tourist visitors to Svalbard. It has always been an international business, mainly involving Germans, Dutch, Russians and Americans.

Local, land-based tourism was kick-started in the 1890s with the opening of a hotel close to where Longyearbyen is today. The project however failed after a couple of years. A second attempt took place in the 1930s in Ny-Ålesund (now a research centre site), with a hotel (which remains open today but only to special guests) and a regular shipping line from Northern Norway. In the decades following World War II, the Norwegian authorities were largely hostile to land-based tourism development, officially due to a concern for the environment. However, the period was not entirely without tourism activities: the trophy hunting of polar bears in Svalbard was a significant business operated from Tromsø, even though that activity never attracted many tourists, and has been forbidden anyway since 1973. Around 1990, some coastal cruise operations started being handled from Longyearbyen, and this coincided with a policy change that gave rise to the third and current period of Svalbard tourism.

Before 'normalisation', there were many practical obstacles to tourism development, including the absence of basic public services. After these were removed, there has been a noteworthy increase in both tourism operations offered and in visitor numbers. For some time, the largest local tourism agency was one that started as a ticket office within the old mining firm. But in the 1990s, many small private companies started operations. Within a decade, there were in fact two major companies, both owning hotels, restaurants and undertaking tour operations, employing together 115 workers. Since then, these two firms have merged, with the resulting firm being very close to exercising a practical monopoly in the provision of tourist accommodation, as well as being by far the largest local tour operator. Clearly, Svalbard tourism is still in its initial phase (Butler, 1980): most investors are more or less local, the majority hailing from the nearest areas in Norway as they mainly have been since the late 1800s, and international visitor numbers remain low.

From Company Town to Tourism Resort

Tourism has recently become a profitable and promising activity in Longyearbyen. The accommodation sector in the town includes two new hotels of international standard, built in 2001 by the same owner, and a couple of smaller guest houses and lodges. There were 210 beds available in 1993, these being former miners' accommodation (Svalbard Industrial Development, 1994, p. 17). In 2003, the corresponding number was 662 (Svalbard Tourism, 2004). The number of restaurants, cafés and bars has also increased, from four in 1993 to eight in 2004, whereas the number of enterprises offering guided tours has increased from four to fifteen in the same period. Today, the tourism industry is vital to the Svalbard community; it provides considerable employment and revenue. In 1992, the tourism industry provided the equivalent of about 20 full-time jobs. In 2002, if both direct and indirect impacts are counted, tourism accounted for an equivalent of 258 full-time jobs, a staggering 25% of the total work force in Longyearbyen (Longyearbyen Community Council, 2003). Together with mining, tourism is today the major contributor to the visibility of the Norwegian state on Svalbard.

The main selling point for Svalbard as a destination is its pristine, natural environment, located at the edge of the world. No other place so close to one of the poles is so easily accessible. And in most eyes, Svalbard is a genuine wilderness. Many people also associate Svalbard with such polar explorers as Nansen, Nordenskiöld, Nobile, André and Amundsen. This certainly attracts many adventurers. Moreover, many Norwegians, comprising the majority of tourists, have had a relative or acquaintance who has stayed on the islands. This explains the broad current popularity of the islands to Norwegians. As Table 10.1 shows, Svalbard is mainly a domestic destination, Norwegians accounting for 74% of guest-nights in 2003.

The number of guest-nights in Longyearbyen has, with few exceptions, increased steadily between 1992 and 2001, stabilising thereafter to around 73,000 annually. Although domestic travel dominates, the number of foreign tourists has tripled in the period shown, whereas domestic tourism has 'only' doubled. Travel statistics for 2003 show that 63% of visitors to Longyearbyen were leisure tourists, 19% were business travellers and 18% were people attending conferences or meetings (Svalbard Tourism, 2004). There is no doubt that the increase in tourist volume presents a challenge, but it is very difficult to identify the carrying capacity limits: this is a problem that Svalbard shares with other destinations (Butler, 1997).

Table 10.1: Number of guest-nights in Longyearbyen: 1995–2004.

Year	Norwegians	Foreigners	Total
1995	26,459	6236	32,695
1996	41,999	6002	48,001
1997	36,925	8023	44,948
1998	37,211	8990	46,201
1999	33,666	9911	43,577
2000	49,522	11,755	61,277
2001	61,034	15,120	76,154
2002	56,704	17,729	74,433
2003	52,382	18,667	71,049
2004	58,574	19,352	77,926

Source: Svalbard Tourism (2004).

With tourism, Longyearbyen has changed: it now carries the visible trappings of the industry. There are souvenir shops and cafés selling flags and banners, advertising bill-boards, hotels and restaurants and tourists strolling in the streets. Remnants from the mining period in town are today declared as heritage. Tourists can visit one of the mines still left within the town; another mine is a museum, and the remnants of the coal transport system are spectacular symbols of the past, flood-lit during the dark winter period. The inhabitants of Longyearbyen have also experienced a change. With the reduced dominance of the mining industry and the majority of miners now commuting to Svea, 90 km away, the type of people that abound in town are no longer blue-collar, industrial workers but mainly professional and well-educated middle-class people (Viken, 1998). This, in turn, is reflected in the social, cultural and political life of the town.

Svalbard Tourists

There are certainly plenty of images of polar tourists (Butler, 2002). Most of them are myths. Thus, one popular misconception is that it requires an expedition to travel to and on Svalbard. This is how it may have been in the past, but not anymore. Longyearbyen is just a 90-minute flight away from Tromsø and three hours away from Oslo, with several daily connections with ordinary jets in the peak seasons, and five weekly connections in the low season. On the islands proper, there is a tourism infrastructure that makes it possible to travel around the islands, in summertime by boat, in wintertime primarily by snowmobile or dog-sledge. Besides, all three Norwegian settlements have airports. Even if many of the tourists are explorers in their own eyes, those who are really on an expedition to more remote parts of Svalbard on foot, on ski or by kayak on a self-prepared tour are few, counting for less than 1000 field-nights per year altogether (Svalbard Tourism, 2004). The bulk of visitors are mostly ordinary tourists who have bought their trip from tour operators. Whereas travelling around on Svalbard 15 years ago required meticulous planning and preparation and was reserved for the well trained and well off, the place has become a destination for almost everybody these days. Svalbard is one other, regular, travel agency option competing with other destinations.

Another myth is that tourists to a place like Svalbard are particularly concerned with the environment. Again, this is largely not borne out by the evidence. According to a visitor survey conducted in 2000 (Viken & Heimtun, 2001), 32% of foreign tourists and 11% of Norwegian visitors were, or had been, members of an environmental organisation; while, in their own judgement, 39% of tourists reckoned their knowledge about the environment to be good. Thus, around two out of every three tourists had never been engaged in environmental organisations, neither looked upon themselves as particularly well skilled in environmental issues. Nor did self-reports on environmental behaviour envisage a particular pro-environmental attitude (*ibid.*). Or at least, not more than one could expect from modern middle-class people. Tourists to Svalbard are well educated, the proportion that have graduated from university is high, and much higher than among tourists at North Cape, a well-known comparable destination on the Norwegian mainland (*ibid.*). Svalbard tourists are also significantly younger on average than those visiting North Cape. The majority of the tourists are male, but not so much to suggest that the place attracts a macho-type tourist fearless of the challenges of extreme weather conditions.

People on Svalbard like to regard their islands as an international location. Many of those working on the islands come from all over the world. This diversity is also evident in the case of tourists. Unlike the Norwegian mainland, where 20–30% of visitors are German, Longyearbyen has no such concentration and remains a global tourist attraction.

What may be a particularity among Svalbard tourists is that small and exclusive group of travellers that go to places that are really far from the beaten track, participating on tours that are so expensive that only a few can afford them. Such a tiny minority turns up mostly as cruise tourists, on board refurbished ice-breakers that cruise in the circumpolar region or go to the North Pole. There are also other minority tourist groups, people who do extreme sports or an ordinary sport under special harsh conditions; Svalbard has, in recent years, been visited by para-gliders, kite-skiers and golfers for an annual Ice Golf Tournament. This may be seen as part of a post-modern search for extreme and extraordinary experiences. However, the majority of the Svalbard tourists continue to be fairly ordinary, middle-class folk.

Cruise Tourism

Overseas cruise tourism, with tourists following the ship from the European mainland and back again, has a long history on Svalbard and is still significant (World Wildlife Fund for Nature (WWF), 2004). In addition, there are today locally based cruise operators, whose passengers arrive at and leave Svalbard by air. In 2002, 16,892 passengers came to Svalbard with overseas cruise ships embarking in a European harbour; 2706 passengers boarded coastal cruise ships handled from Longyearbyen and run by external tour operators; while 7698 passengers enjoyed coastal cruises starting and ending in Longyearbyen and run by local tour operators: 27,296 cruise tourists in all in 2002. Most tourists staying in Longyearbyen in summer go on a cruise, mainly a day-cruise, but some prefer a three and a half day tour along the west coast of Spitzbergen, the biggest island, and a few on even longer cruises, the most prestigious one being a circum-navigation of Spitzbergen.

The major attractions for the cruise passengers are the scenery and the breathtaking views in front of the glaciers that go down into the sea where they 'calf' (that is, break up and produce icebergs). Besides, going ashore is a major anticipated activity, for the sake of hiking, bird watching, looking at other natural features and often to observe heritage from close range. Old whale stations, old mining locations, trapping stations and places used by the explorers of the north are all popular types of heritage sites. In recent years, there has been a tendency for cruise operators to put passengers ashore at new places. It seems to be a competitive advantage to offer new ports of call. This dispersal is not unexpected, but counteracts the policy of the authorities that has been to concentrate tourism in the Ice Fjord and Nordenskiölds Land, the areas closest to Longyearbyen. The number of recorded disembarkations by passengers outside Longyearbyen has in fact increased from 37,508 in 1996 to 69,691 in 2003. Table 10.2 contains indications of the dispersal from 1996 to 2003.

The data reveals that the number of ports of call has almost tripled from 63 in 1996 to 162 in 2003; meanwhile, the percentage of passenger disembarkations that occur in the three major tourist ports outside Longyearbyen (i.e., Barentsburg, Ny-Ålesund and Magdalenefjorden) has decreased from 87 in 1996 to 52 in 2003. The average number of tourists who have disembarked on each site every year has also increased significantly: from 83 in 1996 to 211 in 2003. This suggests that the dispersal provokes more pressure on nature in each port of call. Although the number of tourists that visit these places remains so far relatively small and manageable, the monitoring authorities express concern due to this dispersal of the tourist footprint (Presterud, 2003). Locally based tour operators fear the imminent imposition of restrictions on tourism movements. Meanwhile, this dispersal carries a symbolic significance: more of Svalbard is being conquered by the tourism industry.

Planned or Haphazard?

It is difficult to say to what extent the development of tourism on Svalbard has been planned. One component is an obvious result of national policy: the authorities set up

Table 10.2: Indicators of tourism dispersal on Svalbard.

	1996	1997	1998	1999	2000	2001	2002	2003
Total number of ports of call	63	76	98	111	104	138	153	162
Percent of disembarkments (passengers) in Barentsburg, Ny-Ålesund and Magdalenefjorde	87	76	77	69	74	63	57	52
Average number of disembarking passengers per port in other locations	83	125	96	101	114	186	212	211

Source: The Governor of Svalbard (Cruise-ship visits to Longyearbyen are not included).

Svalbard Næringsutvikling (Svalbard Industrial Development), a company that should stimulate new industries, in the late 1980s. This agency assigned a high priority to tourism and established a department called Info-Svalbard, the local tourist office, which was taken over by a local tourist board called *Svalbard Reiseliv* (Svalbard Tourism) in 2001. Svalbard Industrial Development also initiated a tourism plan in 1991 that was finalised three years later (Svalbard Industrial Development, 1994). This work basically followed a social learning planning model: the goal was to use a planning process in order to achieve a better understanding of the tourism business for all vital actors. The planning process implied interaction between stakeholders, discussions of values and of the knowledge base, led by a task-oriented action group (Reid, 2003, p. 125; Friedman, 1987).

As far as content is concerned, the tourism plan from 1994 corresponds well with the recommendations of Page and Dowling (2002) on the analyses of future product opportunities, resource base, logistic problems and the need for information strategies. The plan states that nature and heritage should be preserved and monitored, and environmental goals adopted. The environmental section was expanded and detailed in a strategic follow-up of the plan in 1997 (Svalbard Industrial Development, 1997). However, other than the goals for environmental preservation, the plan was much more focused on problems than solutions: it was more of a precautionary tale. This may have been due to the fact that tourism was a new economic issue, and no one could accurately predict or foresee its future volume and challenges. Page and Dowling (2002) also recommend a targeted marketing strategy, so that one gets the clients one wants to have. This was not mentioned in the plan: the predominant philosophy seemed to be that Svalbard should be a destination for anybody.

The Svalbard tourism development process has followed Page and Dowling (2002) most thoroughly in regard to their recommendations on networking and close contacts with the authorities. The Svalbard Tourism Board has been vital for some aspects of the development, particularly for the tourist industry to appear as a responsible actor within the environmental area. There has also been external collaboration with other Arctic destinations and with international NGOs, primarily with the World Wildlife Fund. This organisation has used Svalbard as its planning ground for the creation of Arctic Guidelines for Tourism. Ironically, these guidelines have not been much used on Svalbard, in part because they have been set up by an external organisation, and also because the local guidelines are even more restrictive.

Nevertheless, despite these planning initiatives, there are clear indications that traditional entrepreneurial and capitalist principles have been as, if not more, important for tourism development. Mergers, external investment, competition and marketing efforts are all central elements in the development. Environmental concerns do not always take priority, and usually only when seen to be related to cost reductions (Viken & Heimtun, 2001).

The Environmental Situation

"The [Norwegian] Government wishes Svalbard to be one of the world's best managed wilderness areas. [...] In the event of a conflict between environmental targets and other interests, environmental considerations are to prevail within the limits dictated by treaty obligations and sovereignty considerations" (Ministry of Environment, 1999).

A keen sense of environmental stewardship has been the declared governmental policy goal for Svalbard for the last decade. Its objectives require a variety of actions in order to secure their fulfilment. An important instrument for the implementation of this policy has been to establish a good monitoring system: the Environmental Monitoring of Svalbard and Jan Mayen, another remote island (Mosj). Mosj's aim is to "collect and analyse data about pressure on the environment and assess the state of nature and heritage; on the basis of this describe the environmental changes; and give advice about its management" (http://miljo.npolar.no/mosj/start.htm). The information is grouped under environmental pressure, climate, flora and fauna and heritage. Environmental pressure is in turn measured by a series of indicators: pollution, travel, fishery and trapping, hunting, terrestrial damage and introduction of foreign species. In 2004, the system contained extensive information about the environmental situation; but Mosj did not report significant problems with the impact of tourism. For example, there were "no negative changes registered from the snowmobiling on the stocks of reindeer, fox or geese" (Presterud, 2003); and that "with the current volume of activities, tourism will not imply significant damages on vegetation and soil conditions except for places where cruise ships set ashore huge concentrations of tourists" (*ibid.*). Concerning heritage the report claimed: "there are reasons to believe that some heritage sites are threatened due to tourism, but also weather and wind are still significant pressure factors" (*ibid.*). Mosj also reports on climate change, the presence of toxic levels of PCBs (polychlorinated biphenyls) and other toxic substances observed in the area and found in concentrated form in such mammals as the polar bear (http://miljo.npolar.no/mosj/MOSJ/reviews/review015.pdf). These are issues where Svalbard, in spite of its remote and island geography, suffers from pollution transported from the densely populated areas on earth by sea and air currents to the Arctic. Mosj also reports that Svalbard has a warmer climate, more rain and a 10% reduction of glacial ice volume since the 1960s (http://miljo.npolar.no/mosj/MOSJ/reviews/review022.pdf). The polar areas are in fact excellent laboratories for research on environmental and climate change. Research in different sciences is, besides mining and tourism, one of the major industries on Svalbard. Scientists and environmental observers constitute a significant tourist segment. In August 2004, a group of U.S. senators, among them Hillary Clinton, visited Svalbard in order to increase their knowledge about the impact of climate change (Fyhn, 2004).

Despite few negative observations of tourism impacts (Svalbard Tourism, 2004), the Norwegian Polar Institute has expressed some concern and looks at tourism as a possible threat to the Svalbard environment (Johansen, 2004). It must be recalled that tourism as a locally based industry has a very short history. Moreover, given that Svalbard has long been a laboratory for scientists from all over the world, any impact of tourism can be monitored by a vigilant environmental authority in relation to a large array of historical knowledge and data.

The Governance of Tourism

Meanwhile, Svalbard is undergoing another revolution: a shift towards governance practices. Whereas 'government' refers to activities undertaken primarily or wholly by state bodies, " ... the essence of governance is its focus on governing mechanisms, which do not rest on recourse to the authority and sanctions of governments" (Stoker, 1998, p. 17). As the modern society and the modern state has developed " ... no actor has sufficient overview to make the application of particular instruments effective; no single actor has sufficient action potential to dominate unilaterally in a particular governing model", argues Kooiman (1993, p. 4). Thus, governance refers to regulation, management or steering where a multitude of actors are normally involved, both in the decision-making and implementation processes (Pierre, 2000; Pierre & Guy Peters, 2000; Kooiman, 2003; Kjær, 2004). The culture for governing has changed in this direction both due to privatisation processes, new awareness about societal responsibility, and to new opinions about the role of the state. Thus, a normalisation of Svalbard society also implied new ways of governing the islands. One expression of this is the creation of *Svalbard Lokalstyre*, the locally elected steering committee.

There are three major models for governance, according to Kooiman (2003): hierarchical governance or regulation, self-governance or self-regulation and co-governance or co-management. Svalbard now has examples of all three in its management of the environment.

Laws exemplify hierarchical regulation: A recent law, the Svalbard Environmental Protection Act (SEPA) introduces some well-known principles for environmental management in the governing of Svalbard (Goodall & Stabler, 1997). One principle is a duty of care; "Any person who is staying in or operates an undertaking in Svalbard shall show due consideration and exercise the caution required to avoid unnecessary damage or disturbance to the natural environment or cultural heritage"(§5). The 'precautionary principle' (§7) states that if an authority lacks information of the environmental impacts of a plan or an action, they can force the actors in question to provide them with this knowledge. The law also states that "[a]ny activity that is started in Svalbard shall be assessed on the basis of the overall pressure on the natural environment and cultural heritage that would result"(§8), the 'polluter pays principle' (§9), and that "activities in Svalbard shall make use of the technology that puts the least possible pressure on the environment" (§10). Other paragraphs deal with other specific issues.

The law may appear to be an example of hierarchical governance, but is not entirely so. A committee that had several participants from Svalbard, including a representative of the tourism industry, drafted the legislation. Furthermore, the interpretation of this and many other rules requires negotiation between the regulator and the regulated to be properly implemented. The SEPA is first and foremost a warning; if the tourism industry does not act responsibly, the Governor of Svalbard will intervene. This strong signal has given rise to a robust self-regulating and co-governance culture regarding tourism development on the islands.

Self-regulation can be defined "as a legal regime where the rules that steer the behaviour [...] are developed, managed and implemented by those whose behaviour shall be managed" (Sanford & Kimber, 2001, p. 162). One example of self-regulation in Svalbard tourism practice is a set of guidelines for snowmobile use created by the Svalbard Tourism Board and adopted voluntarily by all snowmobile tour operators in Longyearbyen. Another example is a training and certification program for tour guides that the Tourism Board has been running since 1995.

Co-governance has the objective of constituting a shared responsibility for the management of a particular task or area. This can be achieved through communicative rationality: governing actions obtained through joint decisions or through a public–private partnership (Jordan, Rüdiger Wurzel, & Zito, 2003). The model for the 1998 environment project within the tourism industry in Longyearbyen was created by an organisation called Grip, funded jointly by private companies and the Norwegian Ministry of Environment. Another example is that of several tourism networks: perhaps the most interesting is that started in 2003 amongst cruise-ship companies that operate in the Arctic areas (the Association of Arctic Expedition Cruise Operators), with a view to develop a common practice concerning environmental questions, and eventually to adopt a common set of guidelines for cruise operations in the area. This collaboration may yet result in a new regime for Arctic sea-borne tourism, like the one that for years has existed for Antarctica (International Association of Antarctica Tour Operators (IAATO)). Both the tourism development plan from 1994, and its follow-up in 1997 are examples of co-regulation, as is the developed set of guidelines for tourist behaviour (see Figure 10.1).

The crucial question after this is: who is in charge? Does anybody have the power to decide? The authorities seem to be issuing contradictory signals, one being the will and readiness to lead and govern, the other being their inability to govern effectively without collaborating with the powerful tourism lobby. While the SEPA *does* threaten fairly strict regulation, so far there are no such examples, only cases of negotiation and co-operation. The culture today is "let us talk, and see what we can do". There are many formal and informal bonds between the staff of the Governor on Svalbard and other authorities, and those running the local tourism industry. Many share similar backgrounds, have similar interests and values, and belong to the same social networks. This may contribute to a suitable climate for collaboration and co-management (Viken, 1998). It was not like this before. Until very recently, the mining community looked upon tourism as a threat, and most others regarded tourism with scepticism. With the high turnover in the population that exists, the changing attitudes may not so much be a result of altering views and attitudes as of the exchange of people described earlier.

Moreover, there is also an international dimension to this discussion of power. The ambitious goals set for the Svalbard environment by the Norwegian authorities and fleshed out in the new SEPA are very much an answer to an international awareness of the Arctic. Thus, local politics reflects a situation where the Norwegians do not have the power to do what they want. Related to this international responsibility there is also a move beyond: a transfer of power to non-governmental organisations (NGOs) and extranational regimes. On several occasions and in several issues dealing with tourism and environment, international NGOs have acted as pressure groups, but more and more act as collaborating partners and policymakers. The World Wildlife Fund plays a crucial role here, collaborating with both the tourism industry and the Governor of Svalbard. The emerging regime for cruise ships operating in the Arctic area is another example of an outward move of governance. Meanwhile, a prominent 'downward' shift is the more powerful negotiating position that the tourism industry now enjoys. By acting responsibly, the tourism industry has gained power and assumed a more central position in a co-governance system.

Figure 10.1 Common sense rules for Svalbard (From Svalbard Reiseliv AS, Longyearbyen, Norway).

Conclusion

This chapter has described the galloping pace of tourism development on Svalbard: other than cruise ship tourism, the rest of the industry simply exploded after 1990. Except for some nature reserves, there is today hardly anywhere left in the islands where tourism has not ventured. This conquest has at least three dimensions: one is the physical presence of tourists all over the archipelago; the second is the more symbolic transformation of Svalbard away from being the exclusive home of polar bears, reindeer, polar foxes, other mammals and birds and becoming part of the burgeoning empire of tourism; the third is how the industry has become a powerful political institution on the islands. This third conquest means that any decisions that may impact negatively on the tourism industry may be very difficult to take in future. Still, even if no interventions by the authorities have so far been necessary, the regulations are in place, should the tourism industry not act responsibly.

References

Arlov, T. B. (1996). *Svalbards Historie*. [*A history of Svalbard*]. Oslo: Aschehoug.

Butler, R. (1980). The concept of tourist area life cycle of evolution: Implications for management of resources. *Canadian Geographer*, *24*(1), 5–12.

Butler, R. (1997). The concept of carrying capacity for tourism destinations: Dead or merely buried? In: C. Cooper, & S. Wanhill (Eds), *Tourism development: Environmental and community issues* (pp. 11–22). Chichester: Wiley.

Butler, R. (2002). The development of tourism in frontier regions: Issues and approaches. In: S. Krakover, & Y. Gradus (Eds), *Tourism in frontier areas* (pp. 3–19). Lanham, MD: Lexington Books.

Elstad, Å. (2004). Polarturisme [Polar tourism]. In: E.-A. Drivenes, & H. D. Jølle (Eds), *Norsk Polarhistorie 3. Rikdommene* (pp. 477–518). Oslo: Gyldendal.

Friedman, J. (1987). *Planning in the public domain*. Princeton, NJ: Princeton University Press.

Fyhn, M. (2004). Kalde Svalbard tente senatorer [Svalbard turned senators on]. *Aftenposten* (national newspaper), August 24, 8.

Goodall, B., & Stabler, M. J. (1997). Principles influencing the determination of environmental standards for sustainable tourism. In: M. J. Stabler (Ed.), *Tourism sustainability. Principles and practice* (pp. 279–304). Wallingford: CABI.

Johansen, B. F. (2004). Miljøeffekter av turisme på Svalbard [Environmental impacts of tourism on Svalbard]. *Nordlys* (Tromsø regional newspaper), October 14, 54.

Jordan, A., Rüdiger Wurzel, K. W., & Zito, A. R. (2003). 'New' instruments of environmental governance. Patterns and pathways of change. In: A. Jordan, K. W. Rüdiger Wurzel, & A. R. Zito (Eds), *'New' instruments of environmental governance: National experiences and prospects* (pp. 1–26). London: Frank Cass.

Kjær, A. M. (2004). *Governance*. Cambridge: Polity Press.

Kooiman, J. (1993). *Modern governance: New government–society interactions*. London: Sage.

Kooiman, J. (2003). *Governing as governance*. London: Sage.

Longyearbyen Community Council. (2003). *Samfunns- og næringsutvikling på Svalbard: 1989–2002*. [*Societal and industrial development on Svalbard: 1989–2002*]. Longyearbyen: Longyearbyen Lokalstyre.

Ministry of Environment. (1999). *Svalbard*. Report no. 9 to the Storting (1999–2000). Oslo: Ministry of Environment.

Ministry of Industrial Affairs. (1990). *Industrial development on Svalbard.* Report no. 50 to the Storting (1990–1991). Oslo: Ministry of Industrial Affairs.

Page, S. J., & Dowling, R. K. (2002). *Ecotourism.* Harlow: Prentice-Hall.

Pierre, J. (2000). *Debating governance.* Oxford: Oxford University Press.

Pierre, J., & Guy Peters, B. (2000). *Governance, politics and the state.* London: Macmillan.

Presterud, P. (2003). *Vurdering av landmiljøet på Svalbard: Påvirkninger, tilstand og tiltak.* [*Assessment of the land-based environment on Svalbard: Impacts, situation and actions*]. http://miljo.npolar.no/mosj/mosj/reviews/review023.pdf (accessed 20/10/2005).

Reid, D. G. (2003). *Tourism, globalization and development. Responsible tourism planning.* London: Pluto Press.

Riffenburgh, B. (1993). *The myth of the explorer: The press, sensationalism, and geographical discovery.* London: Belhaven Press.

Sanford, E. G., & Kimber, C. (2001). Redirecting self-regulation. *Journal of Environmental Law, 13*(1), 158–185.

Stoker, G. (1998). Governance as theory. *International Social Science Journal, 155*, 17–28.

Svalbard Environmental Protection Act (SEPA). http://odin.dep.no/md/norsk/tema/svalbard/022021-990262/index-dok000-b-n-a.html (accessed 20/10/2005).

Svalbard Industrial Development. (1994). Reiselivsplan for Svalbard [*Tourism plan for Svalbard*]. Longyearbyen: Svalbard Næringsutvikling.

Svalbard Industrial Development. (1997). *Tourism plan for Svalbard: Challenges and strategies.* Longyearbyen: Svalbard Næringsutvikling.

Svalbard Tourism. (2004). *Reiselivsutviklingen i Longyearbyen. En evaluering.* [*Tourism development in Longyearbyen. An assessment*]. Longyearbyen: Svalbard Tourism.

Viken, A. (1998). Miljødiskurs på Svalbard som akademisk hegemoni. [The environmental discource on Svalbard as academic hegemony]. *Sosiologi i dag, 28*(1), 83–109.

Viken, A., & Heimtun, B. (2001). *Miljøbevisst reiseliv på Svalbard?* [*Is tourism on Svalbard environmentally conscious?*]. Report no. 1. Alta: Finnmarksforskning.

World Wildlife Fund for Nature (WWF). (2004). *Cruise tourism on Svalbard — A risky business?* Oslo: WWF International Arctic Programme.

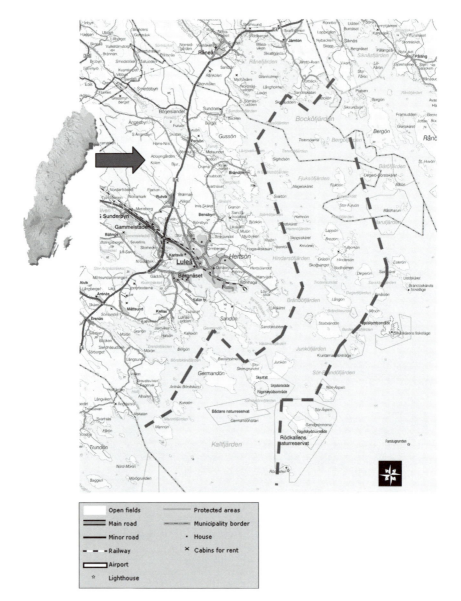

Image 8: Luleå Archipelago and surrounding region.

Chapter 11

The Luleå Archipelago, Sweden

Per-Åke Nilsson and Rosemarie Ankre

Introduction

While a number of coastal areas in Sweden (like the Stockholm archipelago) have been part of larger research projects, the coastal areas of northern Sweden have not been much investigated for their tourism potential. Hence, the Luleå archipelago case is interesting because of its peripheral geographical location as well as because there is a general willingness to develop tourism further during both summer and winter.

The Luleå archipelago is located far up north in Sweden, just 100 km away from the Arctic Circle: this means full moon during daytime in the winter and sun during the whole night in the summer. Since the area's nature and culture landscape is particular, sustainable tourism development involves preserving the environment as well as maintaining a permanent population: "In the future treatment of the housing conditions for a permanent living in attractive areas, it is particularly important to acknowledge the significance the settled population has for a living archipelago" (authors' translation, SOU, 2000, p. 67). In its proposal for the sustainable development of the Swedish coastal areas, the Environmental Advisory Council (SOU, 1996, p. 153) argues that the process of sustainability concerns three inter-linked factors: economy, society and environment. Therefore, sustainable development must include prospects for the local population to be able to live and prosper in the archipelago.

The summer season in the Luleå archipelago is of good quality and to some extent it resembles that of island resorts in warmer climates. Its combination of dry weather, sun, sandy beaches and temperate water is well known in Scandinavia. Visitors from the northernmost parts of Norway and from most of Sweden find the area quite irresistible. In winter however, national and international tourists are not very frequent.

The Bothnia Arc Project

Funded by the European Regional Development Fund (ERDF) (2003), the Bothnia Arc project is a cross boundary cooperation between the Swedish and the Finnish side of the

Gulf of Bothnia. New opportunities for building a strong and competitive region with high international standards in technology, enterprise, tourism, expertise and networking are being developed. In collaboration with the Russian region of Karelia and the Centre for Regional and Tourism Research in Bornholm, Denmark, the project aims to develop a new tourism concept based on sub-arctic climate. The Gulf Stream nurtures both excellent winter and warm summer conditions for tourism in an Arctic milieu and creates a distinct tourism profile, clearly distinguishing the region in relation to Lapland in northern Scandinavia. The project plans attractive trails, waterway routes, related services and other investments in tourism infrastructure and will balance the needs of tourism against environmental and cultural interests in a strategy for sustainable long-term development. Within the project, *special* efforts are being made to extend the tourist season into, and during, wintertime. This development process should ensure that the people of the region obtain security and a better quality of life (ERDF, 2002).

Between 1998 and 2001, three initiatives were concluded under the auspices of the Bothnia Arc project, namely: (a) Vision Strategy and Networks; (b) Communication Systems; and (c) Tourism and the Environment (ERDF, 2003). These projects were designed to generate proposals for planning, investment and other actions aimed at the sustainable development of the region. The most important goals were presented as "… the need to identify possibilities for the future development of the region, to create networks for vital long-term regional cooperation, and to ensure that the Bothnia Arc becomes a well-known project in European Union Terms." (Bothnia Arc Project, 2003, p. 6). The overall vision emerging from this trans-frontier exercise is that, by the year 2010, the Bothnia Arc would become a dominant player on the international scene (www.bothnianarc.org).

There is an agreement between Sweden and Finland regulating the border river system (SFS, 1971, p. 1016). It regulates the use of the water area around the river system and the mouth surroundings in the Gulf of Bothnia. The agreement has turned out to be too weak as a protection for the environment compared with the more developed national laws so the agreement has now been superseded by the European Union's Water Directive (interview with Hans Överby, 2004). Nevertheless, the relations between the different counties and municipalities in northern Sweden are probably more difficult to cope with than the international cooperation between Sweden and Finland. A recent example of that is a decision from the department of the environment at the County Council of Norrbotten which invalidates a decision from the municipality of Luleå about summer house establishments in the archipelago (Norrbotten County Council, 2004).

The thickness of the ice in the northernmost part of the Gulf of Bothnia ranges from 0.5 m to 1.5 m. Thus, in the Bothnia Arc project, the emphasis has been placed on developing a brand image based on the unique fact that this is one of the few inhabited places in the world where the sea is frozen solid during the winter months (www.bothnianarc.org). The hope of tourism authorities on both sides of the border is that more international visitors will be attracted to an area that already lures domestic visitors who take advantage of this unusual environment.

It is important to note that an overarching aim of the Bothnia Arc project is to promote the coastal region as an alternative but also as a complementary year-round destination to Lapland. The latter is a very well known destination concept and attracts international guests because of the existence of such features as Santa Claus in Rovaniemi (www.lapland.fi), the

Ice Hotel in Jukkasjärvi (www.norrbottenlappland.se) and the downhill skiing resorts in the mountain range (Bodén & Rosenberg, 2004). The coast of the Gulf of Bothnia, in contrast, is hardly known internationally.

Questionnaire Survey

At the Mid-Sweden University in Östersund, a research project on planning frameworks for sustainable tourism development has been in progress. Its recommendations are based on the results of a questionnaire survey of visitors who stayed in the Luleå archipelago during the summer of 2003. Questionnaires were mailed to 891 people and the response rate was an encouraging 62% (Ankre, 2005). The survey examined the visitors' activities, attitudes and experiences together with their geographical location and dispersion in the area: the resulting data were applied to land-use planning. By gathering and understanding visitor data, planning frameworks may combine preservation with tourism development. Effective planning requires such knowledge of the visitors and their attitudes since it constitutes the difference between visitor expectations and actual management. Furthermore, if different groups of interests or activities use the same land area, conflicts are likely to arise. These could be reduced by utilising suitable planning methods (Ankre, 2005).

Myths and Image of the Islands

Historically, remote often sparsely populated, frontier island regions have held a high degree of attraction for adventurous travellers, because of their isolation and their marked difference (perceived and/or real) to their visitors' origins. Such characteristics, not to mention the overall 'myth of the frontier,' endow those areas with a degree of the 'exotic,' appealing to travellers who are in constant search of out-of-the-ordinary environs they can add to their list of 'collected destinations' (Butler, 1996). Islands seem to offer something special in comparison to the large mainland, perhaps because one has to travel by boat or airplane to reach the destination. To be detached from the mainland assigns a unique physical and psychological twist to the visit (Baum, 1995).

For many tourists, islands symbolise some sort of paradise. To sell cold water resorts as a paradise where the cold water is not a problem but an asset may be seen as a challenge. The presumptive guest must be someone, who differs from the normal 'paradise seekers' found in summer island resorts. The guest must be atypical since the destination is atypical. Tourism has become a process or organisation containing a complex hierarchy of products, emotions, consumption and stories. Pedersen (2004) is convinced that the atypical tourist is not found where the destination is a typical one. There must be an atypical destination as well. Marketing the Luleå archipelago regionally or even nationally has not been very fruitful so far. For regional tourists, the area is familiar which means swimming, sailing and hunting in the summer and fishing, skiing and snow-scooter driving in the winter. Even if these features are appreciated, they are normal and expected experiences. However, for the national and the international tourist, especially from the south of Europe or from Asia, these experiences are quite unexpected and considered atypical. A trip to the Gulf of Bothnia and the Luleå archipelago would satisfy many such atypical needs.

Something extra must be experienced and by that, experience in itself has become the keyword. To be next to the pool in a tropical environment is no longer an experience, if it becomes humdrum and routine. In comparison, to have dinner on ice in snowmobile attire is not seen as a routine, at least not yet. Boorstin (1962) stresses that for an experience to qualify as a noteworthy tourism event, it should mean something unexpected and extra, and not just be an anticipated pleasure. This is often forgotten and experience is offered as something special but not really exceptional. A lot of effort is made to display the tourist experience in a proper manner; but what this is remains defined by the entrepreneur in the context of *local* cultural patterns and expectations, and not by the tourists themselves in relation to what *they* want and expect (Larsen, 2003).

Turner and Ash (1975) coined the phrase 'pleasure peripheries' and saw the boundaries for tourism traffic steadily expanding into newer and newer territories. Today, many more territories are within the range of tourist exploration and familiarity; thus distance and remoteness are less decisive for impressing neighbours and friends. The different tourist types or typologies presented by Cohen (1972), where he distinguishes between recreational, diversionary, experiential, experimental and existential tourists, seem to have melded together. Today, many tourists feel that they should belong to several or even all of these categories in order to achieve a 'complete' vacation: in her study of tourists to Estoril in Portugal, Wolf (2001) noticed that it was difficult to place tourists into neat, mutually exclusive categories, because in some respects they may belong to one category and in other respects to others. Tourists also change categories depending on when (during their life cycle) they go on vacation and in what context they make up their mind to travel.

The Luleå Archipelago

The Luleå archipelago consists of over 700 islands located in the Gulf of Bothnia. Just adjacent to the archipelago lies the city of Luleå with its 73,000 inhabitants. The harbour is one of the largest in Sweden calculated in terms of tonnage. Iron ore is an important primary product in the region since it is a traditional industry together with steel. The development of industry has initiated a technical university whose research specialisations include the properties of ice and the dynamics of chilling (Luleå Municipality, 2003). During the last 150–200 years, there have been various industries — such as mining, sawmills and ship building — in the Luleå archipelago. Today fishing for a livelihood still exists but on a small scale, farming with raising of livestock has almost disappeared and seal-hunting is forbidden. These economic transformations are related to the ongoing structural changes in Swedish economic life. For people in the archipelago, tourism is a possible solution for survival. Only a few of the islands are inhabited: the entire Luleå archipelago is nowadays only populated all the year round by some 80 people (Hederyd, Wallin, Westerberg, & Blom, 1999; interviews with Göran Wallin et al., 2005).

Tourism is viewed as the next profitable industry. The landscape of the archipelago has special qualities for outdoor life, and many people have access to second homes in the area. The active outdoor life like sailing, fishing, driving snowmobiles, skiing and skating is also intense. During both summer and winter, the archipelago is a place for outdoor life for the inhabitants of Luleå city and other visitors. Pleasure boat riding is a main activity.

With more than 8000 small boats, Luleå is one of the Swedish municipalities with the largest number of boats per person, one pleasure boat for every eight inhabitants (Luleå, 2004).

Several islands in the archipelago have accommodations and other service facilities, such as bridges, barbeque-sites, guest harbours and saunas, which the municipality has built and manages (Hederyd et al., 1999; Luleå Municipality, 2000). There are three to four restaurants open in the archipelago, the number depending on the possibility for Luleå municipality (as the owner) to secure leaseholders. The municipality also owns some campsites and seven summer houses for rent, established on the islands. It is difficult to have the restaurants open all year round: only one is available in winter, and then only for reserved orders. Late in winter, the restaurant may be open during weekends (Malmstad, 2002).

The shallow waters of the Gulf of Bothnia include sandy beaches which permit somewhat warm bathing temperatures in summer. Together, the brackish water and the land rise have created certain prerequisites for a special development (Hederyd *et al.*, 1999). A truly unique natural feature of the Gulf of Bothnia is the coastal land-rising at a rate of 0.8–1 cm per year, or up to 1 m per century. Significantly, this means that within an average person's lifetime the waterline can shift as much as 100 m. This up-lift is related to the retreat of the glaciers since the end of the last ice age over 10,000 years ago. Over time, the phenomenon leads to more land area but also shallower waters, and inevitably it has significant impacts on harbours and communities located in the deltas of the rivers that traverse the region. Authorities on both sides of the border are highly conscious of this phenomenon. It has led to coordinated planning efforts to ensure the protection of the coastal plains, landscape conservation and the reforestation of woodlands (Ioannides, 2004).

Planning and Management

In Sweden, there are national, regional and local levels of responsibility and accountability in the planning systems. The municipalities have a great opportunity to influence land and water use, because of their control over the planning system. Moreover, the county administration boards provide basic data for planning (National Board of Housing, Building and Planning, 1996). A special Department called *Archipelago/Outdoor Life* manages all the municipality's establishments and activities for the active outdoor life on the mainland and in the archipelago (Luleå, 2004). Its work has to be carried out in co-operation with other administrative bodies, various interest groups, organisations and companies, along with the population of the archipelago. The Department's overall objective is to advance the interests of the archipelago's resident population, also doing so by creating more and better possibilities for the tourism industry and related market activities to expand. The Department is also expected to take any appropriate initiatives to safeguard nature and culture, within this overall process. *Archipelago/Outdoor life* is responsible for transportation, waste collection, signage and the maintenance of establishments and excursions (Hederyd et al., 1999).

In the development plan, the municipality has affirmed that tourism and recreation should be carried out in a way that the Luleå archipelago's values and biological variety would not be threatened. The main priority is to uphold recreational life so that the inhabitants of Luleå have access to satisfactory recreational areas and facilities. Keeping the environment intact would after all be the basis for a long-term tourism product: this is important for the municipality's own future (Luleå Municipality, 1990). Land-use planning and zoning connect the preservation of natural, cultural and visual values with the characteristics that correspond to the purposes of tourism and recreation. In Swedish coastal areas, national parks, nature reserves, bird and seal sanctuaries and shore protection areas already exist as zones within development planning strategies (SOU, 2000, p. 67).

The Municipality of Luleå has an unofficial zoning of the archipelago which is recognised and used by the Department of Archipelago/Outdoor Life. According to Göran Wallin, head of the department, the zoning was established after a consideration of how many visitors the area was felt capable of managing:

> *We note that the outer islands are the most vulnerable [areas] and that the islands closest to the mainland can get by with considerably more visitors. It is in relation to how many people can and do tread on vulnerable vegetation. Of course, the vegetation is more sensitive the further out one goes from the mainland.* (authors' translation, Wallin interview, 2004).

A significant 82% of the protected area in Luleå municipality consists of water. A majority of nature reserves and bird sanctuaries are situated in the outer zone; but there are also some in the middle zone and only one in the inner zone (Hederyd et al., 1999).

Permanent Living

Most of the 80 permanent residents of the Luleå archipelago are old people who have always lived in the archipelago and are now retired (Hederyd et al., 1999). Only one family with children lives in the area, on the island of Hindersön. The adults of the family work in Luleå city and during winter, the children go to school in the same city.

There are twelve active fishers in the Luleå archipelago, geographically spread over seven islands, but two of them are now living on the mainland. All of them have apartments in Luleå city. The fishers are single men between 35 and 55 years old and most of them are sons of former fishers. Together with one farmer, these men form the labour force of the old traditional agrarian sector (interview with Malmstad, 2004). In relation to the area's tourism development, Ankre's survey (2005) found that 56% of the respondents think that the local residents are important for their experience of the archipelago. Almost none of the respondents had been disturbed by local inhabitants during the stay.

In the Luleå archipelago, there are people living permanently in second homes. Some of them are retired and some commute while others live there part time or use the second homes as a workplace. Many of them have apartments in Luleå city (interview with Malmstad, 2004). Among the respondents in the questionnaire survey (Ankre, 2005), the willingness to buy a second home was not great. That may be explained by the fact that 38% already had regular access to second homes. Only a few among these could consider using their second homes for permanent living.

Many Swedish coastal areas have witnessed an expansion of second homes. After 1970, the number of newly built second homes in the Norrbotten group of islands within the Luleå archipelago was as many as the ones built in total in the coastal areas of Sweden, but with less density. Only a few permanent houses have been built in the northern coastal area of Norrbotten, Sweden (National Rural Development Agency, 2003).

According to the Environmental Advisory Board, the expansion of second homes in Norrbotten does not create many problems for the municipalities in general. There is enough space in the region so there should be no friction between tourism and recreation on one hand and nature conservation and cultural environment on the other. In the outer archipelago of Luleå, the number of second homes is considerably less. However, according to Luleå municipality, the innermost area of the archipelago has so many second homes that this has led to limited public access to the beaches (Luleå Municipality, 2000).

Müller (1999) discusses counter urbanisation in his investigation of the purchase of second homes by Germans in Sweden. Transaction costs for commuting can be reasonable for some but too costly for others, both financially and psychologically. The purchase of a second home in the hinterland of a metropolitan area may be seen as a substitute for a relocation of permanent residence into a rural area. Second homes nearby on the archipelago can serve as a means to attract people to settle down in Luleå city. The Environmental Advisory Board also states that in order to establish sustainable development, local residents must have a possibility to live and prosper in the archipelago (SOU, 1996, p. 153).

Nonetheless, people who live permanently in existing second homes are viewed as a problem by Luleå municipality due to the poor second home sewage systems and problems with personal means of transport. Despite this, new second home settlements have been established and the number of people living in these settlements has increased (Luleå Municipality, 2002).

Experiencing the Luleå Archipelago in Winter

According to the municipality of Luleå, there is an increasing awareness of the importance of tourism among local residents. The policy of the municipality is to encourage diversification within employment activities from the permanent residents' side: fishing, transport facilities and tourism (interview with Göran Wallin, 2004). Not all the inhabitants are happy with tourism however, even if they are generally in favour of tourism as a source of additional income (Malmstad, 2002).

From the perspective of the Department of Commerce and Tourism Business of Luleå municipality, winter tourism is of utmost importance. The Department is very much aware of the market split between summer and winter tourism. For summer, the traditional regional, national and Norwegian market is intact; but for winter, something else must be found beyond local residents from Luleå (interview with Göran Wallin, 2004). In order to target the winter tourism market, it is necessary to cultivate tour operators from Continental Europe. These generally agree that, with the exception of Santa Claus at Rovaniemi, northern Scandinavia remains untapped for winter tourism purposes (Danielsson, 2004). In Ankre's survey (2005), only 2% of respondents felt that the Luleå region attracted too many tourists. In contrast, 45% deemed the amount of tourists too few. Asked how the future development of tourism should proceed within the next five years, not a single respondent felt that tourism should decrease, while 72% believed that it should rather increase.

In the Luleå archipelago, the sea freezes to ice in January and this condition lasts until March–April. Since the ice is so thick, people can actually ride their snowmobiles onto the frozen sea or with conventional vehicles. These 'winter roads' are cleared from snow on the ice over specific stretches that take travellers to four of the inhabited islands. Luleå municipality pays for this service so that national ice-road standards are observed (interview with Malmstad, 2004). Anders Granberg, Luleå municipality (interview with Anders Granberg, 2004) states that the Luleå archipelago has about 60 km of ice-roads. There are also possibilities for learning how to drive on ice for people with limited opportunities to drive on slippery roads at home. A German automobile club (*Allgemeine Deutsche Automobil Club* — ADAC) sends drivers annually to Luleå for such practice.

During summer, the main transport means is motorboat. As Ankre (2005) illustrates, in summer most tourists come by car and the typical stay is for 1–5 days (35%) followed by 16–30 days (20%). Staying for 5–15 days is remarkably low: just 5%. Moreover, each visitor is probably paying more per stay in winter than in summer. In winter, round-tours by car are rare and the normal pattern for a stay is a one-week package offer. Moreover, winter visitors are not likely to stay at a campsite, tent or in the car, as they might do in summer. In that respect, tourism is much easier to forecast and cope with in winter than in summer because of low numbers and the consistent pattern of tourist visitations and length of stay (Vuorio & Emmelin, 2000; Fredman, Emmelin, Heberlein, & Vuorio, 2001).

Winter Activities in the Bothnian Rim

The Luleå municipality website offers a number of other generalised winter tourism experiences. These include cross-country skiing, snowmobile driving, ice yachting or ice sailing (where the yacht is pushed along by the wind over ice), dog sledging, ice fishing, sauna (followed by a roll in the snow or a dip into the frigid waters for the really daring), picnics and hikes among the pack-ice (formed into majestic walls by the combined forces of wind and weather) and canoeing and kayaking (possibly among the icebergs). All this in a formidable context of wide open spaces.

The idea of the Bothnia Arc project is to connect the offers from Luleå municipality to local or regional people who seek recreation in the frozen archipelago, to the tourists from continental Europe for whom most of these activities are simply not available in their home environments. The winter season can, in that respect, become the peak season for the area, perhaps not in terms of the number of tourists but in monetary terms. One of the options available to wintertime visitors is the ability to take a trip on an icebreaker from Kemi in northern Finland on the same latitude as Luleå (www.vinteripitea.com).

For local residents, the winter activities are quite familiar and typical. For tourists from southern Europe they must seem *atypical*. The major challenge is how to make the continental European market aware of such opportunities. Specific successful inroads into this lucrative market include:

- *Dining on ice:* Dinner is served on the ice of the Gulf of Bothnia in a tent, about 100 m out from the shore. The ice is cleaned from snow so the ground is almost transparent. A stove in the middle of the tent keeps the air relatively warm, although the temperature is normally below 0°C (32°F). The customers are dressed in snow-scooter overalls which make it possible to keep warm during the dinner and during any walking to and from the tent. The customers are first given a glass of champagne outside the tent. The champagne is chilled beneath the ice and brought up by a fishing line through a hole in the surface. The meals served are hot dishes on fine china, just like any first class restaurant. The food and the drinks are brought to the tent by snowmobiles. Any particular needs for facilities on land are met by a ride on the snow-scooter. After dinner, sauna is offered both in the traditional form (indoors) or else outdoors in special vats with hot water.

- *Icebreaker conferences:* The icebreaker can serve as a hotel or just as a congress facility. It takes the customer on an icebreaker tour and the congress is held on the ice. The customers go on the gangway right down on the ice where chairs and other facilities for the congress are placed just beside the ship. Since there is open water behind the ship, diving and swimming opportunities are offered. Special wet suits can be hired but people can also swim in bathing suits. For the winter season 2003/04, conferences have been held with, among others, Spanish customers, originally meant to be travelling to Rio de Janeiro: the challenge of having a conference on an icebreaker changed the minds of the organisers (Dagens Nyheter, 2004).

While each of these activities may be interesting to tourists from continental Europe, tourists also have different views on the value of such and similar attractions. It has, for example, already become clear to some Luleå entrepreneurs that not all tourists from Spain love and enjoy a sauna (Piteå seminar, 2003). The automatic and first reaction to this discovery is to try and convince Spanish tourists that sauna *is* wonderful. However, upon further reflection, perhaps one should accept such an expression of preference and offer alternative experiences.

Conclusions

The Luleå archipelago has two separate tourism seasons. In summer, it is an ordinary seaside resort, remindful somewhat of paradise islands further south. The area is peripheral to many Swedes since one needs to travel to the region by plane or train and, once there, spend at least a week on site. Tourists to Luleå are, above all, from the region with a sprinkle of visitors from the very north of Norway where high temperature, sea and sand is a rare combination. The archipelago also serves as a recreational area for local residents from adjacent Luleå city. The obstacle is the 1,000 km distance from the densely populated parts of Sweden, like the capital city of Stockholm. It is time-consuming to go by train and exhausting to go by car. Normally, a stay is a transit, with airfares and hotel costs included in a package.

In winter, the season is markedly different even though the area continues to serve as a place for recreation. For most Swedes, the winter activities are great experiences but also expected and well known. Visitors are less in number, come from closer regions, but tend to stay longer. Winter activities have normally been conducted in a haphazard way by local residents. In order to live up to expectations of an experience as something totally unexpected, the winter season in the Luleå archipelago should be promoted amongst potential international visitors as a chance to sample that something extra and unique. For an atypical tourist with no direct experience of winter conditions in northern Scandinavia, coming to this atypical destination can make the visit a truly memorable one.

Increased winter tourism is a way to mitigate seasonal swings in the region. The winter season has already been developed and exploited for a couple of decades in Lapland. It follows a trend, which started with Santa Claus, winter cities (like Edmonton, Kiruna, Oulu and Tiumen), and the Ice Hotel in Jukkasjärvi. The latest trend is winter activities taking place on the frozen sea. This shows that an island resort is not bound to be just a sun paradise. The islands in peripheral northern regions can also offer chilly and exotic experiences where frosty dinners, combined with hot saunas, can entertain tourists with a cosy time in front of stoves with open fires on warm reindeer skins and whisky on the rocks at night. This is, anyway, what the marketers are hoping for.

The Luleå archipelago means different things to different actors. For the inhabitants, it is a more or less obsolete way of living. Most of them now have second homes, and may require regular commuting to and from the urban centres. For the local residents of Luleå city and its suburbs, the archipelago is a recreational area where it is possible to conduct a life of leisure close to their urban dwellings. The possibility of owning a second home is a privilege many of them look forward to. For the tourists in the summer, the archipelago is a recreational area of great value since it offers sea and sun in a comfortable mix. For the tourists in the winter, it is an atypical destination with experiences out of the normal.

The interests of these four categories need to match the policies set out by the relevant authorities. The problem for the authorities is that they suffer from internal contradictions and different agendas. For the leisure department, a growth of second homes is desirable. For the town-planning department, it is important to plan this expansion carefully and not accept free development. For the environment department, it is necessary to protect different natural locations and resources from exploitation. And for the department of commerce, it is important to encourage industrial development.

For the moment, the smallest common denominator is a subdued tempo of development where all restrictions can somehow be observed. This is possible so far due to the small number of inhabitants and the manageable number of tourists. If any of these factors expand, however, there are bound to be problems. The most likely factor to expand is second home-owners moving to the archipelago and settling there. Their occupation will be urban and not locally rooted and thereby they are bound to change the character of the settlement. The second most likely factor to expand is tourism. If that happens, the departments of commerce and leisure may gain influence and accept the development of commercial activities on a larger scale. The already tense situation among policy makers could escalate. With the voice of the traditional local residents being overwhelmed and overtaken by that of incoming settlers, sustainability may end up being the main victim of such an escalation.

References

Ankre, R. (2005). *Visitors' activities and attitudes in coastal tourism. A case study of Luleå Archipelago, Sweden.* Working Paper no. 1, Östersund: Mid-Sweden University, European Tourism Research Institute.

Badur, J. (2003). *Analysis of the questionnaire results: Tourism industry in the Bothnian Arc, Bothnian Arc Project.* Frankfurt: Nord Info GmbH Nord Europa Marketing Application form, Baltic Sea Region INTERREG III B. Rostock: BSR Joint Secretariat.

Baum, T. (1995). The fascination of islands: A tourist perspective. In: D.G. Lockhart, & D. Drakakis-Smith (Eds), *Island tourism: Trends and prospects* (pp. 21–34). London: Pinter.

Bodén, B., & Rosenberg, L. (2004). Kommersiell turism och local samhällsutveckling. En studie av sex svenska fjälldestinationer. [*Commercial tourism and local development – a study of six Swedish mountain destinations*]. Östersund: European Tourism Research Institute.

Boorstin, D. (1962). *The image: A guide to pseudo-events in America.* New York: Harper & Row.

Bothnia Arc Project. (2003). *Final plan: Gränslösa möjligheter.* [*Final plan: Unlimited possibilities*]. Bothnia Arc Project.

Butler, R., & Hinch, D. (1996). Indigenous tourism: A common ground for discussion. In: R. Butler, & D. Hinch (Eds), *Tourism and indigenous people.* London: International Thomson Business Press.

Cohen, E. (1972). Towards a sociology of international tourism. *Social Research, 39,* 164–184.

Danielsson, J. (2004). Norra Sverige: En ny exotisk destination med enorm tillväxtpotential. Expertintervjuer med utländska researrangörer i Tyskland, Storbritannien. Italien, Frankrike, Ryssland och Japan. [*Northern Sweden: A new exotic destination with enormous growth potential. Expert interviews with travel agencies in Germany, UK, Italy, France, Russia and Japan*]. Luleå: Norrbotten/Lappland Ekonomisk Förening.

European Regional Development Fund (ERDF). (2002). Interreg III B, community initiative concerning transnational co-operation on spatial planning: 2000–2006. Bothnian Arc: Arctic Coastal Tourism Region – Bothnian Arc-ACTion. Rostock: Application Form.

European Regional Development Fund. (2003). *Application for Interreg III B project: Bothnian Arc-ACTion.* Haparanda: Bothnian Arc Association.

Fredman, P., Emmelin, L., Heberlein, T. A., & Vuorio, T. (2001). Tourism in the Swedish mountain region. In: B. Sahlberg (Ed.), *Going north: Peripheral tourism in Canada and Sweden* (pp. 123–146). Östersund: Mid Sweden University, European Tourism Research Institute.

Hederyd, S., Wallin, G., Westerberg, A., & Blom, L. (1999). Din egen lots till Luleå skärgård. [*Your own guide to the Luleå archipelago*]. Luleå: Luleå Municipality.

Ioannides, D. (2004). *Trans-boundary collaboration in tourism: The case of the Bothnia Arc.* Unpublished paper, Missouri State University and Centre for Regional & Tourism Research, Missouri & Bornholm.

Larsen, S. (2003). The Psychology of the tourist experience. Unpublished manuscript, paper presented at the 12th Nordic Tourism Research Symposium in Stavanger, October.

Luleå Municipality. (1990). Översiktplan Luleå kommun. [*Luleå Municipality development plan*] Luleå: Luleå Municipality.

Luleå Municipality. (2000). Naturvårdsplan Luleå. [*Nature conservation plan for Luleå*]. Luleå: Luleå Municipality.

Luleå Municipality. (2002). Aktualitetsförklaring, översiktsplanen Luleå kommun. [*Declaration of the status, the Luleå development plan*] Luleå: Luleå Municipality.

Luleå Municipality. (2003). Tourism pamphlet, unpublished document, Luleå: Luleå Municipality.

Malmstad, I. (2002). Från Laxfällor till Kärleksmums: Återblickar och episoder från Luleå stad och skärgård. [*From Salmon traps to Chocolate cake: Flashbacks and episodes from Luleå city and archipelago*]. Hammerdal: Hammerdal Förlag & Reportage.

Müller, D. (1999). *German second home owners in the Swedish countryside. On the internationalization of leisure space.* Unpublished dissertation, Department of Social and Economic Geography, Umeå University and European Tourism Research Institute, Östersund.

National Board of Housing, Building and Planning. (1996). Boken om översiktsplan del II. Översiktsplanen i lagstiftningen. [*The development book, part II: The development plan in the legislation*]. Karlskrona: The National Board of Housing, Building and Planning.

National Rural Development Agency. (2003). Sveriges kust och skärgårdar: En faktasamling om boende, arbete, service och kommunikationer. [*Sweden's maritime areas and archipelagos: Facts about living, labour, service and infrastructure*]. Östersund: National Rural Development Agency.

Nilsson, P. Å. (2002). Rekreation og tillgaengelighed i et taetbefolket område: Brug og attituder i det agrare Danmark. [*Recreation and accessibility in a densely populated area: Use and attitudes in rural Denmark*]. Bornholm: Centre for Regional and Tourism Research.

Norrbotten County Council. (2004). Ansökan om dispens från strandskyddsbestämmelser för uppförande av två uthyrningsstugor, en bastu samt kombinerat WC och vedförråd på fastigheten Brändöskär, Luleå kommun. [*Application for exemption from the shore protection regulations to build two cabins, a sauna, WC and woodshed on Brändöskär, Luleå municipality*]. Norrbotten Regional State Authority, 17th November.

Pedersen, K. M. (2004). Turisters rejsevalg i et globalt oplevelsesrum. [*Tourists' choice of travel in a global space of experience*]. Unpublished paper, Centre for Regional and Tourism Research, Bornholm.

SFS. (1971). Gränsälvsöverkommelsen. [*Agreement on border river conditions*]. Stockholm: Riksdagen (The Parliament).

SOU (State Committee Report). (1996). Hållbar utveckling i Sveriges skärgårdsområde. [*Sustainable development of archipelagos in Sweden*]. Stockholm: Ministry of Environment.

SOU (State Committee Report). (2000). Levande skärgård: Miljövårdsberedningens betänkande om de regionala miljö- och hushållningsprogrammen för vissa av Sveriges skärgårdsmiljöer. [*Sustainable archipelago: Report on programmes for regional environmental and economic management for certain areas within the Swedish archipelagos from the committee for environmental management*]. Stockholm: Ministry of Environment.

Turner, L., & Ash, J. (1975). *The golden hordes: International tourism and the pleasure peripheries.* London: Constable.

Vuorio, T., & Emmelin, L. (2000). Naturturism i norr. [*Nature tourism in the north*] Working Paper, no. 6, Östersund: Mid-Sweden University, European Tourism Research Institute.

Wolf, E. (2001). Med charter till Estoril – en etnologisk studie av kulturell mångfald inom modern svensk turism. [*With a charter to Estoril: An ethnological survey of cultural variety within modern Swedish tourism*]. Gothenburg: Etnologiska Föreningen i Västsverige.

Newspapers

Dagens Nyheter. (2004). Norrländsk kyla hett turistmål för Spanjorer. [*Nordic chill: A hot travel target for Spaniards*], 8th February edition.

Internet Sites

Bothnia Arc Project:
    www.bothnianarc.org/index.html (available in English)
    www.bothnianarc.net (available in Finnish, Swedish and English)
Ice Hotel, Jukkasjärvi:
    www.norrbottenlappland.se (available in Swedish and English)

Luleå:
   www.lulea.se (available in Swedish and English)
Santa Claus, Rovaniemi:
   www.lapland.fi (available in Swedish, Finnish, German and English)
   www.vinteripitea.com or www.pitea.se (available in Swedish, Finnish, German and English)

Interviews

Anders Granberg, Director, Business Department, Luleå Municipality, 24/8/2004.
Hans Överby, Department of Environment, County of Norrbotten, 25/11/2004.
Ivar Malmstad, Luleå, author, 29/7/2004.

E-Mail Correspondence

Göran Wallin. Head of Department, Archipelago/Outdoor Life of Luleå Municipality, 14/5/2004.

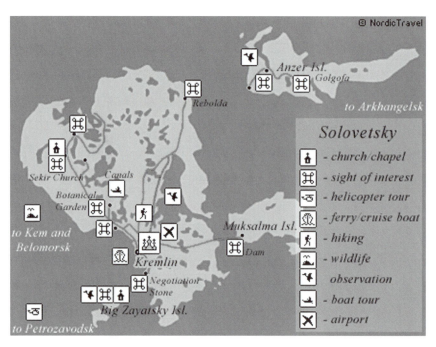

Image 9: Solovetsky map.

Chapter 12

The Solovetsky Archipelago, Russia

Julia Nevmerzhitskaya

Introduction

There are places in the world where nature, culture, history and mystery are in strong collusion. These places attract people's attention and interest over the years. Solovetsky Archipelago is one such place. Located in the western part of the White Sea, 150 km from the Arctic Circle to the south, the Solovetsky Archipelago (or Solovki, as Russians call it) covers about 300 sq. km. The Archipelago consists of six comparatively large islands and scores of smaller ones. Administratively, the Archipelago forms part of the Arkhangelsk region.

The White Sea is a part of Arctic Ocean, but even though it was called 'Freezing Sea' in ancient times (Boguslavsky, 1971, p. 13), the climate there is more continental due to the lack of cold ocean streams and an absence of warm ocean airflow. Still, the average water surface temperature is only +4°C in June and up to +8°C in August.

What attracts thousands of tourists each year to this cold and remote peace of land in the Arctic Ocean? Is it the fascinating nature of the island, with a relatively warm microclimate for these latitudes? A chance to get away from the mainland? An opportunity to visit the famous Solovetsky Monastery? Or is it just to experience the spirit of a former GULAG?

History

The first traces of civilisation on the Solovetsky islands date back to the 3rd century BC, when inhabitants built villages, sacred sites and irrigation systems. On one island, there is a compact group of religious and funerary monuments, including 18 stone labyrinths, over 600 stone burial cairns, and several stone alignments and circles. One labyrinth, over 22 m in diameter, is the largest known in the world (UNESCO, 2005).

The Solovetsky monastery, established in 1436, is what led the Archipelago to become inscribed as an UNESCO World Heritage Site in 1992 (*ibid.*). For six centuries, the

Extreme Tourism: Lessons from the World's Cold Water Islands
Copyright © 2006 by Elsevier Ltd.
All rights of reproduction in any form reserved
ISBN: 0-08-044656-6

Solovetsky Archipelago has been regarded as a holy place. By the mid-16th century, the monastery had become an important religious and political centre in Russia. It had been increasing power and wealth over the years: it owned large tracts of land and traded in salt, fish as well as fat, skin and other products from seals and whales. The Russian Czars were also interested in fortifying Russia's northern borders, and so they financially supported the building of the monastery's defenses, transforming it into a fortress (Frumenkov, 1975).

The tide turned when the Solovki monks refused to accept the reforms suggested by Russian Orthodox Church Patriarch Nikon (Kartashev, 1991; Shickman, 1997). In 1668, Czar Alexei Michailovich sent troops to storm Solovki, which they did after a seven year siege.

With the Great October Revolution of 1917, a new age of Solovetsky history was ushered in: the Solovetsky Concentration Camp of Special Designation (SLON), where political and other prisoners were kept and killed, was set up in 1923. Solzhenitsyn (1974, pp. 25–78) called SLON "GULAG's *alma mater*". The Archipelago's extreme isolation was the basic attraction for its transformation into a maximum security prison:

> [I]t was such a good place, cut off from communication with the outside world for half a year at a time. You couldn't be heard from there, no matter how loud you shouted (Solzhenitsyn, 1973, p. 462).

In 1937, SLON was reorganized as STON (Solovetsky Prison of Special Designation), and prisoners were kept there for two more years.

From 1939 to 1957, the islands were used by the Soviet Navy for training purposes. Only in 1967 were the Solovetsky islands recognized as a unique historical, cultural and natural site, when the Museum Preserve was created. The museum includes about 170 archeological, historical and architectural monuments and memorable places. Since that time, tourists have had the possibility to observe the island, but still access to Solovki was restricted for foreign visitors. In 1990, after having been closed for 70 years, the Monastery was inaugurated again and re-opened. Since then, the Solovetsky islands have become a focus for global pilgrimage. About 30 monks permanently live and work there.

Solovetsk is all about isolation. This is the place where all its components — location, people, nature, culture and tradition — conjure up the same idea that of the transformation of the human mind. This is the place where different epochs are focused: neolithic labyrinths, an Orthodox monastery and a Soviet concentration camp. Perhaps there is nowhere else in the world where such an unlikely combination of features is found in such a small land area. The mixture of great history, Orthodox tradition, extreme isolation, challenging weather and the spirit of a holy place makes Solovki an attractive contemporary tourist destination.

Tourism Characteristics

Most tourists coming to Solovki are eager to see the Monastery, but this is only one of the features that attract people to the islands. The microclimate of the Archipelago and its challenging weather conditions makes certain type of people to come back there again and again. It is due to, or in spite of, the weather that the islands are so popular among American, German and Finnish tourists, who comprise the lion's share of incoming visitors.

The islands lie only some 150 km south of the Arctic Circle, and one should expect frigid climate along with poor nature. In fact, winters are not that severe because of the warming influence of the Norwegian Current, a northern arm of the Gulf Stream. Temperatures get as low as −15° to −20° Celsius, and strong frosts are un-typical. But winters are long and windy. For six months, the islands are practically isolated from the rest of the world. Polar nights bring a peculiar beauty to the place, but there are only a few experts on site to appreciate their true value: there are less than a thousand local inhabitants, and winter tourism is grossly under-developed.

In contrary, summers are normally very short, windy and rainy. The average temperature during summer is not more than +12°C, with the highest temperatures of around 15°C expected around September. The summer sun shines almost permanently: the longest day in June lasts 21 h 56 min — exactly as long as the longest night in December (Boguslavsky, 1971).

Ninety percent of all the tourists visit Solovetsk during summer. This is also an effect of poor access infrastructure: other than small airplanes, the only means of public transport available is cruise ships, able to carry up to 200 tourists per trip.

There is even a botanical garden on the islands — the northernmost one. But the climate is hardly the main reason for people who choose Solovetsk as summer destination. What they value most is its remoteness and isolation, and the image of a 'holy place', while the challenging weather is just an essential part of such image. The influence of orthodox religion that requires suffering for the purification of the soul harmoniously fits with the natural environment of the islands and reinforces its particular brand.

Tourists to the Solovetsky islands can be divided into several types: group tourists, mostly foreign, coming to Solovki as a part of so-called Northern cruises (which include Norway, Finland and Northern Russia); pilgrims and volunteers coming to the island in small groups and usually staying there at least for a couple of weeks, working at the Monastery or the Botanical Garden for food and accommodation; there are city men, usually from Moscow and other big cities, who consider Solovki as a trendy place to visit; and individuals simply looking for peace, isolation and quietness. What unites all these groups is a wish to experience something totally different from a typical tourist destination. To compare: 3–4 days tour to Solovki costs as much as a week's tour to Cyprus or Greece. It means that people expect to get as much value as possible in such a short time. And, if in the case of warm islands tourism, the main attributes are sun, beaches and fun, this type of extreme tourism provides divine inspiration, ability to stay along with the thoughts, virgin nature and lack of civilization, packaged and framed by suitable harsh weather conditions.

Cold Water Island Tourism

Although Solovki is considered to be one of the most isolated and remote tourism destinations in Russia, tourism is becoming one of its main industries. In 2003, there were more than 30,000 summer tourists, a quarter of them were pilgrims coming with the monastery pass. Taking into account that there are only 990 local residents, this number is considerable. Such tourist flows need to be regulated, and the question of regulation is twofold: on one hand, to prevent an erosion of the natural environment and to keep the place isolated and quiet (which, after all, is what makes the place attractive to the tourists in the first place) and on the other to attract capital in order to develop the tourist industry, and support the amenities and products that the tourists expect as part of their stay.

In order to better this situation, an agreement between the Museum and the Monastery was struck in 2001, restricting tourist flows. According to the agreement, the Museum freely allows pilgrims and monastery volunteers to access the Museum's objects, but the visitors are divided into small groups and a strict time slot is allocated in order to avoid overloading. There are also rules of attending and behaving on the Solovetsky islands (Solovestky Local Administration, 1999). Thus, visiting some of the islands for tourism purposes is only allowed with prior permission from the Solovetsky Museum and in organized groups. Visiting some islands of the Archipelago for tourism purposes is strictly forbidden (*ibid.* clause 2). These regulations are made to safeguard the nature of the islands, and its forests in particular.

Solovetsk is not a mass tourism destination. According to the Monastery representative, Archimandrite Josef:

> [O]vergrowth of tourism flows and preservation of divine spirit of the island are incompatible. Nobody even thinks of converting Solovetsk into a trendy resort where the White Sea shore is full of restaurants and … the sky above the Monastery's towers is crossed by para-gliders (International symposium, 2003).

Solovki does need more tourists — all parties agree on that proposition since tourists are seen as the main source of income for the islands. But the type of tourists is an issue of discussion between the local administration, the Monastery and the Museum. Harmony has been an asset of the island for centuries, but what harmony can be achieved between nature and business?

Questions of pollution, erosion and ecosystem balance on the islands do not arise, since there are no mass tourist flows; the main concerns rather have to do with the rational use of natural resources and the preservation of cultural objects. Moreover, tourism is still seen as the hoped-for solution to the development problem by attracting investors and therefore capital to the islands. The situation on Solovki is quite deplorable: there is neither enough financing nor enough qualified responsible persons to control the islands' ecology or to restore and renovate cultural objects. Although some efforts are taken by the Monastery, they are not sufficient and the budget allocated to the islands is unable to cover all needed expenses.

Moreover, there is a real threat of destroying the remains of ancient objects. Some new buildings are built literally on human bones — for example, the building of an administration unit took place on an ancient burial ground. Infrastructure could harm the remains and heritage of the past.

There are still no paved roads, no cars and no gas stations on the islands. Tourists can rent bikes while, for senior tourists and big groups, buses are organized from the mainland. As Vasily Matonin, resident island historian and poet, puts it: "Solovki is either the Monastery or the camp, but in any case it is a cemetery, where discos or parties are intolerable"

(Matonin, 2005). The regulation of tourist flows, in spite of growing popularity, is the main concern shared by the Monastery, Museum and islands' local administration.

Access

Solovetsk is a special place, and in order to access it, one needs to overcome some logistic difficulties. The remoteness of the islands is still an advantage in preserving natural and cultural objects from industrialization and commercialization, but there is a growing interest in creating more convenient and comfortable facilities for Solovetsky guests.

Yet, even before that the question of access must be addressed. Isolated from the mainland by water and ice, the islands — as well as islanders — have almost no connection with the world beyond, especially during winter. There is a ferry service between the mainland and the island during summer time, but it is too expensive for the local population, not to mention small airplanes. As for the long winter, when the sea is full of floating ice, the only feasible (and expensive) form of transportation is by air. So the locals experience isolation for almost 5 months out of every twelve. This situation also affects the transport of food and supplies. Owing to high transportation costs, the prices of goods on the islands are up to 40% higher than the mainland's.

There are three main ways to get to Solovetsk: from Karelian Kem by boat, from Arkhangelsk by air or boat and from Murmansk by boat. The trip is time and money consuming; moreover, if you are travelling by yourself, there is no guarantee that there will be places available on the boats when arriving from Moscow or Petrozavodsk to Kem or Murmansk. There is an ongoing construction of two new passenger lines to Solovetsk from Karelia. As for air transport, there are flights from Arkhangelsk to Solovetsky islands several times per week. Solovetsky airport has been reconstructed and now it is able to receive 50-seater airplanes. There are also irregular charter helicopter flights from Petrozavodsk or Arkhangelsk to Solovetsk. They may be a more convenient and faster means of transport, but are very expensive: it would cost over US$3,000 to charter a helicopter for a return trip.

As for big cruise vessels — the main means of transportation for big foreign groups — all of them require Russian Government permission for each call, which takes few months to get and for sure complicates access to the islands for foreign tourists. Some efforts have been made by shipping agents together with the administration of Arkhangelsk region to simplify this process, but the Government has so far turned down their proposals.

It is unlikely that the situation will change in the near future. There is no developed infrastructure on the islands; the only justification for improving the transportation system is the tourism industry; yet, the small tourism agencies providing services to Solovetsk do not have enough capacity to deal with transport problems; and the local administration considers the current situation as appropriate. Some enthusiastic tourists even consider these difficulties as an integral part of the 'Solovetsky adventure' and fundamental features of their tourist experience.

Tourism-Related Business

The quality of tourist packages does not depend only on transportation and inner island facilities but also on the quality of service providers. Even though the islands' capacity is limited and the tourist market is not large, there are various companies offering tours to Solovetsk. The islands' economy strongly depends on tourism.

Apart from the collection of seaweed, there are no businesses other than tourism on Solovetsk. So, for the local community, tourists are the main source of income. This means that the activities of the local small tour operators determine the development of the islands. Although the competition is tough, the policies and practices of most tour operators are quite similar. There are 6 hotels on the islands, but the quality of services is still to be improved, while the prices are high since demand continues to grow year after year. In 2002, the first winter tour was offered. Tour operators are trying to create a new image of Solovetsk — concentrating on the challenging natural attractiveness of the island and its typical northern environment rather than on cultural tourism.

There is a strong attempt to brand Solovetsk as 'the Northern Pearl', and this is being widely used to attract tourists. Thanks to the promotional efforts of tourism companies, Solovetsk is becoming a popular tourism destination for those interested in traditional Russian style relaxation, including sauna, swimming in a lake and playing billiards. These people are ready to pay, but they expect high-quality service and, as the result, do not care much about nature and traditions. If this tendency will be kept, Solovetsk might lose its real spiritual value, a feature that has helped to differentiate this location from all other northern destinations.

Boon and Bane of Isolation

It is this spirituality, which gives the islands their greatest competitive advantage. People going there expect the unexpected: whether from the environment or from the human services provided. That the poor infrastructure and transportation system are not deliberate, but a consequence of separation, remoteness, lack of funds and facilities, is almost incidental. Solovetsk is famous for its remoteness but at the same time severely curtailed by it. In this age of technology and communication, a place without an Internet café or a permanent hot water supply, with squirrels asking for food and silent monks passing by is of certain interest even for those who are just curious to visit a famous Monastery, without bothering much about history and culture. As for the others, pilgrims in particular, Solovetsk will always be a place to come back to over and over again. This image — of a holy, an orthodox and a mysterious place — is the image of Solovetsk. This is the reason why people visit, the reason why they are ready to suffer low-quality services, Arctic weather, sharp winds and mosquitoes. And thanks to this image, Solovetsk can develop its own tourism strategy.

Conflicts of Interest

Not all parties welcome Solovki's growing popularity. The islanders, acutely aware of their small numbers compared to the hordes of tourist invaders, are afraid that their isolation is coming to an end. There is a great dilemma: tourists as a means of income *versus* tourists as a threat to quietness and natural beauty of the place.

People living on the islands can be called 'local' only to some extent: most of them have come to Solovetsk since the 1990s, after the islands had become an open area. Most islanders are working for the Museum or Botanical garden, since there are no other employment opportunities on the islands. They came to Solovetsk looking for a quiet place, for an almost otherworldly existence, and they have found it there. Island life passes slowly, and for most inhabitants this is the main asset.

On the other hand, locals also understand that, without tourists, the islands will fall quickly into decay and ruin. Local salaries are low compared to other regions. Almost every resident is in some way engaged in the tourism industry: some are working at hotels, some are tourist guides, some sell fish, berries or mushrooms, and almost all of the locals offer accommodation at relatively cheap rates.

There are no conflicts between the local population and tourists or between locals and monks: Solovetsk is a peaceful place, and people here are generally hospitable and hearty, although, to some extent, they might consider tourists as "cash cows". There are, however, two types of power on the Solovetsky islands — temporal and church power, and three main authorities: the local administration, the Museum and the Monastery. All these see themselves as the sole masters of the place — the only head that will rule the Solovk body. Thus, they are striving to advance their own goals without bothering to coordinate with each other. Museum director Mikhail Lopatkin sees the islands as a major tourist centre:

> The trouble is that everything here is associated only with the monastery while the Solovki are much more than that. They should be promoted as a unique territory. Thus far, there is only crude material: It should be made into a saleable product. This is what we are going to work on. Design is of paramount importance: There should be a strong branding exercise (Vylegzhanin, 2003).

Archimandrite Josef, superior of the Solovki monastery, has an entirely different view:

> The Solovki have always belonged to the Church, and this right has been reaffirmed and extended by all Russian Tsars .... We see the Solovki museum as part of the Solovki monastery. Of course, there is no place for uncontrolled, wild tourism on the islands (*ibid.*).

The local administration is responsible for the entire social and associated infrastructure, which constitutes the lion's share of problems on the Archipelago. Yet, the administration has no effective leverage, whether economic (the district administration budget is much smaller than that of the museum) or administrative.

As for the national government, it has other, more pressing problems to address. The press called Solovetsk "No Man's Island" (*ibid.*), perhaps as an allusion to its treatment as a political vacuum. President Vladimir Putin did become the first Russian leader after Peter the Great to visit the islands in 2003. Still, little has changed. One Presidential visit is not enough to change life at Solovetsk. Besides, some local residents believe that change will simply take care of itself: business and tourism development will go on regardless, and facilitating these processes may cause tension among different political and business parties. This remote piece of land is of interest both to the state (as a product for increasing Russia's competitiveness as an international tourism destination) as well as to the regional authorities (as a magnet for attracting capital to the region).

The Solovetsky Islands remain so far a most beautiful site with its polar location, extreme climate, remoteness and isolation together with its fascinating nature, divine spirit of the Monastery and secrets of the past.

References

Boguslavsky, G. A. (1971). *The Solovetsky islands*. Arkhangelsk: North-West Publishing House.

Frumenkov, G. G. (1975). *The Solovetsky monastery and defence of Belomorie in XVI-XIX centuries*. Arkhangelsk: North-West Publishing House.

International symposium. (2003). *Solovetsky: Future insights: May-June 2003*, Solovetsky. Symposium materials. www.museum.ru/N13534 (accessed on 20/10/2005).

Kartashev, A. V. (1991). *Essays on Russian church history — Vol. 2*. Moscow: Nauka.

Matonin, V. (2005). Business on Solovetsky should have spiritual basis. *The Business Class Magazine*, no. 26, Arkhangelsk, 11th July.

Shickman, A. P. (1997). *Public figures in native history: A reference book*. Moscow: ACT-LTD.

Solovestky Local Administration. (1999). *Rules for visiting Forests in the Solovetsky Region*. Approved by decision of the Head of Local Administration, Solovetsky district, 12th June.

Solzhenitsyn, A. I. (1973). *The Gulag Archipelago 1918–1956: An experiment in literary investigation — Vol. 1*. New York: Harper and Row.

Solzhenitsyn, A. I. (1974). *The Gulag Archipelago 1918–1956: An experiment in literary investigation — Vol. 2*. New York: Harper and Row.

UNESCO. (2005). *World heritage list*. Solovetsky Islands entry. http://whc.unesco.org/en/list/632 (accessed on 20/10.2005).

Vinogradov, N. N. (1927). *Solovetsky labyrinths, their origin and place in similar prehistoric architectural monuments — Volume IV*. Solovetsky: Materials of Solovetsky local lore community.

Vylegzhanin, R. (2003). No man's island. *The Moscow News*. no. 14. Available at: http://mn.ru/issue.php?2003-14-59 (accessed on 20/10/2005).

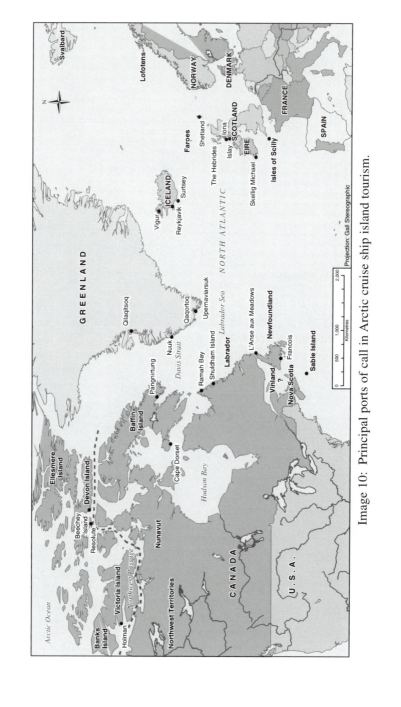

Image 10: Principal ports of call in Arctic cruise ship island tourism.

Chapter 13

Arctic Cruise Ship Island Tourism

Callum Thomson and Jane Sproull Thomson

Introduction

After a two day delay due to bad weather up north, we were finally in the Arctic and anxious to catch up on an itinerary that would take us from Resolute to Devon and Baffin Islands to West Greenland. So here we were, in the semi-light of a summer Arctic night, with parkas hastily thrown on over pyjamas at 2 a.m., travelling by Zodiac over calm, moonlit seas to a gravel beach on Beechey Island, Sir John Franklin's first overwintering stop in 1845. On the shore we could see headstones marking the graves of three of Franklin's men, the first of 128 to die on this most tragic of expeditions to find the Northwest Passage.

Thus began one recent trip on board a Canadian-chartered Russian-owned converted cruise ship. Venturing into remote inlets and squeezing between islands unapproachable by larger cruise liners, these 'adventure' cruises have become increasingly popular with travellers seeking a distinctive sailing experience, and are surely the ideal way to travel among the cold ocean islands of the world. The physical footprint and onboard facilities of the small expedition cruise ship are virtually the same across the board. Almost all are former research vessels or ferries converted to carry approximately 100 passengers, all are ice-strengthened or icebreaker class, and all share a pared-down approach to luxury cruising, emphasizing personal service over amenities, and learning over mindless entertainment.

There are fewer than a dozen companies operating small-ship cruises to remote areas, and most own only one or two ships. However, many travel operators purchase blocks of cabins on these cruises and sell them under their own logo. Examples of this are the many museum, gallery, or society-sponsored expeditions, which fill up the ship owners' cabins while generating income for the organizers. Some tour companies are eventually successful enough with these to charter the entire ship for a cruise tailored to their own clientele.

Much of the passenger experience hinges on the opportunity to quickly and efficiently land passengers by Zodiac (small inflatable boat) in remote locations and small harbours. Because it is expensive to operate in remote areas and carry a large crew and staff relative to passenger numbers, cabin rates aboard these ships are considerably more costly than the average hotel-ship sunshine cruise. Tellingly, expedition cruise companies enjoy a comfortable returning-passenger ratio. Veteran cruise company *Adventure Canada* estimates that between 35 and 40 per cent of their passengers on any trip have sailed with them before (Bradley-Swan, 2004), while relative newcomer *Polar Star Expeditions* found that some passengers on recent voyages had already taken up to four trips with them (Filbee, 2004).

Small-ship cruises offer a unique ecotourism opportunity. On board is a small, captive audience sequestered together for two or three weeks, consisting of well-educated people predisposed to support conservation objectives. Add to this a mixed staff of trained interpreters and university- or museum-based educators expert in a variety of subject areas, and sprinkle in encounters with whales and polar bears, gannets, puffins and skuas, caribou and muskoxen, a variety of onshore visits to hard-to-reach destinations including World Heritage Sites, tiny communities with huge hearts, and other unique points of interest, and you have the makings of an educational vacation experience available in no other format.

The Cold Water Islands Experience

The islands of the North Atlantic visited by adventure cruise lines share some similarities, but each is unique and these comparative characteristics are of great interest to visitors. All share a severe environment, a fauna and flora unique to Northern regions including migratory terrestrial birds, waterfowl and seabirds, seasonal and resident sea mammals, a few species of land mammals, a tundra-like ground-hugging vegetation as well as an exciting history.

The climate in these northern oceanic island regions often yields high winds, erosion and severe limits on the height and variety of those few trees able to germinate and grow. Agriculture is challenging if not impossible, and only the hardiest of domestic animals can be successfully raised. Often, wild animals such as reindeer and eider ducks are farmed instead. On Vigur, a tiny island off northwest Iceland, crevices in the garden walls and stone boxes built by the island's residents are home to dozens of eider, whose soft down is culled from the nests, cleaned and shipped off for making quilts, pillows and parkas.

Although their human populations (if any) differ in origin, all these islands have been subject to or influenced by waves of exploration and/or immigration, especially from the Nordic countries. The result is a thrilling if tragic history of clashing cultures, Viking raids and settlement, whaling and sealing disasters, and vanished adventurers, which cries out to be narrated and shown off to visitors from cruise ships. Cruise themes, such as *On the Trail of the Vikings*, are popular as they help to link northern island and mainland destinations in a cultural and geographic continuum. Here, the lecturer and passengers trace the beginnings of the great Viking adventure from Norway to the northern and western isles of Scotland, moving northward as Norse confidence in their shipbuilding and navigation skills increases, arriving in the Faeroe Islands by 860 A.D. Proceeding northwestwardly across another 400 miles of open ocean to Iceland, the Norse set up small farms, importing sheep, cattle and horses, and accessing the resources of the terrestrial and marine environments around them. Their adventurous spirit saw them extend their dominion to southwest Greenland and, briefly and much less successfully, to northern Newfoundland and Vinland where further colonization was thwarted by resident aboriginal groups.

Following the wake of the Norse longships, though in somewhat more comfort and security, provides a unique and memorable experience for the expedition cruise passenger. The experience is made all the more informative by the ship's naturalists and historians who describe the life history of the mammals, birds and geographic features encountered enroute, and explain how they were exploited by the Norse and aboriginal peoples.

The *Viking Trail* theme is supplanted elsewhere among the cold ocean islands by other themes linking the destinations. *The Search for the Northwest Passage* follows the story of 500 years of daring and often tragic exploits through the islands of the North Atlantic and Arctic oceans. *Inuit Art and Culture* traces the evolution of art styles and media and the people responsible for creating them from the pre-historic period to the present, with visits to some of the most interesting and productive communities like Cape Dorset and Pangnirtung on Baffin Island. Cruises like these are appreciated by art collectors who relish the opportunity not only to study and collect unique original artwork, but also to meet the artists and learn at first hand about their way of life. When a cruise itinerary includes visits to the well-known art centres on Baffin Island, or Holman on Victoria Island, it is customary for the small expedition ships to offer the onboard expertise of an art historian. Typically, lecturers/study leaders provide an introduction before arrival at the anticipated stop, conduct an informal and personalized tour once ashore, and offer advice or moral support while exploration or business is underway.

The storyteller may weave into each of the themes the history of the peoples who have made their living among the same islands and iceberg-studded bays for thousands of years, the European explorers seeking the riches of the Orient or the glory of the Pole, whalers who strove to ply their trade in the same waters, and today's adventurers, the oil, gas and mineral exploration crews. All face the same environmental obstacles and call on strength, prowess, leadership and resilience, although many of the Europeans, too arrogant to adopt indigenous skin clothing and boots, locally available foods and travel strategies, died in the pursuit of their goals.

Knowledgeable expedition staff can connect the region's islands, waterways, fauna, geology and cultures through these and other cruise themes. However, each island is unique, with its own special set of attributes and attractions. Iona, best known for its links to early Christianity in the British Isles, is also the resting place for many of the historic kings of Scotland, and a place of breathtaking beauty: the finest white shell sand beaches lapped by turquoise seas; a brilliant mass of tiny *machair* flowers; a backdrop of calls from dozens of species of terrestrial and marine birds.

In contrast, on the subarctic Shuldham Island and neighbouring Kikkertarsuaq (Big Island) in the mouth of Saglek Bay, northern Labrador, the history buff can gain an impression of a harsher North American native life in the shadow of the Torngat Mountains and on the edge of the Labrador Sea, frozen for eight months of the year. Here, aboriginal people and possibly the Norse on their way to and from Vinland hunted seal and walrus at the precarious ice edge, pursued the caribou on the tundra terraces and fished in glacially cold streams for arctic char. They left their marks in the form of longhouses, tent rings and semi-subterranean sod houses, meat caches, foxtraps and graves, *nangissat* (lines of flat slabs used in a game of balance and stamina) and kayak supports, myriad stone tools made of the local chert (a hard sedimentary rock), and tiny soapstone amulets and figurines portraying polar bears, snowy owls and humans (Sproull Thomson & Thomson, 1991). Here also, geology buffs relish the opportunity to walk on 3.8 billion-year-old gneiss (high-grade metamorphic rock). Along with outcrops on Greenland's west coast, they are among the oldest surface rocks on Earth. The birders will check off a few more species from the tundra, shore, bay and pond, while the avid hiker can stretch the legs over lonely beaches, bogs and bedrock.

Beechey Island, off the southwest coast of Devon Island in the Arctic archipelago, holds a special place in every northern historian's heart as the beginning of the end of Sir John Franklin's last Arctic expedition, 1845–1847. Its graves, traces of the ship's forge brought to shore for the winter and the numerous badly soldered tin cans thought by Beattie, Geiger, and Atwood (2004) to have contributed to the demise of the expedition through lead poisoning, need little interpretation. Northumberland House, a storehouse and refuge established during the Franklin Search period, is situated a brisk walk down the beach. Here, the ship's archaeologist has a formidable challenge: thousands of relics from the Franklin Search expeditions lie scattered around the ruins of the wooden building: coal, barrel staves and hoops, and the ubiquitous rusted tin food cans. The archaeologist is kept busy monitoring the traffic in order to prevent damage to these fragile artefacts.

Qilakitsoq ("the sky is low") on the west coast of Greenland is the 15th century burial place of eight Greenlandic Inuit women and children who were mummified in their cold dry environment. The bodies were excavated in the 1970s and removed for study and ulti-mately displayed in the Greenland National Museum at Nuuk. Visiting the burial cyst is a highly emotional experience, evoking empathetic responses not easily duplicated in a museum visit. (When the ground is wet, however, the passage of dozens of pairs of boots can leave a long-lasting and ugly scar on the soil. This is a common problem at fragile sites, and one that requires monitoring, avoidance when conditions dictate, and perhaps the provision of pathways and barriers.)

Visitors are intrigued to note that the Greenlandic Inuit are today occupying many of the same locations in southwest Greenland's fjord arms where the Norse 1000 years ago successfully raised sheep, goats, cattle and horses, grew winter fodder and exploited the marine environment. The Greenlanders of today also are now raising sheep for their meat and wool, and tending their flocks on horseback. Visitors are invited to inspect new or improved plant species being raised and demonstrated at the Upernaviarsuk experimental farm near Qaqortoq, southwest Greenland, where the isolation offers unique opportunities for agriculture and ecological experimentation with minimal risk of contamination from an adjacent and more populated mainland.

On an island, one senses the opportunity to be able to finish the project, to take it all in. Here, most human settlement will be located near the shoreline. Coastal paths thus offer an opportunity for visitors to walk to archaeological sites, viewpoints and other attractions along a pathway that (like doing a circuit on a ship's deck) will eventually bring them back to where they started. Unlike sunspots, cold ocean islands do not normally cater to hordes of tourists. The visitors to these islands see people conducting normal daily activities un-related to their visit. The tourists observe family and community lives in a setting far removed from North American or European urban experience, and are often invited to join in the activities.

In cases where guest accommodation is non-existent, it may be *only* the cruise ship pas-senger or camper who *can* visit. And in the extreme case of restricted islands, such as Nova

Scotia's Sable Island, only those with ship accommodation can spend the night in the island's vicinity.

The Small-Ship Experience

The small size and shallow draft of these ships allow them to navigate deep into the fjords and island archipelagos of the cold oceans, and to approach close to shore. Many islands are accessible only by ship or helicopter, and most small islands have few roads and thus no traffic congestion. Conversely, many islands offer plenty of good anchorages for private watercraft, and those developed for tourism often have jetties or wharves where boats and sometimes medium-sized ships can tie up alongside. Passengers are then a short stroll away from settlements or tourist sites.

Small adventure cruise ships are like isolated islands themselves, with tiny populations, limited recreational opportunities, environmental challenges and unavoidable expenses. Like islands, they are bounded by water, structured by resource-users and resource-providers, but at the same time at least partly self-sufficient. The notion of *remoteness* is a critical attraction of islands, both those terrestrial islands anchored to the sea floor and those steel-clad ships bobbing about on the surface. Many tourists, especially those who dislike being surrounded by large numbers of other visitors, are lured by the sense of private access that a small island offers.

In many ways, the small expedition cruise ships provide the same sense of privacy. One might think that these ships are small and crowded, but they generally are not. Even out on the front deck by the bridge where people like to watch wildlife, there are seldom more than 15 or 20 people around, and frequently just one or two after the novelty of the fauna and scenery wears off. The crowded times are meals in the dining room and the lectures, when there are often nearly 100 people all eating or listening. Otherwise, sailing with 60–100 passengers, 5–10 staff and 20–40 crew, it is easy to find an isolated corner of the deck, or a quiet nook on the bridge during the midnight shift, or a quiet corner in the library to curl up with a book, apart from one's cabin. On shore, there is always a sheltered little bay or beach that anyone wishing some solitude can call one's own (although in polar bear country this will cause anxiety attacks among the bear monitor/lecture staff who prefer to know where everyone is).

The small expedition cruise ship also functions as a social organism, with all the potential for relationships and shared experiences present in any small island community. Friendship is fostered by the rigours of the weather, the physical demands, the compressed itinerary and the hectic pace: all of which throws people together in support of each other.

The ship's social order is structured along clear organizational lines. The Captain and officers, deck and engine room crew, and the hotel and housekeeping staff stay on the ship for months at a time and interact more closely with each other than with other groups. The passengers, who may also organize themselves along various lines, depending on their place of origin, age or affiliation (e.g., Elderhostel or other groups), form the closest bonds among themselves. The lecture and expedition staff is the exception, freely crossing the lines, as they must interact closely with the ship's crew and also get to know everyone in the passenger group to ensure that the paying customers feel secure and are well looked after. There is generally no formal separation among these groups, and in fact many lasting friendships are made between and among their members.

Many of the passengers on small-ship cruises to remote, cold-water areas are relatively well-off, highly educated and ecologically aware people who feel they have "done it all". They have visited the Caribbean, owned condos in Hawaii, been on safari in East Africa and cruised the Galapagos. They are seeking experiences on less-travelled ground. These fortunate few are joined by less wealthy individuals willing to part with savings in order to experience these opportunities at least once in their lifetime. Neither group may yet have been to the remote Scottish islands, Iceland or the Arctic archipelago. They know that these small ships are well staffed and offer interesting educational programmes in subjects they may know little about. They know that staff will ensure they have companionship and personal attention. There will be a full-time doctor on board. Meals will be nutritious, balanced, varied and served at regular times, and passengers with dietary concerns will be able to elect small portions and individualized requests, a healthy situation quite different from the undifferentiated, 24-h binge buffets available on other cruise ships.

Because of this high level of attention and care, increasing numbers of elderly North Americans are opting to travel nearly full-time with these small ships. Lindquist and Golub (2004) opine that cruising might offer an attractive alternative to nursing homes for the well-off elderly American needing assisted care (see also Staples, 2004). We have noted the beginnings of this trend on some of the more luxurious small vessels in the Arctic, particularly those run by American cruise firms. The cost is similar to high-end nursing facility care in the U.S.A., and the experience infinitely preferable.

Passengers must be flexible, however, and it helps to have a sense of adventure. These trips are truly *expeditions* and despite careful planning, things often go awry. Just as unexpectedly extreme weather can play havoc with a herd of sheep in south Greenland caught outside in a snow storm, the weather, along with other factors, can also change plans for expedition landings or Zodiac cruises. The Expedition Leader and staff must then call on all their skills and resources to complete the itinerary while protecting their charges from harm, to find interesting alternatives to scheduled activities, and to maintain the reputation of their industry and, more importantly, their company as true purveyors of expedition cruises, with the quality of surprising experiences that the term implies. A wee-hours landing on Beechy Island after two days of weather delays, en route to another more distant visit in the early morning, was one such solution. (In that instance, anticipating perhaps a dozen or so takers, the staff was astounded when approximately 100 sleepy heads emerged following the midnight Zodiac call. Back aboard by 3 a.m, most appeared again for a pre-landing breakfast at 7!)

Sometimes things go so well that even staff expectations are exceeded. One cruise brought an unexpectedly calm sea and bright moonlit night, prompting our energetic Expedition Leader to take advantage of the conditions. Even though we had already made three landings that day, he called ahead to a distillery on the Hebridean Isle of Islay and talked the manager into a tour of the facility, with landings *starting* at 9 p.m. Almost all of the weary passengers, some of the ship's crew and all expedition staff clambered once more into the Zodiacs, casting longing eyes at their comfortable cabins, and set off for shore. Three hours later, after meandering through tanks and vats filled with aromatic varieties of alcoholic brews, access to a bountiful gift shop uncluttered by other tourists, and several sample bottles of 9, 12 and 15-year-old single malt whisky, the happy group wove their way back to the ship over obsidian seas reflecting a full moon, with a magical escort of dolphins.

Environmental, Social and Safety Issues

The principal reason for signing on to an expedition cruise is to encounter remote regions that are difficult to visit in any other way. The challenge is to encourage and support such tourism, and create a benefit to the region, while avoiding harm to the very attractions people want to see. In such cold regions, the flora and fauna as well as the archaeological sites are highly sensitive to damage from visitation. The environment itself is fragile and easily disturbed. How do we allow 50–100 people to photograph a polar bear without stressing either the bear or the photographers? How can we visit a remote historic site without having someone dislodge a wall rock or trample an artefact? How is it possible to conduct a hike over the tundra without pummelling the delicate flora or cutting a new path that will endure for decades?

One advantage of the 100-passenger cruise ship visit to communities or sites is that it is of short duration: generally less than 4 h, after which the plant, animal or human host community can relax and return to its natural state. In contrast, the impact of a shipload of 500–2000 passengers can be devastating. As global warming continues to melt the Arctic ice, we might expect more of the behemoths to take advantage of the improved access, potentially placing an even greater strain on the environment and communities.

Small communities are also subject to negative effects when a planned landing at a remote village must be cancelled at the last minute because of weather or unanticipated scheduling problems. In such instances, local operators may be left with unrecoverable expenses, not to mention the disappointed anticipation of local residents who may never have seen a cruise ship before.

The responsible company and its expedition staff attempt to anticipate and address the challenges. Most lay out and monitor strict guidelines for conduct on board ship and Zodiac, and particularly on shore. An introductory address to passengers asks for adherence to basic rules: do not approach animals in a way that alters their behaviour, do not congregate in groups when traversing the tundra, stay within sightlines of staff, do not give money or gifts to children, take nothing but photographs, and leave only pleasant memories behind. The exception to the latter is tourism dollars, as both the ship's operators and the passengers are encouraged to enrich local economies through the local purchase of services and souvenirs. It is only by maximizing local benefits and minimizing negative effects that cruise visits will continue to be welcomed by government authorities and local residents.

When new archaeological sites are discovered in the course of expedition landings at previously unexplored locations, the onboard archaeologist records information with the assistance of the passengers and later submits a full report to the heritage authorities. This offers an opportunity to educate passengers about correct conduct near archaeological resources: avoid dislodging structural elements, do not move or remove anything, take pictures only. In this way, the cruise company that has a qualified archaeologist on board contributes significantly to knowledge of past cultures, particularly in remote island areas unlikely to be targeted for research by cash-strapped archaeologists.

Natural and human disaster planning, beyond the normal safety drills, has become a major factor for small-ship cruise companies operating in Northern waters in recent years. Following on the heels of events such as the 2001 outbreak of the foot-and-mouth disease in Britain, many planned cruise landings around the British Isles had to be altered or cancelled at the height of the spring and summer tourism season, with devastating results for the tourism industry as well as farmers. British authorities have since undertaken studies and outlined new procedures which restrict travel in remote regions (Miller & Ritchie, 2004).

Anti-terrorism measures following the 11 September 2001 attacks have included restricted access to the bridge on some small ships operating within North American waters, access hitherto unfettered and one of the anticipated pleasures for the small-ship passenger. In turn, this has resulted in reduced interaction between crew and passengers, impacting a key social element of the cruise experience. Additionally, passengers and staff boarding vessels for the first time are now subjected to screening by metal detectors and baggage searches, and Customs and Immigration officials in Canada and elsewhere are becoming more insistent in meeting ships at their first port of entry to check passports.

The Expedition Staff

The expedition lecturer is a highly privileged person. A few make the major part of their living on board cruise ships; some are semi-retired or have other means of support at universities and museums; and others, particularly the Expedition Leaders, may spend equal time at head office planning new itineraries, contacting shore agents and guides, hiring staff and working to ensure that the ship and activities all meet and exceed environmental and safety standards. Lecturers are paid and their expenses covered. On board ship, lecturing staff dine with the passengers and are provided a comfortable (shared) cabin. They accompany the passengers throughout the trip and enjoy the same experiences. Because they combine the roles of tour guide, personal companion and boat driver, the character, skill and knowledge of the expedition staff directly affects the quality of the passengers' cruise experience. It requires months of unpaid time to research and prepare new one-hour lectures, and staff might also complain among themselves about the 12+ hour workdays, the 7-day weeks, the multiple stints on board ship, all without a break. Some suffer repeated bouts of seasickness. However, they do it because they love it, and this is evident in their interactions with passengers.

The environment in the polar and cold ocean regions adds to the experience. There is nothing quite so invigorating for staff as being lowered in a Zodiac from the top deck of a cruise ship at 6 a.m., being cast adrift in swells a metre or more high, struggling to start a balky outboard, and then maintaining an impossibly level platform onto which the passengers step with varying degrees of aplomb from the gangway for a pre-breakfast outing. With perhaps 10 passengers, the Zodiac meanders among sparkling icebergs reflecting the rising sun or along the foot of cliffs several hundred metres high alive with nesting seabirds, with thousands of them whizzing by the bow on their way to or from the feeding grounds, or lands on an unknown island beach with the anticipation of finding, exploring and recording a new archaeological site several hundreds or thousands of years old.

Sharing those experiences with the passengers, and seeing the exhilaration and wonder on their windblown faces on the way back to a hot breakfast make so worth while the pre-dawn wake-up call, the cold blasty air, and the drenching while holding the Zodiac steady in a swell on a steep beach.

Conclusion

Ultimately, a cold ocean island is a small, enclosed world, where environmental vulnerability is at its most extreme. Adverse weather, pollution, even too much tourism, can destroy an entire ecosystem. The small expedition cruise ship industry strives mightily to avoid contributing to environmental and social problems by advocating and implementing the aspirations of 'green tourism'. Still more can and should be done to improve host community benefits and minimize or avoid all negative environmental effects. The World Wildlife Fund Arctic Programme has developed ten principles for Arctic Tourism and Codes of Conduct for Arctic Tourists and Arctic Tour Operators that expand upon these and other ideals (World Wildlife Fund, n.d.)

Small-ship expeditions to cold ocean islands offer tourists the opportunity to experience a way of life completely different from that of the average urban Westerner. From the Hebridean crofter to the Inuk hunter in Nunavut, the people encountered invariably treasure their difficult environments. Their closely guarded sense of family and community reinforces for the weary cynic, the sense that real human values lie outside of purchasing power. What better way could there be to gain these experiences than by traveling from island to island in the comfort and security of a small expedition cruise ship? The expedition cruise passenger returns enriched, to a home also made richer for his or her travels among the cold ocean islands of the world.

Acknowledgments

Thanks to the numerous Expedition Leaders, other staff and cruise operators for helping us to bring our knowledge and love of the islands and oceans of the North on countless Trails. Most of all, we express our gratitude to the thousands of passengers we have been privileged to meet for allowing us to share our enthusiasm. We encourage you and all adventurers to return to the sea and seek magic among the cold ocean islands.

References

Beattie, O., Geiger, J. G., & Atwood, M. (2004). *Frozen in Time: the Fate of the Franklin Expedition* (2nd ed.). Vancouver: Greystone Books.
Bradley-Swan, C. (2004). Adventure Canada, personal communication.
Filbee, M. (2004). Polar star expeditions, personal communication.
Lindquist, L. A., & Golub, R. M. (2004). Cruise ship care: A proposed alternative to assisted living facilities. *Journal of the American Geriatrics Society*, *52*(11), 1951–1954.

Miller, G. A., & Ritchie, B. W. (2004). Sport tourism in crisis: Exploring the impact of the foot-and-mouth crisis on sport tourism in the UK. In: B. W. Ritchie, & D. Adair (Eds), *Sport tourism: Interrelationships, impacts and issues* (pp. 206–225). Clevedon: Channel View Publications.

Sproull Thomson, J., & Thomson, J. C. (1991). Prehistoric Eskimo art in Labrador. *Inuit Art Quarterly*, *6*(4), 12–18.

Staples, S. (2004). Cruise ships touted as future old-age homes. *The National Post*, Canada, October 27.

World Wildlife Fund. (n.d.). Ten principles for Arctic tourism, code of conduct for Arctic tourists, and code of conduct for tour operators in the Arctic WWF-Arctic Programme, Oslo. www.panda.org/downloads/arctic/codeofconductforarctictourists(eng).pdf and http://www.panda.org/about_wwf/where_we_work/arctic/what_we_do/tourism/tourism_tips.cfm (accessed 20/10/2005).

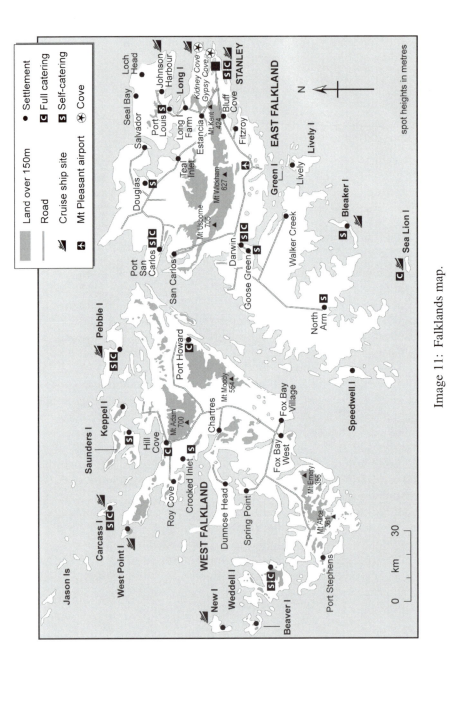

Image 11: Falklands map.

Chapter 14

The Falkland Islands

Stephen A. Royle

Introduction

In Punta Arenas airport at the tip of mainland Latin America, T-shirts on sale enable buyers to boast of having been to *Finisterre*, the world's end. East of this end of the world lie the Falkland Islands. From Punta Arenas every Saturday a flight from Santiago via Puerto Montt, until then a Chilean domestic service, is reincarnated as an international flight to the Falklands, and passengers for the islands must disembark to clear customs and immigration. Once a month the flight includes a leg to Rio Gallegos in Argentina, 483 km off whose coast the islands lie. This service, operated by Lan Chile, is the Falklands' principal commercial access. Their other carrier is the British Royal Air Force (RAF), which accepts civilians on flights from England via Ascension Island about six times a month. This combination i.e. remoteness, difficulty of access, military involvement, and — with limited communications being indicative — poor relations with its nearest neighbour, constrains life in the Falkland Islands including, of course, tourism.

The Falkland Islands comprise two substantial islands, West and East Falkland, and over 700 smaller islands of largely sedimentary and metamorphic origin, mainly quartzite, sandstone and shale. The islands' 12,173 km², combined with a tiny civilian population of 2491 (2001 census; 1989 lived in the town, Stanley) results in low-population density. This, together with the absence of trees, give the islands a spacious feel, especially West Falkland which is less rugged and more rounded than East Falkland, and which has less than 400 residents. The vegetation — principally white grass interspersed with ground hugging shrubs, such as diddle-dee and teaberry, with more substantial tussac grass clumps being confined to coastal areas and especially now, given pastoralism, offshore islets — has to cope with a troublesome climate. The Falklands are at latitude 52°S and, while temperatures are mild with a small annual range (mean daytime temperatures of 2°C in July to 9°C in December), there are persistent strong winds, usually Westrerlies, with a mean of 15 kn, a trial to any organism, vegetable or human, that seeks to elevate itself more than a few centimetres from the surface.

The British probably first sighted the islands in 1592 and landed in 1690, but it was the French who settled first (1764 at Port Louis on East Falkland), and their resultant claim passed through a sale to Spain, and later to Argentina. The British, who had temporarily settled Saunders Island off West Falkland in 1765, sent in a ship to take control of all islands in the archipelago in 1833, after a period of lawlessness in which Port Louis had been destroyed by an American warship. The British moved the capital from Port Louis to the new planned town of Stanley in 1845 and developed the archipelago for sheep ranching (see Royle, 1985, for a brief overview of the early history). The Argentinean claim was never abandoned and in 1982 Argentina, largely for domestic–political reasons, invaded, expelling the British authorities. The British, under Prime Minister Margaret Thatcher who is still revered in the Falklands, countered by sending down a naval Task Force. After ships on both sides had been sunk, the British established a beachhead in the west of East Falkland and troops 'yomped' as the phrase had it (i.e. walked) towards Stanley with engagements at Goose Green and in the mountains to the west of the town amongst a series of clashes. The Argentineans surrendered rather than fight in a major battle for Stanley, and the British resumed control (e.g. Smith, 1984; Middlebrook, 1988).

The Falklands Conflict catapulted the islands onto the world stage and accelerated ongoing modernisation, as Britain had now to be seen to cherish this colonial outpost on which so much blood and treasure had been expended. One change was an extensive programme of land reform that saw the breaking up of many of the huge estates, most owned by expatriate companies, into family farms owned and run by locals. There were 36 farming enterprises in 1979, now there are 90. This reform saw much non-familial labour having to leave the agricultural sector and migrate into Stanley, which as a result and with some immigration from overseas, has grown by about 50% since 1982. The Falklands' economy was until then based on wool production and not, as was popularly believed, on transfer payments from Britain (Shackleton, 1976, 1982). It has now been transformed with fishing, especially for two squid species, *loligo* and the migratory *illex*, becoming dominant, foreign vessels paying for licences to fish within the Falklands Conservation Zone, declared in 1986. The money raised from the licensing accounts for over half government revenue (£25.9 million of an estimated £50.5 million (51.3%) in 2003–2004 (Falkland Islands Government (FIG) 2003)), and has facilitated development and infrastructure projects. In Stanley, most prominent is the community school, which also serves as leisure centre and library, while in Camp (everywhere outside Stanley) the expanding road network is notable. Previously overland journeys were without benefit of roads. The government's Falkland Islands Development Corporation (FIDC) has used some of the income, together with private sector involvement, to promote diversification. Thus, an EU-standard abattoir now enables sheep meat as well as wool to be exported, and textile producers add value to some of the islands' product by making sweaters from local wool.

The Falkland Islands remain under British administration as an Overseas Territory, one of a series in the Atlantic stretching south from Bermuda, incorporating the Turks and Caicos Islands, St. Helena and its two dependencies, Ascension Island and the Tristan da Cunha group, and, moving beyond the Falklands, South Georgia and the South Sandwich Islands, which were separated administratively from the Falklands after the Conflict. Links within the British South Atlantic are functional and not administrative. Ascension is a staging and refuelling post for Falklands traffic coming down the Atlantic, and St. Helena is the source of much of the Falklands' immigrant labour supply. The tiny population of the Falkland Islands rather precludes independence nor would there be any wish for it (Summers, 2003); local suspicions of Argentine ambitions remain strong and the British defensive shield is considered vital. The islands have a British Governor, but are self-ruling with Legislative and Executive Councils. The Governor is obliged to consult the latter in the exercise of his function under the 1985 Constitution. The Falklands are self-supporting, the British pay only for defence, which, with foreign affairs, remains a reserved responsibility.

Tourism to the Falkland Islands

Another diversification product, part of the post-Conflict search for growth in which FIDC was much involved, is tourism. This now vies with agriculture to be the islands' second industry — passenger tax from cruise ships alone brought £300,000 to government coffers in 2003–2004. It is of growing long-term importance as a sustainable sector in an economy otherwise dependent on fickle uncertainties — the breeding and migration of squid and the world market price of wool (see *The Economist*, 2004). The islands' tourism was studied by the author in September 2004. Interviews were held with legislators, tourism officials, managers in tourism companies and providers of tourism services on the ground. Site visits took place to Camp, both in West and East Falkland, as well as in Stanley.

Tourism Categories

Cruise ship passengers comprise the vast majority of Falkland visitors, 34,000 in 2003–2004 (Table 14.1); closer to 50,000 if crew visits are included. This business, dating from 1968, in 2004–2005 saw 39 ships make 85 voyages to the islands. Cruising is seasonal, from October until late March/early April, the southern hemisphere summer providing somewhat warmer weather, calmer seas, longer hours of daylight and being the time when all the migratory species that breed on the islands are present, wildlife being an important factor in Falklands tourism.

There are different types of ships. The biggest are 'luxury' cruisers, as might be seen in the Caribbean, some with over 1000 passengers. Their voyages usually start in mainland Latin America, often incorporating Ushuaia in Argentina, cruise around Tierra del Fuego and come across to the Falkland Islands. Passengers tend to be American and elderly, usually between 60 and 79 years of age. Other ships present 'soft adventure' cruises, catering for a bolder passenger; and finally there are 'expedition' ships, usually under 200 passengers with a younger age profile, certainly under 65 years (Ingham & Summers, 2002), engaged in adventure tours to and beyond the Falklands. One company operating in this market is called Expeditions Antarctica Journeys. An example of its wares is the two 19 day cruises of the 2004–2005 season of M/V *Polar Star*, (1500 t), an 'expedition cruise vessel' accommodating 98 passengers within its ice-hardened hull. Two days in the Falklands at Stanley and New Island are part of the trip:

Table 14.1: Falkland Islands visitor statistics.

	1995–1996	1996–1997	1997–1998	1998–1999	1999–2000	2000–2001	2001–2002	2002–2003	2003–2004
Ships						26	23	24	28
Voyages	26	34	48	55	65	54	59	68	84
Cancelled voyages						10	12	4	9
Mean stay (days)						1.9	2.1	2	1.7
Passengers:									
• Mean per voyage						409	462	404	413
• Voyages <200 passengers						32	38	45	52
• Voyages > 1000 passengers						9	12	13	17
Total arrivals	3490	7008	19,523	19,638	22,370	22,125	27,230	27,461	34,691
Passenger origins (%):									
• USA						55.3	58.2	58.7	58.9
• Canada						6.1	7.2	7.7	6.4
• Latin America						7.5	10.5	7	7.7
• UK						15.4	8.1	17.6	7.5
• Other Europeans						13	13.5	5.7	13.8
• Africa						0.2	0.03	0.3	0.4
• Asia						0.7	0.8	1.1	1.6
• Oceania						1.7	1.7	2	2.7
• Other countries						52	68	67	66

Source: Adapted from data supplied by the FITB & Sullivan Travel. Collected by Falkland Islands Customs.

We sail from Ushuaia, Argentina to the Falkland Islands — home to a collection of flora and fauna dependent on the surrounding sea, and scene of the 1982 Falkland Islands Conflict between Great Britain and Argentina. We then move on to South Georgia where we spend four days. During our unforgettable landings, we experience its unique concentration of wildlife (imagine penguins and reindeer side-by-side), marvel at the awe-inspiring landscape, and examine the remnants of the whaling industry from a bygone era. When we leave South Georgia, we head southwest to the Antarctic Peninsula where we spend another four days immersed in the 'White Continent', before returning to South America through the Drake Passage. (Antarctica Journeys.com, 2005)

The few hundred land-based tourists each year are less seasonal than those on ships; they stay longer — normally at least a week, given the infrequent flights — and spend more, needing accommodation and food, and spread tourism beyond the ten sites used by cruise ships (Ingham & Summers, 2002). They often have niche interests in, say, wildlife or military history and tend to be reasonably wealthy, given the cost of reaching the islands. Mostly they are middle aged or above, and come without young children.

The third major tourist sector is an unusual captive market: the military posted to the islands. In 1985, the British established an airbase at Mount Pleasant (MPA) about 63 km from Stanley to secure the defence of the Falklands. Perhaps 1500 service personnel are stationed there, each entitled to R&R (rest and relaxation, military speak for holidays), which they may choose to spend away from the base. A guesthouse owner at Port Howard attributed their motivation to being able to have a bath instead of a shower, to enjoy home cooked food, to have their own bedroom and to be able to set their own agenda. Whether this is to go trekking, fishing or see wildlife is less important than the fact that the choice of activity is theirs. They might also play golf: the Port Howard course has the unique hazard of a minefield within it, giving a whole new interpretation to 'out of bounds'. The military sector has no connection with the generalities of cold water or small island tourism. Little more will be written about it, except to emphasise its importance, in that it is not as seasonal as other sectors, focuses on Camp rather than Stanley, and serves as a base, 'home', market that bulks up tourism and helps to support suppliers.

Tourism Motivation

Elderly Americans, sated with Caribbean cruises and moving on to take one in Latin America, arrive in the Falklands without necessarily having consciously chosen to do so, the islands might just be a small part of an extensive cruise. Thus, will passengers of the 59,652 t *Rotterdam* with its 658 cabins and four restaurants sailing in November 2005 from Rio de Janeiro via Montevideo, Buenos Aires, Stanley, Usuahia, Punta Arenas and Puerto Montt to Santiago's port of Valparaiso choose to take ship because a nine hour visit to Stanley is included (Holland America Line, 2004)? Anecdotal evidence suggests that passengers from some of the luxury cruises are not well prepared: 'Does the sea go all the way round the islands?' 'How do you cut the grass on the minefields?' and 'Do penguins fly?' were all genuine questions repeated to the author. Further, material given to passengers on some large cruisers is flawed: warnings not to leave main roads for fear of crime may be necessary for Latin American cities, but not in Stanley where there has never been a mugging or pick pocketing (Penguin News, 2004). One set of passengers was told that they 'may' find people who speak English, a nonsense regarding this thoroughly Anglophone destination. Some nervous passengers just cluster around the jetty and the visitors' centre adjacent, not even stepping further into Stanley for fear of the unknown. Others ask to be whisked to the nearest penguin to complete their Falklands experience. These people gain nothing and contribute little. The FITB and tourism providers are keen to get accurate information on board ships, to reassure passengers, encouraging them to be more adventurous, but not raising their expectations unrealistically. One business, which includes off-road driving as part of the tourist experience, wants the realities made known before passengers innocently board their Land Rovers.

Others, particularly those on expedition cruises and land-based tourists, are more 'inquisitive' about their destination as one tourism official stated and have chosen the Falklands. Why? Not for their sophistication. Food artfully arranged in a tower, a benchmark of contemporary cuisine, can be bought in Stanley restaurants; however, menus are limited. There is no professional entertainment, just a lively local music scene, also amateur dramatics and sports events to which visitors are welcome. One tourism company wanted to see accommodation standards rise 'to another level', for hotel accommodation in Stanley is not of the highest quality, while some Camp lodges are basic in facilities. 'Cold-water tourism is coping without a hair dryer' said a guesthouse operator, explaining the constraints of managing without main electricity.

Choices may be made because of the islands' difference. They are curious, not of Latin America but an English-speaking British Overseas Territory where people drive on the left and celebrate the Queen's birthday with 21 gun salutes. (Further north, Bermuda also profits from these, to mainlanders, 'quaint' characteristics.) Some like to add the Falklands to their list of countries seen; some are attracted to the historic ships condemned and abandoned here (Smith, 1985); and some come because the islands are quiet and safe. There are the famous stone runs, notable peri-glacial formations prominent especially on East Falkland, which look like rivers of stone and are spectacular when seen from the air (Stone & Aldiss, 2000). There is no pollution, the light's clarity giving the landscape deep, vibrant colours, attracting photographers. Some cherish the traditional sheep-ranching economy: tourism providers might arrange shearing demonstrations; all will be able to show shearing sheds, their distinct odour the olfactory symbol of Camp for islanders apparently. One farm on East Falkland draws bus loads of cruise ship passengers from Stanley to demonstrations of horse and sheepdog management, peat cutting and sheep shearing. It brings guests into the traditional farmhouse to see the peat stove and have 'smoko' (the local term for a break, usually with a snack) with bread, butter and cream all being home made. Follow-up questionnaires with clients of one company picked up on these themes: 'unspoilt', 'hospitable', 'friendly' and 'authentic' were terms used. Further, there is excellent angling, especially for sea trout, in little fished, uncrowded rivers, where the angler will probably not see another fisher: some will come round the world for such experiences.

Others come because of the 1982 conflict. Tour companies arrange focused visits to battlefields, plane crash sites (souvenir hunting is discouraged), cemeteries and memorials. Islanders can be sensitive about the conflict, attitudes remain hard, but those involved in tourism at least are aware that this is an important part of the island story and it can be marketed, although the Falkland Islands Tourist Board (no date) (FITB) is keen to promote other attractions. One operator in particular specialises in battlefield work, often for film companies, although he will also arrange other tours (www.discoveryfalklands.com).

Overwhelmingly, however, people choose to visit the Falklands for the wildlife (Strange, 1992). Here, at last, is commonality with other cold water islands: remote, relatively little disturbed and sparsely populated, such places still display nature writ large, red here not in tooth and claw, given the absence of terrestrial mammalian carnivores, but red in beak and talon. The star of Falklands' postcards and T-shirts is the penguin. The islands are of global importance for the breeding of Gentoos and Rockhoppers, less so for Kings and Magellanics. Dolphins, whales, sea lions, fur and elephant seals can be seen and one popular offshore destination is Sea Lion Island. Everywhere, there are surprisingly sizeable birds: upland geese

(Stanley's major hotel is the Upland Goose, on the grass outside pairs of which always graze), the Falklands flightless steamer duck, grebes, shearwaters and petrels. The Cobb's wren is an important endemic; few will see another, the splendidly named Dark-faced Ground-Tyrant. Turkey vultures scavenge; falcons, hawks and caracaras, both striated and crested, are birds of prey. Avian life is spectacular, abundant and relatively tame. One tourism firm reported that the icon of the luxury cruise tourist, the penguin, was replaced for the expedition ship traveller by the black-browed albatross, the Falklands accommodating 70% of the world's population, ca. 380,000 pairs, of this near threatened species (see Huin, 2001).

Access

Access is an important issue for Falklands tourism, particularly given the continuing dispute with Argentina. In 2003, Argentina imposed restrictions on air space clearance. Except for the RAF link through Ascension, all flights, including those from Chile, have to traverse Argentinean airspace. The restriction could not affect the established weekly flight from Punta Arenas, but made it more difficult, virtually impossible, for shipping companies to organise charter flights for passenger exchanges in the Falklands. There were 16 such turn-arounds in 2002–2003; only one, organised through the Lan Chile link, was held in the year following the restriction. Cruisers, which once might have remained in the South Atlantic, now have to return to South America to board new passengers, with less time available for island visits. Almost every respondent in the fieldwork interviews brought up this issue, and it is discussed at inter-government level with British involvement, this involves foreign affairs.

The other access choke point is the Lan Chile flight being only weekly. Thus, most land-based tourists have to come for units of whole weeks. This precludes the islands from the growing short-break tourism market. With the need for all but Chileans to get first to Santiago or Punta Arenas, another couple of days might be required on top, so a visit to the Falklands is of the duration of an annual holiday for those in work, limiting the islands' market. There is a demand to have a second flight weekly, which would ease matters; however, given the current position of Argentina, this seems to be unlikely. Without better access, one legislator thought tourism could only 'tick over'.

The RAF flights are slightly more frequent but are tedious — two long legs from RAF Brize Norton in southern England to Ascension and on to MPA — often taken in noisy, slow, Tristar aircraft without modern facilities; the RAF is not part of the hospitality industry. Only to some civilians does the cachet of flying in an RAF Tristar outweigh the rigours of the experience. There are possibilities with the opening up of Ascension Island for civilian use to develop two-centre holidays on both British possessions, but as Ascension's infrastructure presently is limited, such schemes are for the future. So there is little chance for considerably increasing land-based tourism, even when there is the demand. For cruise ships there is no such problem and passenger numbers have increased markedly in recent years, despite the ending of passenger exchanges (see Table 14.1).

Cold Water Tourism and Its Management

Falkland Island tourism is unusual as it is cold water based, free from the paradise island tag — these are *Darwin's desolate islands* (Armstrong, 1992, commemorating the fact that

Charles Darwin spent longer here than he did in the Galapagos Islands). There are splendid beaches, but the islands are not suitable for beach holidays; it is not warm enough, it is too windy and the sea is unwelcoming. A sixth-generation islander reported that she and her friends when young had swum in the sea on hot summer afternoons but this was not undertaken with relish, more as a dare, and the immersion was brief. Sadly, too, many beaches near Stanley will be forever off limits after being mined in 1982. In any event, the tiny scale of society and the resultant limited infrastructure, together with the remoteness and consequently expensive travel, preclude the Falklands' catering for mass tourism, whatever the water temperature. The islands get some backpackers, often through last minute bookings with Lan Chile, but they can find the Falklands difficult, there is little cheap accommodation, especially outside Stanley and hitchhiking is problematic with a skeletal road network and few vehicles.

At one time, there was a notional cap of 200 on land-based tourists as a conservation measure (Royle, 1997). Now, government policy is to increase long-stay tourist visits (FIG, 2002). Nevertheless, the self-regulation of remoteness, restricted access and limited infrastructure makes this difficult. For example, Stanley has only about 50 hotel beds and about the same number in guesthouses. A former Chief Executive thinks that:

> [T]he finite limit to the numbers that can be transported and accommodated is probably less than 500 per year. (Gurr, 2001, p. 223)

Cruise ships have fewer infrastructural constraints. Only the smallest of them berth alongside, so there is no competition for wharf space. Most remain in the ample anchorages where more than one ship at a time can be accommodated. When this happens — on 'clash days', as they are termed in the trade — considerable overcrowding is caused on land. Usually ships make two stops in the islands, one at Stanley where tourists who will venture beyond the visitor's centre.

> [D]rift as though they were inhabitants of another dimension, like giants observing a model village … [without] concept that the roads carry traffic and real people are doing real work in real offices while they shamble around. (Gurr, 2001, p. 221)

Full information is not yet available, but it seems that mean passenger spend is rather low, if it could be raised, more money would be made from tourism without increasing pressures. One development is more substantial souvenir outlets, the most prominent being the new Capstan Gift Shop that, like the Upland Goose Hotel, belongs to the Falkland Islands Company, a long established firm, which still owns much land used for sheep ranching as well as being dominant in the islands' commerce, including retailing (www.the-falkland-islands-co.com).

It is necessary to manage a delicate environment when the tourist gaze is towards iconic wildlife whose very presence might be affected by these tourists. There is one site easily accessible by road from Stanley, Gypsy Cove, a penguin rookery. Falklands Conservation regards this site as having been 'ruined'. Tourist pressures including quick trips of passengers from cruise ships anchored off Stanley, up to 1000 people per day in high season, led to trampling, damaging the burrows of Magellanic penguins and reducing their numbers, although others claim that excess predation by an elephant seal was the reason for their decline. The site is now protected with marked and roped pathways and there are still some penguins to be observed, though not the numbers of other sites. Gypsy Cove provided a valuable lesson that care has to be taken to manage tourists.

Elsewhere, site visits require a certain amount of endurance, for they can only be reached after travelling in off-road vehicles and walking. This difficulty of access helps reduce environmental pressures, reported several respondents, although there remain worries about visits to offshore islands especially where rats and other introduced vermin could cause problems: the endemic Cobb's wren cannot survive where there are rats, for example, and a rat-eradication programme has been put into operation on several offshore islands. A carelessly managed barbecue from a private yacht party irretrievably destroyed much of the habitat of Green Island when not only tussac grass but also the peat soil caught fire, as reported by an environmentalist.

Tourist visits are usually better handled. Consider cruise ship passengers' visits to Kidney Cove on East Falkland. These see them taken from the liner by ships' boats or tourist company's launch to a small jetty, collected by Land Rover and driven to penguin sites. Some find the off-road 'safari' challenging; to others it is part of the attraction. The principal site has two 'bucket and chuck it' toilets, benches and a hut selling souvenirs, otherwise the area is natural, except for ropes keeping tourists a few metres away from the disturbingly malodorous mass of penguins to minimize the problems caused by disturbance (see Regel & Pütz, 1997). Such visits do not see tourists left unsupervised. Further, many tourist operators have completed a Tour Guide course organised by the FITB that includes substantial input from Falklands Conservation, which has taught them how to 'assist visitors to view wildlife and habitats while protecting against damage or disturbance: that is 'sustainable tourism' according to the Powerpoint presentation they use, and which the author was allowed to see. Firms such as Kidney Cove Safari Tours mention their Registered Tour Guides in their marketing (Falkland Island Tourism, 2003).

A positive feature affecting conservation is the major significance tourism has on the economy of some farm enterprises, leading farmers to cherish their wildlife, their 'golden geese'. Farmers on some of the subdivided estates whose 4–8000 ha (10–20000 acres) have proved to be rather too small (Gurr, 2001, p. 108) reported that tourism now accounted for around half their income. Some islands, including Sea Lion and Weddell, are now almost completely reliant on wildlife tourism. Some locals, especially in Camp, also earn tourism cash by making crafts, though there are also stuffed toy penguins made in China in some Stanley outlets.

Conclusion

Tourism is now an essential, integral part of the Falkland Islands economy. Its operation and management consequently has to be and indeed is professional, thus the FITB is efficiently run, a stand-alone agency working closely with government, operators, Falklands Conservation and local people to develop an effective, sustainable strategy and policy. On the ground there is the Tour Guide course, while internationally there is attendance at tourism events in Latin America and Europe, although the absolute spend on marketing can only be tiny. Falklands Conservation not only studies the islands' flora and fauna (e.g. Jones, 2004) but also keeps a watching brief on the impact of tourism (Ingham & Summers, 2002), and has produced a visitor's guide advising on behaviour as well as detailing wildlife sites (Summers, 2001). It has a seat on the FIG Environment Committee, has helped designate protected land, including Ramsar (wetland) sites, and is involved in bodies such as the International Association of Antarctic Tour Operators which establishes good practice for Antarctic tourism. The British government, through the Governor and his staff, regards tourism development as a local responsibility, encourages it as a necessary economic diversification, but would not like to see the islands become a 'theme park'. Local government, less focused on agriculture than it used to be, requires one of eight councillors to take the tourism portfolio and it is to the incumbent that FITB reports. Local companies involved in arranging tours for the military, land based tourists and cruise ship passengers liaise with each other and with partners in Stanley and Camp, custodians of the tourism product. Most Falkland Islanders now see tourists, even those crowding Stanley on cruise ship days, as worthwhile; though societal norms do not see locals defer to people just because they are 'from away'. Another issue is that there is no unemployment here, more a labour shortage given that St. Helenians are increasingly going to the UK rather than the Falklands for work. This colours some local attitudes to tourists: 'who needs them?' Some landowners with important historic or wildlife sites on their property will not allow tourist access, even though this would be profitable: the Islanders are often individualists. However, at least Stanley shops are likely to open now for ship visits, a flexibility not always seen in the past.

Would the Falklands be an example of extreme tourism? Many respondents begged to differ, since they did not recognise their tourism product as belonging to such a category. 'Extreme' to them implied hardship, endurance and privation, characteristics not integral to the Falkland Islands tourism experience. One legislator and a tour company owner independently both proposed instead the word 'raw', in the sense of being unprocessed or unrefined, rather than crude or unfinished. The title of one FITB leaflet (no date) serves as an apt summary: *Falkland Islands … naturally.*

Acknowledgments

The author received a Scholarship from the Shackleton Fund, which supports Falklands research. He was assisted by the Falkland Islands Tourist Board and acknowledges also the kindness of interviewees who shared their time and expertise.

References

Antarctica Journeys.com (2005). www.antarctica-journeys.com/antarctica/journey_types/expedition/polar_star/Falkland_Islands_SGeorgia_Antarctica/ (accessed on 20/10/2005).
Armstrong, P. (1992). *Darwin's desolate Islands.* Chippenham: Picton.
Falklands Conservation. (2003). *Wildlife conservation in the Falkland Islands issue 3.* Stanley and London: Falklands Conservation.

Falkland Islands Government. (2002). *The Islands plan 2002/05*. Stanley: Falkland Islands Government.

Falkland Islands Government. (2003). *Falkland Islands: Securing a sustainable future*. Stanley: Falklands Islands Government.

Falkland Island Tourism. (2003). *Kidney Cove Safari Tours*. www.tourism.org.fk/pages/kidney-cove-tours.htm (accessed on 20/10/2005).

Falklands Islands Tourist Board. (no date). *Falkland Islands … naturally*. Stanley: Falkland Islands Tourist Board.

Gurr, A. (2001). *A little piece of England: My adventures as chief executive of the Falkland Islands*. London: John Blake.

Holland America Line. (2004). http://cruises.hotwire.com/b/c/sc.asp?d=10/1/2004&d2=3/31/2006&i=847980&c=24&v=113. (accessed on 20/10/2005).

Huin, N. (2001). *Census of the black-browed Albatross population of the Falkland islands*. London: Falklands Conservation.

Ingham, R. J., & Summers, D. (2002). Falkland Islands cruise ship tourism: An overview of the 1999–2000 season and the way forward. *Aquatic Conservation: Marine and Freshwater Ecosystems, 12* (1), 145–152.

Jones, A. G. (2004). *Insects of the Falkland Islands*. London: Falklands Conservation.

Middlebrook, M. (1988). *Task force: The Falklands war, 1982*. New York: Penguin.

Penguin News. (2004). *Visitors guide: 2004–2005*. Stanley: Penguin News.

Regel, J., & Pütz, K. (1997). Effect of human disturbance on body temperature and energy expenditure in Penguins. *Polar Biology, 18* (4), 246–253.

Royle, S. A. (1985). The Falkland Islands 1833–1876: The establishment of a colony. *Geographical Journal, 151* (2), 204–214.

Royle, S. A. (1997). Tourism to the south Atlantic Islands. In: D. G. Lockhart, & D. Drakakis-Smith (Eds), *Island tourism: Trends and prospects* (pp. 323–344). London: Pinter.

Shackleton, Lord. (1976). *Economic survey of the Falkland Islands*. London: HMSO.

Shackleton, Lord. (1982). *Falkland Islands economic study 1982*. London: HMSO.

Smith, J. (1984). *74 days: An islander's diary of the Falklands occupation 1982*. London: Century.

Smith, J. (1985). *Condemned at Stanley*. Chippenham: Picton

Stone, P., & Aldiss, D. (2000). *The Falkland Islands: Reading the rocks — a geological travelogue*. London: British Geological Survey for Department of Mineral Resources, Falkland Islands Government.

Strange, I. (1992). *Field guide to the wildlife of the Falkland Islands and south Georgia*. London: HarperCollins.

Summers, D. (2001). *A visitor's guide to the Falkland Islands*. London: Falklands Conservation.

Summers, M. (2003). Self-determination in the Falkland Islands. In: L. Ivanov (Ed.), *The future of the Falkland Islands and its people* (pp. 68–74). Sofia: The Atlantic Club of Bulgaria and the Manfred Wörner Foundation.

The Economist. (2004). Virtue rewarded: Conservation in the Falkland Islands. London: The Economist Intelligence Unit (13th October).

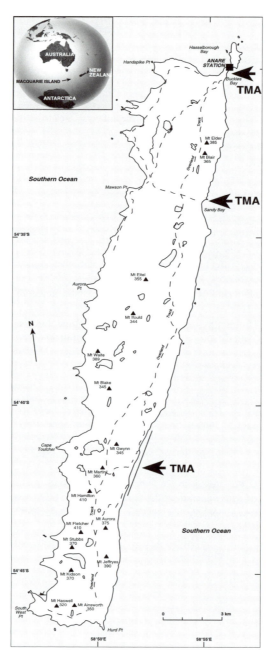

Image 12: Map of Macquarie Island. (TMA=Tourism Management Areas.)

Chapter 15

Macquarie Island, Australia

Lorne K. Kriwoken, Claire Ellis and Nick Holmes

Introduction

Located in the Southern Ocean 1500 km SSE of Tasmania, Macquarie Island is a remote and isolated island located roughly half-way between Australia and the Antarctic continent. This sub-Antarctic island is only 34 km long and up to 5 km wide with a land area of 12,785 ha. Because it is situated in the path of the 'Furious Fifties', the winds that circle the high southern latitudes, on average there are over 300 days of precipitation a year. Macquarie Island lies just north of the Antarctic Convergence zone where cold Antarctic waters mix with relatively warmer northern water. This results in a rough ocean, cold mists, sea-fogs and strong average wind speeds. Steep rocky beaches rise sharply to an undulating plateau roughly 100–300 m above sea level, with the highest point being Mt Hamilton (433 m). These extreme sub-Antarctic environmental conditions are key factors in the overall distribution and abundance of island flora and fauna.

Macquarie Island is home to an abundant and diverse array of wildlife. Approximately, 3.5 million seabirds arrive annually to breed and moult. Most of these visiting seabirds are penguins including 850,000 endemic royal penguins, over 100,000 breeding pairs of king penguins, 5000 breeding pairs of gentoo penguins and rockhopper penguins. Other seabirds include the endemic king cormorant, skuas and four albatross species. Of particular importance are the 15 pairs of the endangered wandering albatross. Four species of seal breed on Macquarie Island, including Antarctic fur seals, sub-Antarctic fur seals, New Zealand fur seals and one-seventh of the world's population of elephant seals (80,000) (PWS, 2003). The limited land mass in the Southern Ocean makes this a particularly important location for birds, seals and sub-Antarctic vegetation.

Macquarie Island is also one of the earliest sites occupied by Europeans in Australia. Sites of historical interest from fur seal, elephant seal and penguin oil gathering work gangs are scattered around much of the island and since 1948 there has been a permanent scientific base staffed by Australian National Antarctic Research Expeditions (ANARE), now known as the Australian Antarctic Program (AAP). In addition, the Tasmanian Parks and Wildlife Service (PWS) operate year-round research and management programs. The station occupies a low flat isthmus at the north of the island. The only access is by sea usually with inflatable rubber craft such as zodiacs. There are no jetties or landing facilities for ships. Helicopters gain access from ships anchored off the northern eastern coast.

From 1987 to 2004, just over 5000 tourists visited the island with commercial tour operators (see Table 15.1). Tourists arrive on expedition-style ships, typically ice-strengthened or ice breakers, with usually no more than 100 passengers. The nature-based experience is supported by a high level of onboard interpretation from lecturers and expedition staff. Visitation is strictly controlled and, in some cases, severe weather does not allow tourists to disembark. The island is often included as a stop over in a longer expedition to Antarctica or to the New Zealand sub-Antarctic islands.

This chapter begins by outlining the management process including the reasons for its World Heritage Area status. The numbers and types of tourists and permitted activities are then discussed. Tourist impacts and issues revolving around tourism supply and demand are then introduced. The chapter concludes by arguing that the harsh environment and the physical challenge of getting to the island enhance the intensity of the experience surrounding this type of cold-water tourism. Tourism is undertaken in a very controlled manner and at present numbers do not seem to adversely impact the ecology of the island. The only host community consists of researchers and field staff and these people play a role in educating tourists and in the planning and management of the island.

Protection and Management

Macquarie Island was discovered in 1810 and almost immediately fur seals were targeted for their skins, which were exported to Europe. Within 10 years this resource became depleted and elephant seals were targeted for their blubber. By the late 1880s, penguin oil was the dominant industry, but by 1919 this too was no longer commercially viable.

Scientific interest dates back to the 1820s, yet it was not until 1933 that Macquarie Island was declared a Wildlife Sanctuary. The island became a Tasmanian State Reserve in 1972 and was recognised internationally in 1977 as a Biosphere Reserve under the United Nations Educational, Scientific and Cultural Organisation's (UNESCO) 'Man and the Biosphere' Program. It was declared a restricted area in 1979 thereby requiring all visitors, including tourists, to acquire permits from the managing authority.

In 1997, the World Heritage Committee (WHC) inscribed Macquarie Island and waters out to 12 nautical miles on the World Heritage List for its outstanding geoconservation significance, satisfying two of four natural criteria as a location that is 'an outstanding example representing major stages of the Earth's evolutionary history, including the record of life, significant on-going geological processes in the development of landforms, or significant geomorphic or physiographic features' and a site 'containing superlative natural phenomena or areas of exceptional outstanding natural beauty and aesthetic importance' (PWS, 2003, p. 16). It is the only island in the world composed entirely of oceanic crust and rocks from the earth's mantle where rocks from the mantle are being actively exposed above sea level (PWS, 2003, pp. 16, 17). Interestingly, Macquarie Island was not inscribed on the World Heritage List for its rich biological values.

In October 1999, the Macquarie Island Marine Park, representing over 16.2 million ha, was declared to protect the unique and vulnerable marine ecosystems of the south-eastern portion of the Macquarie Island Region (Environment Australia, 2001). The Marine Park was divided into three zones: a Highly Protected Zone (assigned International Union for Conservation of Nature (IUCN) category Ia) and two Habitat/Species Management Zones (IUCN category IV) either side of the Highly Protected Zone.

The State Government of Tasmania, through the PWS, a unit of the Department of Tourism, Parks, Heritage and the Arts, and the Nature Conservation Branch, a unit of the Department of Primary Industries, Water and Environment (2001), are responsible for research and management of Macquarie Island and the surrounding waters out to three nautical miles. The Commonwealth Government of Australia has responsibility for the management of the area from three nautical miles to the 200 nautical mile Exclusive Economic Zone (Environment Australia, 2001).

Legislation providing for the conservation of Macquarie Island is present at both the federal and state levels and includes the *Environment Protection and Biodiversity Conservation Act 1999* (Commonwealth) (EPBC Act) and the *National Parks and Reserves Management Act 2002* (Tasmania). An objective of the EPBC Act is to provide for the protection of the environment, in particular those aspects of the environment that are matters of national environmental significance. World Heritage is one of six environmental aspects to be considered of national environmental significance (Padgett & Kriwoken, 2001). Macquarie Island is managed in accordance with the Macquarie Island Nature Reserve and World Heritage Area Draft Management Plan 2003 (the Plan) (PWS, 2003), which is currently under review by the Tasmanian Resource Planning and Development Commission. A management objective of the Plan permits tourist visits under strictly controlled conditions and allows visitors to experience the island's natural values.

The Parks and Wildlife Service charge a fee of US$115 (PWS, 2004) for each passenger aboard a tourist ship that makes a shore visit. The guidelines for tourist operations on Macquarie Island state that the revenue will be used for the management and promotion of the island, which may include the provision of staff, facilities to protect the environment and visitor impact monitoring programs. For instance, the eradication of feral cats was supported financially from this fee.

There is no host community on Macquarie Island in the traditional sense. AAP and PWS researchers, field and support staff mostly live in Australia and spend the austral summer or sometimes a winter on the island. In most cases they are working in paid positions, but volunteers are sometimes used. The Plan stipulates that a maximum of 80 people can stay overnight (60 on station and 20 in the field huts during changeover and resupply operations). Those involved in the scientific or management community act in many ways as a host community. Staff often form a strong and long-lasting bond with the location and maintain an interest in a range of island issues. Compared with many small host communities on remote islands, this type of host community is well educated, sometimes politically well connected and more readily able to influence management decisions concerning the island, including management issues pertaining to tourism. As a result researchers, field and support staff are integrally connected with both mainland and island communities (e.g. Baldacchino, 2004).

Tourism on Macquarie Island

A series of New Zealand Government expeditions to the Auckland Islands, Campbell Island and Macquarie Island from 1882 to 1927 provide the earliest evidence of tourists to Macquarie Island (Headland, 1994). These expeditions were made at least annually with some of the passengers described as tourists. Early tourism continued up to the mid-1950s with a number of tourists travelling aboard ships on voyages to Antarctica for a variety of purposes, including the relief of scientific staff, the provision of supplies, castaway searches and the provision of mail services. For the purpose of this chapter, the term 'tourist' will be used in accordance with the current views of the Parks and Wildlife Service and be restricted to commercial tourist visitation (although a few individuals in private yachts occasionally visit and are also considered tourists).

The only tourism product currently available for tourist visits to Macquarie Island is expedition-style ship-borne tourism. Although there is no agreed definition between academics or within the industry concerning niches within the cruise market, expedition-style ships are characterised by their style of operating which includes exploring new and often hard-to-reach locations, and an emphasis on ecotourism with onboard lecturers and expedition staff providing a high level of interpretation (Ellis, et al., 2005). Generally, expedition-style ships are small, taking a maximum of around 100–150 passengers, which permits rapid disembarkation at locations with little or no infrastructure. Macquarie Island, with its rough weather and no landing infrastructure, means this type of visitation is currently the only possible type. Fast manoeuvrable and inflatable zodiac-style craft are used to ferry passengers ashore and to cruise the coastline for wildlife viewing.

Expedition-style tourist ships have visited sporadically since 1970 (PWS, 2003) but regular tourist visits to Macquarie Island did not commence until the 1990/1991 season when 559 tourists visited. The number of tourists visiting Macquarie Island between the 1990/1991 and 2004/2005 season has fluctuated with an average annual visitation rate of just 334 visitors (Table 15.1).

These tourist numbers would have been marginally higher, except for the fact that bad weather prevented some ships from landing passengers. On average, 27% of tourists given approval were not able to land. Despite this, interest is expected to continue to grow. The media, particularly through film and photography, has been extremely important in raising public awareness of the island's World Heritage Area site status and the high conservation values of the reserve. The Tasmanian State Government has also supported tourism as part of Tasmania's Antarctic, sub-Antarctic and Southern Ocean Policy (Tasmania, 2004) and in marketing strategies (Abel & Ellis, 2003). Growth in Antarctic tourism also affects tourist numbers on Macquarie Island. Most tourist operators include the visit as part of a longer expedition to the Antarctic continent or as part of an expedition that includes other destinations, such as the New Zealand sub-Antarctic islands (Kriwoken & Rootes, 2000; Sanson, 1994; Cessford & Dingwall, 1994). One reason for including Macquarie Island in

Table 15.1: Ship visits and tourist landings for Macquarie Island: 1987–2005.

Season	Approved ship visits	Actual ship visits	Approved tourist landings	Actual tourist landings
1987/1988	1	1	n/a	18
1988/1989	0	0	n/a	0
1989/1990	0	0	n/a	0
1990/1991	4	4	n/a	559
1991/1992	0	0	n/a	0
1992/1993	4	4	n/a	416
1993/1994	4	3	n/a	128
1994/1995	5	5	432	342
1995/1996	9	8	421	351
1996/1997	6	6	526	490
1997/1998	6	6	376	313
1998/1999	6	6	458	374
1999/2000	7	4	558	329
2000/2001	9	7	818	556
2001/2002	8	7	522	371
2002/2003	4	4	352	202
2003/2004	5	5	454	433
2004/2005	5	5	358	303
Total		75		5185

Source: Cusick (2005).

the itinerary of longer voyages is to accommodate a break in lengthy periods of sea travel. Other significant reasons for tourist visits to Macquarie Island include its wildlife, flora, historic sites from the sealing era and visits to the ANARE research station to witness station life in the sub-Antarctic.

Although no specific research has examined the motivations or characteristics of tourists to Macquarie Island, other researchers have noted differences between types of ecotourists (Weaver, 2002, Weiler & Richins, 1995). Distinctions have often been related to the length of the trip, but more often to levels of ecotourism activities undertaken, the extent to which an interest in science was specialised, intense or scientific, or on the basis of physical difficulty, challenge and/or discomforts (Lang, O'Leary, & Morrison, 1996). According to each of these, tourists to Macquarie Island would be considered hard-core (sometimes termed dedicated, specialist, active or deep). Although this type of tourist is sometimes considered to prefer a 'personal experience', Weaver's (2002) Australian research noted a preference by hard-core eco-tourists for an escorted or interpreted tour to enhance learning, such as exists with expedition-style cruise ships. These characteristics relate to the ecotourism trip, and in addition, the tourist is assumed to have certain preferences, or values, because of their trip choice including higher levels of environmental concern or pro-environmental behaviours.

Permitted Tourism Activities on Macquarie Island

The Draft Management Plan maintains that 'the impacts of tourism have been negligible compared to the impacts of year round occupation of the island to support scientific, monitoring, conservation and management personnel and programs' (PWS, 2003, p. 114). PWS has a set of tourism guidelines for Macquarie Island found in Appendix 8 of the Plan. Island visits are restricted to between 07:00 and 19:00 hours as pre-arranged with the PWS and no overnight stays are permitted. Adventure activities such as ocean kayaking, diving and camping, permitted in Antarctica, are not permitted on, or adjacent to, Macquarie Island. Ships that carry more than 200 passengers are not allowed to land visitors on the island. These limitations are intended to protect wildlife and the environment and to ensure the quality of the experience.

Tourist landings are restricted to two locations zoned as Tourism Management Areas (TMAs): the beach at Sandy Bay and the ANARE research station on the isthmus. The guidelines allow a maximum of 60 people ashore at any one time at Sandy Bay and a maximum of 100 people ashore at any one time at the isthmus area. Concurrent landings at each site are not permitted, therefore a maximum of 100 tourists can be ashore at any one time. All shore parties are organised into groups with no more than 15 people per group (one guide and 14 clients). The scientists, field and support staff volunteer as guides and represent an excellent human resource with their first-hand knowledge of the flora, fauna and historic sites. Tourists are not permitted to land at any other location however, zodiac cruising is allowed at the Waterfall Bay to Lusitania Bay TMA, the home of a spectacular king penguin colony. Guidelines and restrictions apply concerning the distance from shore, speed and movement near the main penguin access channel. The Draft Management Plan includes specific guidelines for small boat operations that must be followed by guides and zodiac drivers.

Tourists visiting the Sandy Bay area are restricted to the beach and two boardwalks. The first boardwalk takes tourists to the periphery of a royal penguin colony and the second to a king penguin colony. Elephant seals, fur seals and a number of non-breeding penguin species are seen on the beach. Visitors to the isthmus are restricted to the beach, boardwalks, the network of roads at the ANARE station and the station itself, if a visit has been arranged. Boardwalks in the isthmus area allow tourists to visit a lookout over the research station and a cultural site containing digesters from the sealing era. Digesters were used to render down seal blubber; however, the climate has caused substantial deterioration of artifacts and hut materials.

In addition to on-shore restrictions, the permit process for tourist operators includes eight criteria that operators must meet to gain a permit. Most of these are associated with safety, accreditation and environmental controls. One criterion requires that the tourist operators demonstrate benefits to the State of Tasmania through employing Tasmanians or re-supplying in the State. Another criterion insists on high levels of education concerning the natural and cultural values of the island and the role that visitors play in protecting these values. As expedition-style cruise ships generally focus on having high levels of interpretation and having a range of qualified lecture staff on-board, the last criterion is easily met. In the 2004/2005 season, two tourist companies (one New Zealand-based, one USA-based) and in the upcoming 2005/2006 season four different tourist companies were granted permits to land. The permit application is assessed on a case-by-case basis by the PWS and takes into account the tour operator's ability to deliver desirable outcomes as outlined in the Plan.

Tourism Impacts

Any level of recreational or tourist use of a natural area inevitably results in some level of environmental impact. According to Cole (1994), the total impact to a natural area depends on a number of principal factors that are unique to each individual site. These factors comprise frequency of use, type and behaviour of use, season of use, environmental conditions and spatial distribution of use. The tourist management guidelines on Macquarie Island include restrictions based on these principal factors of impact, with the exception of environmental conditions, such as the weather.

The number of visiting tourists is managed by a quota system. Up to the late 1990s, 500 tourist landings *per annum* were permitted (although in 1990/1991 there were 559 actual tourist landings) and this was increased for the 2000/2001 season to 750. Table 15.1 indicates both the approved and actual tourist landings. The spatial distribution and activities of tourists using Macquarie Island are restricted and managed by PWS staff. As most tourist operators include Macquarie Island in their itineraries either on the way to, or from, Antarctica, the season is restricted to the summer months of November to March to enable ships to reach the Antarctic continent when sea ice is at its minimum.

The strict control of tourist visits to Macquarie Island and their restriction to hardened sites and beach areas suggests that tourists presently have little impact on flora and fauna. Tourist visits to wildlife colonies via the boardwalks do not extend beyond the periphery of the colonies, therefore it is expected that the impact on the wildlife is negligible to very low.

Tourists encounter a variety of wildlife on the beach in the Sandy Bay area, therefore the potential exists for disturbances to wildlife if tourists approach too closely. Research by Holmes et al. (2003) has indicated that giant petrels can be sensitive to human activity, including small boat activity. To minimise the affects of tourism, the PWS undertakes monitoring and maintains strict controls on the movement of tourists.

Tourism Demand and Supply Issues

The demand to visit Antarctica and sub-Antarctic islands has grown significantly and during the 2003/2004 season, 19,771 tourists visited Antarctica with another 4939 having cruised the area but not disembarked (International Association of Antarctica Tour Operators [IAATO], 2004). Most of this visitation occurs in the Antarctic Peninsula where the passage through rough water is limited and the range of landings and tourism activities is broader than from Australia. In 2001/2002, less than 3% of visitors to Antarctica visited the Ross Sea region, south of New Zealand (Maher, 2003) and the numbers of tourists to Macquarie Island was also quite low (see Table 15.1) and expected to remain relatively low compared with visitation to Antarctica via South America.

Motivations for visiting Antarctica include wildlife, curiosity, scenery, remoteness, adventure, photography and the pristine environment (Bauer, 2001). But the attractions of Macquarie Island, a small island with no icebergs or glaciers, may differ. For many visitors, Macquarie is an interesting stop on the way to Antarctica, but for others it is one of the highlights of a trip, together with other New Zealand sub-Antarctic islands. Much like Antarctic tourists, visitors to Macquarie Island are generally well educated, well travelled, financially well-off and tend to be older. They seek the unique experience of visiting Macquarie Island as well as viewing the unique wildlife.

The key tourist attraction of Macquarie Island is its vast congregation of unusual and visually interesting wildlife. The richness or intensity of a wildlife tourism experience is influenced by the authenticity, intensity, uniqueness, duration, species popularity and species status (Reynolds & Braithwaite, 2001) and Macquarie Island as a destination rates highly for each of these. Closely related is the rapid growth in bird-watching as a niche within ecotourism and the above average education and income levels of this group (Sekercioglu, 2002). This also contributes to the demand to visit Macquarie Island.

Macquarie Island has additional attractions such as its wild nature and wilderness, the lure of an unusual, hard-to-reach site that few others have visited and these are compounded by concepts within 'islandness' that recognise the psychological importance visitors place on the feeling of being separate and cut-off from the more familiar mainland environment (Baum, 1997). The emotive richness of a natural experience, sometimes considered spiritual, has been noted as a key outcome for visitors undertaking wilderness trips (Webb, 2002). Part of the appeal of wilderness areas is the feeling of isolation and closeness with nature. Visitors to Macquarie Island gain this in small tightly controlled groups during short carefully constructed periods ashore or zodiac cruises offshore. The harsh and intense nature of the environment is also experienced by visitors during the voyage, and on deck, as well as on-shore, and each contribution adds to the visitor's personal experience of being separated from the familiar. The small size of the ship and the relatively small passenger and crew numbers makes the overall ship experience akin to a floating island in the Southern Ocean. The physical challenge of coping in a harsh environment (such as moving about in small zodiacs in rough seas) can also intensify the experience and add elements of excitement and adventure. Maher's (2003) research on the Ross Sea region of Antarctica noted that this challenge was a motivator for visitors. It practically demonstrates the difficulties of visiting the location and intensifies the sense of remoteness and isolation.

Despite the allure of the location, the increase in interest in Antarctica, and the growth of specific segments of the wildlife tourism market, such as bird-watchers, current visitation remains low. Although the Tasmanian State Government has encouraged visitation to Macquarie Island, the cost of a trip, seasonality and weather issues, short time on the island, chance of not being able to disembark, and alternative opportunities, are all likely to continue to limit visitation.

However, visitor numbers could increase marginally without significant environmental impacts, provided that tourist visits continue to be restricted to the two landing areas and one zodiac cruising area and the visits remain strictly controlled. Both landing areas are either beaches or hardened areas, therefore, an increase in tourist numbers should result in only a minimal increased impact on the environment. Because an excellent management system was put in place while tourism numbers were low, and the continued difficulties of access, degradation of the site or significant change from increasing visitor numbers over time (as outlined in wildlife tourism by Duffus and Dearden (1990)) is unlikely to occur, at least in the near future.

Researchers and logistical staff, whose work has a significant on-going influence on the management of the island and the tourism industry, generally support continued restrictions on tourist activities. Despite the acknowledgement of very limited environmental impacts from tourism and the broad political encouragement of tourism to Macquarie Island, there has not been support for proposals to improve or extend access, such as overnight stays and extension of walking areas. Physically, the island is not well suited to further track development as access to higher ground would be steep and require extensive infrastructure costs, increase human safety concerns and potentially disturb wildlife. Overnight stays require accommodation infrastructure, food supplies, rubbish removal, toilet waste disposal and first aid capabilities and these are not presently considered appropriate given the area's high conservation value.

Conclusion

Wet, wild and windy Macquarie Island is a distinctive cold water tourist destination. The distance from Australia and New Zealand and the severe weather make any tourist visit a physical challenge. Yet this challenge, together with the island's natural values, contributes to its attraction. Presently, tourism is highly regulated and the numbers do not seem to adversely affect the flora or fauna. However, management guidelines ensure that visitor numbers are limited and their on-shore activities are tightly controlled. Tourists visit in groups on small-scale expedition-style cruise ships. Their on-shore visits are for short periods only, yet the sense of isolation and remoteness of the location, and the rewarding views of large numbers of wildlife, appear to have a profound impact on visitors.

Unlike many remote islands with small isolated host populations, researchers, field and support staff constitutes the host community of Macquarie Island. They are often dedicated and highly motivated to protect and conserve the island. They provide research and information that influences ongoing planning and management such as strict guidelines established for tourism visitation. The host community also plays an important role in the interpretation and education of tourists during visits yet their involvement with tourism operators does not include any accrual of commercial benefits.

As visitor numbers are slowly increasing, it is essential that the PWS support long-term research on the impacts of tourist visits. It is also essential that natural resource managers continue to work closely with commercial tourist operators to ensure that the outstanding natural and cultural World Heritage values of Macquarie Island are not compromised. The results of long-term impact monitoring will assist in determining whether the increase in tourist visits is sustainable on Macquarie Island.

Acknowledgments

The authors thank the Cooperative Research Centre for Sustainable Tourism, the School of Geography and Environmental Studies and the Antarctic Climate and Ecosystems Cooperative Research Centre, University of Tasmania for their support. A special thanks to the editor for his comments and suggestions. All errors and omissions remain the responsibility of the authors.

References

Abel, J., & Ellis, C. (2003). *Cruise Tasmania marketing strategy.* Hobart, Australia: Cruise Tasmania, Hobart Ports Corporation.

Baldacchino, G. (2004). The coming of age of island studies. *Tijdschrift voor Economische en Sociale Geografie, 95*(3), 272–283.

Bauer, T. G. (2001). *Tourism in the Antarctic: Opportunities, constraints and future prospects.* New York: The Haworth Press.

Baum, T. (1997). The fascination of islands: A tourism perspective. In: D. G. Lockhart, & D. Drakakis-Smith (Eds), *Island tourism: Trends and prospects* (pp. 21–35). London: Pinter.

Cessford, G. R., & Dingwall, P. R. (1994). Tourism on New Zealand's sub-Antarctic islands. *Annals of Tourism Research, 21*(2), 318–332.

Cole, D. N. (1994). Backcountry impact management: Lessons from research. *Backcountry Recreation Management/Trends, 31*(3), 10–14.

Cusick, P. (2005). Personal communication. Senior Ranger, Parks and Wildlife Service, Hobart, Tasmania, Australia.

Department of Primary Industries, Water and Environment. (2001). Macquarie Island. Hobart, Tasmania, Australia: DPIWE.

Duffus, D., & Dearden, P. (1990). Non-consumptive wildlife oriented recreation: A conceptual framework. *Biological Conservation, 53*(3), 213–231.

Ellis, C., Barrett, N., & Schmieman, S. (2005). Wilderness cruising: Turbulence, cruise ships and benthic communities. *Tourism in Marine Environments, 2*(1), 1–12.

Environment Australia. (2001). *Macquarie Island marine park management plan.* Canberra, Australia.

Headland, R. K. (1994). Historical development of Antarctic tourism. *Annals of Tourism Research, 21*(2), 269–280.

Holmes, N., Giese, M., & Achurch, H. (2003). Conservative management required for pedestrians and small boating near Giant petrels. *Australasian Ornithological Conference 03 Program & Abstracts.* Manning Clarke Centre, ANU, Canberra, 98-98.

International Association of Antarctica Tour Operators (IAATO) (2004). *2003–2004 Summary of sea-borne, air-borne and land-based Antarctic tourism.* www.iaato.org/tourism_stats.html (accessed 25/10/2005).

Kriwoken, L. K., & Rootes, D. (2000). Tourism on ice: Environmental impact assessment of Antarctic tourism. *Impact Assessment and Project Appraisal, 18*(2), 138–150.

Lang, C.-T., O'Leary, J., & Morrison, A. (1996). Trip driven attribute segmentation of Australian outbound nature travellers. *Proceedings from the Australian tourism and hospitality research conference*, Southern Cross University, Australia.

Maher, P. T. (2003). One hundred years after Scott: Visitor's anticipation of an experience in the Ross Sea region. Proceedings of 'Taking Tourism to the Limits' conference, University of Waikato, New Zealand, December.

Padgett, R., & Kriwoken, L. K. (2001). The Australian 'Environment Protection and Biodiversity Conservation Act 1999': What role for the commonwealth in environmental impact assessment? *Australian Journal of Environmental Management, 8*(1), 25–36.

Parks and Wildlife Service. (2003). *Macquarie Island nature reserve and world heritage area draft management plan.* Hobart, Tasmania, Australia: Parks and Wildlife Service & Department of Tourism, Parks, Heritage and the Arts.

Parks and Wildlife Service. (2004). *Guidelines for tourist operations and visits to Macquarie Island nature reserve world heritage area 2004/2005.* Hobart, Tasmania, Australia: Parks and Wildlife Service.

Reynolds, P. C., & Braithwaite, D. (2001). Towards a conceptual framework for wildlife tourism. *Tourism Management*, *22*(1), 31–42.

Sanson, L. (1994). An ecotourism case study in sub-Antarctic Islands. *Annals of Tourism Research*, *21*(2), 318–331.

Sekercioglu, C. H. (2002). Impacts of birdwatching on human and avian communities. *Environmental conservation*, *29*(3), 282–289.

Tasmania. (2004). Tasmania's Antarctic, sub-Antarctic and southern ocean policy. Hobart, Tasmania, Australia: Ministry for Economic Development.

Weaver, D. B. (2002). Hard-core ecotourists in Lamington National Park, Australia. *Journal of Ecotourism*, *1* (1), 19–35.

Webb, D. (2002). Investigating the structure of visitor experiences in the Little Sandy Desert, Western Australia. *Journal of Ecotourism*, *1*(2,3), 149–161.

Weiler, B., & Richins, H. (1995). Extreme, extravagant and elite: A profile of ecotourists on earth-watch expeditions. *Tourism Recreation Research*, *20*(1), 29–36.

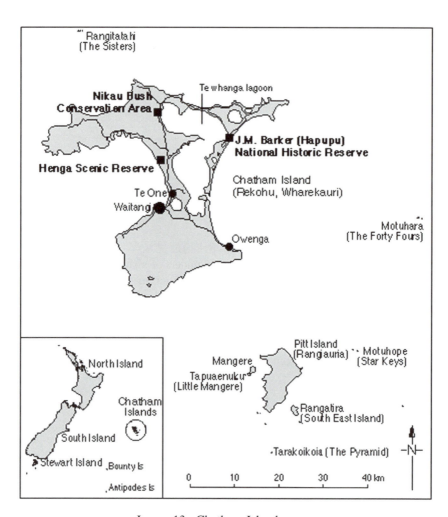

Image 13: Chatham Islands map.

Chapter 16

Chatham Islands, New Zealand

Peter Wiltshier and Andrew Cardow

Introduction

> Tourism can be a significant source of income and employment for local
> people. It can also pose a threat to an area's social fabric and its natural and
> cultural heritage, upon which it ultimately depends, but if it is well planned
> and managed it can be a force for their conservation. (Vourc'h, 2003, p. 7)

Life on the Edge – This was the marketing slogan dreamed up by the Chatham Island
Visitor Industry Group prior to the start of the third Christian Millennium. The phrase was
designed to evoke images of the frontier, harsh windswept Islands on the edge of the
Southern Ocean and at the edge of continuous inhabited settlement by New Zealanders.
The Chatham Islands receive few but growing numbers of visitors keen to experience life
on the edge. As the interest in the Islands as a destination increases, so too does the need
to examine the willingness and acceptance of tourism by the inhabitants. An important
issue in a remote and poorly developed tourism location such as the Chatham Islands is the
competence and ability of both the public and private sectors to manage the impacts of visitation. Unlike some other industries, tourism is a highly complex activity resulting from
interaction between airlines, accommodation providers, tour operations, surface transportation, souvenirs, food and beverage outlets and tour guides. This complexity is compounded by the critical difference that tourism brings the consumer to the product and not
the reverse. Effectively all complications, depredations, management errors and impacts
occur at the point of delivery which is always the destination. In addition, a destination
needs to supply products and services that help create the tourist experience generating
jobs and business opportunities while doing so. The destination also needs to find ways of
mitigating the negatives that may include pollution, crime and, frequently in remote locations, inadequate service provision. In isolated locations such as the Chatham Islands the
cost of ensuring adequate infrastructural services may be borne without an adequate
income from the tourism activities to meet the full cost of services. The cost of such services are then subsidised by the local inhabitants.

Extreme Tourism: Lessons from the World's Cold Water Islands
Copyright © 2006 by Elsevier Ltd.
All rights of reproduction in any form reserved
ISBN: 0-08-044656-6

In more cases than ever before, destinations are challenging the rights of tourists to consume services and products without paying a fair and equitable fee for those services and products (e.g. CSI, 2005). Many destinations are seeking a solution that offers development, while maintaining the local quality of life, species diversity and preservation of heritage and culture. This chapter will illustrate the context in which the Chatham Islanders have historically offered a tourism product and discuss avenues by which a new tourism industry can be developed that meets the needs of the expectant visitor and also satisfies the residents and local politicians. So far, new tourism operations on Chatham are being established without really coordinating activity by public sector stakeholders or reference to the existing players in the market. Still, a coordinated approach between the different stakeholders appears to be in the offing.

History

The Islands lie approximately 700 km off New Zealand on the edge of the roaring forties in the deep south of the Pacific Ocean, 2 hours flying time due east of Christchurch, New Zealand. The Islands form the most remote continuously inhabited offshore Islands of New Zealand and are part of the Rongotai, Wellington, Electorate. The Islands were first settled by the Moriori, an early indigenous Polynesian people, sometime in the 1600s then by the Europeans from the late 1700s and invaded by Maori from Wellington and Taranaki during the 1830s (King & Morrison, 1990). By the time of the Maori invasions the Moriori had developed a different language and culture from the mainland Maori tribes. Such differences can be seen in the petroglyphs and dendroglyphs still evident in the Island (*ibid.*).

Since 1984, the Government of New Zealand has delegated responsibility for implementing regional development to the local territorial authority and has empowered that authority with policy and legislation (mostly through resource-management control) to develop and regulate industry and economic development. On the Chatham Islands, as will be illustrated, the response to such devolution was to establish an enterprise trust that would oversee and provide guidance concerning the nature of new Islands-wide initiatives. It was envisaged that such an enterprise trust would also integrate new development along with stronger social development agenda issues. On the New Zealand mainland local authorities established similar operations geared toward bottom-up solutions to economic development such as Enterprise North Shore, on Auckland North Shore, and the Canterbury Development Corporation, in Christchurch, South Island.

A 'bottom-up' solution to regional development is dependent on a well-organized, competent and informed public–private sector partnership at the destination under examination. As with many well-examined tourism destinations in the northern hemisphere, like Majorca, St. Lucia and Malta, it is the engagement of the political process by the community that can be considered the key to future development initiatives, addressing both regional under-development and under-performance relative to the host nation (Howarth & Howarth, 1989; Jayawardene & Ramajeesingh, 2003; Lockhart, 1997; Paniagua, 2002). Meanwhile, community groups are engaged in response to local problems and local good practices that are appropriately communicated to and among all concerned stakeholders.

Action that is global in practice and local in implementation might also prove, in the long-term, to be most productive and best interpreted by these stakeholders. However, on the Chathams, such a coordinated political approach is currently missing.

This chapter reviews a decline in economic resources and activities on the Chatham Islands and the subsequent reaction by some to utilize tourism as a new and alternative activity for the destination, improving in the process the Islands' economic diversification. This situation also highlights crucial institutional blockages to the proposed development.

In presenting the Chathams as a tourism destination, a number of particular aspects will be addressed. Some are endemic to remote cold water islands: such as the impact of oligopolistic practice on the destination; the difficulty of improving access to the destination; the authenticity of local products as tools for tourism interpretation and marketing; and conflicts between operators and the few established owners of the marketing channels. Other issues are more specific to the Chathams and include the actual activity content and management strategies of the various tourism operations, and a need to focus on marketing of known tourism services and products (MacDonald & Jolliffe, 2003; Cai, 2002; Reed, 1997; Ioannides & Petersen, 2003; Mitchell & Reid, 2001).

The Lure of the Islands

There are just 696 people living on 2,500 km^2 of rugged terrain with plentiful supplies of seafood, pasture and fresh water. The Chatham Islands have a diverse and unique indigenous flora and fauna that has attracted both colonists and invading Maori tribes. Today, the rich tradition is one of the platforms for the development of an incipient tourism industry based on natural resources and the collective sharing of resources amongst visitors and residents alike.

The Islands comprise 10 outcrops including two main islands, the largest being named Rekohu or Wharekauri (and commonly referred to as Chatham) and the second largest being Rangiauria (also known as Pitt Island). The Chathams are cold, ranging from an average high of 15°C in February to an average low of 7°C in July (NIWA, 2005). The Islands are often regarded as a desolate remote outpost of New Zealand, but they are nevertheless well endowed with natural beauty, as any image would attest. Moreover, the Chatham group boasts a coastline that is both rugged and endowed with long white sandy beaches, clear deep blue sea, unique flora and home to some of New Zealand's most endangered birds, including a waterfowl, the taiko, and the New Zealand black robin.

The Islands' remoteness has required the Islanders to remain dependent on shipping for most capital goods, including the fossil fuel used for energy generation. But the same remoteness has served as a curiosity motivator for visitors, and ironically also provided a barrier to the tourism industry's growth and its development.

Strangely, Chatham Islanders welcome visitors, but they express a reluctance to embrace tourists. The Chatham Islanders we spoke to describe their differentiation of visitors and tourists in the following way; visitors were people who had been invited to the Islands, or had a personal tie to the Islands. Tourists, on the other hand, engendered visions of unattached people just walking around, without any personal tie to the islands, or else simply people who were uninvited and there just to look — not to experience. As an illustration, note the following interchange reported by an independent British journalist between Islanders and a visitor at the time of the 2000 millennium celebrations: "Visitors are welcome," said the islander, shaking my hand. "Tourists can **** off." It was an inauspicious start' (Newton, 2005).

One possible reason for such hostility could be the bond that most of the Islanders have with the land: they are very protective of their stewardship of the local fauna and flora. Moreover, regardless of the tourist possibilities on the Islands, the majority of the land is privately owned, including land held by both the Maori and Moriori people. Thus, tension exists on the Chathams in relation to increased accessibility: there are people in the visitor industry who express a desire to increase visitor numbers, yet the majority of potential tourist sites are located within the boundaries of privately held land. Such contradictions are amongst the basic barriers to tourism development on the Chatham Islands.

Living on isolated Islands has led to a social development that is varied and dynamic. The census reveals that there is a dearth of young, marriageable women who flee the Islands after completing their secondary education and seek security in employment career and partnership in New Zealand (New Zealand Census, 2001). Throughout the 20th century there was a repeated failure in development of local social capital through further education on the Islands, which has been well documented (Arbuckle, 1971). A lack of social capital is therefore perceived as critical to future socio-economic and cultural success of any development agenda. There is a collective feeling within the Chathams' community that in recent years they find themselves just holding on, perched if you like, in the face of economic and social change sweeping in from New Zealand.

The situation in the islands has not always been so gloomy. There has been a history of successful fishing and agriculture. At one stage in the early 19th century this group of islands were a store of fresh vegetables, seafood and seal and whale meat and oil products to supply the vessels plying the great circle route from the south through to the west coast of the Americas (King & Morrison, 1990). In the 1960s, the establishment of a crayfish tail exporting industry became a cornerstone of economic survival for the Chathams. However, this boom industry that saw millions of dollars of export income from crayfish tail exports to the United States did not survive the decade. Rising fuel costs associated with the oil price hikes in the early 1970s, plus over fishing of crayfish led to the eventual demise of an unsustainable activity. The Islands at one time had a fleet of helicopters ferrying crayfish tails to refrigerated freighters and there were in excess of a dozen fish packing plants located throughout the Islands (Arbuckle, 1971, p. 23). Today, there are only three packing plants at Waitangi, Kaingaroa and Port Hutt. Moreover, a race to the sea in order to diversify into fishing was halted by the introduction of fishing quotas in 1986. The down side to the diversification away from agriculture into fishing has created a boom-bust effect on the Chathams, a phenomenon common to many small isolated communities. Fishing did not turn out to be the economic goldmine that many had hoped for. The desire to make easy money from the plentiful supplies of fish that inhabit the water around the Chatham Islands only contributed to economic woes rather than to their solution. By the end of the 1980s, Chatham Islanders were facing a dilemma resulting from an easy over-dependence on one economic activity: they had over-fished their waters and had under-resourced their land. With a net decrease in farm income, and neglect of pasture, scrub had begun to take over vast areas of previously deforested and grassed land. This meant that any income for agriculture declined just as the same was happening to any income from fishing. The reasons visitors come to the Islands in the 21st century have little to do with primary agriculture. Instead most visitors are seeking a sensation of isolation, which could not be provided by more mass market-oriented destinations and tours (personal communication, Kea Travel, in-bound tour operator, 2004).

The Chathams competed with other isolated islands in the Pacific Ocean to be the first inhabited Island to witness the start of the third Christian millennium. As a result, there were spectacular celebrations organized on the Chathams in December 1999, and January 2000, funded by the New Zealand Government to a tune of NZ$500,000 (US$320,000). However, due to the nature of the reporting of these celebrations, some on the Islands received the review of these celebrations with mixed feelings. The infrastructure, services and built environment on the Chathams were never intended for mass-tourism consumption. The residents can accommodate no more than 100 visitors in any one week. In the month of January 2000, over 1,000 visitors descended on the Islands. Despite such numbers, the publicity that surrounded the celebrations on the Chathams was less than complementary. Excerpts from a story in the *New Zealand Herald* carried such gems as: "Many Pitt Islanders were still hung over from partying all night in the woolshed, the corrugated tin hut where they usually shear their sheep"; and "Despite its status as the place that would usher in the first sunrise of the year 2000, the islands millennial countdown clock [a mantle clock] was carried to the woolshed". Within the same article were various references to farmers "swigging from a scotch bottle", and "sipping from a wine bottle". Quite understandably some Islanders were unhappy with such negative publicity that ridiculed their efforts as hosts. This prompted the Mayor of the Chatham Islands District Council to speak on New Zealand National Radio in February 2000 in order to refute claims of incompetence and to protect the reputation of the Islanders. Such an experience gave rise to the suggestion that the tourism industry on the Chathams would be better served if based on indigenous skills and modelled to suit the local community, rather than striving (unsuccessfully) to meet a tourism blueprint created elsewhere. Local leadership and management of tourism is not only vital to endogenous models of community-based development but critical to brand, image and integrity of products and services (compare, for example, a longitudinal study on Gomera in the Canary Islands in the 1990s by Macleod (2002) and in the Guianas by Sinclair (2003).

Conflict between visitors and tourists was not just limited to the millennium event, however. It is one of long standing history. In an attempt to resolve this issue, the development of a collective host/guest management plan was recommended. This would generate interest in taking local action to address concerns over competencies and capacity. In particular, it was recommended that the feasibility of a collective internet portal and a modestly upgraded tourism infrastructure (with such items as backpacker accommodation, a larger variety of activity and the provision of public facilities) be seriously considered (Wiltshier & Cardow, 2001). A feasibility study is underway to assess these proposals and may eventually lead to a redressing of this situation.

The current tourist supply to the Chatham Islands is somewhat limited to small tour groups arranged by Auckland, Christchurch and West Coast based tour operators and the occasional international nature-based, independent traveller. The tour groups typically consist of seniors (aged over fifty) and prepared to pay relatively high airfares for the two to three hour turbo-prop airline services between the New Zealand mainland and the Chathams. Tour packages are not competitively priced when compared to other island destinations within the same three hour jet service of New Zealand, such as Eastern Australia, Norfolk Island, Fiji, Cook Islands, New Caledonia or Vanuatu (personal information, Seymour Tours, 2004). Yet, as expected, when we spoke to the tour operators servicing the Chathams, there was general agreement that the price was not a limiting factor. Tourists generally appeared quite prepared to spend the money to visit a place that was decidedly off the beaten path. Moreover, given the present air service and infrastructure, there would be difficulty in developing a new market for the Islands. This is in part due to a lack of inspiration and commitment to tourism development and the lack of perception of a visitor industry as a way to achieve economic development by both the local government and major non-governmental coordinating groups on the Islands. Neither did we witness much aspiration by stakeholders to models of tourism development available in other, somewhat similar locations. Such reluctance for tourism makes it difficult for those in the community who are interested in tourism to develop any alternative community growth strategy.

Methodological Issues

As a result of the Radio New Zealand interview with the Chatham Island Mayor, the two writers contacted the mayor to suggest the proactive development of a tourism industry group: bringing together Chatham Island tourism operators who would work co-operatively to promote the Chathams as a destination and to assist in the development of any required tourism infrastructure. The offer was taken up: when we arrived on the Island, we set about introducing ourselves, and through the local closed circuit television channel, called a public meeting of all interested persons.

Subsequently the bulk of the material for this research into the state of play of the Chathams tourism industry was conducted using in-depth unstructured interviews and one focus group in September 2001, and updated in the light of emergent events. In following grounded theory methodology (Glaser & Strauss, 1973), the structure of an action model incorporating supply, demand and regulatory functions involving the complex range of actors on the Islands was assembled. This model was then used to define and then attempt to create a desirable outcome model for sustainable tourism development (Wiltshier & Cardow, 2001). The focus group was a self-selected group that responded to a radio and television appeal for participants to take part in a discussion intended to raise the profile of the visitor industry. The balance of informants was selected on the basis of their roles with tourism supply/demand and governance/regulatory factors. With such a small island community, it was relatively easy to target and involve all the key decision makers.

The underpinning literature for this study is based on the community sustainable tourism model best illustrated by the work of such authors as Brent-Ritchie (1999), Inskeep (1991) and Woodley (1993). The work also broadly draws on Scheyvens (1999) and her study of empowerment at political, economic, psychological and social levels. Added to these resources is an overwhelming sense of purpose in the conservation, regeneration and regulatory environment, which is particular and perhaps peculiar to the Chatham Islands. These latter factors are indeed the core principles for the destination's future governance and management.

Participants for this research included the local Mayor, the Council's administration officer, the owner of the largest local hotel along with current and potential operators of the tourism industry on the Islands. The operators spoken to included inbound operators, resident in New Zealand, handicraft retailers, fishing and dive providers, guide operators and potential entrants into the industry.

Political Issues

The Chatham Islands constitute the smallest and most remote of New Zealand's, local territorial authorities. The local district council oversees the governance of 696 residents (NZ Census, 2001) and is responsible for administering the infrastructure of the Islands with the rateable income from some 200 family groups. In addition, the Local Council is doubly unique amongst local authorities in New Zealand in that it can levy import and export dues on all goods landed and exported from the Islands regardless of eventual destination. In addition the council is unique in that it does not own the majority of the 'Islands' infrastructure. In 1991, as part of on-going neo-liberal reforms in New Zealand, the "Minister of Internal Affairs, acting for and on behalf of the Government of New Zealand" (Chatham Islands Enterprise Trust 1991, p. 1) established the Chatham Islands Enterprise Trust with a grant of NZ$8 million (US$5 million). The Trust was established with five trustees, of which only two were living on the Chatham Islands. The other three were a barrister, a retired public servant and an accountant, all from Wellington. The Trust was established to operate several business activities that were being operated by both the local and central government and transfer those central and local government assets from the state to private control. The Trust was established for the benefit of the community and future inhabitants of the Chatham Islands (*ibid.*) 5. As a result of these changes, the Trust now enjoys the ownership of the wharf at Waitangi and at Flower Pot, the airport at Karewa, the electricity generation facilities and facilities for waste disposal. In addition, the Trust administers the sales of fishing quota, the radio and television broadcasting system and has purchased forestry on the New Zealand mainland in Hawke's Bay. Although the Chatham Islands do not have a television station as such, there is a closed circuit broadcasting facility, which is used to deliver the government broadcasters main evening bulletin and deliver taped programmes from Television New Zealand. Apart from the forestry the remainder were all functions that were previously controlled by central and local government on the Islands. As a consequence the council and the Trust share, and to some extent duplicate, some aspects of administration and strategic management. The only infrastructure items funded by the Council are the roads. The democratic processes that see Council members elected every three years are not mirrored in the Trust. For example the original trust deed prevented a trustee serving more than three terms; however in 1995 the Trust deed was amended to allow a trustee to serve an indefinite number of terms (Chatham Islands Enterprise Trust, 1995, p. 2). The Trust Board has seen re-elected Trustees serving more than two consecutive terms and the process of elections has been largely subverted as existing trustees are apparently re-elected. Despite the commercial activity of the Trust, and the trust ownership of the airport, the current members of the Trust Board have not been keen in the past to see any spending on developing or marketing the tourism product.

Socio-economic Issues

The reluctance to spend on tourism infrastructure is caused by both social and economic factors. In terms of social reluctance there is the widely held belief indicated above that tourists are unwelcome, whereas visitors are to be encouraged. This is based on the assumption that the infrastructure of the Chatham Islands could not cope with tourist development. A related issue regarding tourism development on the Chathams is a common issue that concerns the development of tourism in isolated communities, which relates to the presence of an oligopoly in terms of tourism infrastructure. The Chathams are no exception. Creating a tourism industry on the Chathams involves making concessions to local interpretations of tourism. The primary route of access into the Chathams remains via Air Chathams, a privately owned and operated airline which runs the only direct scheduled air service from mainland New Zealand, which according to Air Chathams, is seeing a growing number of visitors per year (personal communication, Air Chathams, 2005). This service is supplemented by infrequent private charter aircraft and intermittent calls by scheduled freighters. Added to this transportation mix is the occasional adventure cruise ship, often en route to the sub Antarctic or Antarctic Islands. The Chief Executive Officer of the Council in April 2005, was unable to suggest how many visitors arrived by ship, except to say "a few" and indicated that it was, in his opinion, a very small number.

All this adds up to an imperfect market situation in terms of tourism access. Air Chathams operates as a *de facto* gatekeeper for the tourism industry and, along with the accommodation opportunities on the islands, has given rise to the belief that the local tourism industry is limited and even constrained by the scheduling of Air Chathams and the available bed nights provided by the two main accommodation providers. Island tourist accommodation is provided by a small number of 'bed and breakfast' operators, one backpacker and motel operator, two dive operators who also provide bunk accommodation for their guests, and two hotel operators. The majority of visitors are directed towards these two hotels; the Travellers Rest/Waitangi Hotel and the Chatham Islands Lodge. The Travellers Rest is a converted villa offering a high standard of overnight accommodation. It is located at the top of a bluff overlooking the port of Waitangi and sits directly above the hotel. The Travellers Rest has been host to New Zealand Prime Ministers, and is used, along with the hotel, by visiting government and business officials. The hotel, under the same ownership as the Rest, provides accommodation, meals and operates the town's only tavern. The Lodge, by comparison, is located in the centre of Chatham Island and is a self-contained unit providing meals, accommodation and the organization of tourist activity. The Lodge caters mainly to package tours rather than people visiting the Islands on business. Both the Lodge and the Travellers Rest/Hotel deal directly with inbound travel agents and as a result are seen by many operators on the New Zealand mainland as the only two options for accommodation on the Chathams.

The oligopoly that exists on the Chathams is not due to any formal design but to the outcome of historical and commercial accident. Nevertheless, the existence of this oligopoly has provided real blockages for the development of additional tourism infrastructure, which has meant that there are problems when recommending a new course of action or a new strategy for development that will meet all partners' expectations. In particular, this situation creates friction between stakeholders, as Haikai Tane, who in a professorial address at Unitec in

2000, reported, when put alongside emergent tourism operators, such as those seeking to expose mainly European tourists to indigenous practices and beliefs. Europeans bred in an economic culture that does not question the 'growth imperative' may find rewarding lessons in observing at close range the sustainable, multi-purpose agriculture and aquaculture developed over generations by the indigenous Polynesians, the Moriori of the Chatham Islands (Tane, 2000). Another way of enhancing the tourism presence on the Island is to build upon the developing desire of tourists to have a wilderness and adventure experience. Eroding the current oligopoly and introducing more wilderness/adventure/culture tourism will require a rethinking of the way tourism is approached by the Island's operators. At the time of writing, each operator remains responsible for their own marketing. There was no official central portal, no official clearing house, no official coordination for tourism policy or development. This could be as a direct effect of the existing tourism market demand structure.

The socio-cultural makeup of the Chathams makes it necessary for any future development to be in sympathy with both residents and potential visitors. Visitors are searching for an authentic experience in regards to the uniqueness of flora, fauna and indigenous culture of the Chathams. Developments that mirror core values are fundamental to future success in this tight knit community. One operator noted to the researchers: "We're doing OK in a slow sort of way" (personal communication, October 2000).

Recommending the establishment of a socially responsible body to oversee tourism developments could be preceded by a resource audit which would be accompanied by a resident expectation and perceptions survey. Recent developments in local government practice indicate that social responsibility must be reflected in the outcomes of Council driven, business operations. In this case, the accountability and responsibility for such coordination lies with the Chatham Islands Enterprise Trust. Even though the Trust is not a Council controlled business operation, it does have the responsibility for economic development on the Chatham Islands and so appears as the vehicle by which any programme should be delivered.

The Tourists

At a public meeting held on the Chathams in October 2001, at least three potential tourism operators expressed a desire to enhance the traditional tourist profile for the Chatham Islands. The historical visitor to the Chathams is part of a package group, is aged fifty or older and is staying either at the Lodge or the Hotel/Travellers Rest. In addition, the typical Chatham Island visitor is well travelled, interested in flora and fauna and is informed about the destination. The particular group that expressed a desire to enhance the profile was aware of a growing number of younger people seeking an adventure/wilderness experience. Among the ideas floated at that stage were; paraponting, where a person makes a controlled descent from a cliff top utilising a parachute type wing, sand yachting, horse riding, lagoon kayaking and shark viewing. All these ideas are low impact and entirely feasible, however they were also ideas that ran contrary to the existing tourist paradigms and at the time were quickly out voted by the majority of the participants at the meeting.

Subsequently, an operator has established a deep sea fishing and shark viewing operation whereby customers are taken into the Southern Ocean in a secure launch and then lowered in baited cages to view great white sharks. This operation is attracting a younger audience and, as the activity is offered as a package holiday, it is a pull activity for the Chathams. The fact remains however that this operator is not part of a coordinated approach and is reliant solely on word of mouth and an internet site for customer take-up (Starkey's website 2005). Although there are backpacker accommodations available, the main Chatham Islands web page still insists that people wishing to travel to the islands should have their accommodation booked before purchasing their air ticket (Chatham Islands web-site 2005).

Self-determination

A combination of aquaculture, agriculture and tourism is suggested as a way of smoothing the 'boom-bust' effect of the economic history of the Chatham Islands. Fisheries and the provision by government legislation in 2003 of a 321-km exclusive fisheries zone protecting fishing rights is a critical element of the economic future of the Islands. Both central and local government as well as the fishing industry now recognize the unsustainable extractive nature of past fishery activity. Both central and local government have, in their indirect fashion, supported the establishment of a wider base of economic activity. The Enterprise Trust Board has the mandate to oversee such an economic diversification process and is a cornerstone to the future survival of economic activity for residents and business people alike.

The Chatham Islands are recognized worldwide for their important contribution to the preservation of unique and endangered flora and fauna. In effect, the unique Chatham Islands forget-me-not and three endangered bird species — the guillemot, taiko and the ground-dwelling black robin — have been protected by New Zealand's Department of Conservation for more than 100 years. This unfortunately brings the Islands to the attention of horticulturalists, ornithologists and adventurers. Features such as the black robin and the taiko have in effect created a new demand, which the local inbound tourism estimate to be a growing trend for such idiosyncratic tourism. (Although there are no firm figures to be found regarding exact numbers of visitors to the Chathams, an aspect which makes reporting difficult, all operators contacted in relation to this work expressed the opinion that their numbers were up and were growing.) Such tourism, unless accompanied by education and interpretation specialists (usually New Zealand university experts) could further endanger species by intrusion, introduction of exotic pests and opportunists seeking the unusual.

Conclusion

In March 2004, the return of important tracts of land in the northeast corner of Chatham Island to an indigenous trust marks the beginning of a new era of cooperation between residents and landowners. The 4,116 hectare Kaingaroa Station includes 247 hectares of protected reserve. This land is significant to the indigenous Moriori people. It contains remnant broadleaf forest at Hapupu that features *dendroglyphs*, carvings by Moriori ancestors into living trees that are among the only remaining memorials of past habitation and culture for Moriori. These carvings, known in Polynesian as *rakau momori*, are both sacred and endangered by further visitation and by the inevitable destruction by the ravages of time. In addition late 2004 saw the establishment of a joint Moriori and Maori hospitality centre capable of providing food and lodging to a large number of visitors. The establishment of such a facility in conjunction with the developing backpacker accommodations may lead to the emergence of a different tourist profile. Already there are tourists willing to go to the Chathams for shark viewing and deep sea diving. These people are helping to illustrate to the Chatham Islands tourism industry that there may be more to offer the visitor than sanitised package holidays for seniors.

The Chatham Islands are a remote cold water island destination and until recently seen as a destination for the middle aged or senior adventurer. In order to build upon the trend for younger adventure and wilderness tourists, a more coordinated approach needs to be considered. The power of the status quo must be harnessed in order for this transition to happen. A more differentiated tourism industry could cater for a wider swathe of tourism interests on the islands. Moreover, such an activity could incorporate the image and branding of *Living on the Edge.*

References

Arbuckle, G. A. (1971). *The Chatham islands in perspective*. Wellington: Hicks Smith & Sons Ltd.

Brent-Ritchie, J. R. (1999). Policy formulation at the tourism/environment interface: Insights and recommendations from the Banff-Bow valley study. *Journal of Travel Research, 38*(2), 100–110.

Cai, L. (2002). Cooperative branding for rural destinations. *Annals of Tourism Research, 29*(3), 720–742.

Chatham Island Enterprise Trust. (1991). Deed of trust. Wellington: Department of Internal Affairs.

Chatham Island Enterprise Trust. (1995). Deed of trust. Wellington: Department of Internal Affairs.

Chatham Islands website. (2005). Experience the edge, www.chathams.com/ (accessed 25/10/2005).

CSI. (2005). Alaska cruise ship initiative launched. www.conservationinstitute.org/csireport2_05.htm (accessed 25/10/2005).

Glaser, B. G., & Strauss, A. L. (1973). *The discovery of grounded theory: Strategies for qualitative research*. Chicago, IL: Aldine Publishing.

Howarth & Howarth (1989). *Maltese islands tourism development plan*. London: Howarth & Howarth Inc.

Inskeep, E. (1991). *Tourism planning: An integrated & sustainable tourism approach*. New York: Van Nostrand Reinhold.

Ioannides, D., & Petersen, T. (2003). Tourism non entrepreneurship in peripheral destinations: A case study of small and medium tourism enterprises on Bornholm, Denmark. *Tourism Geographies, 5*(4), 408–435.

Jayewardene, C., & Ramajeesingh, D. (2003). Performance of tourism analysis: A Caribbean perspective. *International Journal of Contemporary Hospitality Management, 15*(3), 176–179

King, M., & Morrison, R. (1990). *A land apart: The Chatham islands of New Zealand*. Glenfield, NZ: Random House.

Lockhart, D. G. (1997). We promise you a warm welcome: Tourism to Malta since the 1960s. *Geo Journal, 41*(2), 145–152

MacDonald, R., & Jolliffe, L. (2003). Cultural rural tourism: Evidence from Canada. *Annals of Tourism Research, 30*(2), 307–323.

Macleod, D. (2002). Disappearing Culture? Globalisation & A Canary island fishing community. *History & Anthropology, 13*(1), 53–67.

Mitchell, R., & Reid. D. (2001). Community integration island tourism in Peru. *Annals of Tourism Research 28*(1), 113–139.

New Zealand Census. (2001). Wellington: New Zealand Department of Statistics.

Newton, R. (2005). Chatham Islands: the end of the world. www.travelintelligence.com/wsd/articles/art_3303.html (accessed 25/10/2005).

NIWA (2005). www.niwa.cri.nz/edu/resources/climate/overview/map_chathami (accessed 25/10/2005).

Paniagua, A. (2002). Urban rural migration, tourism entrepreneurs and rural restructuring in Spain. *Tourism Geographies, 4*(4), 349–371.

Reed, M. (1997). Power relations and community based tourism planning. *Annals of Tourism Research, 24*(3), 506–591.

Scheyvens, R. (1999). Case study: Ecotourism and the empowerment of local communities. *Tourism Management, 20*(2), 98–108.

Sinclair, D. (2003). Developing indigenous tourism: Challenges for the Guianas. *International Journal of Contemporary Hospitality Management, 15*(3), 140–146.

Starkey's website (2005). www.starkeys.co.nz/ (accessed 25/10/2005).

Tane, H. (2000). Professorial address. Auckland, New Zealand: Unitec Institute of Technology.

Vourc'h, A. (2003). Tourism & local agenda 21: The role of local authorities in sustainable Tourism. New York: International Council for Local Environmental Initiatives, www.food-mac.com/Doc/200411/la21.pdf (accessed 25/10/2005).

Wiltshier, P., & Cardow, A. (2001). *Public meeting of Chatham islands' visitor industries stakeholders group*. Unpublished document, October 2001. Available from authors upon request.

Woodley, A. (1993). Tourism & sustainable development: The community perspective. In: J. G. Nelson, R. Butler, & G. Wall (Eds), *Tourism and sustainable development: Monitoring, planning, managing* (pp. 135–146). Waterloo: Heritage Resources Centre, University of Waterloo.

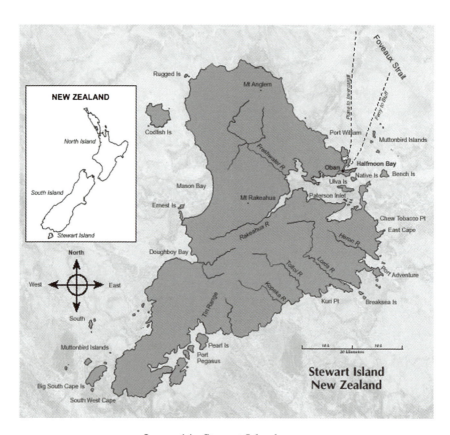

Image 14: Stewart Island map.

Chapter 17

Stewart Island, New Zealand

C. Michael Hall

Introduction

> From several vantage points we had seen glimpses of the dim and some-what forbidding outline of Stewart Island. Rain storms had scudded across Foveaux Strait and inky storm clouds brooded over it. There had been no indication of the beauty that lies across the pendant island .... Inland the green forests mount upwards, threaded by tracks which lure the visitor further and further into the bird-frequented bush which opens up here and there to reveal white sands lapped by the ever-changing water below, while overhead a horizon-wide gold and crimson sky is set on fire by the sinking sun. (Reed, 1954, pp. 404, 410)

> Stewart Island draws conservationists, eco-tourists and anybody wanting to experience one of the more obscure and most special outposts of the world. (Stewart Island Flights, 2005)

Stewart Island is New Zealand's third largest island. Lying at the southern end of the country, the island has long been a location of which New Zealanders have talked of in glowing terms as to its natural beauty but usually never visited themselves. Stewart Island is less than 35 km from the southern coast of the South Island of New Zealand. The island is separated from the mainland by the relatively shallow Fouveaux Strait which has a max-imum depth of 36 m. Although Maori have had a presence on the island since the 1200s and Europeans from the late 18th century, the biology of the island is relatively undis-turbed when compared to the New Zealand mainland.

Maori referred to the island as Rakiura, meaning red or glowing sky. This is interpreted as relating to sunsets visible from the island, night-time displays of Aurora Australis (the Southern Lights), or even the blushing of a Maori chief, Raki tamau (Reed, 1954, p. 405). The island is also known to Maori as Te Puka a te Waka a Maui (The Anchor of Maui's Canoe), a reference to the tradition of Maui's discovery of New Zealand and his use of the

South Island as a canoe or platform by which he fished up the North Island. Stewart Island anchored his canoe (Braithwaite, 1985). The island was also known to Maori as Motunui or Large Island (Department of Conservation (DoC), 2004a). Although the island was too far south for Maori to grow staple crops, such as kumara, the island's marine resources supported a small permanent population as well as frequent visits from mainland Maori. Of special importance was the migratory titi (the sooty shearwater), which Maori harvested every autumn. The right to harvest titi is still held by descendants of the Maori who live on Stewart Island.

Although covering an area of 1746 km^2 (670 miles^2) (Braithwaite, 1985), similar in size to Singapore, the island has only 25 km of road, 245 km of walking tracks, and a permanent population of approximately 400 people in 2001 (Statistics New Zealand, 2003). However, the island presently receives over 60,000 visitors a year, apart from a significant number of second homes (Table 17.1).

The island's permanent population has rarely risen over 500 people during the course of its European history. Cumberland and Fox (1970) noted that the population fluctuated between 571 in 1951 and 332 in 1966, with the higher figure being attributable to Maori visiting the island for muttonbirding (the harvesting of the sooty shearwater or muttonbird). The permanent inhabitants are concentrated around the township of Oban, which is located at Halfmoon Bay, in the north of the island. On the southeast coast of the island another township, Point Pegasus (also referred to as Port Pegasus) was established after declaration of British sovereignty of the island in 1840 and once had a post office and several shops, serving as a base for gold and tin mining and fishing until the end of the 19th century. However, the township ceased to be permanently inhabited in the 1950s, although the presence of offshore coastal islands means that the coastal waters are often used for shelter by fishing boats, yachts and small craft.

Tourism has long been recognised as one of the economic development options for the island. Unfortunately, no accurate visitation figures exist for Stewart Island. Reader's

Table 17.1: Visitors to Stewart Island: 1992/1993–2002/2003.

Year	Annual visits	% Change
1992/1993	40,047	
1993/1994	48,748	21.7
1994/1995	48,921	0.4
1995/1996	47,778	−2.3
1996/1997	45,534	−4.7
1997/1998	47,042	3.3
1998/1999	52,470	11.5
1999/2000	56,320	7.3
2000/2001	57,572	2.2
2001/2002	61,772	7.3
2002/2003	62,021	0.4

Source: Visitor Information Network, in Skjelde (2003).

Digest (1981) reported that in the late 1970s Stewart Island attracted 30,000 visitors a year, a figure still used in official documents in the late 1990s (Lovelock & Robinson, 2005). In 2003, this figure had grown to at least 60,000 visits, although this figure is still only a rough estimate as it only records visits to the Visitor Centre, which therefore may include double-counting, but does not account for second home visitors, and various degrees of boat access to many other parts of the island outside the township of Oban. Nevertheless, according to the Southland District Plan (Southland District Council, 2001, p. 155).

> Tourism is growing, reflecting an increase in interest throughout the world in plants, animals and 'unspoilt' or remote places. Stewart Island offers the tourist the opportunity to see large numbers of seabirds, bush birds uncommon on the mainland and a largely unmodified flora, as well as spectacular scenery. The challenge is to provide for the needs of the residents while retaining the quality of the environment.

Reader's Digest (1981) reports that the first boatload of organised sightseers arrived at Halfmoon Bay from Bluff on the South Island in the mid-1870s. This route is still used by the ferry service in the present day, while the connection to the Southland District remains important in tourist terms because the island is used for fishing and hunting trips as well as for second homes and boating by Southland families. In recent years, the island has served to attract tourism interest from elsewhere in New Zealand and, perhaps more significantly, from international visitors who are interested in its natural attractions.

Cumberland and Fox (1970, p. 197) noted that "isolation and inaccessibility are essential features of the region". Thirty-five years on, this observation still holds true. Although international cruise ships pass by the island during the Southern Hemisphere summer, they do not access the island for passenger day-trips. The nearest international airports are in Queenstown and in Dunedin, both of which only serve Australia, and are over two hours' drive away from the ferry connection at Bluff. Invercargill Airport, which provides the passenger connection to Stewart Island, has been upgraded to take Boeing 737s from Australia; but regular passenger services have not yet materialised. Invercargill is connected to the Air New Zealand network via Christchurch International Airport. Indeed, such is the lack of air network connectivity for Stewart Island that to fly from New Zealand's largest city and main international gateway, Auckland, requires a minimum of three different legs and approximately six to seven hours travel at best. Apart from visitors from the Southland district in the adjacent mainland, travellers to the island therefore tend to be undertaking their travel as part of extended stays in the country, usually of at least 10 days to 2 weeks as in the case of the Australian market that is visiting South Island. International travellers to the island are more likely to be those visiting New Zealand for several months, and who usually meet the profile of a backpacker or early retirees who have a substantial time budget. Similarly, domestic travellers to the island outside of the Southland or Otago regions or the South Island aviation hub of Christchurch will usually be including Stewart Island as part of an extended travel itinerary through the South Island rather than a single-trip destination. Furthermore, difficulty in access also means that the relative cost of access in both time and monetary cost is also a significant deterrent for short-term visitation (Lovelock & Robinson, 2005) affecting not just the cost of travel to the island but also the relative cost of goods and services on the island.

Despite accessibility issues, tourism has long been regarded as the mainstay of the island's land economy. Tourism is estimated to be growing annually at the rate of 10–15 per cent on the island (Brook, 2001) although the empirical basis for such assertions is rather weak. Nevertheless, tourism is seen as the best future economic option for the island along with the further development of marine fisheries, although much of the latter catch is landed at the mainland harbour of Bluff. A key element of economic development as well as a conservation measure was the establishment of a national park on the island with both the New Zealand Tourism Board (1997) and the DoC (1997a, b) publishing studies that argued for potentially positive economic impacts that would follow the creation of a park. The impact of park establishment and its relationship to tourism-related issues are discussed in detail below. However, this chapter first outlines Stewart Island's economic and natural history which serve as the basis for its tourism potential.

Economic and Natural History

The high natural values of Stewart Island have long been one of the key tourist attractions of the island. However, despite its somewhat peripheral location, it should be noted that there has been significant exploitation of the island's natural resources. Stewart Island was first incorporated into European geographies with its sighting by Captain James Cook during his circumnavigation of New Zealand in 1769–1770. However, it was initially mapped as a peninsula as Cook did not sail the Endeavour through Fouveaux Strait. European settlement on the island was initially seasonal and consisted of temporary settlements established by sealers and whalers as they harvested the seas around the island and the sub-Antarctic islands. However, some sealers and seafarers married into the local Maori and semi-permanent settlements were recognised from 1825 on. Apart from marine mammal exploitation, some attempts were made to harvest timber from the island for shipbuilding and other purposes, although such timber cutting tended to be sporadic and was not successful because of the availability of more accessible timber closer to the main Australian and New Zealand markets. The island's fishing industry, which has long been an economic mainstay, was initially established in 1868 with the discovery of deep-water oyster beds in Foveaux Strait. Although even here primary access to the oyster beds and other fisheries had moved to the mainland (Bluff and Invercargill in particular) by the end of the 19th century, salmon and oyster farming continued to be significant commercial activities with a development of other fish farms being one potential avenue of economic development. At the same time as the fisheries were initially developed, a cable connection and a regular steamer service to the mainland was also established. As with many other parts of New Zealand, a freezer works was built in order to improve export opportunities, primarily to Australia in the case of the Stewart Island development, but the expected economic development potential did not materialise. Arguably, the last significant attempt at large-scale economic development of the island was the establishment of the Norwegian Rosshavet whaling enterprise at Patersons Inlet in 1923 in order to exploit Ross Sea whale stocks. Whales were never brought to the site with the location instead used for fleet maintenance. The site was abandoned in 1933 following a glut in the whale-oil market and the company instead operated primarily out of South Africa. The site is now a part of the tourist itinerary for the island with buildings from the site also being relocated to the main settlement at Oban, where several are still in use today.

As the only current township on the island, Oban acts as an important gateway as well as the centre for social and economic activities. Oban contains around 20 accommodation establishments and is the base for fishing and tourism operations as well as for retail businesses. Its 'fishing village' character is regarded as extremely important from the perspective of amenity landscapes. The Southland District Plan, which guides planning and development, has been written to provide clear guidelines for sympathetic development (Southland District Council, 2001). Indeed, according to the Council:

> The landscape of Stewart Island is outstanding, and supports significant plant and animal communities. These attract visitors from around the world and at the same time support the community in Halfmoon Bay. The residents value the character and quality of their life-style and are looking for ways to allow them to retain those values while also developing new opportunities to create economic sustainability.

The planning objectives identified for Stewart Island include:

- the continued conservation of the island's landscape and ecology;
- the sensitivity of the coastal environment to the effects of urbanisation;
- the retention of a balance between bush protection and further housing development in and around Oban;
- the adverse effects of the growth of the township due to a lack of services; and
- the need to mitigate the effects of further commercial fishing and recreation shore facilities on landscape and ecology values (Southland District Council, 2001, p. 155).

Like many islands, Stewart Island has developed a relatively unique flora and fauna as a result of its relative isolation. The biogeographic significance of the island has been long recognised. Following his botanical survey, Cockayne (1909) described the flora of the island as 'primeval', with the natural history and landscape being regularly described as a 'paradise' in books and brochures from the early 20th century on.

Although the biology of the island has been modified by fire, logging and the accidental and deliberate introduction of animals by both Maori and Europeans, the island demonstrates the effects of Pleistocene changes in climate and primarily pre-human vegetation patterns (Wilson, 1987). A number of tree and shrub species that are present on the mainland are absent on Stewart Island, including *Nothofagus solandri* (mountain beech), *ladus alpinus* (mountain toa toa) and *Halocarpus bidwillii* (bog pine). The absence of *Nothofagus* (beech) forest is particularly significant given its widespread distribution in locations with similar soils and climates on the South Island and its role as an indicator of Gondwanic distribution (Wardle, 1984).

The current vegetation of the island is a complex mosaic of forest, open ground and scrub. A mainly hardwood forest covers some 64% of the island, and just over 25% is covered by scrub (Wilson, 1987). What remains is a combination of wetland, sedge fields, grass land and dune vegetation. The absence of several woody species from the island which are present on the mainland is attributed to failure to disperse and the limited time that suitable habitats have been available following the last ice age.

> The spatial variation in plant cover is related to the island's strongly oceanic, windy climate, its altitudinal range from maritime cool temperate to upper subalpine, its generally low but variable soil fertility and pH, and its wide diversity of soil drainage. Effects of historical events such as fire, milling, and landslides, which would tend to obscure the primary pattern, are both limited in extent and readily identifiable. (McClone & Wilson, 1996, p. 371)

As with the New Zealand mainland, the most significant indigenous fauna is the bird population. This includes the native parakeet, wood pigeon, tui, bellbird, tomtit, weka, robin, fernbird and kaka. Arguably, the most significant species is the Stewart Island kiwi, known as the southern tokoeka, which behaves differently from mainland species maintaining family groups and engaging in daytime feeding activity. Both these factors are extremely significant from a tourist perspective as it increases the likelihood of the birds being viewed by visitors, unlike the mainland species that feed at night. Because of its isolation, Stewart Island was also a stronghold for the flightless, nocturnal parrot/kakapo, although the population was relocated to the pest-free nature reserve on Codfish Island in order to increase the likelihood of survival. A number of introduced species (such as red and white-tailed deer, cats, rats and possums) have also had an impact on the island; in the case of the deer, these also constitute a significant tourism resource because of their attraction to hunters (Lovelock & Robinson, 2005).

Given the conservation significance of Stewart Island's flora and fauna and the relatively undisturbed nature of much of its landscape, New Zealand's 14th national park, Rakiura National Park was established and opened on the island in 2002. The park covers about 157,000 ha, comprising about 85% of the island, and integrating a pre-existing network of former nature reserves, scenic reserves and State Forest areas (DoC, 2004a). The Park's establishment has not been without some controversy, in part because of the extent to which its creation may serve to restrict some recreational activities within its boundaries, particularly with respect to hunting (Reid, 2001; Lovelock & Robinson, 2005), while its dominance on the island's economy may reinforce certain types of development options and restrict others. Nevertheless, the landscape and ecological values of the island are wider than just those contained in the park area and include the coastal and settled landscapes around Oban that have been identified in the plan document.

Landscape and ecological values of Stewart Island urban resource area:
- the outstanding landscape features of the island — mountains, bush, coast, etc.;
- the visual and ecological sensitivity of the small-scale coastal landscapes;
- the delicate visual balance of buildings and bush around Halfmoon Bay;
- the view of Oban from the bay;
- the 'fishing village' character of Oban;
- the rural character of urban roads;
- the diversity of the plants and animals;
- the numbers of seabirds and the health of their populations;

- the diversity and health of the coastal and marine plant and animal communities;
- large areas of intact plant community sequences from coast to mountain tops; and
- the presence of highly visible native birds in the residential area (Southland Regional Council, 2001, p. 155).

Thus, the potential development strategies for the island are constrained both by the value of the conservation estate in the national park and by the amenity values associated with private land. These issues are dealt in more detail in the next section that examines the impact of the establishment of the park and the growth of tourism.

National Park as Development Strategy

The establishment of the Rakiura National Park was cited by central government agencies as providing significant economic development opportunities for Stewart Island. Indeed, the incorporation of such a high percentage of the land area of Stewart Island into the national park virtually ensures future dependence on nature-based tourism. Nevertheless, the island's inhabitants envisaged both positive and negative impacts arising from the national park establishment on the island's community.

Just prior to the setting up of the park, Reid (2001) conducted a study on the implications of its establishment. The research was undertaken through a combination of key informant interviews, survey and media analysis. A summary of his findings and contemporary community and media responses is reported in Table 17.2.

In terms of perceived social impacts, several respondents to Reid's (2001, p. 118) study 'predicted that increased visitor numbers would put pressure on existing services on the island', with some referring to further pressure on the already busy health services because of greater use of the outdoors. A small number of respondents suggested that increased visitors and 'short stop visitors' would increase crime and drug use on the island.

Reid (2001, p. 119) also revealed that respondents feared that increased tourism 'may make costs generally unaffordable for many of the Island's population'. The likely increase in local property taxes (rates) was perceived as another difficulty for the local residents to cope with, and could also prevent new families from settling down on Stewart Island. Indeed, substantial concerns related to the indirect effect of tourism growth is on rise in property values. There were also widespread concerns over the consequences of increased visitor numbers on facilities and amenities such as the rubbish disposal system: a number of residents feared that " … the local rating base would be expected to pay for services that were primarily for tourists' benefit" (Reid, 2001, p. 135).

In relation to economic development issues, concerns were expressed regarding the potential displacement of small local firms by larger companies connected to mainland businesses and/or new migrants. It was being feared that larger non-local tourism operators would take "business away from smaller, and locally run, tourist operators" (Reid, 2001, p. 119). However, one of the perceived positive impacts of increased visitor numbers to Stewart Island is 'an increase in the quality of services on the Island' (*ibid.*). Many also saw the potential "for growth in the accommodation, restaurant and catering, retail, transport and guiding sectors" (Reid, 2001, p. 120).

Table 17.2: Implications of establishing Rakiura National Park as perceived by respondents.

Impact issue	Perceived costs	Perceived benefits
The impacts of increased visitor numbers on the Stewart Island 'lifestyle'	– National park will attract a more semi-permanent population – Close-knit community spirit may be compromised – Potential increase in crime and drug use – Visitor numbers will put stress on existing services and facilities on island (e.g. health and education) – Island will become more attractive to major tourist operators and this will have a detrimental effect on small and locally owned tourist operations – Island may become unaffordable to local residents	– A larger population – An increase in the quality of services on the island – Greater tolerance and acceptance of tourists
Tourism and economic growth	– Perceived shortage of freehold land available for building – Shortage of accommodation available for workers – Seasonality: 'feast or famine' situation makes it difficult for small businesses to sustain themselves over the slow season – High cost of building on the island – Physical constraints, such as the changeable climate and the moody Foveaux Strait, perceived as a barrier to development	– Increasing opportunities to become involved in the tourism industry, particularly in the provision of accommodation – Secondary benefits such as increased employment opportunities, rise in property values, better facilities for the community and a higher standard of service for locals
Hunting	– Residents are concerned with the extermination requirements of the National Parks Act because of the potential loss of deer as a hunting and wild food resource.	– Conservation groups on the mainland were encouraging of the extermination requirements of the National Parks Act with respect to introduced mammals

National park boundaries	– While majority of residents appeared satisfied with the newly extended buffer zone, a number suggested that the zone was still inadequate and that it should be larger to allow for future development. Others suggested it should have been smaller, as initially proposed by DoC	– General satisfaction
Infrastructure and amenities	– Residents felt that the national park would have a profound impact on existing infrastructure and amenities on the island. In particular, they highlighted a need to: (i) increase footpaths around Oban, (ii) improve rubbish disposal system, (iii) extend sewerage system, (iv) upgrade airstrip and wharf and (v) increase township amenities and 'tidy up' the township	
	– Residents were also concerned about who would pay for the necessary upgrades	
Tangata Whenua (Maori) issues	– Concerns were expressed that the park did not acknowledge the Treaty of Whaitangi partnership	
Recreational use	– Tracks will become too developed	– Possible advantages that national park status would have for recreational opportunities, and specifically the upgrading of tracks
	– More rules applying to outdoor behaviour, such as camping, fires	

Sources: Reid (2001) and contemporary media reports.

As with all types of economic development, community responses to tourism-related development as a result of national park establishment often seem contradictory, although the central concerns of the resident community were clearly related to the desire to maintain a satisfactory quality of life while improving services at minimal economic and social cost.

Since the establishment of the park, two pieces of research have been undertaken that indicate how the island has responded, at least initially, to park-related nature-based tourism developments. Utilising some of the issues raised in Reid's (2001) study, Skjelde (2003) mailed a one-page questionnaire to all 204 households on the island. Eighty surveys were returned, a response rate of 39.2%. A summary of the results is presented in Table 17.3.

Almost 70% of the respondents reported that they were aware that the national park would attract an increased number of visitors, although the level of awareness that tourist numbers had actually increased was considerably smaller. Half of the respondents agreed

Table 17.3: Stewart Island resident perception of the impact of establishment of Rakiura National Park.

	Disagree	Neutral	Agree	N
Rakiura National Park will attract more visitors to Stewart Island	9 (11.4%)	15 (19%)	55 (69.9%)	79
I have noticed that an increased number of tourists are visiting Stewart Island	16 (20.3%)	26 (32.9%)	37 (46.8%)	79
Pressure upon health services on Stewart Island has increased	12 (15.4%)	27 (34.6%)	39 (50%)	78
There is a noticeable increase in crime on the island	34 (43.6%)	29 (37.2%)	15 (19.2%)	78
Non-local tourism operators have been established on Stewart Island	31 (39.7%)	19 (24.4%)	28 (35.9%)	78
The quality of services on the island have been improved	33 (41.8%)	21 (26.6%)	25 (31.6%)	79
Overall, the costs on Stewart Island have increased	15 (19.2%)	13 (16.7%)	50 (64.1%)	78
Property costs on the island have increased	7 (8.9%)	10 (12.7%)	62 (78.5%)	79
I am positive towards enlarged visitor numbers to Stewart Island	21 (27.3%)	18 (23.4%)	38 (49.4%)	77
I find the rubbish disposal system sufficient to deal with increased visitors	40 (53.3%)	20 (26.7%)	15 (20%)	75
The local community has been charged for expenses used to improve facilities	11 (13.9%)	22 (27.8%)	46 (58.2%)	79

Source: Skjelde (2003, p. 43).

that there was an increased pressure on health services on the island, although there was not a perceived increase in the extent of crime. There were considerable differences in the perception of respondents on several issues, such as views on increasing quality of services and views on the establishment of non-local tourism operators. Nevertheless, there was a greater agreement on issues related to the increase in costs on Stewart Island. Over 60% of the respondents agreed that overall costs on the island had increased, with almost 80% agreeing that there has been an increase in costs of properties. The cost issue is significant because of the potential to impact on the existing Stewart Island community, and particularly in relation to the capacity to attract younger people to the island who may live there permanently in comparison with second home and retirement home purchases. Indeed, one of the objectives of the Southland District Council (2003) is to "[D]evelop a well-balanced population made up of all groups, in particular families". The increase in real estate costs is therefore "seen as a potential barrier for increasing the residential population" (Southland District Council, 2003; Skjelde, 2003). Still, to blame the national park for such increased costs of housing and services is problematic: there has been a nation-wide increase in such costs in New Zealand; yet, the increase in land value on Stewart Island appears to above the regional average for Southland.

Another key issue that emerged out of the development of the national park was its impact on hunting. The introduction of white-tailed deer in the 1900s has long-since provided the basis for recreational hunting. Indeed, half of the 450 submissions on the initial national park proposal came from hunters, worried that with a change in status of the land, they would no longer be allowed to hunt white-tailed deer (Asher, 2001). Part of the attraction of white-tailed deer for hunters, apart from being a different species from the main species of deer hunted in New Zealand (red deer), is their reputation for being extremely elusive. This characteristic is well demonstrated by the average number of days spent by hunters to be successful in bagging a white-tailed deer, which is high at around 10 days per kill (Lovelock, 1987). There are 35 hunting blocks and an Open Hunting Zone in the Rakiura National Park and 13 blocks in the Rakiura Maori Land area. Permits are required for all hunting and must be applied for in advance from the DoC or the Rakiura Maori Land Trust. The DoC blocks can be booked up to one year in advance and are limited to one party of 12, for up to 10 days. This ensures exclusive access to the permitted area for the reserved period. The Open Zone is a shared area and access may be permitted for up to 90 days. Access to some blocks is determined by a lottery system (DoC, 2004b). Lovelock and Robinson (2005, p. 153) comment that the local community 'generally supports the retention of the herd'. Many local (island) hunters argue their case either in terms of 'traditional rights' to hunt deer, or through the subsistence value of the deer meat (venison) that they bring home. In addition, there is a substantial support for hunting in relation to the expenditures of hunter-tourists who come from outside the island and who may ultimately contribute to the island's economy through their expenditures. Nevertheless, as Lovelock and Robinson (2005) identified, total hunter expenditure on the basis of average daily spend was NZ$50 (around US$35), which is much less than many islanders believe. Worked out on 2000 data, total expenditure on Stewart Island hunting-tourism would reach NZ$1.1 million (less than US$800,000) (Lovelock & Robinson, 2005; Robinson, 2002).

Significantly, however, the actual proportion of hunter expenditure on the island was relatively small and estimated at 32.1% of total expenditure. Transport was the only item that contributed a significant amount to the island, 57% of total transport expenditure going to island-based operators. Equipment, food and beverage expenditures all contributed little to the island relative to total hunter expenditure on these items. The economic benefits of hunting tourism to Stewart Island tourism are therefore small when compared to other forms of tourism. The average daily spend at NZ$50 was considerably lower than that for domestic tourists, based upon expenditure data for domestic visitors to Southland, which was NZ$81 (US$57) per night (Gravitas, 2002). By far, the biggest proportion of hunter expenditure is off-island. The underlying reason for this is the physical nature of the destination in terms of its distance from the mainland, its ruggedness and the difficulty of access (in terms of both time and expense) to hunting blocks. These characteristics, along with the small scale of the retail community and the lack of retail choice on the island, dictate that hunters travel directly to their blocks, often bypassing Oban, purchasing their food and equipment from their hometowns or the mainland points of embarkation. Nevertheless, despite such a minimal economic impact, support continues to be maintained for hunting tourism. Arguably, this may be because of the 'rights' argument for hunting deer or, because in such a peripheral area, *any* marginal increase in expenditure is welcome. Indeed, DoC's role in supporting the hunting effort lend support to the argument that the establishment of the national park on the island and the conservation activities engaged in by government agencies are as much related to economic development as they are to conservation priorities.

Conclusion

Stewart Island is not a tourism paradise in the traditional sense of a sun, sand and sea destination but it has frequently been referred to as such in promotions and travel writing for almost a century. The sea waters are cold as well as often stormy but its relative isolation and high levels of natural beauty have contributed to the development of a perception of an idyllic island existence. Of course, the realities are quite different. Although the island clearly does have high-amenity values that serve to attract tourists and second home owners and helps retain some residents, the reality is that you cannot eat a landscape. Economic development through fisheries and tourism operations therefore becomes a crucial component towards providing an economic base for the inhabitants of the island and to provide essential and desirable services.

The recent creation of a national park was in part justified on the basis of its potential economic contribution through tourism. However, as surveys of Stewart Island residents have demonstrated, genuine concerns exist over the extent to which tourism and the promotion of amenity values may add further pressures to the island's services as well as lead to competition for increasingly scarce land and property in the longer term. Indeed, the desire to maintain both natural and urban amenity values has already led to the development of specific planning and development guidelines for the island by the Southland Regional Council. The value of such practices undoubtedly depends on which side of the development fence one sits on. In the case of Stewart Island, the sheer amount of land in government ownership (and especially with the establishment of the national park) actually limits the long-term economic strategy of the island to one based on tourism and fisheries. Many will argue that, given the conservation value of the land, this is a good thing. Yet, it does mean that in the case of downturns in the tourism market (such as through increased cost of travel due to fuel price increases) or damage to fisheries resources (such as through disease or decline in stock), then the long-term economic options for the island have become even more limited, with the possibility of further loss of its permanent population. Stewart Island therefore faces the difficulty of balancing conservation and tourism growth issues that face many of the peripheral areas of New Zealand (Hall & Boyd, 2005).

Yet, it is likely that the final arbiter of the future for the island will not be the islanders themselves. As the history of the island demonstrates, changes in the global economy and the nature of personal consumption in countries and locations far away from the island are likely to determine the economic fate of the island, located as it is on New Zealand's economic and geographical periphery.

Acknowledgments

The funding of graduate student research by the Department of Tourism at the University of Otago as part of the department's research foci on peripheral and rural areas is gratefully acknowledged as are the comments of Brent Lovelock.

References

Asher, J. (2001). From island to Rakiura National Park. *Southland Times*, *12*(May), 1.

Braithwaite, E. (1985). *Beautiful New Zealand*. London: Hamlyn.

Brook, K. (2001). Concerns in paradise. *Southland Times*, *6*(July), 5.

Cockayne, L. (1909). *Report on a botanical survey of Stewart Island*. Wellington: Government Printer.

Cumberland, K.B., & Fox, J.W. (1970). *New Zealand: A regional view* (2nd revised ed.). Christchurch: Whitcombe and Tombs.

Department of Conservation (DoC). (1997a). *Stewart Island/Rakiura National Park investigation: Discussion document*. Invercargill: Department of Conservation.

Department of Conservation (DoC), Southland Conservancy. (1997b). *Stewart Island/Rakiura National Park investigation: Report to the New Zealand conservation authority*. Invercargill: Department of Conservation, Southland Conservancy.

Department of Conservation (DoC). (2004a). *Rakiura National Park*. http://www.doc.govt.nz/Explore/001~National-Parks/Rakiura-National-Park/index.asp. (accessed on 25/10/2005).

Department of Conservation. (2004b). *Stewart Island/Rakiura*. http://www.doc.govt.nz/Explore/Hunting-and-Fishing/Southland-Hunting-Information/Stewart-Island-(Rakiura)-Hunting-Information.asp. (accessed on 25/10/2005).

Gravitas. (2002). *New Zealand domestic travel survey 2000*. Wellington: Tourism Research Council.

Hall, C.M., & Boyd, S. (Eds). (2005). *Nature-based tourism in peripheral areas: Development or disaster?* Clevedon: Channelview Publications.

Lovelock, B.A. (1987). *Northern Stewart Island wild animal survey 1986*. Invercargill: Department of Conservation.

Lovelock, B., & Robinson, K. (2005). Maximizing economic returns from consumptive wildlife tourism in peripheral areas: White-tailed deer hunting on Stewart Island/Rakiura, New Zealand.

In: C.M. Hall, & S. Boyd (Eds), *Nature-based tourism in peripheral areas: Development or disaster?* (pp. 151–172). Clevedon: Channelview Publications.

McClone, M.S., & Wilson, H.D. (1996). Holocene vegetation and climate of Stewart Island, New Zealand. *New Zealand Journal of Botany, 34,* 369–388.

New Zealand Tourism Board. (1997). *Stewart Island tourism strategy: A strategy for sustainable growth and development.* Wellington: New Zealand Tourism Board.

Reader's Digest. (1981). *Wild New Zealand.* Surrey Hills: Reader's Digest Services.

Reed, A.H. (1954). *The four corners of New Zealand.* Wellington: A.H. & A.W. Reed.

Reid, A. (2001). *Stewart Island/Rakiura National Park: Community perspective on the process and the implications.* Unpublished Master's dissertation, University of Otago, Dunedin.

Robinson, K. (2002). *Hunter visitation to Stewart Island: An exploratory estimation of expenditure.* Unpublished dissertation, University of Otago, Dunedin.

Skjelde, M. (2003). *The Stewart Island residents' perceptions of Rakiura National Park.* Unpublished dissertation, University of Otago, Dunedin.

Southland District Council. (2001). *Southland district plan.* Invercargill: Southland District Council.

Southland District Council. (2003). *Stewart Island — Rakiura: Guidelines for development.* http://www.southlanddc.govt.nz/sdc_shadomx/library/l90906_6.pdf. (accessed on 20/10/2005).

Statistics New Zealand. (2003). *Stewart Island community profile.* www2.stats.govt.nz/domino/external/web/CommProfiles.nsf/FindInfobyArea/613000-au. (accessed on 20/10/2005).

Stewart Island Flights. (2005). *History of Stewart Island.* www.stewartislandflights.com/sections/theIsland/historyofSI/. (accessed on 20/10/2005).

Wardle, J. (1984). *The New Zealand beeches: Ecology, utilisation and management.* Wellington: New Zealand Forest Service.

Wilson, H.D. (1987). Vegetation of Stewart Island, New Zealand. *New Zealand Journal of Botany* (Supplement).

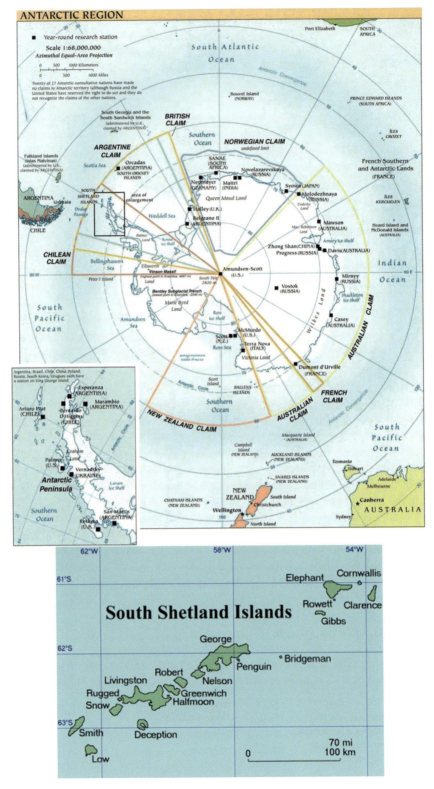

Image 15: (a) Map of Antarctica, with the Antarctic Peninsula as inset.
(b) South Shetlands map.

Chapter 18

Antarctica and the South Shetlands

Thomas G. Bauer

Introduction

Many 'exotic' tourist destinations are associated with warm climates and with the 4ses of sun, sea, sand and sex. Antarctica in general and the South Shetland Islands in particular do not offer these attributes. Nevertheless, during the brief southern summer season from November to March, an increasing number of adventurous travellers make the voyage south to experience the beauty of the islands and the nearby Antarctic Peninsula aboard ice strengthened or ice-breaking vessels.

More than 2000 years ago, the Greeks thought that a southern continent must exist in order to 'balance' the Northern Hemisphere and in 1773, Captain James Cook and his crew crossed the Antarctic Circle and subsequently circumnavigated Antarctica. Other explorers followed including Bellingshausen in 1819, Weddell in 1823, Dumont d'Urville in 1835 and Ross in 1839, but it was not until 1894 that the first human set foot on the continent itself at Cape Adare in the Ross Sea section of the continent (Stonehouse, 1994, p. 195). Following the early explorers were the whalers and sealers who exploited the biological resources of the Southern Ocean until it became uneconomical to venture south to continue to do so. These were followed by the explorers of the 'heroic' age including Scott, Shackleton and Mawson, and more recently by adventurers such as Kagge, Messner, Fuchs, Mortimer, Fiennes and Swan who have looked to Antarctica for personal challenges The reports of the early explorers and modern adventurers (e.g. Scott, 1987; Shackleton, 1932; Swan, 1990; Fiennes, 1993), combined with the curiosity to discover new places and an increasing interest in unspoiled destinations, have stimulated the interest in this remote region in the minds of intrepid travellers. An increasing number now travel south to experience the southern continent first hand.

Tourism in Antarctica

Antarctica is the fifth largest continent and covers 13.9 million km^2. It is almost completely covered by a thick layer of ice and snow that holds some 70% of the world's fresh water and 90% of its ice. It is the highest, windiest, coldest, driest and remotest of all the continents. The vast interior is a polar desert devoid of life but during the brief summer months the coastal regions and offshore islands, such as the South Shetlands provide seasonal habitat to large numbers of penguins, flying sea birds and seals. Marine wildlife comes ashore to court, mate, nest and breed and to raise their offspring before returning to the sea prior to the onset of winter.

Antarctica is the only continent that has never had an indigenous human population. Even today the only semi-permanent residents are scientists and their support staff at the over 40 scientific research stations. The absence of a local population means that no on-shore tourist infrastructure is available. There are no markets, churches or museums to visit, no pubs and restaurants to explore and no locals to mix-and-mingle with. The only shopping opportunities for visiting tourists are provided by the souvenir shops of the scientific stations. The range of products sold is limited to T-shirts, sweatshirts, baseball caps, coffee mugs, key rings, postcards as well as postage stamps of the countries that operate the stations. In the absence of a local population that could benefit economically or socially from tourist activities, tourism exists predominantly for the benefit of the tourists and tour operators.

Ship-Based Tourism

There are several types of tourism in Antarctica. These include sightseeing overflights of parts of the continent (predominantly from Australia), air-supported land-based adventure tours that explore the interior of the continent, fly-cruise tours and ship-based cruise tourism. Among these, ship-based tourism is by far the most popular and important. Since there are no hotels in Antarctica, cruise vessels provide tourists with all the amenities they need during their visit — transport, accommodation, food and beverages as well as education and entertainment. The level of luxury offered to tourists varies with the type of vessel they select for their trip south. The capacity of vessels that make landings in Antarctica ranges from yachts with 4 passengers to vessels carrying over 400 tourists. An increasing number of large vessels carrying over 1000 passengers are also visiting Antarctic waters but fortunately they do not attempt to land passengers ashore, thus minimizing the possible negative environmental impacts.

Regular commercial cruising began in 1966 when Lars-Eric Lindblad chartered the Argentinean vessel *Lapataia* to take 94 passengers to the Antarctic Peninsula region, the closest Antarctic region to the other continents being located some 1000 km from the southern tip of South America (May, 1989, p. 18). Most cruises depart from Ushuaia, the southernmost town in the world located in the south of Argentina on Tierra del Fuego. During the past decade the city has evolved into the gateway to Antarctica and has improved its port infrastructure, hotels, restaurants as well as shopping opportunities. By comparison, the other departure points to Antarctica including Port Stanley, Punta Arenas, Hobart, Bluff and Cape Town only play minor roles. Cruises to the Peninsula take place from mid-November to mid-March. Cruises last between 8 and 20 days depending on whether voyages include the Falklands (Islas Malvinas), South Georgia and the South Orkney Islands or not. After sailing the Beagle Channel, cruises bound for Antarctica face the two to three day crossing of the sometimes rough waters of the Drake Passage. During this time passengers are educated by experts on Antarctic wildlife, geology, history and biology and they are required to attend a mandatory briefing on the dos and don'ts of going ashore.

Antarctica lacks purpose-built tourism infrastructure and hence there are no landing piers or docks that cater to cruise ships. To transport passengers from the ship to the landing sites, tour operators depend on inflatable rubber boats, usually Zodiacs. These sturdy vessels can carry up to 14 passengers and can operate even under fairly severe ice conditions.

The Antarctic is a wildlife paradise. On land, visitors may encounter penguins, seals and flying seabirds, such as terns and giant petrels. In the Drake Passage, birdwatchers delight in observing a variety of albatross including the wandering albatross with its wingspan of over 3 m. In the seas a variety of whales including minke, humpback and, with luck, sei or even blue can be observed. Orcas are also common and an encounter with these great creatures while seated in a Zodiac is an experience not easily forgotten. During the height of the summer in December/January, daylight can last 24 hours and this allows energetic passengers to enjoy the beauty of the place virtually around the clock. The Antarctic scenery is the most beautiful cold climate scenery in the world. The unique mix of snow and ice covered mountains that fall off steeply into the freezing waters of the Southern Ocean, floating and grounded icebergs of varying shapes, colours and sizes and glaciers that calve into the sea, all provide visitors with unsurpassed vistas.

Where passengers go ashore and what they see during their voyage is determined by the expedition leaders who have to be aware of the constantly changing weather, wind and ice conditions as well as the movements of other passenger vessels in the area. Most cruise vessels are ice-strengthened and thus can handle ice conditions up to approximately 8/10-ice concentration. At 10/10, the sea is completely covered with ice and an icebreaker is required to navigate under such conditions.

Management of Antarctic Tourism

Antarctica is a land without a sovereign government. Argentina, Australia, Chile, France, New Zealand, Norway and the United Kingdom claim territories in the south but their claims are not universally accepted. South of 60°S, the Antarctic is managed under the Antarctic Treaty and its associated instruments, such as the *Convention on the Conservation of Antarctic Marine Living Resources,* the *Agreed Measures for the Conservation of Antarctic Fauna and Flora* and the *Convention for the Conservation of Antarctic Seals* as well as the *Protocol on Environmental Protection to the Antarctic Treaty* (Madrid Protocol). The Antarctic Treaty Parties meet annually to discuss how best to manage issues, such as scientific research, commercial fishing and tourism. Officially Antarctica is the domain of government funded scientific expeditions and private, non-governmental expeditions are tolerated but not encouraged.

The high concentration of visits at a limited number of sites has raised concerns regarding the possible negative impacts of tourism activities on the fauna and flora of these sites. Concern about possible impacts on scientific research and the potential need for search and rescue has also been raised. Of course there is also the possibility of pollution by sewage, waste, oil, fuels as well as the introduction of microbes, plants and animals.

Because of the remoteness of Antarctica, commercial tourism depends on the close co-operation of the governments of the Antarctic Treaty Parties, tour operators, the Council of Managers of National Antarctic Programs (COMNAP) and the tourists. The establishment of the International Association of Antarctica Tour Operators (IAATO) in 1991 and its close links with the various governments have significantly contributed to the successful manage-ment of Antarctic tourism. All accounts to date suggest that tourists and tour operators alike have complied with the visitor and tour operator guidelines established by IAATO and by the Treaty Parties and that the negative impacts caused by Antarctic tourists and tour operators have been negligible. Beginning with Lars-Eric Lindblad, the pioneer of Antarctic tourism, and continuing with IAATO members, tour operators have been proactive in their measures to protect the resource on which their businesses depend. As the author has previously stated (Bauer, 2001a, p. 524), the good cooperation between tourists, tour operators and Treaty Parties has led to Antarctic tourism being the best-managed tourism in the world.

Antarctica is a difficult place to reach and those visitors who want to experience her beauty will first have to endure long flights from their home countries to Ushuaia in the far south of Argentina. For the author, his annual pilgrimage south involves 30 hours inside an aircraft just to get to the ship, followed by the often uncomfortable crossing of the Drake Passage. Thus, only intrepid travellers are willing to endure the long-trip south to experience Antarctica. The rewards of putting up with the difficulties of getting there are high: once the first icebergs are sighted and the snow covered beauty of the first land mass appears, all financial pain and seasickness sufferings are forgotten.

Chart 18.1 retrieved from the IAATO website highlights the substantial growth of Antarctic tourism during the past decade. To get an appreciation of how special a visit to Antarctica is it is useful to keep in mind that, according to the World Tourism Organisation (WTO, 2005), some 763 million international visitor arrivals were recorded during 2004.

IAATO (2005) reported that, during the 2004–2005 season, a total of 22,926 passengers landed in Antarctica. The breakdown by nationality is as follows: USA 36.5%, United Kingdom 15.9%, Germany 13.7%, Australia 10%, Canada 3.7%, Japan 3.2%, Switzerland 1.9%, Netherlands 1.8% and others 13.5%.

Station Visits

Antarctic tour operators like to visit scientific research stations because it provides tourists with a human perspective on Antarctica. At the stations, the scientists and their support staff act as a substitute host population. Being visited by boatloads of curious tourists does have its positive and negative aspects. On the positive side, tourists provide diversions from the daily routine. They bring with them stories from the 'outside', and may be keenly interested in the work that is being carried out. On the negative side, tourists can disrupt the routine of a station as well as the scientific work that is being conducted, particularly if there are too many visits over a short period. Tourist visits may also inadvertently dis-turb areas that are under observation and they may bring infectious diseases ashore, which may infect station staff. To minimize the potential negative impacts of tourist visits,

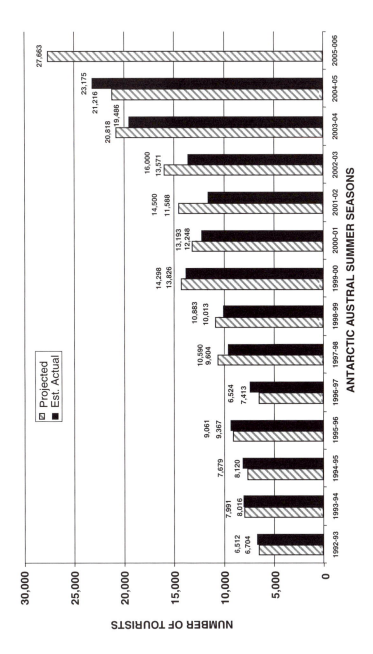

Chart 18.1: 1992–2006 Antarctic tourist trends – landed (includes ship and land-based passenger numbers. 1997–1998 includes commercial yacht activity).

Source: www.iaato.org.

Antarctic stations operated by the USA (Palmer on Anvers Island, McMurdo in the Ross Sea and Amundsen-Scott at the Geographic South Pole) require prior notification of intent to visit. Such visits are scheduled and pre-arranged during a meeting between the representative of the National Science Foundation (NSF) of the United States and the tour operators at the annual IAATO meeting. In this way, NSF can be reasonably assured that the industry is aware of what the requirements for station visits are and operators know what is expected of them prior and during their visits to research facilities. Most other stations can be visited on relatively short notice and many are happy to have visitors who buy souvenirs from their gift shops.

The Antarctic Peninsula and the South Shetland Islands

Antarctic tourism is highly concentrated in only a few locations and most of the continent never sees any tourists. Some of the sub-Antarctic islands and the Ross Sea are visited; but most ship-based tourism takes place in the relatively easily accessible and climatically milder Antarctic Peninsula region. Many of the landings take place on islands located off the west coast of the Peninsula, in particular, in the South Shetland Islands; islands off the Trinity Peninsula and Anvers Island opposite to Danco Coast are also visited.

After the crossing of the Drake Passage, the South Shetlands are frequently the first sight cruise passengers get of Antarctica. They are also often the last stop before ships return to South America and as such they play an important role in Antarctic tourism. The climatic conditions of the islands are relatively mild with summer temperatures ranging from –5 to +5°C. The islands provide all the attractions the visitors expect and they can be seen as the core product of ship-based Antarctic tourism.

The South Shetland Islands take their name from the Shetland Islands located to the north of Great Britain at approximately the same latitude (60°), but north. The islands form a chain of 11 major islands with a total area of 3687 km^2, 120 km to the west of the coast of the Antarctic Peninsula. Nearly 90% of the islands are covered permanently by ice. The highest peak is Mt. Foster on Smith Island (2105 m). The islands lie within the region of 61°00' to 63°37'S, 53°83' to 62°83'W and were discovered by William Smith on 19 February 1819, and named New South Britain. He returned in October of the same year and landed on King George Island, claiming it in the name of King George III. In 1920, the islands were renamed to South Shetland Islands (McGonigal & Woodworth, 2001, p. 156). Despite this legitimate claim by Great Britain, the South Shetland Islands are also claimed by Argentina and Chile who see these islands, and indeed the whole of the Antarctic Peninsula, as the natural southern extension of their respective countries. Because the islands are located south of 60° they, like the rest of Antarctica, are covered under the Antarctic Treaty. Under the Treaty all existing claims have been suspended for the time being and nothing that a country does (such as establishing scientific research stations) or does not do can strengthen or weaken a claim. For Smith, as for other early 'entrepreneurs' that came to this region, the islands were primarily of interest as a hunting ground for seals and whales; these were hunted to near extinction.

In 1956, one of the first Antarctic tourism activities took place in the region when a sightseeing flight passed over the South Shetland Islands and parts of the Antarctic Peninsula.

Today, the South Shetlands form an integral part of the Antarctic Peninsula tourism product. The archipelago can be seen to consist of four main groups: Clarence and Elephant islands; King George and Nelson islands; Robert, Greenwich, Livingston, Snow and Deception islands; and Smith and Low islands.

King George Island

At 1295 km^2 King George is the largest of the South Shetland Islands. The island is approximately 69 km long and 26 km wide (McGonigal & Woodworth, 2001, p. 157). By Antarctic standards the island is easily accessible and as a consequence it is home to a high concentration of national year-round stations including the following: Argentina (station name and year of establishment: Teniente Jubay, 1948); Brazil (Commandante Ferraz, 1984); Chile (Presidente Eduardo Frei, 1969); China (Chang Chen/Great Wall, 1985); Poland (Henryk Arctowski, 1977); Russia (Bellingshausen, 1967); South Korea (King Sejong, 1988); and Uruguay (Artigas, 1985). Ecuador, Germany, Peru and the USA also maintain summer bases on the island. The stations conduct research in such areas as atmospheric physics, biology, geomagnetism, human physiology, oceanography, geology, glaciology and Antarctic fauna and many carry out meteorological observations. The high concentration of research facilities in such a small area can, however, not be justified on scientific grounds alone. Instead most of these stations were established to either strengthen sovereignty claims (Chile and Argentina) or for the purposes of becoming an Antarctic Treaty Consultative Party that allows the country to have voting rights. Previously, a country had to show that it was actively involved in carrying out scientific research in Antarctica and establishing a station was seen as a proof. Only the stations operated by Chile, Russia and Poland are regularly visited by the tourists. Tourists are welcomed warmly at all three stations and they are given a tour of the facilities. Invariably they end up in the souvenir shops (or a table set up for this purpose) and many prove to be very obliging shoppers taking away with them unique Antarctic souvenir items. The Chilean Airline Aerovias DAP provides tourist air access to the only air strip in the South Shetlands, the 1292 m long military air strip at the Chilean Teniente Rodolfo Marsh Base. On their website (www.aeroviasdap.cl), the company offers the option of a one-day visit for US$2100 and a two day one night excursion for US$2700. As the author previously reported (Bauer, 2001b), from 1984 to 1993 the Chilean government actively promoted tourism to King George Island. The Chilean air force operated flights using C-130 Hercules transport planes, which took less than 3 hours to cross Drake Passage from Punta Arenas. Packages included a stay in the air force owned 'Hotel Polar Star', a basic hostel. Today a limited number of passengers join fly-cruise excursions that allow them to fly into King George Island (from Punta Arenas using the aviation services of DAP) where they can board a cruise vessel for their exploration of the region.

Deception Island

Deception Island has some of the most popular landing sites in the South Shetlands. It is a dormant volcano and the most recent eruptions were recorded in 1991–1992. Thermal activity is still evident in several places. The interior of the island is a collapsed volcanic cone and the crater rim has been breached in one spot (Neptune's Bellows), allowing the sea to enter the interior of the island and forming a large sheltered harbour. The island previously served as the base for the Norwegian Hektor whaling station as well as a British scientific station. Inside the caldera there is very little wildlife but on the outer rim, at Bailey Head, a colony of some 75,000 pairs of chinstrap penguins can be found. This site is one of the greatest concentrations of wildlife in Antarctica. Deception Island has become well known as a place where it is possible to bath in thermally heated waters. This activity takes place at locations on the beach in Whalers Bay and at Pendulum Cove and is popular with tourists.

Livingston Island — Hannah Point

As on other islands in the South Shetland group, Livingston Island has a sad history as the slaughtering ground for tens of thousands of seals. Today the island's main attraction is the landing site at Hannah Point where 3873 passengers went ashore during the 2004/2005 season. It boasts a diversity of wildlife, including several species of penguin as well as elephant seals. Because of its biotic diversity, the site is often included as the last stop of Antarctic cruises before passengers face the return voyage across Drake Passage.

Half Moon, Greenwich and Aitcho Islands

Half Moon is a 2 km long crescent-shaped island that provides easy walking conditions and a variety of wildlife viewing opportunities. Its backdrop is the magnificently glaciated mountain scenery of Livingston Island. It is home to the only occasionally operating Argentinean summer base of Teniente Camara. The island received 9819 passengers during the 2004/2005 season. Nearby is Greenwich Island and its main site, Yankee Harbour, which was visited by 1872 passengers during the same season. The Aitcho Islands have extensive coverage of mosses and this can make walking on the islands tricky because at times it is impossible to avoid stepping on them. Many gentoo and chinstrap penguins as well as elephant seal can be found on the islands.

Penguin Island

After crossing the Drake Passage, Penguin Island is often one of the first specks of land that is spotted by cruise passengers. The highest point, Deacon Peak (170 m), is an extinct volcano and climbing it allows passengers to stretch their sea legs. The island has populations of chinstrap and Adélie penguins. Its most vulnerable inhabitants are the giant petrels that nest near the easier approaches to Deacon Peak and care must be taken not to disturb these magnificent birds.

Elephant Island

This island played an important role in the heroic age of Antarctic exploration. It is here that 22 members of Sir Ernest Shackleton's expedition were stranded in 1915 after their ship *Endurance* was crushed in the Weddell Sea. The men spent 135 days on the island before being rescued. Zodiac landings on Elephant Island are difficult and as a result the island only receives very few visitors.

Conclusion

The island continent of Antarctica and the nearby South Shetland Islands are proof that cold climate islands can indeed attract tourists. While visitor arrival numbers are much smaller than on most temperate or warm climate islands, an ever increasing number of wealthy and intrepid travellers make their way south to experience the most beautiful and most undisturbed cold climate scenery in the world. With the assistance of all who are involved in Antarctic tourism it has so far been possible to manage tourism in the south in a way that little or no damage has occurred at the sites visited. It is hoped that, with the continued good-will of all parties involved, the far south of the planet will continue to remain the most unspoiled part of our world.

References

Bauer, T. G. (2001a). Antarctic tourism. In: D. McGonigal, & L. Woodworth (Eds), *Antarctica: The complete story*. Noble Park, Victoria, Australia: The Five Mile Press.

Bauer, T. G. (2001b). *Antarctic tourism. Opportunities, constraints and future prospects*. Binghamton, NY: The Haworth Hospitality Press.

Fiennes, R. (1993). *Mind over matter*. London: Sinclair-Stevenson.

International Association of Antarctica Tour Operators (IAATO). (2005). *IAATO Overview of Antarctic tourism 2004–2005 season*. www.iaato.org (accessed: 25/10/2005).

May, J. (1989). *The greenpeace book of Antarctica*. French Forest: Child and Associates.

McGonigal, D., & Woodworth, L. (2001). *Antarctica: The complete story*. Noble Park: The Five Mile Press.

Scott, R. F. (1987). *Scott's last expedition: The journals*. London: Methuen.

Shackleton, E. (1932). *The heart of the Antarctic*. London: William Heinemann.

Stonehouse, B. (1994). Ecotourism in Antarctica. In: E. Cater, & G. Lowman (Eds), *Ecotourism: A sustainable option*? (pp. 195–212). London: Wiley

Swan, R. (1990). *Icewalk*. London: Jonathan Cape.

World Tourism Organisation (WTO). (2005). *WTO tourism barometer*. Madrid: World Tourism Organisation.

SECTION III

CONCLUSION

Chapter 19

Epilogue: Contrasting Coldwater and Warmwater Island Tourist Destinations

Richard Butler

Introduction

The dominance of the physical setting is one of the strongest images that emerges when tourism on coldwater islands is examined. Ignoring for the moment the often dramatised relationship between humankind and climate, it is clear, that human existence, let alone tourism, on these islands is continuously vulnerable to physical conditions. While the "cocooning" of tourists on tropical islands is almost over-discussed (Dann, in this volume), such shielding of the pleasure seekers from the physical (and sometimes human) elements is essentially for comfort, rather than survival. On at least some of the cold-water islands discussed here, it is survival that necessitates such sheltering from the elements, not just tourists, but locals also. Such conditions, along with other factors, have inevitably kept the number of visitors to low levels, even where the islands may have many, often unique, attractions. Thus one can deduce from even a brief examination of the chapters in this volume, the fact that to be a tourist to such destinations means that one must have a specific motivation to visit the particular island or island group. None of these islands, or their equivalents in other cold-water areas, can be visited "by accident" and none of them represent a generic form of tourism except in a very broad way. Each is unique, and grouping them into categories, other than by such adjectives as "coldwater" or "extreme", is not convincing. To draw together some common themes and issues, therefore, is somewhat difficult and inevitably subject to personal bias and interpretation.

It might be appropriate therefore, to make some reflexive commentary here. This writer has had a lifelong interest in such islands, beginning from spending holidays as a child on some of the islands off the west coast of Scotland, and continuing this experience through bird-watching holidays to the northern isles of Scotland, and also visiting Irish, Scandinavian, and Baltic islands, before moving to North America and visiting Canadian northern islands, along with Iceland. It should not be assumed, however, that such visitation

Extreme Tourism: Lessons from the World's Cold Water Islands
Copyright © 2006 by Elsevier Ltd.
All rights of reproduction in any form reserved
ISBN: 0-08-044656-6

developed a longing for cool vacations (in the temperature sense), and it was with at least equal delight that I managed to visit Turks and Caicos, Dominican Republic, Fiji, Bali, and Java among other warmwater islands. This is an important point to bear in mind. While we may discuss the perhaps distinct characteristics of coldwater island tourists, we should not imagine that they do not also visit warmwater islands and do not enjoy a "Blue lagoon" on the veranda of a villa as the sun sets just as much as a malt whisky on a cold wet afternoon, watching a gale or snowstorm near one of the poles. While there may be specific characteristics of coldwater island tourists, these have not been determined definitively, although we are able to generalise about them, or at least those who visit the more extreme examples of such island destinations.

Definitions, Characteristics, and Themes

The descriptions of the islands and those like them that are discussed in this volume have not been well defined. This is perhaps because, as noted above, they do not easily fall into distinct and mutually exclusive categories. Some are remote, but so too are many islands; some are small and/or have small populations, as do many others; some have rare and distinctive environments and species, yet so do the Galapagos and other groups; and some have fascinating human histories but none more unique than, for example, Easter or Christmas Islands. So to describe them in normal geographic or cultural terms is not practical or satisfactory. Instead, and appropriately for a book which has its focus on tourism, we are best served by interpreting them in terms of tourism and its characteristics, for it is these characteristics which make these islands similar and appropriate to study as a specific form of destination, and it is perhaps through tourism that they may be better understood and sheltered from some of the negative effects of globalisation and uniformity.

Attributes

First and foremost the determining characteristic of these islands is that they are each *specific* rather than generic destinations. Without meaning to downplay the uniqueness or appeal of any warmwater island, there is a great deal of substitutability between many of those islands. To the millions of tourists who visit Spain's islands each year, many do not make a great distinction between Mallorca and Minorca, or between Lanzarote and Tenerife. One might anticipate in fact that as the Canaries belong to Spain, it is highly likely that many tourists consider them to be in the Mediterranean, not the Atlantic, only 100 kilometres off the coast of Africa. The principal appeal of such islands is the climate, both in the summer for Mediterranean islands and year round for those such as the Canaries or in the South Pacific and Caribbean. The sunshine, the beaches, and a hedonistic atmosphere, as discussed by Dann (this volume) and other authors (e.g. Conlin and Baum, 1995; King, 1997) are well known. While the islanders themselves and even their marketing agents may argue that each island is unique and has a distinct appeal, the brochures and promotional material tell a different and more uniform story. This is not the case for coldwater islands. Where there is promotional material for such destinations, and some of the chapters in this volume reveal that this is often limited and not wildly appealing to a large market (Berry, in this volume), it tends to focus on specific and often unique features, whether they be wildlife, physical land, or water forms, climate, cultural artefacts, or historical associations. Thus, tourists who visit these islands come specifically to the island or island group as a destination in order to experience something specific. It may be Iceland's geysers and volcanic activity (or its Blue Lagoon and night life in more recent years), the Falkland's bird life and military connections, Greenland's glaciers, the Canadian and Alaskan islands' Inuit populations, Macquarie's bird life, Chatham's flora, or the general landscape and historical heritage of Antarctica or the Far North. What is on offer at such destinations has few substitutes. Inuit live only in the Arctic, albatrosses in the southern hemisphere (except for the odd lost soul in Shetland occasionally), Iceland's volcanic activity is recent, even present, but safe and accessible, the Falkland's conflict is recent enough to be of current interest and safer than the sites of other military events such as the Middle East. Thus the attractions are specific and strong enough to outweigh the difficulties and costs in time and money of reaching these destinations, and their less attractive features such as inhospitable climates and often minimal facilities. This is not to argue that some tourists do not seek out remote and undeveloped warmwater island destinations. They certainly do; but their reasons for doing so relate less to the specific destination than they do to the generic form of a remote island and perhaps the Robinson Crusoe gene that some people appear to possess.

Tourism Elements

If we accept this first proposition that the most distinctive feature of these islands is that they are *specific* rather than generic destinations, several other features emerge that differentiate them from their warmwater equivalents and other tourist destinations. The *nature of tourism* engaged in can be best described as active rather than passive. People visit these islands to engage in specific activities, rather than in rest and relaxation. This is not to say that rest and relaxation are not activities, they are at least planned and deliberate uses of time, and some visitors to coldwater islands also clearly engage in rest and relaxation. The Shetland Islands' advertising slogan for some years was "Shetland: Get Away To It All", a rather clever ploy to promote itself as a location for both a change of place and with a wide range of activities, but even then, the emphasis was put upon the things one could engage in while on the islands. The range of activities listed in Greenland for example (Kaae, this volume) is indicative of the options available to visitors to participate in various forms of physical activity.

A second characteristic is that of the *spatial spread* of this tourist activity. While for the majority of warmwater destination tourists, their activity is frequently confined to the beach and a small area around their accommodation, often strengthened or even controlled by the design of their resort (e.g. Club Med, with a boundary fence, albeit normally to keep locals and non-residents out rather than residents in), in coldwater islands the activities themselves tend to take visitors into the hinterland and by their nature (walking, skiing, snowshoeing, dogsledding, climbing, nature exploration) often involve covering considerable distances from their places of accommodation. While such activities may not bring visitors into contact with local populations *per se*, they often require local resident participation in the form of guides and instructors.

A third feature of the tourism experienced on these islands is its *extreme seasonality*. While many tourist destinations experience seasonality (Baum & Lundtorp, 2001), either because of their climate or the climatic range in their market origin regions, coldwater island destinations tend to be in the higher latitudes and thus experience greater seasonal extremes than their more equatorial counterparts. Not only may the summer periods be short (although long in daylight), the winter and off seasons may be extreme and hazardous for access and travel within the region. Thus, the tourist season may be a matter of a few weeks rather than a few months, and even then may be subject to an extreme fluctuation in the weather conditions. Extreme seasonality makes destinations unattractive to investment, uneconomic for many businesses, and difficult for labour recruitment (Butler, 2001). The tourist season often coincides with peak farming or fishing periods and there may be no labour available for tourist services because of the priorities of the basic essential activities on which survival depends. Still, seasonality is not necessarily bad: it keeps the tourist numbers down (more on this below); and residents can sometimes strategically switch to non-tourism related tasks during the rest of the year, as well as benefiting from a "rest" from the presence of visitors.

Fourthly, there is the fact that the basic attractions are based on *inherent features* of the destination, rather than modified or added elements. Thus wildlife, natural physical features, "authentic" local artefacts, and perhaps current activities, tend to be what visitors come to witness. Again, similar attractions are present in many warmwater destinations: the rainforests, coral reefs, wildlife, and local populations in mainland as well as some island destinations. However, many are supplemented by additional elements and in some cases modified to cater to large numbers of visitors (e.g. local cultural performances hosted several nights a week in hotels or local villages). In coldwater island destinations, the attractions are mostly those experienced by the indigenous residents, including the residents themselves, engaged in genuinely local activities such as hunting and fishing.

Small scale tourism is another defining characteristic of these locations. While there may be several hundred thousand visitors to Iceland (Gössling, this volume), this is very much an exception, and other destinations count tourists in tens or hundreds (Berry, Marsh & De La Barre, Kriwoken et al., this volume), and even the cruise ships that venture into these waters have hundreds rather than thousands of passengers (Bauer, Thomson, & Thomson, this volume). These figures are in marked contrast to the scale of both the resorts and the cruise ships, which visit most warmwater islands. The small-scale nature of tourism is both a reflection of facilities available on the islands and transport services to them, and their appeal to a small market. Economies of scale do not apply in these situations, without a quantum leap in either demand or appeal, and in the short term at least, neither is likely. Thus, the small scale of tourism is likely to remain a long-term characteristic of visitation to these islands.

Access

A key element in the issue of scale is *difficulty of access*, for none of these islands, with the possible exception of Iceland, could be described as easily reached. While many are now accessible by air, such access for tourists is mostly relatively recent. Air access in many of the destinations discussed in this volume has come in the recent past and was often in the form of military or emergency service aircraft rather than regularly scheduled commercial services. Interestingly enough, in several locations it was the potential of limited but lucrative tourism traffic which stimulated the broadening and even provision of commercial services, a scenario reminiscent of the role of tourism in supporting the initial transcontinental railroad lines across Canada (Hart, 1983). Warmwater island destinations, on the other hand, have often had air services for a considerable time, in some cases originating from them being refuelling stops for transoceanic services, as until recently was the case of Fiji and other Pacific islands. Longer-range aircraft have placed such functions in jeopardy, sometimes along with the services on which the tourism industry has come to depend. Many of the warmwater island destinations now have frequent and often low-cost air services from their major markets, geared to a mass tourist market, which has resulted in significant airport expansion, along with related services such as shopping and car hire. In the case of coldwater islands, most of them were totally dependent upon boat service for the delivery of supplies as well as visitors, an often infrequent and time-consuming method of access. In some cases (as with St. Helena in the South Atlantic), access by boat is still the only method of reaching the island and services are limited to only a few visits a year. Many smaller islands off the coast of Britain and Scandinavia are still dependent on sea transport for all but emergency services, and most of these services are not geared to carrying tourists, meeting their demands for short periods between visits, or offering decent accommodation and on board facilities.

Such services often date back to a long time, and this raises another attribute of tourism in coldwater islands, and that is the often *long history of visitation*, albeit in small numbers, of tourists. The unique features of these islands, noted above, have served to attract small numbers of curious visitors over a long period in many cases. Islands off the coast of Scotland e.g. Staffa, with its unusual volcanic features such as Fingal's Cave, drew scientific, artistic, and literary figures from the 18th century onwards, including musicians such as Mendelssohn, artists like Turner, and scientists such as Banks (President of the Royal Society) (Butler, 1985). Thus, tourism of a form in a number of such islands predates conventional tourism in many warmwater islands, most of which experienced little if any tourism before the beginning of the 20th century and almost never in the 18th, except for a few Caribbean islands hosting visitors to the Great Houses (Husbands, 1983). This may be occasioned in part by the fact that most of the coldwater island destinations lie in the northern hemisphere and are, therefore, considerably closer to the then major sources of such visitors, compared to those in warmer climes. They would, therefore, be much better known, particularly ones which featured in literary works of the period, such as those of Sir Walter Scott, Mary Shelley, or other European authors.

Image and Markets

Image is therefore important, as it is with every tourist destination. Potential visitors must have some image of a destination to allow it to enter their consideration as a destination. No knowledge of the existence of a place means no image and no thought of visitation. The image of coldwater island destinations might be defined as generally being one of *oddity and uniqueness*, especially when compared to their warmwater counterparts; the image of the latter, as Dann (this volume) notes, is stylised, and embodies sexual and erotic elements. One might therefore, be tempted to characterise the differences as being between *exotic* images for coldwater destinations and *erotic* ones for warmwater ones. Allied with such images is the issue of 3 or 4 "Ss". Warmwater island destinations have long been linked with sun, sand, and sea, and increasingly with sex. If one has to characterise coldwater destinations, it would not include the "sea" — by definition normally too cold to swim in — and neither sun nor sex comes instantly to mind, but rather perhaps a series of "Is"— like ice (and many associated derivatives), indigenous people, and isolation.

Ageist though it might be to see a relationship between this last point and the tourist market, one has to admit that the present market for coldwater island destinations is at least a *mature one* (in age). All of the locations examined in this volume demonstrate this characteristic. These islands attract a senior segment of the tourist market, with few visitors being accompanied by children. Thus, family groups are generally absent, reflecting perhaps the difficulty of access, the cost of such a holiday, and the specific appeal of the destinations, none of these factors being particularly child friendly (although that is certainly not to say that children would not enjoy a holiday at such destinations, in fact the physical nature of such holidays may well appeal to them). The market is made up very much of couples or small groups of friends (often comprised of couples), who are well travelled and have definite interests which are met by these destinations. Cultural tourists and nature tourists are the main segments which appear; people interested in history, in cultural artefacts, in historic populations, in birds and other wildlife, and in natural physical features. Despite the potential, relatively few of the already small number of visitors appear to come for extractive forms of recreation such as hunting and fishing, although at least in Scotland and other parts of western Europe, these were major attractions in the 19th century (Butler, 1985). As with these predecessors of modern tourists, the current market is predominantly from the upper rather than lower income brackets and of an above average educational attainment, reflecting no doubt the maturity and perhaps comfortable retirement of this segment. The market in warmwater island destinations is much more varied, comprising a large number of families with children and ranging widely across income and educational levels.

Facilities

These differences in market segments are mirrored in the supply of facilities for visitors. On coldwater island destinations for the most part, facilities are *limited in range and variety*, often relatively primitive and lacking many of the comforts found in the market segment's own homes. Accommodation establishments are generally small and basic, mostly owned and operated by local residents, and frequently are adjoining or part of their own living quarters. On some warmwater island destinations, while such facilities also exist, the vast majority of guests stay in relatively luxurious accommodation, often better equipped with facilities such as en suite bathrooms and air conditioning than the market segment's own residences.

Prices, on the other hand, are often the reverse. Cost of living on remoter islands can be *high* and this is often reflected in accommodation charges and particularly the cost of food and drink. On warmwater counterparts, given the intense competition and the buying power of tour operators, accommodation is often cheap in absolute as well as relative terms, and there is often a surplus of restaurants: again, all highly competitive. When combined with bulk priced travel on charter or budget airlines, the overall cost of a holiday on warmwater islands, even considerable distances from markets, is often much lower than an equivalent stay on a coldwater island, a shorter distance from the market. This situation accentuates the need for the visitor to coldwater island destinations to specifically desire to visit that destination and be prepared to pay a premium for doing so. In the case of cruises to the remoter polar islands, cost per guest per day may be several times the cost on a warmwater cruise, reflecting economies of scale for boats holding over 2000 passengers, compared to those carrying 200 or less. The larger boats also have a wider range of facilities such as swimming pools, casinos, theatres, and entertainment, and a greater opportunity for guests to spend money than they could do in the small coldwater boats. On the other hand, the latter tend to feature educational elements and interpretation from distinguished experts, access to rare features, and highly specialised and personal services, with a higher staff to passenger ratio on many smaller vessels than on their larger counterparts.

Resident Involvement

In many coldwater island destinations, resident involvement in tourism is *minimal* and often at the most peripheral. In the cases discussed in this volume, tourism is often catered to on a part-time and occasional as-needed basis by local residents whose principal source of income is some other, often more traditional activity such as farming or fishing. Tourism is very much an "add-on" to most residents' lives, if they are involved at all, and it is clear that many islanders are not involved in tourism at all. On warmwater island destinations, while there may be sizeable groups of residents, particularly those not living in the tourist resort communities, who are not directly involved in tourism, it is highly likely they will benefit from tourism indirectly in terms of taxation from tourism enterprises, better access, and better services generally. Tourism on the major warmwater island destinations is often the major source of income and employment and may have created a "monoculture" in the few decades it has been present. Dependency on tourism may be very great for the population as a whole, whereas on coldwater islands, it tends to be of much less significance, albeit growing in many cases. Whether tourism will assume the dominance in such islands that it has elsewhere is something that is discussed below. None of the examples discussed in this volume revealed much dislike, resentment, or opposition to tourism, perhaps because of its low levels in those locations, unlike some warmwater locations (Doxey, 1975). Only in those places in which visitors have expressed concern or opposition over traditional activities such as seal hunting (e.g. in northern Canadian islands) have attitudes towards tourists become negative. Even there, residents have generally differentiated between "normal" tourists or "visitors" (Wiltshier & Cardow, this volume) who are welcomed or tolerated, and those whom they characterise as "environmentalist freaks" who are ignored or refused services such as guiding (personal observation).

Conclusions

The previous discussion has attempted to draw out the characteristics of coldwater island tourism that makes such destinations distinct from other island tourist destinations (generally the warmwater ones). It is now appropriate to conclude with an overall evaluation and express some thoughts on the probable future of coldwater island tourism destinations and areas for research. Table 19.1 lists the characteristics discussed above comparing those of coldwater and warmwater island destinations.

Perhaps the most overriding characteristic is that coldwater islands are *both the attraction and the setting* for the holidays there, whereas in the case of warmwater islands, the islands are much more the setting in which activities or inactivity take place. In that sense, the island itself may be of only a marginal significance, whereas in the case of coldwater island destinations, the individual island is of very great significance. How important the island nature of warmwater island destinations is remains to be determined and could be a fruitful area of research. The opportunities offered by many such destinations are often indistinguishable from those of warm mainland destinations (e.g. sun, sand, integrated resorts), while the opportunities offered on coldwater islands vary greatly from island to island, as to the specific attractions, of which the island nature of the destination is usually of high significance.

Another research question, which might be raised is the nature of the process of tourism development on such islands. Many warmwater destinations have followed a well-documented evolutionary cycle (Butler, 1980), although with a variety of variations from the principal pattern (Butler, 2006a,b). This is characterised by an initial slow growth period with local involvement, giving way to a rapid development phase involving external agencies, culminating in many cases in overdevelopment, loss of quality of experience and environment, and stagnation or decline in visitation. This is finally followed by often elaborate and sometimes frantic efforts to rejuvenate the destination to regain market share, and all too often results in a price war with competing destinations and a downward spiral of prices and quality of supply, matched by a downward trend in market segment. Efforts to revision destinations all too often result in a move towards a supposed but often

Table 19.1: Summary characteristics of island destinations.

Coldwater islands	Warmwater islands
Specific destinations	Generic destinations
Active nature of tourism	Passive nature of tourism
Wide spatial dispersion	Concentrated spatial pattern
Highly seasonal tourism	Seasonal to year round tourism
Inherent attractions	Inherent plus added "artificial" attractions
Small-scale tourism	Large scale and mass tourism
Difficult infrequent costly access	Easy frequent low-cost access
Long history of visitation	Short period of intense visitation
3 I image (ice, isolation, indigenous people)	4 S image (sun, sea, sand, sex)
Mature adult market	Wide market including families
Limited range of facilities	Wide range of facilities and opportunities
High cost of vacation and travel	Wide range of costs from low to high
Exotic image	Erotic image
Limited local involvement	High degree of local involvement

false "sustainable" tourism, frequently confused with attempts to move upmarket and attract a higher spending and lower impacting type of visitor.

Coldwater island destinations appear not to follow such a cycle, although it may be that they simply have a very long initial period before there is extensive development and growth, if that does occur. Coldwater mainland destinations such as the resorts of the United Kingdom have had lifecycles of more than a century, compared to warmwater destinations that appear to have cycles of two or three decades, perhaps a reflection of natural growth, for example of plants, which is more rapid in warm than in cold climates. It is questionable if coldwater island destinations will go through such a cycle or at least that they will ever experience large-scale mass tourism. Their locations, their relative or absolute inaccessibility, high costs of access and stay, extreme seasons, and limited specific attractions all militate against the large-scale growth of facilities or markets. It was on the basis of such arguments that this author argued for the potential sustainability of tourism in destinations such as the Shetland Islands (Butler, 1996) and these arguments are still valid. The market, a senior one, is growing, as are educational attainment (at least on paper) and level of affluence in most developing and developed countries, and interest in the natural and historic environments also appears to be increasing. Such considerations suggest that these destinations should be able to continue to tap into this market successfully, providing they maintain their attractive qualities that draw this market at the present time and have continued to do so for more than a century.

With such characteristics, however, also goes vulnerability. Many coldwater island destinations depend very greatly on two features, their natural environment and external providers of access, characteristics they share with some warmwater island destinations. Dependence on external providers of access leaves such destinations very vulnerable to market shifts in travel patterns, to factors such as rising oil prices, and to the whims of large corporations with relatively little investment in these destinations compared to their global scale of operations. There is little which can be done about this situation. Most destinations in this category are too small in terms of local population or capital to own and operate their own transport facilities and thus dependency is a fact of life. In recent years, even relatively rich industrial western nations such as Belgium and Switzerland have seen the demise of their national airlines, while some of the largest airlines in the world from the richest country (the USA) seem to be in a semi-permanent state of bankruptcy following the events of 2001 and high oil prices.

The natural environment of these destinations is not immune to threat either. Ignoring the propensity of some of these destinations to volcanic and marine natural disasters, the effects of climatic change and global warming in particular pose very real threats. While most of the destinations examined in this volume are not likely to be submerged by rising sea levels, as are some of their warmwater counterparts, they may lose a significant part of their attractiveness through the disappearance of indigenous wildlife. Warmer water temperatures may cause a relocation of fish stocks, making survival of some bird populations in specific locations doubtful, resulting either in massive losses or migration of species to more appropriate conditions, which would probably mean to higher latitudes and cooler water. Thus, some of the attractions could disappear. Concerns over the long-term survival of polar bears, for example, could be mirrored by the disappearance of musk ox and arctic foxes from Canadian Arctic islands such as Banks and Baffin. Marine mammals such as whales and seals could relocate to follow food sources, not only threatening the continuance of tourism but even the very survival of the indigenous population in its traditional locations.

In the short term, such longer term events may stimulate a tourism mini-boom to these destinations, driven by a "see them before they disappear" motivation, but that is hardly to be seen as a positive development. One may be cynical and conclude that if such a scenario did develop with the extreme range of negative climatic changes forecast, a decline in tourism to coldwater island destinations would not be high on the list of the world's concerns when compared to other problems, but that is hardly comforting to anyone either. Coldwater island destinations, like everywhere else in the world, must hope (and there is little else the residents of these areas can do but be passive observers) that climatic change can be halted or even reversed, and that conservation of oil stocks allows reasonably priced travel to continue for the foreseeable future. Research can obviously look at alternative scenarios of development or contraction of tourism given the different economic and environmental conditions and potential responses from destination communities. There is a great need to explore in much more detail the specific motivations of tourists to these destinations. It is likely that, as well as committed cultural and natural history tourists, there are island "collectors" and those desiring esteem from visiting remote and therefore potentially, in their minds perhaps hazardous locations, to boost their prestige. Others may just be curious, as were their predecessors in the 18th and 19th centuries, to see such anachronisms in a globalised and increasingly sanitised world. Research is also needed to inform those involved in tourism development generally what can be learned from long-term limited tourism in these destinations, and whether the continually inappropriate and short-term development of many warmwater island destinations could or should be modelled more on their coldwater counterparts. It would be ironic but somewhat satisfying if such were found to be the case, and would confirm this volume as a useful contribution to the debate over the appropriate way of allowing tourism into sensitive environments such as these islands.

References

Baum, T. G., & Lundtorp, S. (2001). *Seasonality in tourism*. Amsterdam: Pergamon.

Butler, R. W. (1980). The concept of a tourist area cycle of evolution: Implications for management of resources. *The Canadian Geographer*, *2*(1), 5–12.

Butler, R. W. (1985). The evolution of tourism in the Scottish highlands in the 18th and 19th centuries. *Annals of Tourism Research*, *12*(3), 371–391.

Butler R. W. (1996). Problems and possibilities of sustainable tourism: The case of the Shetland Islands. In: L. Briguglio, R. Butler, D. Harrison, & W. Filho (Eds), *Sustainable tourism in islands and small states: Case studies* (pp. 11–31). London: Cassell.

Butler, R. W. (2001). Seasonality in tourism: Issues and implications. In: T. G. Baum, & S. Lundtorp (Eds), *Seasonality in tourism* (pp. 5–22). Amsterdam: Pergamon.

Butler, R. W. (2006a). *The tourism area life cycle: Applications and modifications*. Clevedon: Channelview Press.

Butler, R. W. (2006b). *The tourism area life cycle: Conceptual and theoretical issues*. Clevedon: Channelview Press.

Conlin, M. V., & Baum, T. G. (1995). *Island tourism management: Principles and practice.* Chichester: Wiley.

Doxey, G. V. (1975). A causation theory of visitor-resident irritants: Methodology and research inferences. *Proceedings of the sixth annual conference, Tourism and travel association*, (pp. 195–198). San Diego, CA: TTRA.

Hart, A. (1983). *The CPR and the selling of Banff.* Banff, Canada: Altitude Press.

Husbands, W. (1983). The genesis of tourism in Barbados: Further notes on the welcoming society. *Caribbean Geography*, 2(1), 107–120.

King E. M. (1997). *Creating island resorts.* London: Routledge.

Author Index

Subject Index